Wissenschaftliche Untersuchungen
zum Neuen Testament · 2. Reihe

Herausgeber / Editor
Jörg Frey (Zürich)

Mitherausgeber / Associate Editors
Friedrich Avemarie (Marburg)
Markus Bockmuehl (Oxford)
James A. Kelhoffer (Uppsala)
Hans-Josef Klauck (Chicago, IL)

301

Timothy P. Henderson

The Gospel of Peter and Early Christian Apologetics

Rewriting the Story of Jesus' Death, Burial,
and Resurrection

Mohr Siebeck

TIMOTHY P. HENDERSON, born 1971; 2010 PhD, Marquette University; Adjunct Professor of New Testament at Bethel Seminary since 2006, and also currently Adjunct Professor at Concordia University (St. Paul, MN).

ISBN 978-3-16-150709-0
ISSN 0340-9570 (Wissenschaftliche Untersuchungen zum Neuen Testament, 2. Reihe)

Die Deutsche Nationalbibliothek lists this publication in the Deutsche Nationalbibliographie; detailed bibliographic data are available on the Internet at *http://dnb.d-nb.de*.

The book was printed by Laupp & Göbel in Nehren on non-aging paper and bound by Buchbinderei Nädele in Nehren.

Printed in Germany.

Preface

This book is a lightly revised version of my dissertation submitted to the faculty at Marquette University. It was during my first semester at Marquette that I was in a doctoral seminar on the formation of the gospel tradition. What I did not know at the time was that one of the papers I submitted in that course was a mustard seed of sorts, since it is that 12-page effort that has eventually grown to become this book. Many people deserve recognition for their part in seeing this project to its completion.

I first would like to thank Dr. Julian Hills, who was my advisor from day one of my time at Marquette and who directed my dissertation. His encouragement to be continuously improving my work has been a rewarding challenge for which I owe a debt of gratitude. I hope to emulate his commitment to the highest standards of scholarship.

Thanks to Dr. Michel Barnes, who, in addition to being on my dissertation committee, has frequently helped me better understand the development of Christian thought during the second and third centuries. I would also like to thank Dr. Andrei Orlov for his interest in my work and for his generous willingness to help me in a variety of areas during my studies at Marquette. Gratitude is also due to Dr. Deirdre Dempsey, who graciously volunteered to be a member of the dissertation committee and whose enthusiasm for biblical studies has been apparent to me. The feedback I received from these fine scholars has allowed me to improve several aspects of this book.

The community of graduate students in Marquette's Theology Department was an oasis of encouragement, rewarding dialogue, and friendship. This was one of the most pleasant surprises of my doctoral journey. Thanks to everyone who walked this path with me.

I would like to extend my gratitude to two individuals for their role in seeing this work through the publication stage. Dr. Jörg Frey, editor of WUNT II, enthusiastically accepted the work for inclusion in this prestigious series. Anna Krüger, from Mohr Siebeck's production department, provided invaluable help in formatting this project for publication.

My family deserves the highest thanks of all. My oldest son, Justin, was only a toddler when I began my research, yet today he can read nearly every word of this book. His regular barrage of questions about its contents never ceases to put a smile on my face. I am grateful for the recent arrival of his younger brother Joshua during the time that I have been working toward publication. Lastly, I am certain that I would not have seen this project to its completion if it were not for the patient love and sacrifice of my wife, Jenny. She has been a constant source of strength and encouragement beyond what I deserve, and for this I am most grateful.

St. Paul, Minnesota, February 2011   Timothy P. Henderson

Table of Contents

Introduction

Gospel studies witnessed the rise of several new methodological approaches during the 20th century. Karl Schmidt, Martin Dibelius, and Rudolf Bultmann pioneered the form-critical study of these texts, giving attention to the period in which stories about Jesus were transmitted orally. They then classified these stories according to their form in an effort to ascertain the particular context in which a given form would have been most valued in early Christian communities. Research on this period of oral tradition has been enhanced by subsequent studies of memory and orality, as reflected in the publications of Werner Kelber, Birger Gerhardsson, and others. Soon after form criticism entered the scene redaction criticism arrived in the work of Willi Marxsen, Günther Bornkamm, and Hans Conzelmann. This approach sought to understand the ways in which the authors of the gospels edited their sources. In doing so, these scholars attempted to recover each evangelist's unique theology and setting.

These New Testament (NT) practitioners of form- and redaction-criticism were preceded by their Hebrew Bible counterparts in some regards. Hermann Gunkel had already been employing form-critical methods in the study of Genesis and Psalms. And the Documentary Hypothesis – in the version proposed by Julius Wellhausen in the 19th century – had a strong redaction-critical component. Wellhausen detected four sources behind the pentateuchal books and judged that each had been edited and creatively integrated with one another by later editors.

The vast majority of form- and redaction-critical research on Christian gospels has been devoted to those gospels that came to be included in the NT. Over the past several decades, however, there has been a growing interest in noncanonical gospels. This resurgence began in 1945 with the discovery of the *Gospel of Thomas* and the eventual publication of this text at the end of the 1950s. Most recently, a copy of the long lost *Gospel of Judas* was found and subsequently published in 2006 with much media fanfare.

Although it has been over one hundred years since an ancient copy of the *Gospel of Peter* was discovered in an Egyptian cemetery, this gospel continues to intrigue those with an interest in early Christian literature. On the one hand, it bears striking similarities to the accounts of Jesus' death, burial, and resurrection that are found in the NT gospels; but on the other hand, it deviates significantly from those stories at points. This has made it difficult to understand the specific relationship between this noncanonical gospel and its canonical companions. Furthermore, while scholars have offered various descriptions of the religio-social context in which this text was composed, many have been unconvinced by what has been suggested thus far in this area.

The path I follow in this study is important because it revisits old questions and offers new answers. As previous gospel critics have shared the same methodological insights as their Hebrew Bible counterparts in utilizing form and redaction criticism, I wish to do likewise in my suggestion about the proper analogy for understanding the *Gospel of Peter*'s relationship to the NT gospels.

Specifically, I will be appealing to a category of Second Temple Jewish literature that has come to be identified as "Rewritten Bible." These texts, though differing in genre, authorship, and date, are united in that they retell portions of the Hebrew Bible in order to address the new situations of their authors and readers. It will be my contention that the relationship between these "Rewritten Bible" texts and their biblical antecedents is precisely the type of relationship between the *Gospel of Peter* and the NT gospels. As such, my work is largely redaction-critical in nature, and my focus is on the apologetic nature of the editorial work in this gospel.

While previous scholarly literature has often referred in passing to the apologetic interests of the *Gospel of Peter*, the issue has rarely been documented and analyzed in a systematic fashion. What has not been addressed specifically is the influence that criticism from those outside the Christian movement may have had on the development of the traditions in this gospel. Various sources of the first few centuries C.E. preserve some of the thoughts of those who were critical of emerging Christianity. Included among these are critiques of details found in the NT gospels. Justin Martyr purports to give many of these in his *Dialogue with Trypho*, and the remnants of Celsus' similar objections, written originally in his *True Doctrine*, have been left behind in Origen's reply to him. These and other works provide evidence of the types of criticisms that were made against some of the accounts in the NT gospels. To date, though, no significant work has been done to explore how these might shed light on the situation in which the material in the *Gospel of Peter* developed and how this background may provide an explanation for the heightened apologetic tendencies in this text. My study seeks to fill this gap that currently exists in scholarship.

Many have continued to explore the factors that influenced the transition of the early Christian movement from what was originally a small Jewish sect to what became an almost entirely Gentile religion that in most outward respects was distinct from Judaism. This "parting of the ways" has been studied extensively by James D. G. Dunn, Judith Lieu, and others. Because of its strong anti-Jewish polemic, the *Gospel of Peter* potentially sheds some light on the question of the relationship between Christians and Jews in the communities where the text originated. At this point I will go beyond the results of my textual analysis in an attempt at social reconstruction and it is here that my thesis is more speculative and thus its results less certain. But if this reconstruction over-interprets the text in my search for the original setting of this gospel, it is still the case that I have presented more accurately than previous studies the relation between the *Gospel of Peter* and the canonical gospels.

As for technical matters, unless otherwise noted, I use the NRSV for all English Bible translations. All English translations of modern German and French scholarship are my own. Except where noted, I follow the English translation of the *Gospel of Peter* in the critical edition edited by Tobias Nicklas and Thomas Kraus, and I am also dependent on this source for the Greek text. When providing block quotations of ancient texts, I include the title and citation followed by the English translation used and its page number(s) (e.g., *1 Apol.* 48; Falls 85). In these instances see the "Primary Sources" section of the bibliography to locate a specific author.

Chapter 1

The History of the Gospel of Peter and
Its Status As Rewritten Gospel

The purpose of this first chapter is to review the history of the *Gospel of Peter* (hereafter, GP) itself and of the research on it, and to set out my own claims and procedure for this study. After reviewing the patristic references to GP, I will summarize the details surrounding the discovery of a fragment from it near the end of the 19th century. I will then outline the history of scholarship, noting in particular the ways in which its relationship to the NT gospels has been understood and referring to some proposals that have been made concerning the social and religious background to it. Following this, I will present my own thesis and procedure for this study.

1.1 The Early History of GP

As is true of many works written in antiquity, the sands of history once swallowed GP, leaving behind not a single manuscript containing any of its words. For centuries this gospel was known only from the testimonies of patristic writers. There are, in fact, seven such authors or texts to be discussed – Serapion (preserved in Eusebius of Caesarea), Eusebius himself, Origen, Didymus the Blind, Jerome, Theodoret, and the *Decretum Gelasianum*. In addition, I will review a statement from Justin Martyr that has been claimed by some to be an allusion to GP. As I will point out, however, this should not be understood as a reference to our gospel.

The earliest writer to refer to GP is Serapion, bishop of Syrian Antioch near the end of the second century. He composed a short tract entitled "Concerning the So-Called *Gospel of Peter*" (περὶ τοῦ λεγομένου κατὰ Πέτρον εὐαγγελίου). While this work has been lost, some of its contents have been preserved by Eusebius of Caesarea, who apparently possessed a copy of it.[1] The entire passage from Eusebius' *Ecclesiastical History* is worth quoting:

---

[1] On Serapion's comments, see already Henry B. Swete, *The Akhmîm Fragment of the Apocryphal Gospel of St. Peter* (London: Macmillan, 1893), ix–xi; Léon Vaganay,

Now it is likely, indeed, that other memoirs also, the fruit of Serapion's literary studies, are preserved by other persons, but there have come down to us only those addressed To Domnus, one who had fallen away from the faith of Christ, at the time of the persecution, to Jewish will-worship (τὴν Ἰουδαϊκὴν ἐθελοθρησκείαν); and those To Pontius and Caricus, churchmen, and other letters to other persons; and another book has been composed by him *Concerning what is known as the Gospel of Peter*, which he has written refuting the false statements in it, because of certain in the community of Rhossus, who on the ground of the said writing turned aside into heterodox teachings. It will not be unreasonable to quote a short passage from this work, in which he puts forward the view he held about the book, writing as follows:

"For our part, brethren, we receive both Peter and the other apostles as Christ, but the writings which falsely bear their names we reject, as men of experience, knowing that such were not handed down to us. For I myself, when I came among you, imagined that all of you clung to the true faith; and, without going through the Gospel put forward by them in the name of Peter, I said: If this is the only thing that seemingly causes captious feelings among you, let it be read. But since I have now learnt, from what has been told me, that their mind was lurking in some hole of heresy, I shall give diligence to come again to you; wherefore, brethren, expect me quickly. But we, brethren, gathering to what kind of heresy Marcianus belonged (who used to contradict himself, not knowing what he was saying, as ye will learn from what has been written to you), were enabled by others who studied this very Gospel, that is, by the successors of those who began it, whom we call Docetae (for most of the ideas belong to their teaching) – using [the material supplied] by them, were enabled to go through it and discover that the most part indeed was in accordance with the true teaching of the Saviour, but that some things were added, which also we place below for your benefit." (*Hist. eccl.* 6.12.1–6; Lake and Oulton, 2:39, 41, 43; all parentheses and brackets are original)

Unfortunately, Eusebius does not proceed to quote the items from GP to which Serapion alludes as having been added to the "true teaching of the Saviour."

We may note several features of this excerpt. First, there was a text known as the "Gospel according to Peter" (τὸ κατὰ Πέτρον εὐαγγέλιον) circulating in the regions around Cilicia and Syria near the end of the second century. Second, Serapion was apparently unfamiliar with this gospel prior to his first visit to Rhossus.[2] This is the best way to explain his change of opinion concerning it. Had he already been acquainted with this work, it is doubtful that he would have given his initial approval to read it. Since Serapion's episcopacy is most frequently dated to the last decade of the second century, a *terminus ante quem* of 180–190 C.E. can be established for GP. Third, and only at a time after his first visit to Rhossus, Serapion learned that certain "Docetae" (heretics, in his estimation) had

---

L'Évangile de Pierre (2d ed.; EBib; Paris: Gabalda, 1930), 1–8; Thomas J. Kraus and Tobias Nicklas, *Das Petrusevangelium und die Petrusapokalypse: Die griechischen Fragment mit deutscher und englischer Übersetzung* (GCS[2] 11; Berlin: de Gruyter, 2004), 12–16.

[2] Swete, *Akhmîm Fragment*, xi.

been using this gospel to support their teachings. He goes even further in claiming that it originated with the Docetae. Fourth, Serapion himself finally read the gospel and judged that it was largely "in accordance with the true teaching of the Saviour," although it had added some things to what he considered to be orthodox ideas.

Fifth, it should be asked whether Serapion's opinion of this gospel was influenced by his acquaintance with those who were reading it. Clearly, he knows members of the group led by Marcianus and is in disagreement with them. How much of Serapion's judgment about GP has been colored by his theological differences with those who held it in esteem? Sixth, it is interesting to note that Domnus, an acquaintance of Serapion's, had left the Christian movement to join a Jewish group during a time of persecution. The source of this conflict is not stated, but this may be indicative of tension between Jews and Christians in the time and place in which GP was composed and/or circulated. There is a strong anti-Jewish tone permeating this gospel, and Eusebius' comment here adds intrigue to the background to our text. At the very least, it appears that Christian and Jewish groups were in close social proximity to one another in the area where GP was being read in the latter part of the second century.

At a previous point in his *Ecclesiastical History*, Eusebius had provided his own opinion about GP after having discussed the question of the authenticity of the two epistles written in the name of Peter:

On the other hand, of the Acts bearing his name, and the Gospel named according to him (τὸ κατ' αὐτὸν ὠνομασμένον εὐαγγέλιον) and Preaching called his and the so-called Revelation, we have no knowledge at all in Catholic tradition, for no orthodox writer of the ancient time or of our own has used their testimonies. (*Hist. eccl.* 3.3.2; Lake and Oulton, 1:192–93)[3]

In light of his comments regarding Serapion, Eusebius undoubtedly judged that the gospel known to him as the "Gospel according to Peter" was the one of which Serapion wrote. We must remember that Eusebius had access to the writings of numerous Christian authors and was familiar with a very wide range of early Christian texts.[4] With this in mind, while Eusebius was acquainted with two letters written in Peter's name, he knew of only one gospel attributed to the apostle. It seems virtually certain that the text

---

[3] Treatments of this passage appear in Swete, *Akhmîm Fragment*, ix; Vaganay, *Évangile de Pierre*, 9–11; Kraus and Nicklas, *Petrusevangelium*, 17.

[4] Summaries of this topic typically show up in works addressing the role of Eusebius in the development of the NT canon. Two recent estimates of the scope of texts with which Eusebius was familiar appear in Everett R. Kalin, "The New Testament Canon of Eusebius," in *The Canon Debate* (ed. Lee M. McDonald and James A. Sanders; Peabody, Mass.: Hendrickson, 2002), 386–404; David L. Dungan, *Constantine's Bible: Politics and the Making of the New Testament* (Minneapolis: Fortress, 2007).

known to this early church historian is the same one that was circulating in
and around Syria and Cilicia at the end of the second century.

Origen makes a passing reference to GP in his commentary on Matthew.[5] After quoting a passage that mentions Jesus' family members (Matt
13:55–56), he comments on how those outside Jesus' family viewed him:

> They thought, then, that He was the son of Joseph and Mary. But some say, basing it on a
> tradition in the Gospel according to Peter (κατὰ Πέτρον εὐαγγέλιου), as it is entitled,
> or "The Book of James," that the brethren of Jesus were sons of Joseph by a former wife,
> whom he married before Mary. Now those who say so wish to preserve the honour of
> Mary in virginity to the end. (*Comm. Matt.* 10.17; *ANF* 9:424)[6]

The "Book of James" is most likely the text known today as the *Protevangelium of James*, since there are several points at which this work alludes
to Joseph having children from a previous marriage (*Prot. Jas.* 9.2; 17.1;
18.1). Origen eventually affirms his belief in the perpetual virginity of
Mary, though he seems to trace this idea back to GP or the *Protevangelium
of James* rather than to Matthew. Where Serapion condemned the use of
GP among Christians, Origen found in it an ally for his own theological
position. However, there is no passage in the extant fragment of GP that
would fit with a scene like the one mentioned by Origen.

In the middle of the fourth century, Didymus the Blind used the gospels
attributed to Thomas and Peter as examples of books falsely ascribed to
authors (βιβλία ψευδεπίγραφα), which were not to be read by Christians.[7] It is unclear whether Didymus had firsthand knowledge of GP or
was dependent on hearsay.

Moving to the end of the fourth century, we find two references to GP
in Jerome's *Lives of Illustrious Men*, a work that Jerome acknowledged as
owing a large debt to Eusebius' *Ecclesiastical History*.[8] Jerome refers to
GP in the context of discussing the various writings that have been attributed to Peter:

> He wrote two epistles which are called Catholic, the second of which, on account of its
> difference from the first in style, is considered by many not to be by him. Then too the
> Gospel according to Mark, who was his disciple and interpreter, is ascribed to him. On
> the other hand, the books, of which one is entitled his Acts, another his Gospel, a third
> his Preaching, a fourth his Revelation, a fifth his "Judgment" are rejected as apocryphal.
> (*Vir. ill.* 1; *NPNF*[2] 3:361)

---

[5] See Swete, *Akhmîm Fragment*, x; Vaganay, *Évangile de Pierre*, 8–9; Kraus and
Nicklas, *Petrusevangelium*, 16–17.

[6] Greek text in Kraus and Nicklas, *Petrusevangelium*, 16.

[7] Greek text, German translation, and discussion in Kraus and Nicklas, *Petrusevangelium*, 18–19.

[8] Summaries of these excerpts in Swete, *Akhmîm Fragment*, ix, xii; Vaganay,
Évangile de Pierre, 11.

Later, in his brief summary of Serapion's accomplishments, Jerome again mentions the gospel:

[Serapion] wrote a volume also to Domnus, who in time of persecution went over to the Jews, and another work on the gospel which passes under the name of Peter, a work to the church of the Rhosenses in Cilicia who by the reading of this book had turned aside to heresy. (*Vir. ill.* 41; *NPNF*[2] 3:372)

Nothing new can be learned from either of Jerome's comments, as they appear to be restatements of what he has found in Eusebius. They indicate that the two writers share the same perspective on GP.

In the fifth century, Theodoret refers to GP in his description of the sect known as the Nazoraeans:

The Nazoraeans are Jews who honor Christ as a righteous man and use the so-called Gospel according to Peter. (*Haer. fab.* 2.2)[9]

It is uncertain how much direct knowledge Theodoret had regarding this group, but one feature that characterized its members is that they used a "Gospel according to Peter."

Efforts among some early Christian leaders to ban the use of noncanonical texts were strong in the sixth century. This is reflected in the so-called *Decretum Gelasianum*, which lists over fifty texts that were to be rejected by everyone in the church.[10] Among the gospels to be excluded is a "Gospel under the name of the apostle Peter," which in all likelihood is the gospel mentioned by the previous authors I have surveyed. The compilers of this decree knew that multiple gospels were associated with other names, since they list "the Gospels under the name of Bartholomew" and "the Gospels under the name of Andrew," but they are aware of only one gospel written in the name of Peter.

One final reference needs to be addressed, and it is in fact earlier than all of the others discussed thus far. Justin Martyr, writing in the middle of the second century, frequently mentions texts that he identifies as ἀπομνημονεύματα τῶν ἀποστόλων ("memoirs of the apostles").[11] He

---

[9] I am unaware of any published English translation of this work. My translation is based on the Greek text found in Vaganay (*Évangile de Pierre*, 11): οἱ δὲ Ναζωραῖοί Ἰουδαῖοί εἰσιν τὸν Χριστὸν τιμῶντες ὡς ἄνθρωπον δίκαιον καὶ τῷ καλουμένῳ κατὰ Πέτρον εὐαγγελίῳ κεχρημένοι. On this passage, see also Swete, *Akhmîm Fragment*, xi–xii; Vaganay, *Évangile de Pierre*, 11; A. F. J. Klijn and G. J. Reinink, *Patristic Evidence for Jewish-Christian Sects* (NovTSup 36; Leiden: Brill, 1973), 51–52; Kraus and Nicklas, *Petrusevangelium*, 18.

[10] ET and background information in *NTApoc*[2] 1:38–40. The inclusion of GP in it is discussed in Kraus and Nicklas, *Petrusevangelium*, 20.

[11] On Justin's use of this phrase, see Arthur J. Bellinzoni, *The Sayings of Jesus in the Writings of Justin Martyr* (NovTSup 17; Leiden: Brill, 1967); Charles H. Cosgrove, "Justin Martyr and the Emerging New Testament Canon: Observations on the Purpose

refers to these memoirs thirteen times in *Dial.* 98–106, and it has been suggested that one such occasion concerns GP:

And when it is said that [Jesus] changed the name (μετωνομακέναι) of one of the apostles to Peter; and when it is written in the memoirs of Him (καὶ γεγράφθαι ἐν τοῖς ἀπομνημονεύμασιν αὐτοῦ) that this so happened, as well as that He changed the names (ἐπωνομακέναι) of other two brothers, the sons of Zebedee, to Boanerges, which means sons of thunder. (*Dial.* 106.3; *ANF* 1:252)[12]

There are two questions to address about this passage. First, in the phrase ἀπομνημονεύμασιν αὐτοῦ, who is the antecedent of αὐτοῦ: Jesus or Peter? Second, in light of our answer to the first question, how should we understand the expression? There have been three main responses to these questions: 1) the phrase means "memoirs of Jesus," in which case they are memoirs *about* Jesus; 2) it indicates "memoirs of Peter" and refers to a text known as the "Gospel of Peter"; and 3) it means "memoirs of Peter" and refers to the Gospel of Mark. The first and third options, in my judgment, are more probable than the second.

The translation in *ANF* has taken αὐτοῦ to be a reference to Jesus, as indicated by the capitalization of "Him" in the phrase "the memoirs of Him." This has been the judgment of the majority of scholars.[13] Paul Foster has contended that grammatically "the pronoun αὐτοῦ is far more likely to refer to the same person who changes the names of the sons of Zebedee, since the infinitive ἐπωνομακέναι assumes Jesus as its subject without signaling any change from the previous subject designated by the

---

and Destination of the *Dialogue with Trypho*," *VC* 53 (1982): 209–32; Martin Hengel, "The Titles of the Gospels and the Gospel of Mark," in idem, *Studies in the Gospel of Mark* (trans. John Bowden; Philadelphia: Fortress, 1985), 75–77; Helmut Koester, *Ancient Christian Gospels: Their History and Development* (Philadelphia: Trinity Press International, 1990), 36–43; Paul Foster, "The Writings of Justin Martyr and the So-Called *Gospel of Peter*," in *Justin Martyr and His Worlds* (ed. Sara Parvis and idem; Minneapolis: Fortress, 2007), 104–12; Katharina Greschat, "Justins 'Denkwürdigkeiten der Apostel' und das Petrusevangelium," in *Das Evangelium nach Petrus: Text, Kontexte, Intertexte* (TU 158; ed. Thomas J. Kraus and Tobias Nicklas; Berlin: de Gruyter, 2007), 197–214.

[12] Throughout this project I will typically utilize the translation of Thomas B. Falls (*Saint Justin Martyr* [FC 6; Washington, D.C.: The Catholic University of America Press, 1948]) for Justin's works. However, his translation is inadequate here: "Now, when we learn from the Memoirs of the Apostles that He changed the name of one of the Apostles to Peter (besides having changed the names of the two brothers, the sons of Zebedee, to that of Boanerges, which means 'sons of thunder')" (313). The rendering "Memoirs of the Apostles" is not accurate and it glosses over the question that ἀπομνημονεύμασιν αὐτοῦ poses. For this reason, I have opted not to use Falls here.

[13] Foster, "Writings of Justin Martyr," 107.

pronoun αὐτοῦ."[14] In this view, αὐτοῦ is an objective genitive, and the expression means "the memoirs about Jesus."

However, what if ἀπομνημονεύμασιν αὐτοῦ is taken to signify "the memoirs of Peter"? There are two alternatives. The first is that Justin is, indeed, referring to a text known as the "Gospel of Peter." Walter Cassels was among the first to claim that Justin had GP in mind here.[15] More recently, Peter Pilhofer has advocated this position.[16] He has argued that whenever Justin uses a modifier with ἀπομνημονεύματα elsewhere, it is to indicate that the memoirs are associated with the apostles (e.g., ἀπομνημονεύματα τῶν ἀποστόλων).[17] So, following this logic, combined with the nearby antecedent Πέτρον, it is best to understand αὐτοῦ as referring to the apostle. However, Foster's point about there being no indication of a change in the sentence's subject lessens the force of Pilhofer's argument here. But what if Pilhofer is correct in his claim and the phrase should be understood to mean "the memoirs of Peter"? Does this necessarily mean that Justin is writing about a text he knows as the "Gospel of Peter"?

Graham N. Stanton and others have taken a middle way, so to speak.[18] Stanton suggests that the phrase probably does mean "memoirs of Peter," but that by this expression Justin is referring to the Gospel of Mark. In support of this contention he refers to the early tradition among some proto-orthodox Christians of the second century – such as Papias and Irenaeus – that behind Mark's gospel was the testimony of the apostle Peter. Furthermore, in the passage from Justin that we are examining, the apologist refers to Jesus changing the names of both Peter and the sons of Zebedee in the memoirs. However, only Mark, and no other known gospel, includes something like Justin's phrase "Boanerges, which means sons of thunder" when giving the new name of the sons of Zebedee (Mark 3:17). While it is of course possible that GP also included such a phrase, we have nothing to indicate this.

Papias, writing 120–130 C.E., included a similar tradition about Mark as the preserver of Peter's preaching, and he traced this claim to an individual

---

[14] Ibid., 108.

[15] Cassels, *The Gospel according to Peter: A Study by the Author of "Supernatural Religion"* (London: Longmans, Green, 1894), 20–25.

[16] Pilhofer, "Justin und das Petrusevangelium," *ZNW* 81 (1990): 60–78.

[17] Ibid., 68.

[18] See, for example, Stanton, *Jesus and Gospel* (Cambridge: Cambridge University Press, 2004), 100–101. Stanton (101) claims that Adolf von Harnack and Theodor Zahn shared his view, but he cites no sources for this.

whom he identifies as "John the Presbyter."[19] Eusebius relays the words of Papias as follows:

And the Presbyter used to say this, "Mark became Peter's interpreter and wrote accurate-ly all that he remembered, not, indeed, in order, of the things said or done by the Lord. For he had not heard the Lord, nor had he followed him, but later on, as I said, followed Peter, who used to give teaching as necessity demanded but not making, as it were, an arrangement of the Lord's oracles, so that Mark did nothing wrong in thus writing down single points as he remembered them. For to one thing he gave attention, to leave out nothing of what he had heard and to make no false statements in them." (*Hist. eccl.* 3.39.15; Lake and Oulton, 1:297)

In light of this widespread early tradition connecting Peter to Mark, Stan-ton's suggestion is at least as plausible as the idea that Justin is referring to a text he knows as the "Gospel of Peter."

In the end, I am not persuaded that Justin is referring to a writing identi-fied as the "Gospel of Peter." It is most likely that he has in mind the "memoirs about Jesus" or possibly that he is associating Mark's gospel with the apostle Peter. For this reason, Justin is not to be included among the earliest witnesses to GP.

This survey of the evidence from the first six centuries indicates that many Christian writers were acquainted with GP, either through firsthand knowledge or via hearsay. These authors represent a broad geographical area, too. However, like most gospels that were excluded from the emerg-ing NT canon, GP eventually was attributed to heretics and condemned by proto-orthodox church leaders, and finally faded from the pages of history for well over a millennium. It is ironic and perhaps fitting that around the very time that GP vanished from the ancient historical record, a manuscript containing an excerpt from it was buried in an Egyptian cemetery. And it is this artifact that would one day allow us to have access once again to this long lost text.

1.2 The Discovery and Identification of GP

In the winter of 1886–87 a group of archaeologists from the French Ar-chaeological Mission at Cairo discovered a manuscript which contained the Greek text of a writing that would come to be identified as a portion of GP.[20] To be more precise, the manuscript is a codex containing all or part

---

[19] Clement of Alexandria is familiar with this same tradition, which Eusebius pre-serves in *Hist. eccl.* 6.14.6–7.

[20] The *editio princeps*, which details the discovery, appears in Urbain Bouriant, "Fragments du texte grec du livre d'Énoch et de quelques écrits attribués à saint Pierre," in *Mémoires publiés par les membres de la mission archéologique française au Caire* 9.1

of the *Apocalypse of Peter*, *1 Enoch*, the *Martyrdom of Julian of Anaz-arbus*, and GP. It was found in a grave located near Akhmîm (ancient Panopolis), Egypt. While the earliest commentators and many subsequent ones have specified that the grave belonged to a Christian monk, Peter van Minnen has noted that, aside from the Christian texts found with the body, there is nothing to indicate that it was the burial place of a monk.[21] This manuscript has been officially catalogued as P.Cair. 10759, although it is most commonly referred to as the Akhmîm manuscript.[22]

The codex is a collection of fragments which were penned by four different scribes.[23] In the *editio princeps*, Urbain Bouriant included no photographs or other images of the manuscript. The Greek text was included as a transcription. The following year, Adolphe Lods, another member of the French Archaeological Mission at Cairo, re-transcribed the text and also provided heliographic images of the manuscript.[24] It is generally agreed that Lods' transcription was an improvement over that of Bouriant.

(Paris: Libraire de la Société asiatique, 1892), 91–147. Although the codex was discovered during the winter of 1886–87, Bouriant did not publish his work until 1892. Very recently, the circumstances of the discovery have been recounted in Foster, "Are There Any Early Fragments of the So-Called *Gospel of Peter*?" *NTS* 52 (2006): 1–3; idem, "The Discovery and Initial Reaction to the So-Called Gospel of Peter," in Kraus and Nicklas, *Evangelium nach Petrus*, 9–14; Peter van Minnen, "The Akhmîm *Gospel of Peter*," in Kraus and Nicklas, *Evangelium nach Petrus*, 53–60.

[21] Minnen, "Akhmîm *Gospel of Peter*," 54.

[22] The "P.Cair." designation signifies "Papyrus Cairo," indicating that it was housed at the Coptic Museum in Cairo, Egypt. A few years ago confusion arose about whether this manuscript had been lost. At one point, Foster stated that the Cairo museum could no longer locate the manuscript and had not been able to do so for several years ("The Gospel of Peter," *ExpTim* 118 [2007]: 320). Thomas J. Kraus, in personal correspondence with me (May 22, 2009), confirmed that it is currently housed at Bibliotheca Alexandrina in Alexandria, Egypt. However, subsequent attempts by others to locate the manuscript at this location have been unsuccessful. It is catalogued in the Leuven Database of Ancient Books (Trismegistos) at the following website address: http://www.trismegistos.org/ldab/text.php?tm=59976 (accessed May 23, 2009). Photographs of the manuscript were taken in the 1980s and are available in Kraus and Nicklas, *Petrusevangelium*, 165–85. These same photographs are available online in higher resolution images that can be expanded and allow for more viewing precision: http://ipap.csad.ox.ac.uk/GP/GP.html (accessed May 23, 2009). The website is maintained by the Centre for the Study of Ancient Documents, at Oxford University (http://www.csad.ox.ac.uk).

[23] Minnen, "Akhmîm Gospel of Peter," 53–58. The fragments of GP and the *Apocalypse of Peter* were copied by one scribe, and the remaining fragments were composed by three different scribes.

[24] Lods, "L'Évangile et l'Apocalypse de Pierre avec le texte grec du livre d'Hénoch: Text publié en facsimile, par l'héliogravure d'après les photographies du manuscrit de Gizéh," in *Mémoires publiés par les membres de la mission archéologique française au Caire* 9.3 (Paris: Libraire de la Société asiatique, 1893), 217–31, 322–35. Foster ("Dis-

Scholars have reached diverse conclusions regarding the date of the codex. Bouriant dated it to the 8th–12th centuries.[25] In the past few decades, however, most have tended to place it at or before the early end of this range. Foster judges it to be from the 7th to the 9th centuries, while Minnen places it in the late 6th century.[26]

It was Bouriant himself who first identified one of the works in the codex as the text known in antiquity as the "Gospel according to Peter."[27] Recently, however, Foster has suggested that the Akhmîm text might not be a fragment of GP.[28] He notes that Bouriant, in his initial publication of this text, "contemplated no other possibility than identifying the first fragment as being a detached episode from the previously non-extant apocryphal Gospel of Peter."[29] One of Foster's reasons for questioning the identification of this text with GP is that there were numerous texts that circulated in the name of Peter during the first few centuries of the Christian movement. Because of this, there is "the possibility that more than one gospel-like text may have been associated with that apostolic figure."[30] He concludes in one of his articles that "it is no longer possible to assert that the first text discovered in the Akhmîm codex is definitely a witness to an archetype [of GP] dating to the second century."[31]

A few comments might be made by way of reply to Foster's suggestion that our text is not to be identified with the ancient "Gospel according to Peter." Regarding his argument that the proliferation of Petrine literature means that there may have been more than one "gospel-like text" in the name of this apostle, we may recall my earlier review of the early witnesses to GP. Beginning at the end of the second century and continuing into the sixth century – which is very near the time that the Akhmîm text was copied – the testimony is entirely consistent: there was only one gospel in the name of Peter. Serapion, Origen, Eusebius, Didymus, Jerome, Theodoret, and the compilers of the *Decretum Gelasianum* all knew of one, and only one, "Gospel according to Peter." Furthermore, several of these writers were acquainted with additional texts in Peter's name (e.g., two epis-

---

covery and Initial Reaction," 22) describes the process of creating heliographic images: "[It] involves the formation of an engraving obtained by a process in which a specially prepared plate is acted on chemically by exposure to light."

[25] Bouriant, "Fragments," 93.

[26] Foster, "Are There Any Early Fragments?" 1; Minnen, "Akhmîm Gospel of Peter," 54.

[27] Bouriant, "Fragments," 94.

[28] Most notable is Foster, "Are There Any Early Fragments?" 1–28; idem, "Discovery and Initial Reaction," 13–14, 16.

[29] Foster, "Discovery and Initial Reaction," 13–14.

[30] Ibid., 16.

[31] Foster, "Are There Any Early Fragments?" 27.

tles, the *Acts of Peter*, the *Preaching of Peter*, and the *Apocalypse of Peter*). More importantly, they were aware that some apostolic figures had more than one *gospel* written in their names. For example, the sixth-century *Decretum Gelasianum* indicates that there were multiple gospels in the names of Bartholomew and Andrew, but reflects familiarity with only one in the name of Peter. In addition, each of our other witnesses affirms that there was only one "Gospel according to Peter." Therefore, in order for Foster's suggestion to be correct regarding the possible existence of more than one "gospel-like text" being associated with Peter, we would have to say that if multiple texts (say, two) existed, then at least one of them completely escaped the notice of every early Christian writer whose works are known to us. We would have to conclude that every author with knowledge of multiple Petrine writings knew of one and only one Petrine gospel. This is not likely, as there is not a trace of evidence to indicate multiple gospels attributed to Peter.

So, if there was only one "Gospel according to Peter" that existed in the earliest centuries of Christianity, how do we know that the Akhmîm text is to be identified with it? First, what we have in the Akhmîm fragment almost certainly belongs to the gospel genre. In addition to the passion, burial, and resurrection stories, the extant text seems to presuppose certain other features of the missing portion of the work. For example, the reference to the "twelve disciples of the Lord" (GP 14:59) points back to them having a role earlier in the narrative, and the mention of Levi and Jesus together in 14:60 appears to be recounting an earlier incident with which the readers would be familiar. To what degree the entirety of GP might resemble one or all of the canonical gospels cannot be determined with certainty, but it is undeniable that the Akhmîm text, when compared to every other genre of early Christian literature, most closely resembles certain other gospel texts. Furthermore, by having Peter as the narrator, it is highly probable that this gospel would have been associated with this apostle.

Let us look again at Foster's claim that "it is no longer possible to assert that the first text discovered in the Akhmîm codex is definitely a witness to an archetype [of GP] dating to the second century."[32] Of course, the addition of the word "definitely" makes the statement immune to disproof, considering that there are no other manuscript witnesses that have a very high probability of representing the text of GP.[33] Fortunately, historical

---

[32] Ibid.

[33] Some have claimed that other manuscript fragments may contain excerpts of GP (e.g., P.Oxy. 2949, P.Oxy. 4009, P.Vindob. G 2325, P.Egerton 2). See, for example, Dieter Lührmann, *Die apokryph gewordenen Evangelien: Studien zu neuen Texten und zu*

judgments need not reside in the realm of certitude; we should instead be content to base them on probability. Without further manuscript discoveries, it is impossible to determine the degree to which the Akhmîm text reflects the "original" form of GP, so any arguments to this effect are wholly speculative. As it stands, then, we can say that the likelihood is strong that the Akhmîm text is a representative of the work known by early Christian writers as the "Gospel according to Peter."[34] What once was lost has now been found, or at least a portion of it.

1.3 GP Among the Gospels

The Akhmîm fragment of GP begins with the condemnation of Jesus by Herod, and continues by recounting the crucifixion, burial, and resurrection. Next, it describes the disciples returning to their homes, as some of them take their nets and go to the sea, apparently to resume their work as fishermen. The text then ends, but this seems to be the beginning of an appearance story, perhaps similar to the one found in John 21.

In its narrative framework GP is very similar to the parallels in Matthew, Mark, Luke, and John. But in the details, it diverges significantly at numerous points. For example, whereas Jesus is condemned to death by Pilate in the NT works, Herod plays this role in GP. In the NT gospels, the Romans crucify Jesus; the Jews do this in GP. With the exception of a Roman centurion named Petronius (GP 8:31), all of the named characters in GP appear in at least one of the canonical gospels, although often their role and/or actions in GP differ from what is found in the NT texts.

It is this combination of similarities and differences that has led to a variety of descriptions of the relationship between GP and Matthew, Mark, Luke, and John. Has the Petrine evangelist used one or more of the canonical texts as a source for his own work? Or did the writer compose his gospel independently, with no knowledge of the NT texts? Or is GP, in fact, an earlier narrative and thus the potential source for Matthew, Mark, Luke, or John? Versions of these three proposals have been advocated in the history of study on our gospel.

In addition to the issue of literary relationship, the question has occasionally been asked about the social context in which GP was written.

---

neuen Fragen (NovTSup 112; Leiden: Brill, 2004), 55–104. Foster ("Are There Any Early Fragments?" 1–28) rejects all of these possibilities. I, too, remain unconvinced.

[34] Even Foster seems to have changed his opinion on the matter. In a more recent publication, he writes, "While [the Akhmîm text] may, more likely than not, be the same text as the *So-called Gospel of Peter* mentioned by Serapion, certainty is not possible" ("Gospel of Peter," 325).

What has influenced its author? What motivated him to arrange the narrative in the manner he did? What were his theological interests? Some of the answers that have been given to these questions will be outlined in what follows, before I present my own proposal.

1.4 The History of Scholarship

The publication of the Akhmîm discovery in 1892 set off a flurry of research during the final decade of the 19th century.[35] This initial research focused on two areas: 1) determining the relationship of GP to the NT gospels; and 2) judging whether GP promotes "heretical" ideas such as docetism. The docetic question arose in light of the testimony of Serapion, who claimed that the gospel was used by docetists. I will survey the contributions of four of the earliest scholars: J. Armitage Robinson, J. Rendel Harris, Henry B. Swete, and Adolf von Harnack.[36] All of these men published short books on GP within one year of Bouriant's first edition.

Robinson stated that the text of GP was first available at Cambridge University on November 17, 1892.[37] This is telling because it allows us to see the speed with which the Cambridge professors could publish their works.[38] Robinson gave his first public lecture on GP on November 20, 1892, a mere three days after his initial access to the text, and he published his work in December 1892, within no more than six weeks of first laying eyes on his subject matter.[39] While the book itself covers nearly one hun-

---

[35] A thorough summary of the first publications on GP appears in Foster, "Discovery and Initial Reaction," 9–30.

[36] Robinson and Montague R. James, *The Gospel according to Peter, and the Revelation of Peter: Two Lectures on the Newly Discovered Fragments together with the Greek Texts* (London: Clay, 1892); Swete, *Akhmîm Fragment*; Harris, *A Popular Account of the Newly-Recovered Gospel of Peter* (London: Hodder & Stoughton, 1893); Harnack, *Bruchstücke des Evangeliums und der Apokalypse des Petrus* (2d ed.; TU 9.2; Leipzig: Hinrichs, 1893).

[37] Robinson and James, *Gospel according to Peter*, 7. This detail is more or less confirmed by Swete (*Akhmîm Fragment*, v), who writes that he provided his own Cambridge students with a corrected text of GP "at the end of November, 1892, shortly after the appearance of M. Bouriant's *editio princeps*."

[38] Robinson, Harris, and Swete were all at Cambridge University at this time. I will be referring solely to Robinson when discussing the work he published with Montague R. James, since Robinson composed the half of the book on GP while James did the same for the *Apocalypse of Peter*.

[39] Robinson and James, *Gospel according to Peter*, 7–8. This is determined by noting that the book has a publication date of 1892. The preface is dated December 1, 1892 and the authors refer to their publication as a "hurried work" (8). They are keen enough,

dred pages, only twenty-four are commentary on GP. The remaining pages discuss the *Apocalypse of Peter* and include transcriptions of the Greek text of the two works.

Robinson divided GP into fourteen sections, included an English translation, and then provided his own summary remarks. In contrast to some of the first modern commentators, he placed GP "closer to the beginning than to the middle of the second century."[40] He made frequent mention of similarities between GP and the NT gospels and other early Christian literature. It is not uncommon to find him categorizing GP as "perverting" or being a "perversion" of the NT gospels, especially in what he sees as the Petrine evangelist's effort to promote docetic ideas.[41] Robinson found no compelling reason to conclude that GP employs any texts other than the four canonical gospels as source material.[42] The author of this gospel altered the NT gospels in order to present "history as it should be" and he "uses and misuses each in turn."[43] One is led to believe that for Robinson the NT gospels are bare history, devoid of any authorial bias or agenda, while GP alone bends history to suit its theology.

Harris' publication, as its title indicates, was styled as a popular account of GP.[44] It included no Greek text. In his opening remarks, Harris issues a reminder about the need to distinguish between modern conventions of writing and those of the ancient world:

[T]here is much more organic connection between early books than we have any idea of from the study of modern books. The materials which were at hand were always worked over by an author, who never suspected that in the nineteenth century we should call such a proceeding plagiarism; as a matter of fact, it was much more like piety than plagiarism; even the modern euphemism "newly-edited" was unknown. To rewrite a good author was a virtue, and it is to this feeling that we owe some of our best Patristic tracts, which are

---

however, to acknowledge that in their haste it would be "presumptuous to pretend to give the final verdict" on GP and the *Apocalypse of Peter* (30).

[40] Ibid., 32.

[41] See the following examples: "Here is a strange perversion in the narrative" (ibid., 17); "Note here, too, one of the many strange perversions in this Gospel: ... 'the breaking of the legs' is strangely perverted" (19); "'The power' then, ... is here, by a strange perversion of our Lord's quotation from Ps. xxii. I, described as forsaking him" (21); "Perversion is a form of witness to the thing perverted" (30).

[42] Ibid., 32.

[43] Ibid., 32–33.

[44] Harris, *Popular Account*. Although the book is ninety-seven pages in length, the margins and line spacing allow for only about 150 words per page. For this reason, it is actually significantly shorter than Swete's publication, which utilizes much smaller font, wider margins, and far more lines per page than that of Harris. Foster ("Discovery and Initial Reaction," 20) also makes this point.

recognised to have some genealogical relation one to the other, as well as to incorporate common traditions.[45]

This reveals a notably different perspective on the issue from what we found in Robinson and shall see in Swete. Where GP's alterations of the NT gospels are "perversions" or distortions of a purer version of the story for some, these comments suggest that the rewriting of the story might, in reality, be virtuous or akin to an act of piety. But as we will discover, this statement does not represent the final judgment of Harris on this extra-canonical gospel.

Harris concluded that the Petrine author "had a good acquaintance with St. John's Gospel" and drew upon it frequently.[46] When it comes to the Synoptic Gospels, "the material is very freely handled, and the writer makes all sorts of fantastic combinations; but he leaves enough of the language in agreement with the originals to make identification of its sources comparatively easy."[47] Matthew is the gospel most often employed. In addition to using these canonical works, the writer may also have used Tatian's *Diatessaron* and very probably possessed a *testimonia* collection similar to the one that Justin Martyr had.[48] Harris was reluctant to commit to a specific date for GP, saying that it "may turn out to be between Tatian and Serapion, ... or [it] may be between the time of the translator Aquila (in the reign of Hadrian) and the time of Serapion."[49] This includes the range of decades roughly from 130 to 190 C.E.

In the estimation of Harris, GP is clearly docetic and probably also contains elements of Gnosticism and Marcionism. In his closing remarks, he describes the author of GP in this way:

If the rest of the early gospel-makers who produced non-canonical texts were like our Docetist, we can only say that they were wanting, not merely in regard for truth and reverence for the subjects which they handled, but in every other quality which makes history possible.... [A]nd however fantastic the fathers of the second century may have been, we can see the reasonableness of their reiteration that the Gospels are four in number, ... not less than four, nor more than four, nor other than the approved and tested four.[50]

---

[45] Harris, *Popular Account*, 21–22.

[46] Ibid., 68.

[47] Ibid.

[48] Ibid., 75–87. Harris was one of the first champions of the *testimonia* hypothesis, as exemplified in his *Testimonies* (2 vols.; Cambridge: Cambridge University Press, 1916–1920). I will address this in further detail in Chapter Two.

[49] Harris, *Popular Account*, 87.

[50] Ibid., 97.

So, despite his earlier comments about the potential piety that might moti-
vate an author to alter his sources, Harris landed in the same place as Robinson. This gospel is a perversion of the four pure gospels.

Swete's contribution stands apart from those of his two Cambridge
peers in its level of detail.[51] After two earlier editions, he published his
most comprehensive work on GP in May 1893.[52] It contains thirty-eight
pages of background material and twenty-eight pages of commentary and
translations of the text. Rather than merely assuming that the Akhmîm
fragment is to be identified as a portion GP, Swete offered several reasons
for this conclusion. Foremost among these are that it purports to be a personal narrative of Peter's, appears to be part of a larger work that is best
classified as a gospel, is at least consistent with docetic sympathies yet is
generally orthodox in tone, and resembles other second-century Christian
texts.[53] In his introductory section, Swete also addressed issues such as
other Petrine writings, the relation of GP to the NT gospels, whether GP
used a harmony, its OT allusions, place of origin, and more. [54] He concluded that this gospel was written around 165 C.E. but not before 150 C.E., and
that it "presupposes a knowledge and use of the Four Gospels."[55]

In Swete's judgment, the theological vocabulary of GP's author includes items associated in modern research with numerous groups commonly deemed "heretical," as the following remarks from him reveal:

> His Docetism is not of the type which was familiar to Ignatius; his Gnosticism connects
> itself with the schools of Valentinus and Julius Cassianus; his anti-Judaic spirit is worthy
> of Marcion; his apocalyptic tone finds its nearest parallels in the literature which passes
> under the name Leucius Charinus.[56]

We see that, like the other two British scholars surveyed, Swete emphasized the "orthodoxy" of the NT gospels over against the "heresy" of GP.

The second half of Swete's book is arranged in the manner of a commentary. The Greek text is set at the top of each page with comments
below, and there is an English translation given at the end of the book. As
Foster has noted, this latter section of Swete's publication is still today the

---

[51] Foster ("Discovery and Initial Reaction," 14) also notes that "Swete was the most
prolific among the Cambridge trio in his work upon this text."

[52] Swete, *Akhmîm Fragment*.

[53] Ibid., xii–xiii.

[54] Throughout this study, I will use the terms OT and Hebrew Bible interchangeably,
recognizing that both are anachronistic when used to refer to second-century Christian
usage of these texts. At the time GP was composed there was no "New Testament," thus
there could not have been an "Old Testament" or "First Testament." Similarly, because
the author of GP – like the vast majority of Christians of the second century – did not
know Hebrew, it is not entirely accurate to speak of his use of the *"Hebrew* Bible."

[55] Swete, *Akhmîm Fragment*, xlv.

[56] Ibid.

closest approximation to a commentary on GP in the English language, and it stands at only twenty-four pages.[57] But this is not to say that these pages lack significance. On the contrary, Swete compressed a great deal of information into this work. A focus of his commentary is to indicate connections between GP and the canonical texts, and he often noted the ways in which the Petrine author has altered, added to, or omitted material from the earlier gospels. According to Swete, the four NT gospels tell a single unified story that GP has corrupted. This is indicated, for example, by Swete's use of the singular "canonical narrative" when comparing GP to the four NT gospels:

A careful study will shew that even details [in GP] which seem to be entirely new, or which directly contradict the canonical narrative, may have been suggested by it.[58]

On this point, he shared the perspective of Robinson and Harris that GP is a perversion of the more pristine and unbiased canonical gospels.

German scholars were very active writing on GP during the 1890s, as exemplified in the publications of Adolf von Harnack, Oscar von Gebhardt, Adolf Hilgenfeld, and Theodor Zahn, among others.[59] I shall review Harnack – who was the first German to publish on this gospel – in some detail, but before doing so a few remarks about the other three are in order. Gebhardt focused on the Akhmîm codex itself, describing its physical characteristics and proposing possible variant readings that differed from Bouriant's initial Greek transcription. It is thus primarily a work of paleography and not a study of the contents of GP itself.[60] Hilgenfeld published two articles on GP, the first of which summarized Eusebius' references to Serapion, provided the Greek text of GP with a critical apparatus, included approximately nine pages of comments on the text, and concluded with the judgment that this gospel belongs to the second century.[61] Unlike the British scholars surveyed earlier, Hilgenfeld judged GP to be independent of the NT gospels even though it was written after them. In

---

[57] Foster, "Discovery and Initial Reaction," 16. In the publishing particulars (e.g., binding, font, Greek text above and double-column commentary below), Swete's book reflects what had become the common format for commentaries on biblical and patristic texts.

[58] Swete, *Akhmîm Fragment*, xv.

[59] Harnack, *Bruchstücke des Evangeliums*; Gebhardt, *Das Evangelium und die Apokalypse des Petrus: Die neuentdeckten Bruchstücke nach einer Photographie der Handschrift zu Gizeh in Lichtdruck herausgegeben* (Leipzig: Hinrichs, 1893); Hilgenfeld, "Das Petrus-Evangelium über Leiden und Auferstehung Jesu," *ZWT* 36/1 (1893): 439–54; idem, "Das Petrus-Evangelium," *ZWT* 36/2 (1893): 220–67; Zahn, *Das Evangelium des Petrus: Das kürzlich gefundene Fragment seines Textes* (Erlangen/Leipzig: Deichert, 1893).

[60] Gebhardt, *Evangelium und die Apokalypse*.

[61] Hilgenfeld, "Petrus-Evangelium über Leiden," 439–54.

a second article, he built on his previous work in an effort to demonstrate a second-century date for the gospel.[62] Zahn, however, followed the same tack as Robinson, Harris, and Swete, concluding that GP is entirely dependent on the canonical texts.[63]

Among the German scholars, it was Harnack who was the first to publish on GP and provided the most detailed examination of it. His monograph, which was based on earlier published notes, was finished by the end of 1892, though it has a publication date of 1893.[64] The title, *Bruchstücke des Evangeliums und der Apokalypse des Petrus*, gives the impression that equal space is devoted to each text, but this is not the case. Approximately 80% addresses GP, while the remaining 20% concerns the *Apocalypse of Peter*.

Harnack gave the Greek text followed by his own German translation, dividing GP into sixty verses.[65] In addition to discussing the relationship between GP and the canonical gospels, he explored parallels with Justin Martyr, the *Apostolic Constitutions*, the *Pericope Adulterae,* the textual tradition of Luke 23:48, Codex Bobbiensis (Mark 16), *Didache*, Ignatius of Antioch, Origen, and Jerome. When addressing the question as to whether GP is dependent on the NT gospels, Harnack strove to present both sides of the argument, to the point that his own view was sometimes unclear.[66] Writing a few decades later, Léon Vaganay expressed frustration with Harnack in this regard, claiming that the German scholar had originally stated in his first published notes that GP was dependent on the NT gospels, could be read as a docetic text, and belonged to the second century, only for him to give a different impression later.[67] Even today, scholars offer differing summaries of Harnack's position. John Dominic Crossan has described Harnack's book as "so vague as to be frequently infuriat-

---

[62] Hilgenfeld, "Petrus-Evangelium," 220–67.

[63] Zahn, *Evangelium des Petrus*, 38–56.

[64] The preface is dated December 15, 1892 (Harnack, *Bruchstücke des Evangeliums*, iv). The revised and expanded edition has a preface date of February 1, 1893.

[65] Harnack, *Bruchstücke des Evangeliums*, 8–16. Robinson, as noted, divided the text into fourteen sections. The standard practice today when giving a citation for GP is to provide the enumerations of both Robinson and Harnack, that of Robinson given first. Thus, it goes GP 1:1; 1:2; 2:3; 2:4; 2:5; 3:6; ... 13:55; 13:56; 13:57; 14:58; 14:59; 14:60. This means that there is no 2:1; 2:2; 3:1; 3:2; 3:3; etc., when citing GP.

[66] In the preface, he stated that he sought to present both sides of disputed matters (Harnack, *Bruchstücke des Evangeliums*, v).

[67] Vaganay, *Évangile de Pierre*, 18. He is referring to the two articles that Harnack originally published under the same title as his later book: "Bruchstücke des Evangeliums und der Apokalypse des Petrus," *SKPAWB* 44 (1892): 895–903; "Bruchstücke des Evangeliums und der Apokalypse des Petrus," *SKPAWB* 45 (1892): 949–65.

ing."[68] Foster states that Harnack "not only suggested that there is a literary relationship between the canonical gospels and the Akhmîm text, but he saw the Gospel of Peter as being later than, and dependent upon the canonical accounts."[69] But as we will see in a moment, it is certainly not accurate to say, as Foster does, that Harnack judged GP to be dependent on the canonical accounts It would be fairer to describe his position as exhibiting greater nuance and caution than that of his contemporaries, and he undoubtedly came to conclusions that differed from his British counterparts.

Harnack contended that GP's author knew Mark's gospel, but when it comes to Matthew, he found it "more likely" ("wahrscheinlicher") that the Petrine evangelist used a gospel related to Matthew, not the Gospel of Matthew known to us.[70] He reached a similar conclusion regarding Luke, which he judged as having only two possible parallels to our gospel, GP 1:1–2:5; 4:13. Harnack left open the question as to whether GP is dependent on Luke or merely on the same tradition that Luke has employed.[71] He was also tentative about judging GP to be dependent on John, despite the many parallels between the two texts.[72] The reticence of Harnack to attempt to provide the final word on the question of GP's relationship to the NT gospels should mark his scholarship as perhaps the most careful of all the earliest scholars. He understood Justin's statement in *Dial.* 106.3 to be a reference to GP, and in order to account for the apologist's familiarity with the gospel, he dated it to 100–135 C.E.[73]

While Harnack's evenhanded discussions have often made it difficult for subsequent writers to classify his position, in some ways he was ahead of his time. Where Robinson, Harris, and Swete were quick to juxtapose the purity of the NT gospels with the "heretical" nature of GP, and thereby diminish the latter, Harnack frequently was more cautious in his treatment of such matters.

There were others early on who agreed with Harnack to a greater or lesser degree in concluding that GP was not entirely dependent on the

---

[68] Crossan, *The Cross That Spoke: The Origins of the Passion Narrative* (San Francisco: Harper & Row, 1988), 13.

[69] Foster, "Discovery and Initial Reaction," 24. He has quoted Harnack, "Ich habe oben bemerkt, unser Evangelium scheine auf den kanonischen Evangelien zu fussen und also jünger als diese zu sein" (*Bruchstücke des Evangeliums*, 32). But the determinative word in this sentence is "scheine" ("seems"), since in the subsequent pages Harnack will explain why matters may not always be as they first appear.

[70] Harnack, *Bruchstücke des Evangeliums*, 33–34.

[71] Ibid., 34.

[72] Ibid., 35–36.

[73] Ibid., 37–40.

canonical texts.[74] Two general schools soon developed around the question of GP's relationship to the NT gospels. Vaganay, writing his commentary nearly forty years later, would divide the early debate into two camps: 1) the party of Harnack (independence); and 2) the party of Zahn (dependence).[75]

As quickly as the flood of publications on GP covered the scholarly world in the two years after the appearance of its *editio princeps*, the waters rapidly receded to a virtual trickle. Granted, there were a few works written in the thirty-five years after this period, but they were few and far between, and typically contributed little new to this particular conversation. Most notably, Percival Gardner-Smith went even further than Harnack in postulating that GP was not dependent in any way on any of the NT gospels: "The many divergences of 'Peter' from the canonical gospels are best explained, not by supposing that the author had an inexplicable passion for tampering with his sources, but by supposing that he did not know the work of Matthew, Mark, Luke, and John."[76] Gardner-Smith dated GP to 80–100 C.E., which was a few decades earlier than Harnack's estimate.[77] But it would not be until 1930 and the publication of Vaganay's commentary that another full-length work would appear.[78]

Vaganay produced what is still widely regarded as the most significant study of GP ever to have been written. Foster boasts that it "still has no rival."[79] Vaganay's publication is divided into two sections, the first addresses introductory matters and covers nearly 200 pages, and the second provides nearly 150 pages of text, translation, and commentary. Following Zahn, Swete, and others, Vaganay concluded that all four NT gospels were used by the author of the noncanonical gospel. He dubbed this author a "forger" ("faussaire"), a moniker he uses frequently throughout his work.

After summarizing the patristic references to GP and the studies of previous scholars, Vaganay thoroughly reviewed the parallels between GP and each of the NT gospels before doing the same with GP and variants in the textual tradition of those gospels.[80] He judged Matthew to be the gospel on

---

[74] See, for example, Hilgenfeld, "Petrus-Evangelium über Leiden," 439–54; idem, "Petrus-Evangelium," 220–67; Hans von Soden, "Das Petrus Evangelium und die kanonischen Evangelien," *ZTK* 3 (1893): 52–92; Cassels, *Gospel according to Peter*.

[75] Vaganay, *Évangile de Pierre*, 18–27.

[76] Gardner-Smith, "The Gospel of Peter," *JTS* 27 (1926): 270. Gardner-Smith (*Saint John and the Synoptic Gospels* [Cambridge: Cambridge University Press, 1938]) also argued for the independence of John over against the Synoptics, attributing the similarities to a common oral tradition.

[77] Gardner-Smith, "The Date of the Gospel of Peter," *JTS* 27 (1926): 401–7.

[78] Vaganay, *Évangile de Pierre*.

[79] Foster, "Discovery and Initial Reaction," 29.

[80] Vaganay, *Évangile de Pierre*, 43–75.

which GP is most dependent, and John the one used least by our "forger." Where Vaganay differed from earlier commentators who promoted the dependency of GP on the NT gospels was in his description of the specific manner in which the NT texts were employed. He rejected the idea that GP is a harmony or a mere compilation.[81] Instead, "there is in the Akhmîm fragment a personal note, a freedom in the composition."[82] Rather than GP being a simple but poor cut-and-paste version of the earlier texts (e.g., Swete, Zahn) or representative of independent tradition (e.g., Harnack), Vaganay argued that GP is a freely composed work. While nearly every previous scholar argued for a strong docetic influence, Vaganay was reluctant to do so, claiming instead that "despite its docetic tendencies, it is not a work of the sect."[83] Rather than being from a docetic group, GP is a product of popular, relatively unsophisticated Christianity:

The author of our apocryphal work seems to have been one of those common Christians whose faith is not always guided by very firm doctrine. He must have belonged to one of those cosmopolitan areas where the infiltration of heresy occurred easily.[84]

Though well intentioned, the Petrine evangelist lacked the theological ability to create an "orthodox" gospel on a par with the canonical texts. By no fault of his own, he fell prey unknowingly to heretical influences. Vaganay arrived at a date of 120–130 C.E. and proposed Syria as the place of origin.[85]

This French scholar was the first to include an extended discussion of the gospel's apologetic tendencies. While devoting some thirty pages under the topic heading, "The apologetic tendencies of the *Gospel of Peter*," half of this treatment addressed the question of docetism and potential indicators of it.[86] Aside from this issue, Vaganay identified four types of apologetic features: 1) those related to the resurrection of Jesus; 2) those related to the conduct of Peter and the apostles; 3) the tendency to augment passages via prophetic biblical exegesis; and 4) divergence from the NT gospels' chronology.

In his discussion of resurrection apologetics and the ways in which GP differs from the NT stories, Vaganay noted aptly that these changes "constitute, in effect, a pertinent response to common objections."[87] Vaganay, however, only occasionally referred to particular objections in the course of his later commentary on the text. While the author of GP is a "forger,"

---

[81] Ibid., 77–81.
[82] Ibid., 81.
[83] Ibid., 112.
[84] Ibid., 121.
[85] Ibid., 163, 179–80.
[86] Ibid., 90–122.
[87] Ibid., 92.

he is also an apologist. His apologetic tendencies related to Peter and the apostles served the interests of the church.

Vaganay listed approximately thirty potential examples of passages in GP that have been shaped by exegesis of biblical prophecy. Where he was unable to cite specific parallels to his claims regarding resurrection apologetics and apologetics related to Peter and the apostles, Vaganay was thorough in cataloging numerous examples from other early Christian literature that reflect the same type of exegesis of prophecy that he contended is present in GP. In discussing the alteration of chronological details, Vaganay focused solely on the timing of the crucifixion and the actions of the disciples. The changes made in these areas functioned to defend the church and its claims.

Although Vaganay offered many examples indicating the apologetic nature of GP that had not previously been mentioned by others, his judgment was sometimes influenced by his apparent desire to defend the interests of "the church." In some ways it might be fair to say that Vaganay, a Roman Catholic priest who seemed to be intent on protecting some of the church's claims in the 20th century (e.g., the "orthodoxy" of the NT gospels over against the "heresy" of GP), had projected some of his own apologetic interests onto the author of GP. This is not to say that he was necessarily always wrong in his judgments in this area, but he may have been overstating his case at some points. In addition, as I hope to demonstrate in this study, there are several more examples of apologetic tendencies in GP that Vaganay has not included in his discussion, some of which are arguably central to better understanding this text. This French scholar was writing at a time when social-scientific studies of early Christianity were in their infancy. In contrast, I will be employing some of the knowledge that we have gained during the past eighty years about the social world of the developing Christian movement.

Because of the monumental scale of Vaganay's commentary, it appeared for some time that he had pronounced the last word on GP.[88] Between his publication in 1930 and the appearance of Crossan's in the late 1980s, only four works merit attention.[89] Benjamin A. Johnson, under the direction of Helmut Koester, wrote his dissertation on the empty tomb traditions in GP and used a form-critical methodology to argue that GP has

---

[88] Montague R. James (review of Léon Vaganay, *L'Évangile de Pierre*, *JTS* 32 [1931]: 296–99) opened his lengthy review of Vaganay's book by stating that it is "the most extensive that has ever been produced on the Gospel of Peter" (296). Similar sentiments can be found in René Draguet, review of Léon Vaganay, *L'Évangile de Pierre*, *RHE* 27 (1931): 854–56.

[89] To be sure, there were perhaps close to twenty publications during these decades (see the Bibliography). However, the four I discuss here are the ones that are still cited frequently today.

combined two earlier empty tomb stories which are each older than the canonical accounts.[90] Even the guard story in GP is more primitive than Matthew's, according to Johnson. It is entirely independent from the canonical works, having been written near the end of the first century. This short work (only 132 pages) was never published and its thesis does not appear to have been developed by subsequent scholars.

In 1973 Maria G. Mara published a French commentary that in many ways is similar to Vaganay's.[91] She concludes that GP's author was familiar with the NT gospels and also employed a significant amount of oral tradition. The OT background is also an important feature of GP, according to Mara. She criticizes Vaganay's use of the derogatory term "forger," preferring instead to describe the Petrine evangelist as one "inspired by a simple but profound theology."[92] The real value of this gospel is not in its historical accounts of Jesus' life, death, and resurrection, but in its theological claims about him – the very feature that lends worth to the canonical gospels. This helpful corrective moved the discussion beyond a false dichotomy between history and theology that was frequently present in many earlier commentators. She issues a reminder that the NT gospels are every bit as theological as GP, a point that, despite its obviousness, often seemed to be missed or at least neglected by many who had written before her.[93] The Synoptic Gospels, according to Mara, provided the narrative structure for GP, while John was the primary source for its theology.[94]

Jürgen Denker published a dissertation in which he argues on source-critical grounds that GP is not dependent on the canonical gospels, is not anti-Jewish, and arose in a Jewish-Christian setting.[95] The OT and oral tradition account for almost the entirety of GP. The gospel itself did not emerge in a docetic sect but does reflect a naïve docetism not unlike that opposed by Ignatius of Antioch, whose letters were written very near the time Denker claims that GP was composed.

Jerry W. McCant, in his dissertation, questions the long-held assumption surrounding the docetic nature of GP, contending that most such ele-

---

[90] Johnson, "Empty Tomb Tradition in the Gospel of Peter," (Th.D. diss., Harvard University Divinity School, 1965).

[91] Mara, *Évangile de Pierre: Introduction, Texte Critique, Traduction, Commentaire et Index* (SC 201; Paris: Cerf, 1973).

[92] Ibid., 29.

[93] I do not mean to imply that the history-to-theology ratio is the same in GP as in the four NT gospels. Instead, like Mara, I wish to emphasize that all five gospels are primarily theological texts, regardless of the amount of history preserved in any one of them.

[94] Mara, *Évangile de Pierre*, 214.

[95] Denker, *Die theologiegeschichtliche Stellung des Petrusevangeliums: Ein Beitrag zur Frühgeschichte des Doketismus* (Europäische Hochschulschriften 23/36; Frankfurt: Lang, 1975).

ments are better understood as part of a martyriological motif that pervades the gospel.[96] As part of his argument, McCant claims that the evangelist revised four stories from the NT gospels: the Matthean guard episode, Mark's empty tomb story, Luke's account of the trial(s) before Herod and Pilate, and the Joannine epiphany story set in Galilee.[97] The differences between GP and the NT gospels exist because "the author of GP knew and used the four canonical gospels and altered and expanded them according to his own redactional purposes."[98] McCant is largely successful in demonstrating that GP need not be understood as reflecting docetic ideas, but his examination of particular "redactional purposes" is narrow and limited to those surrounding this question of docetism. Issues of apologetics and polemics are not a focal point of his work.

The general lack of interest in GP during the middle decades of the 20th century came to a rapid end with the appearance of Crossan's original thesis. His first full-length publication on GP appears in his book, *The Cross That Spoke*, but his ideas about this gospel were present in an earlier work.[99] Although he has nuanced some aspects of his hypothesis over the last two decades, he remains a staunch defender of it.[100] By Crossan's own admission, however, his proposal has been met with "almost universal scholarly rejection."[101]

It is not easy to summarize Crossan's thesis about the composition of GP as it relates to the NT gospels. The earliest stratum or version of GP was composed in the middle of the first century, and Crossan has dubbed this text the "Cross Gospel."[102] This was the original Passion Narrative, the one used by Matthew, Mark, and Luke when composing their accounts.[103]

---

[96] McCant, "The Gospel of Peter: The Docetic Question Re-Examined," (Ph.D. diss., Emory University, 1978).

[97] Ibid., 35–115.

[98] Ibid., 114.

[99] Crossan, *Four Other Gospels: Shadows on the Contours of Canon* (Minneapolis: Seabury, 1985); idem, *Cross That Spoke*.

[100] See, for example, Crossan, "Thoughts on Two Extracanonical Gospels," *Semeia* 49 (1990): 155–68; idem, *Who Killed Jesus? Exposing the Roots of Anti-Semitism in the Gospel Story of the Death of Jesus* (New York: HarperCollins, 1995); idem, *The Birth of Christianity: Discovering What Happened in the Years Immediately after the Execution of Jesus* (San Francisco: HarperCollins, 1998); idem, "The Gospel of Peter and the Canonical Gospels: Independence, Dependence, or Both?" *Forum* n.s. 1 (1998): 7–51. His most recent publication on GP that appeared in 2007 is "The *Gospel of Peter* and the Canonical Gospels," in Kraus and Nicklas, *Evangelium nach Petrus*, 117–34. This is simply a reiteration of his previous position; it appears to offer nothing new.

[101] Crossan, "*Gospel of Peter* and the Canonical Gospels," 134.

[102] Crossan, *Cross That Spoke*, 16–17.

[103] Matthew and Luke, in addition to having the Cross Gospel as a source for their Passion Narratives, also used Mark. See Crossan, *Cross That Spoke*, 17–21.

The earliest version of GP contained most but not all of the text known to us from the Akhmîm fragment.[104] To be precise, Crossan argues that the original version of GP (i.e., his "Cross Gospel") included 1:1–2 (Herod condemning Jesus); 2:5b–6:22 (abuse and crucifixion); 7:25 (lament of the Jews); 8:28–10:42 (guarding of the tomb and the resurrection); and 11:45–49 (guards' report to Pilate). This earliest account of Jesus' death is the "independent" portion of Crossan's hypothesis. As the first such text, it is dependent on nothing else known to us. The remaining sections – GP 2:3–5a (Joseph requesting the body); 6:23–24 (Joseph receiving the body); 7:26–27 (mourning of the disciples); 11:43–44 (second descent of an angel); and 12:50–14:60 (women's visit to the tomb and the disciples return to their homes) – were added to GP later, most likely by a second-century redactor. Many of these additions were drawn from the canonical gospels in order to harmonize the accounts. It is in this sense, then, that GP is dependent on the NT gospels. Hence, Crossan describes his proposal as an "independence-and-dependence solution" to the question of GP's relationship to the NT gospels.[105]

Crossan has remained unconvinced that any theory of writing, orality, or memory can account for the peculiar nature of GP when compared to the canonical gospels. He has recently summarized his perspective as follows:

If anyone can show me how a person who knows the canonical versions either as scribal documents or oral traditions got from them to the present *Gospel of Peter*, I would withdraw my proposed solution. It is not enough to speak of memory and/or orality in general theory without explaining how memory and/or orality worked in this particular instance. What theory of memory and/or what exercise of oral tradition or scribal transmission gets one from any or all of our intracanonical gospels to the very coherent narrative in the *Cross Gospel*?[106]

The coherence of GP, according to Crossan, is such that it cannot be explained by a cut-and-paste use of the NT accounts, as though the author had those texts in front of him. Similarly, Crossan has not been persuaded that oral tradition can account for this narrative unity. He therefore has concluded that his unique proposal carries the most explanatory power for the text of this gospel as we have it.

As with many provocative hypotheses, Crossan's work ushered in the latest era of studies on this gospel. Some have responded directly to Crossan's claims regarding his Cross Gospel, particularly the suggestion that it

---

[104] Crossan, of course, realizes that the Akhmîm manuscript preserves only a portion of the much longer original work.

[105] Crossan, "*Gospel of Peter* and the Canonical Gospels," 134.

[106] Ibid.

is a mid-first-century document composed prior to all of the NT works.[107] Others, though not endorsing every aspect of Crossan's proposal, have agreed with the idea that GP was independent from the canonical texts.[108]

Crossan and Raymond E. Brown soon developed a rivalry over this issue, their exchanges lasting until Brown's death in 1998. Brown suggests that, although the author of GP did not have copies of the NT works before him when composing his own gospel, he was still dependent on them. He offers the following reconstruction to account for the relationship:

> I doubt that the author of *GPet* had any written Gospel before him, although he was familiar with Matt because he had read it carefully in the past and/or had heard it read several times in community worship on the Lord's Day, so that it gave the dominant shaping to his thought. Most likely he had heard people speak who were familiar with the Gospels of Luke and John – perhaps traveling preachers who rephrased salient stories – so that he knew some of their contents but had little idea of their structure....
>
> Intermingled in the *GPet* author's mind were also popular tales about incidents in the passion, the very type of popular material that Matt had tapped in composing his Gospel at an earlier period. All this went into his composition of *GPet*, a gospel that was not meant to be read in liturgy but to help people picture imaginatively the career of Jesus.[109]

For Brown, the overall lack of agreement in vocabulary and word order between GP and any NT gospel renders improbable the idea of literary dependence. The later evangelist would not have created a work like GP if he had been working with written copies of his source material, in Brown's estimation. Thus, he promotes the idea of the "oral dependency" of GP on the canonical works.[110]

Brown presents a modern analogy to explain his idea. Imagine a Christian today "who had read or studied Matt in Sunday school or church education classes years ago but in the interim had not been reading their NT.

---

[107] See, for example, Joel B. Green, "The Gospel of Peter: Source for a Pre-Canonical Passion Narrative?" *ZNW* 78 (1987): 293–301; Raymond E. Brown, "The *Gospel of Peter* and Canonical Gospel Priority," *NTS* 33 (1987): 321–43; Susan E. Schaeffer, "The *Gospel of Peter*, the Canonical Gospels, and Oral Tradition" (Ph.D. diss., Union Theological Seminary, 1991); Raymond E. Brown, *The Death of the Messiah: From Gethsemane to the Grave, A Commentary on the Passion Narratives in the Four Gospels* (2 vols.; ABRL; New York: Doubleday, 1994), 2:1317–49; Alan Kirk, "Examining Priorities: Another Look at the *Gospel of Peter*'s Relationship to the New Testament Gospels," *NTS* 40 (1994): 572–95.

[108] See, for example, Koester, *Ancient Christian Gospels*, 216–40; Arthur J. Dewey, "'Time to Murder and Create': Visions and Revisions in the *Gospel of Peter*," *Semeia* 49 (1990): 101–27.

[109] Brown, *Death of the Messiah*, 2:1334–35.

[110] Brown's student, Susan E. Schaeffer, also argued for this position in her dissertation ("The *Gospel of Peter*, the Canonical Gospels, and Oral Tradition"). On the various types of dependency at work in ancient texts and the criteria that have been proposed to detect this, see, for example, Richard B. Hays, *Echoes of Scripture in the Letters of Paul* (New Haven: Yale University Press, 1989).

Yet they had heard the canonical passion narratives read in church litur-
gies. Also they had seen a passion play or dramatization in the cinema, on
TV, or on the stage, or heard one on the radio."[111] If we were to ask such a
person to tell the passion and resurrection stories from his or her own
memory, Brown contends, it is possible that (s)he would give an account
similar to what we find in GP. Crossan has rejected this claim, stating that
he had unscientifically tested Brown's hypothesis among undergraduate
students at DePaul University.[112] Having asked thirty-two students to recount from memory alone their recollection of the trial, crucifixion, and
burial of Jesus, Crossan points out that not one "[came] up with anything
even remotely resembling the passion version of the *Gospel of Peter*."[113]

We see in the work of Brown, Crossan, and others the struggle to recon-
cile the clear parallels between GP and the NT gospels with their glaring
differences. I shall argue in this study that Brown's approach underesti-
mates the Petrine evangelist's knowledge of his source material, while
Crossan's theory unnecessarily posits an earlier stratum of GP to account
for matters. Our author was not working with faint memories of stories
heard long ago (so Brown), but rather was well acquainted with written
versions of the NT texts.

While a general calm has returned to the debate over the depend-
ence/independence issue as scholars have taken the time to examine the
question anew in light of the numerous publications during the 1980s and
1990s, the first decade of the 21st century has seen more studies. Two of
these are especially noteworthy. The first complete critical edition of GP
was published by Thomas J. Kraus and Tobias Nicklas in 2004.[114] It contains a survey of patristic references, an examination of the Akhmîm manuscript, the Greek text with critical apparatus, German and English translations, a discussion of other Greek manuscript fragments that have been
proposed as possibly containing portions of GP, and photographs of the
Akhmîm codex, in addition to these treatments of the *Apocalypse of Peter*.

The same two scholars in 2007 edited a volume of essays on a wide
range of issues concerning GP.[115] This publication contains twenty essays
written by twenty contributors and represents the most up-to-date research.
Topics such as the Greek style of GP, its use of the OT, parallels between
GP and other early Christian texts, its Christology, and many more are
included. This volume indicates that there is much more to harvest from
this gospel and that there are further issues to explore beyond the question

---

[111] Brown, *Death of the Messiah*, 2:1335–36.
[112] Crossan, *Birth of Christianity*, 57–58.
[113] Ibid., 58.
[114] Kraus and Nicklas, *Petrusevangelium*.
[115] Kraus and Nicklas, *Evangelium nach Petrus*.

of the gospel's relationship to the NT texts. Some of the essays revisit long-standing subjects (e.g., the relevance of Justin's "memoirs of the apostles"), while others represent new methodologies (e.g., a narrative approach of "reading GP under Empire").

The future of GP studies will need to reckon with the recent appearance of Paul Foster's commentary, which is the first full-length commentary written in English.[116] Interest in noncanonical Christian texts is as high as it has ever been, both in the scholarly world and among non-scholars.[117] We have come to recognize that these sources shed a different kind of light on the development of Christianity during its earliest, highly formative centuries. Conversely, our increasing knowledge of the movement allows us to understand better some of the factors that influenced the formation of GP. I am hopeful that more will continue to be written on this gospel and its place in the emerging Christian movement.

1.5 Thesis: GP As "Rewritten Gospel"

No thorough study of GP can proceed without a hypothesis regarding its relationship to the NT gospels. I will contend that previous scholars, most notably Vaganay, were near the mark in their judgment regarding GP's dependence on the NT gospels, though the term "dependence" is too imprecise to be entirely helpful. In one sense, it is true that GP is dependent on these earlier texts. But this is not the type of dependence we find among the Synoptic Gospels, regardless of how we solve the Synoptic Problem. While it appears, assuming Markan priority, that Matthew and Luke have copied portions of Mark, often sharing the exact vocabulary as their source, a different sort of "dependence" is at work in GP. Matthew and Luke are more conservative than the Petrine evangelist in the handling of source material. Undoubtedly, the canonical authors do alter details, and rearrange, add to, and omit stories from their sources, but certainly not

---

[116] Foster, *The Gospel of Peter: Introduction, Critical Edition and Commentary* (TENTS 4; Leiden: Brill, 2010). I regret that this was published shortly after I completed my own work, thus not providing me the opportunity to interact with it.

[117] This is exemplified in the new series, Oxford Early Christian Gospel Texts, published by Oxford University Press. Volumes in this series aim to be critical editions of key noncanonical gospel writings, complete with full translation, introduction, and commentary. The two volumes published thus far are Christopher Tuckett, ed., *The Gospel of Mary* (Oxford Early Christian Gospel Texts; New York: Oxford University Press, 2007); Thomas J. Kraus, Michael J. Kruger, and Tobias Nicklas, eds., *Gospel Fragments* (Oxford Early Christian Gospel Texts; New York: Oxford University Press, 2009). The volume by Kraus, Kruger, and Nicklas covers several fragments of early gospel texts, including P.Egerton 2, P.Oxy 840, P.Oxy 1224, and more.

nearly to the degree that we find with GP. We must therefore leave behind the relationship among the Synoptic Gospels as the most fitting analogue for understanding GP's relationship to the NT gospels.

I noted earlier that Vaganay referred to GP as exhibiting "a freedom in composition."[118] Harris, although he later rejected the following as being applicable to our gospel, remarked that in antiquity, "to rewrite a good author was a virtue, and it is to this feeling that we owe some of our best Patristic tracts, which are recognised to have some genealogical relation one to the other, as well as to incorporate common traditions."[119] These sentiments from Vaganay and Harris emphasize the loose manner in which the Petrine evangelist handled his sources. So in one sense our evangelist is dependent on the NT gospels, which provide the framework for his own narrative. But in another very real sense his own gospel is a new creation that significantly alters many of the details in the antecedent gospels. He felt under no compulsion to tell the stories in the same way that the previous evangelists had told them.[120]

I want to build upon these ideas and offer a new descriptor that may assist us in better understanding GP's place within early gospel literature. To this end, I suggest that we think of a particular type of relationship between GP and the NT gospels, one that leads me to propose "rewritten gospel" as the best term for GP.[121] This label recalls the category "rewritten Bible" that is frequently used of certain Jewish texts from the Second Temple literature. It is this category of "rewritten Bible texts" (RBTs) that serves as the most helpful analogue for fully appreciating the relationship of GP to the canonical gospels.[122]

---

[118] Vaganay, *Évangile de Pierre*, 81.

[119] Harris, *Popular Account*, 22.

[120] I do not mean to say that the four NT writers tell a single unified story. Each offers his own version. In addition, I am saying something entirely different from Crossan when he speaks of his own "independence-and-dependence" solution. Crossan is referring to layers or strata of GP as being independent or dependent, the earliest being independent of the NT works and the latest being dependent on them. I am referring to a single unified composition that does not fit neatly into the typical understanding of "dependency," especially as it is commonly found in gospel studies.

[121] It was several months after coining the term "rewritten gospel" for GP that I first encountered the expression in a publication, in Adele Reinhartz, "'Rewritten Gospel': The Case of Caiaphas the High Priest," *NTS* 55 (2009): 160–78. Reinhartz, however, applies "rewritten Gospel" (capitalized) to two works from the 20th century: Dorothy Sayers' play, *The Man Born To Be King*, and Sholem Asch's novel, *The Nazarene*. So while there is some overlap between her use and mine, we are applying the category to works that are vastly different from one another.

[122] This study is an exercise in redaction criticism. Where it differs most substantially from typical redaction-critical studies of gospels is in the specific sources being proposed – namely, all four NT gospels. Furthermore, in my hypothesis there is a gap of 80–120

The origin of the term "rewritten Bible" can be traced back to Geza Vermes.[123] The specific parameters of the category itself are debated, and numerous texts have been proposed as belonging to it.[124] Four that are usually included as reflecting this type of literature are *Jubilees*, the *Genesis Apocryphon* (1Qap Gen[ar]), *Liber antiquitatum biblicarum* (Pseudo-Philo), and Josephus, *Jewish Antiquities*. Others often mentioned are the *Assumption of Moses*, the Qumran *Temple Scroll*, the *Ascension of Isaiah*, the *Apocalypse of Moses*, and *2 Baruch*. These texts "rewrite" biblical (OT) stories by including numerous supplements, interpretations, and legendary additions. By "rewriting," then, I mean the modifying, clarifying, enhancing, and/or coloring of previous texts. Daniel J. Harrington remarks that what is of significance in these texts is that they "try to make the biblical story more attractive, edifying, and intelligible."[125] Their primary purpose is "the clarification and actualization of the biblical story," which is to make the accounts "meaningful within new situations."[126]

---

years between the earliest proposed written source (Mark) and the composition of GP itself. This has allowed a significantly greater amount of time to elapse for evidence of reactions to the source material than is the case with redaction-critical studies of the NT gospels. Because of this, in many cases I am able to muster textual support for certain contentions I make about the reception of GP's source material. This larger pool of evidence, in my estimation, allows me to have a better understanding of the particular interests at work in the Petrine evangelists handling of his sources than is the case with the canonical gospels.

[123] Vermes, *Scripture and Tradition in Judaism* (StPB 4; Leiden: Brill, 1961), 67–126. This section of his book is titled "The Rewritten Bible," and scholars today acknowledge this as the source of the term. For example, in the introduction to her work on the subject, Sidnie White Crawford (*Rewriting Scripture in Second Temple Times* [Grand Rapids: Eerdmans, 2008], 2) notes that "it was Geza Vermes in 1961 who first identified a group of late Second Temple works as examples of a particular form of interpretation, a group that he identified as a genre dubbed 'Rewritten Bible' texts." Likewise, James C. VanderKam ("Questions of Canon Viewed through the Dead Sea Scrolls," in McDonald and Sanders, *Canon Debate*, 96) refers to "rewritten Bible" as "Geza Vermes's rubric."

[124] Introductions to the subject of rewritten Bible can be found in Vermes, *Scripture and Tradition*, 67–126; Daniel J. Harrington, "Palestinian Adaptations of Biblical Narratives and Prophecies: I. The Bible Rewritten," in *Early Judaism and Its Modern Interpreters* (ed. Robert A. Kraft and George W. E. Nickelsburg; BMI 2; Atlanta: Scholars Press, 1986), 239–47; Philip S. Alexander, "Retelling the Old Testament," in *It is Written: Scripture Citing Scripture, Essays in Honour of Barnabas Lindars, SSF* (ed. D. A. Carson and H. G. M. Williamson; Cambridge: Cambridge University Press, 1988), 99–121; Erkki Koskenniemi and Pekka Lindqvist, "Rewritten Bible, Rewritten Stories: Methodological Aspects," in *Rewritten Bible Reconsidered: Proceedings of the Conference in Karkku, Finland August 24–26 2006* (ed. Antti Laato and Jacques van Ruiten; SRB 1; Winona Lake, Ind.: Eisenbrauns, 2008), 11–39; Crawford, *Rewriting Scripture*.

[125] Harrington, "Palestinian Adaptations," 239.

[126] Ibid., 239–40.

Though it is difficult to arrive at a specific definition for the category "rewritten Bible," Philip S. Alexander has offered nine principal characteristics exemplifying these texts: 1) RBTs are narratives that follow a sequential and chronological order; 2) they are freestanding works that follow the form of the biblical texts on which they are based; 3) they are not intended to replace the Bible; 4) they typically rewrite a significant portion of Scripture while making use of additional legendary material, integrating it within the biblical narrative; 5) RBTs follow the general order of biblical accounts but are selective in what they include; 6) "the intention of the texts is to produce an interpretative reading of Scripture" by offering "a fuller, smoother and doctrinally more advanced form of the sacred narrative"; 7) because the texts are in narrative form, they can reflect only a single interpretation of the original; 8) the narrative form also renders it implausible for the writers to offer their exegetical reasoning; 9) RBTs use extrabiblical tradition and non-biblical sources (oral and written), and utilize legendary material by fusing it with the biblical narrative, thereby creating a synthesis of the whole tradition (biblical and non-biblical).[127]

I will now offer examples of the ways in which RBTs rewrite biblical texts. These are important, because the types of redaction found here are the very types I will point out later in my discussion of GP. The *Genesis Apocryphon* rewrites the Genesis stories about Abraham and Sarah. Vermes aptly summarizes the manner in which this is accomplished:

The author of GA does indeed try, by every means at his disposal, to make the biblical story more attractive, more real, more edifying, and above all more intelligible. Geographic data are inserted to complete biblical lacunae or to identify altered place names, and various descriptive touches are added to give the story substance. There were, for example, three Egyptian princes, and the name of one of them was Harkenosh.[128]

When there are unexplained or apparently contradictory statements in the biblical text, they are reconciled in the *Genesis Apocryphon* "in order to allay doubt and worry."[129] For instance, the original story in Genesis 12 does not specify how Pharaoh learns of Sarah's identity. In the *Genesis Apocryphon*, however, it is explained that Lot was the one who relayed this information to Pharaoh.

Another feature of RBTs is that difficult biblical texts are occasionally suppressed. Along these lines, Vermes refers to the *Genesis Apocryphon*'s omission of the story of Abraham receiving gifts from Pharaoh on account of Sarah (Gen 12:16). He argues that this is "due to an apologetic preoccupation and a desire to avoid scandal; retention of the passage as it stands would offend pious ears. But although this leaves the enrichment of Abra-

---

[127] Alexander, "Retelling the Old Testament," 116–18.

[128] Vermes, *Scripture and Tradition*, 125.

[129] Ibid.

ham unexplained, it is made good later on in such a way as to preserve, rearranged, all the details of the story."[130]

RBTs occasionally alter the authorial perspective in order to lend greater authority to their own text. For instance, the author of the *Temple Scroll* frequently quotes from the Pentateuch, but when doing so he omits the name of Moses where it appears. Michael Wise, Martin Abegg, Jr., and Edward Cook have remarked on the motivation behind this practice:

> The effect of these omissions is electric. The *Temple Scroll* is made to seem a direct revelation from God to the author. Many scholars believe that the author was claiming to present a new, previously hidden, writing from the hand of Moses.[131]

This change in narrative perspective effectively lends greater authority to the newly rewritten text.

Authors of RBTs sometimes integrate material from multiple biblical texts. The *Temple Scroll*, for example, reorganizes material from Exodus, Leviticus, Numbers, and Deuteronomy, not adhering to any one of them consistently for its own account.[132] But the foundational narratives, the biblical texts, always serve as the primary basis for the new literary creation, albeit sometimes in greatly altered form. According to James C. VanderKam, these alterations were often done in order to "counter contemporary claims," as, for example, in the concern of the author of *Jubilees* to "demonstrate that the laws [i.e., pentateuchal legislation] were not an innovation from Moses' time but had been practiced long before by the heroes of Genesis."[133] The religious and social context of these authors thus serves as an important lens through which to read RBTs, and this will also be true of GP.

This practice of rewriting earlier texts was not unique to Jewish literature, either. In the larger ancient Greco-Roman world the notion of μίμησις or *imitatio* was held in esteem. To imitate or emulate a respected writer was a means of showing respect or admiration for the author being imitated. Appealing to both Jewish RBTs and Greco-Roman imitative works, Thomas L. Brodie has proposed them as the means of explaining John's relationship to the Synoptic Gospels.[134] These Greco-Roman works, however, are typically not religious texts. Harry Y. Gamble summarizes this matter:

---

[130] Ibid., 125–26.

[131] Wise, Abegg, Jr., and Cook, *The Dead Sea Scrolls: A New Translation* (New York: HarperCollins, 1996), 457–58.

[132] VanderKam, "Questions of Canon," 100–104.

[133] Ibid., 106.

[134] See the discussion of Thomas L. Brodie (*The Quest for the Origin of John's Gospel: A Source-Oriented Approach* [New York: Oxford University Press, 1993], 42–46) and the sources he cites for an overview of *imitatio* in ancient literature .

Among the many religious movements of antiquity, only Christianity and Judaism produced much literature at all. Greek and Roman religions appear to have been largely
indifferent to the use of texts.... No Greco-Roman religious group produced, used, or
valued texts on a scale comparable to Judaism and Christianity, so that apart from Jewish
literature, there is no appreciable body of religious writings with which early Christian
literature can be fruitfully compared.[135]

RBTs, because of their religious nature, will serve as the category that
provides the best model for understanding GP's handling of the NT gospels.

With a few slight modifications to the category "rewritten Bible," I shall
apply the concept of "rewritten gospel" to GP. The first and most significant modification is the distinction between "Bible" and "gospel."[136] It is
anachronistic to speak of a "canon" of gospels in place by the middle of
the second century, if one means by this a collection of texts whose contents has been mandated by church councils, bishops, or other ecclesiastical authorities. However, I do think that an argument can be made that
Matthew, Mark, Luke, and John were, practically speaking, the only four
gospels that carried an authoritative status among *some* Christians of this
era. Furthermore, I think that it is likely that the Petrine evangelist held
these particular four gospels in high esteem and considered their stories
about Jesus' life, death, and resurrection to be a type of "sacred narrative,"

---

[135] Gamble, *Books and Readers in the Early Church: A History of Early Christian
Texts* (New Haven: Yale University Press, 1995), 18.

[136] Some might object that the literary genre of "gospel" was not yet a clear category
in the mid-second century. Koester (*Ancient Christian Gospels*, 24–43) is among those
who have argued that it was not until the latter half of the second century that certain
texts came to be identified as "gospels." On the other hand, Martin Hengel (*The Four
Gospels and the One Gospel of Jesus Christ* [trans. John Bowden; Harrisburg, Pa.:
Trinity Press International, 2000], 78–115) claims that Mark, the first to write a gospel,
intentionally created a new literary genre to fit within the broader classification of Greek
writings known as βίοι, biographies of famous figures. It is not necessary, however, to
arrive at a definitive answer to this question here. Regardless of whether Matthew, Mark,
Luke, John, and other writings were referred to as "gospels" in the mid-second century, it
remains the case that there was a group of works that shared common features, characteristics that readers would recognize as uniting them in some way. Therefore, whether or
not the author of GP identified certain earlier texts as "gospels," he modeled his own
literary creation after them in terms of form and content.

For classification purposes, Koester has suggested a criterion for determining whether
any early Christian writing deserves to be called a gospel. Gospels are those texts that
"are constituted by the transmission, use, and interpretation of materials and traditions
from and about Jesus of Nazareth" (*Ancient Christian Gospels*, 46). He includes GP
among these works and I concur with his judgment. Because GP came to be known as a
gospel, the term "rewritten *gospel*" is appropriate.

in the sense that they speak of what holds great religious significance.[137] Undoubtedly, these stories were foundational religious narratives in early Christian communities in the same way that, say, the stories in the Pentateuch held significance for the writers of certain RBTs.

To return to the question of canon, just as it is anachronistic to speak of a fixed canon of gospels in the mid-second century C.E., it is true that the status of the Hebrew Bible canon was not settled during the period when most RBTs were composed (2nd century B.C.E. – 1st century C.E.). As VanderKam notes, "there was no canon of scripture in Second Temple Judaism [i.e., pre-70 C.E.]."[138] At the same time, however, it is clear that during the Second Temple era "some books were regarded by certain writers as sufficiently authoritative that they could be cited to settle a dispute, explain a situation, provide an example, or predict what would happen. In that limited sense there is evidence for a set or sets of authoritative works in Judaism from an early time."[139] Because of this, perhaps the term "Rewritten Scripture" is more accurate since "Scripture" does not necessarily imply a closed collection of authoritative texts.[140]

There are indications that some Christians held Matthew, Mark, Luke, and John in a similar type of esteem by the middle of the second century C.E.[141] Papias, writing circa 120–130 C.E., appeals to the authority of Peter as the source for Mark's gospel, is acquainted with a tradition that Matthew compiled sayings of Jesus in Hebrew, and may know stories about the composition of John's gospel.[142] He refers to the apostolic sources of these texts as a reason for recognizing their authority.

---

[137] Cf. Alexander's sixth characteristic above, which refers to the "sacred narrative" of RBTs.

[138] VanderKam, "Questions of Canon," 91.

[139] Ibid.

[140] This same issue also leads Crawford (*Rewriting Scripture*, 3–15) to conclude that "Rewritten Bible" is anachronistic; she instead proposes "Rewritten Scripture" as a more apt descriptor, and I concur with her judgment. However, because "Rewritten Bible" is more common, I will use it and the corresponding abbreviation "RBT" in my discussions.

[141] Other arguments have been presented for a four-gospel canon being present by the middle of the second century. For instance, Darrell D. Hannah ("The Four-Gospel 'Canon' in the Epistula Apostolorum," *JTS* n.s. 59 [2008]: 598–633) argues that the *Epistula Apostolurm*, in the 140s C.E., evidences the four-gospel canon of Matthew, Mark, Luke, and John. He contends that the author of the *Epistula Apostolorum* "is quite happy to correct [noncanonical] sources, whereas he never corrects our four canonical gospels" (633).

[142] Preserved in Eusebius, *Hist. eccl.* 3.39. Richard Bauckham (*Jesus and the Eyewitnesses: The Gospels as Eyewitness Testimony* [Grand Rapids: Eerdmans, 2006], 412–37) has recently argued that Papias was familiar with John's gospel.

Justin Martyr provides more telling evidence on this front. He describes the reading of gospels during the times when Christians gathered to worship:

> On the day which is called Sunday we have a common assembly of all who live in the cities or in the outlying districts, and the memoirs of the Apostles or the writings of the Prophets are read, as long as there is time. Then, when the reader has finished, the president of the assembly verbally admonishes and invites all to imitate such examples of virtue. Then we all stand up together and offer up our prayers, and, as we said before, after we finish our prayers, bread and wine and water are presented. (*1 Apol.* 67; Falls 106–7)

The "memoirs of the apostles" surely refers to gospels, as indicated elsewhere in Justin's writings.[143] Martin Hengel contends that, while Justin is here writing about worship practices in and around Rome, "the description probably did not apply only to the Western churches dependent on Rome but at least also to Asia Minor, where Justin was converted around A.D. 130 and was first active."[144] Justin's many references to the "memoirs of the apostles" and gospel material demonstrate that he was familiar with Matthew (*Dial.* 106; Matt 2:1), Mark (*Dial.* 106; Mark 3:16–17), Luke (*Dial.* 103; Luke 22:42, 44), and John (*1 Apol.* 61; John 3:3).

The indication reflected in Justin's description of Christian worship is that among some Christians of the mid-second century, the four NT gospels were used in worship alongside OT texts. Koester states that "it is clear here that these 'memoirs' are indeed gospel writings and that they are used liturgically as instructions for the sacrament and as texts for homilies."[145] For Justin and others, these gospels were sufficiently authoritative to do the things that the OT texts could do in Jewish and Christian communities: they were cited to settle a dispute, to explain a situation, to provide an example, and to be read in worship. These particular "memoirs of the apostles" were unique in their status. They were the texts being "rewritten" by the author of GP and they were supplemented with oral tradition and legendary material in the same way that the authors of Second Temple RBTs rewrote biblical (OT) texts.

To return to the characteristics of rewritten Bible (OT) texts that have been proposed by Alexander, it is striking that nearly all of the features suggested by him are present if we think of GP as a "rewritten gospel." As

---

[143] In *1 Apol.* 66 Justin identifies the memoirs as "gospels": "The Apostles in their memoirs, which are called Gospels, have handed down what Jesus ordered them to do."

[144] Hengel, *Four Gospels*, 279 n. 472. Gamble (*Books and Readers*, 204–41) discusses the reading of gospels in early Christian worship and includes commentary on Justin's account.

[145] Koester, *Ancient Christian Gospels*, 38.

I hope to demonstrate in this study, eight of Alexander's nine traits can be applied to GP and its handling of the NT gospels:

1. GP is a narrative that follows a chronological order.
2. GP is a free-standing work that follows the form of the texts on which it is based.
3. The Petrine evangelist rewrites a significant portion of earlier gospels, not just a small section or single scene.
4. GP typically, though not always, follows the order of the NT accounts but is selective in what it includes.
5. The intention of the author of GP is to produce an interpretative reading of earlier gospels by offering a fuller, more advanced form of the narrative.
6. Because GP is in narrative form, it tends to reflect only a single interpretation or harmony of the originals.
7. The narrative form of GP makes it difficult or implausible for the Petrine evangelist to offer his exegetical reasoning frequently.
8. The author of GP creates a synthesis of the whole tradition, employing additional sources beyond Matthew, Mark, Luke, and John – probably oral and written traditions and legends – and combines this material with that of the canonical narratives.[146]

As RBTs reorganize the material from multiple sources to form an original, coherent, and cohesive narrative that is based primarily on one or more religiously authoritative texts from the OT, so GP uses the NT gospels as the building blocks for the development of a new gospel. To be clear, I do not think that the Petrine evangelist was familiar with Second Temple RBTs. Rather, RBTs provide us with examples of the type of imitative religious text that we find in GP, and these texts reflect the prevalence of this mimetic practice in late antiquity. The examples from RBTs that I have provided above serve as representative models of the type of omissions, adaptations, and additions that also occur in GP's handling of the NT gospels. Richard Bauckham has also suggested that RBTs are the model for explaining the relationship between other early Christian texts, particularly early Acts literature.[147]

---

[146] I have omitted Alexander's third characteristic, which is that RBTs are not intended to replace the Bible. It is possible that GP was composed in order to provide a new meta-narrative through which to understand the death and resurrection of Jesus.

[147] Bauckham, "The *Acts of Paul* As a Sequel to Acts," in *The Book of Acts in Its Ancient Literary Setting* (ed. Bruce W. Winter and Andrew D. Clarke; vol. 1 of *The Book of Acts in Its First Century Setting*, ed. Bruce W. Winter; Grand Rapids, 1993), 105–52. He contends that the *Acts of Paul* employs canonical Acts and material from the Pauline corpus (esp. 2 Timothy) in the same way that RBTs use the Hebrew Bible: "Jewish literature of the kind often called 'rewritten Bible' has provided a model – as well as exegetical methods – for the use of scriptural texts as starting-points for developing non-

Most importantly, many of the alterations that GP makes to its sources can best be explained as a means of responding to contemporary claims that were being made at the time of its composition. This is the very motivation that Vermes and VanderKam have identified as central to many of the amendments made in RBTs. The free reworking of religiously authoritative narratives seeks to make the earlier stories able to address new contexts and audiences. As Harrington has suggested, this rewriting has as its focus an effort to "make [a religious tradition] meaningful within new situations."[148] So what is the particular new situation in which the author of GP was writing?

Koester has claimed that those advocating GP's dependence on the NT gospels have failed to clarify the particular *Sitz im Leben* in which this text was composed.[149] My goal is to offer a description of the social context in which the Petrine evangelist wrote, an environment in which those outside the Christian movement had influenced the formation of the gospel traditions that were being handled and reworked by our author. Apologetics and polemics were his primary interests; they are what led him to rewrite the NT stories in the particular manner that he has done. I shall describe some of the criticisms that those outside the Christian movement made against the sect – especially those concerning Jesus' death, burial, and resurrection.

This will include both Jewish and non-Jewish critics of early Christianity, though as this study proceeds it will become apparent that there is a strong anti-Jewish tone in GP. This indicates that our writer probably composed his work in a time and place where exchanges between Christians and Jews were present. I shall argue that we have in our gospel evidence of the early parting of the ways between emerging Christianity and its elder sibling, Judaism.

There are a range of possible referents for the frequent mention of "Jews" in GP. One possibility is that this is purely a symbol for unbelief or a failure to believe in Jesus. But this is doubtful. Another possibility is that the Petrine evangelist has no firsthand knowledge of Jews but is borrowing them from the NT gospels and using them as hostile characters in his own work. A third option is that our author knows Jews in his area and these individuals are not hostile towards Christians, but he has chosen to assign

---

scriptural narratives about a scriptural character.... [T]hese generic precedents would have helped to determine the first readers' understanding of the kind of work they were reading when they read the *Acts of Paul* – no doubt in varying degrees according to their own literary experience" (150).

[148] Harrington, "Palestinian Adaptations," 239–40.

[149] Koester, "Apocryphal and Canonical Gospels," *HTR* 73 (1980): 127; repr. in *From Jesus to the Gospels: Interpreting the New Testament in Its Context* (Minneapolis: Fortress, 2007).

negative traits to them. A final possibility is that the author knows Jews who have opposed the Christian movement, either through violence or simply verbal polemics, and he is casting these Jews in the role of "Jews" in his gospel.

My conclusion is that the author of GP does have some familiarity with Jews in his region and that, at the very least, there has been tension between Christians and Jews. As a result of his perception of Jews as those opposed to Jesus and Christians, he has taken the Jewish characters of the NT gospels and assigned to them the worst possible traits. So this is a combination of the second and fourth options discussed above.

In using the terms "apologetics" and "polemics," I am indicating two different types of reactions to outside critics by our author. I use "apologetics" in its defensive sense. It indicates the defense and explanation of a particular assertion. So an author may rework a particular story in order to defend a significant theological or historical claim. Polemics, on the other hand, refers to an assertive – or offensive – use of language towards opponents or outsiders. This includes words used to attack, disparage, or disprove competing claims. GP contains both apologetic and polemical alterations in its reworking of the earlier gospels.

My approach to apologetics in GP stands in contrast to that of Crossan, who focuses on its *internal* apologetics:

> The emphasis [in GP] is not on external apologetics directed to outsiders and especially to critical or opposing outsiders. It is rather on internal apologetics directed to insiders and believers, to those who might be shocked, surprised, or disedified by certain elements in the narrative of the Passion and Resurrection.[150]

As I shall argue in detail later, however, external apologetics are indeed an integral aspect of GP. Responses to those who were critical of Christian claims and earlier gospel stories function as a constitutive part of the narrative.

My thesis, then, is comprised of two propositions: *1) that GP is a form of "rewritten gospel," a text whose author has reworked earlier gospels by clarifying, expanding, and revising them in order to make the narrative meaningful within the new situation of him and his readers; and 2) that the criticisms from those outside of the Christian movement were the primary factor that influenced the Petrine evangelist's rewriting of the earlier stories.* Our author modeled his gospel after the NT accounts, reworking them to address his own context and supplementing the material from them with oral tradition, legends, and his own imaginative creations. Most likely, GP was written sometime between 150 and 180 C.E. in or near the region of Syria by someone who was familiar not only with the NT gospels

---

[150] Crossan, *Cross That Spoke*, 29.

but also with many of the objections that were being directed against those works and against the Christian movement in general.

1.6 Procedure

The remaining five chapters of this study are each devoted to a section of GP. I have divided the text as follows: GP 1:1–5:19 (condemnation, abuse, and crucifixion); 5:20–8:28 (signs of judgment); 8:29–9:34 (guard at the tomb); 9:35–11:49 (resurrection); and 12:50–14:60 (empty tomb and appearance). In each case the goal is to argue 1) that each section of GP shows signs of being a reworking of one or more of the NT gospels that has sometimes also been supplemented with material from other written and oral traditions, and 2) that the rewritten narrative has been heavily influenced by the apologetic and polemical interests of the author.

The format of each of these chapters is identical. First, I will provide a synoptic table showing the parallels between GP and the four NT gospels, and I will also include a brief and general discussion of these parallels. In the second section I will argue for the particular way(s) that our author has rewritten the antecedent texts. This discussion will serve as the main sub-thesis for each unit within GP. Third, I will review other instances in early Christian texts that exemplify the same apologetic or polemical interest that I am claiming for GP. This is done in order to demonstrate that my observations regarding GP are not unique to this text but instead are representative of a broader interest within early Christianity. The fourth section will seek to provide a rationale behind the apologetic and polemical interests being proposed. In other words, it attempts to answer the question, "Why is the author concerned with such things?" Each chapter will end with a review of the conclusions that I have drawn from my examination.

No text, ancient or modern, is composed in a vacuum. Rather, each is written within a particular context that has shaped the author, his interests, and his motivations. This study seeks to offer a better and fuller explanation in these areas than what has previously been suggested by others concerning GP.

Chapter 2

Rewritten Passion Narrative: GP 1:1–5:19

This chapter examines the depiction of Jesus' death, focusing specifically on the parties who are responsible and not responsible for this act. To this end I will show how GP's author rewrites earlier gospel texts and traditions in order to assign blame solely to Jews. The first section of this chapter will provide a synoptic analysis of GP 1:1–5:19 and review the numerous parallels between this material and the canonical gospels. In the second section I will explore in detail the many ways in which Jews are depicted as the sole executioners in GP and are sometimes more malevolent in this role than are their NT counterparts. I will also demonstrate how OT allusions and quotations function to heighten Jewish guilt and the disparagement of the Jewish people. Furthermore, I will briefly discuss the reduced role of Pilate in these events. Early Christian parallels to these shifts will then be surveyed before I propose some ways in which specific apologetic and polemical interests played a part in shaping GP's reworking of antecedent texts and traditions.

2.1 Synoptic Analysis of GP 1:1–5:19

GP 1:1–5:19	Matt 27	Mark 15	Luke 23	John 19
¹:¹τῶν δὲ Ἰουδαίων οὐδεὶς ἐνίψατο τὰς χεῖρας οὐδὲ Ἡρῴδης οὐδὲ τις τῶν κριτῶν αὐτοῦ. καὶ μὴ βουληθέντων νίψασθαι ἀνέστη Πειλᾶτος	²⁴ἰδὼν δὲ ὁ Πιλᾶτος ὅτι οὐδὲν ὠφελεῖ ἀλλὰ μᾶλλον θόρυβος γίνεται, λαβὼν ὕδωρ ἀπενίψατο τὰς χεῖρας ἀπέναντι τοῦ ὄχλου, λέγων, Ἀθῷός εἰμι ἀπὸ τοῦ αἵματος τούτου· ὑμεῖς ὄψεσθε.			²⁴καὶ Πιλᾶτος

GP 1:1–5:19	Matt 27	Mark 15	Luke 23	John 19
			ἐπέκρινεν γενέσθαι τὸ αἴτημα αὐτῶν	¹⁶τότε οὖν
²καὶ τότε κελεύει Ἡρῴδης ὁ βασιλεὺς παραλημφθῆναι τὸν κύριον εἰπὼν αὐτοῖς ὅτι ὅσα ἐκέλευσα ὑμῖν ποιῆσαι αὐτῷ ποιήσατε.	²⁶ᵇ[Πιλᾶτος] παρέδωκεν ἵνα σταυρωθῇ. ²⁷Τότε οἱ στρατιῶται τοῦ ἡγεμόνος παραλαβόντες τὸν Ἰησοῦν εἰς τὸ πραιτώριον συνήγαγον ἐπ' αὐτὸν ὅλην τὴν σπεῖραν.	¹⁵ὁ δὲ Πιλᾶτος... παρέδωκεν τὸν Ἰησοῦν φραγελλώσας ἵνα σταυρωθῇ. ¹⁶Οἱ δὲ στρατιῶται ἀπήγαγον αὐτὸν ἔσω τῆς αὐλῆς, ὅ ἐστιν πραιτώριον, καὶ συγκαλοῦσιν ὅλην τὴν σπεῖραν.	²⁵ᵇ...τὸν δὲ Ἰησοῦν παρέδωκεν τῷ θελήματι αὐτῶν.	παρέδωκεν αὐτὸν αὐτοῖς ἵνα σταυρωθῇ. Παρέλαβον οὖν τὸν Ἰησοῦν
	⁵⁷Ὀψίας δὲ γενομένης	⁴²Καὶ ἤδη ὀψίας γενομένης...		
²:³εἱστήκει δὲ ἐκεῖ Ἰωσὴφ ὁ φίλος Πειλάτου καὶ τοῦ κυρίου. καὶ εἰδὼς ὅτι σταυρίσκειν αὐτὸν μέλλουσιν,	ἦλθεν ἄνθρωπος πλούσιος ἀπὸ Ἀριμαθαίας, τοὔνομα Ἰωσήφ, ὃς καὶ αὐτὸς ἐμαθητεύθη τῷ Ἰησοῦ	⁴³ἐλθὼν Ἰωσὴφ [ὁ] ἀπὸ Ἀριμαθαίας εὐσχήμων βουλευτής, ὃς καὶ αὐτὸς ἦν προσδεχόμενος τὴν βασιλείαν τοῦ θεοῦ, τολμήσας εἰσῆλθεν πρὸς τὸν Πιλᾶτον καὶ ᾐτήσατο τὸ σῶμα τοῦ Ἰησοῦ. ⁴⁴ὁ δὲ Πιλᾶτος ἐθαύμασεν εἰ ἤδη τέθνηκεν, καὶ προσκαλεσάμενος τὸν κεντυρίωνα ἐπηρώτησεν	⁵⁰Καὶ ἰδοὺ ἀνὴρ ὀνόματι Ἰωσὴφ βουλευτὴς ὑπάρχων [καὶ] ἀνὴρ ἀγαθὸς καὶ δίκαιος ⁵¹οὗτος οὐκ ἦν συγκατατεθειμ ένος τῇ βουλῇ καὶ τῇ πράξει αὐτῶν ἀπὸ Ἀριμαθαίας πόλεως τῶν Ἰουδαίων, ὃς προσεδέχετο τὴν βασιλείαν τοῦ θεοῦ,	³⁸Μετὰ δὲ ταῦτα ἠρώτησεν τὸν Πιλᾶτον Ἰωσὴφ [ὁ] ἀπὸ Ἀριμαθαίας, ὢν μαθητὴς τοῦ Ἰησοῦ κεκρυμμένος δὲ διὰ τὸν φόβον τῶν Ἰουδαίων,
ἦλθεν πρὸς τὸν Πειλᾶτον καὶ ᾔτησε τὸ σῶμα τοῦ	⁵⁸οὗτος προσελθὼν τῷ Πιλάτῳ ᾐτήσατο τὸ		⁵²οὗτος προσελθὼν τῷ Πιλάτῳ ᾐτήσατο τὸ	ἵνα ἄρῃ τὸ

GP 1:1–5:19	Matt 27	Mark 15	Luke 23	John 19
κυρίου πρὸς ταφήν. ⁴καὶ ὁ Πειλᾶτος πέμψας πρὸς Ἡρῴδην ᾔτησεν αὐτοῦ τὸ σῶμα.	σῶμα τοῦ Ἰησοῦ. τότε ὁ Πιλᾶτος ἐκέλευσεν ἀποδοθῆναι.	αὐτὸν εἰ πάλαι ἀπέθανεν ⁴⁵καὶ γνοὺς ἀπὸ τοῦ κεντυρίωνος ἐδωρήσατο τὸ πτῶμα τῷ Ἰωσήφ.	σῶμα τοῦ Ἰησοῦ	σῶμα τοῦ Ἰησοῦ, καὶ ἐπέτρεψεν ὁ Πιλᾶτος. ἦλθεν οὖν καὶ ἦρεν τὸ σῶμα αὐτοῦ.
⁵καὶ ὁ Ἡρῴδης ἔφη· ἀδελφὲ Πειλᾶτε, εἰ καὶ μή τις αὐτὸν ᾐτήκει, ἡμεῖς αὐτὸν ἐθάπτομεν, ἐπεὶ καὶ σάββατον ἐπιφώσκει· γέγραπται γὰρ ἐν τῷ νόμῳ, ἥλιον μὴ δῦναι ἐπὶ πεφονευμένῳ.				³¹ᵃΟἱ οὖν Ἰουδαῖοι, ἐπεὶ παρασκευὴ ἦν, ἵνα μὴ μείνῃ ἐπὶ τοῦ σταυροῦ τὰ σώματα ἐν τῷ σαββάτῳ, ἦν γὰρ μεγάλη ἡ ἡμέρα ἐκείνου τοῦ σαββάτου,
καὶ παρέδωκεν αὐτὸν τῷ λαῷ πρὸ μιᾶς τῶν ἀζύμων, τῆς ἑορτῆς αὐτῶν.	²⁶ᵇ[Πιλᾶτος] παρέδωκεν ἵνα σταυρωθῇ.	¹⁵ὁ δὲ Πιλᾶτος... παρέδωκεν τὸν Ἰησοῦν φραγελλώσας ἵνα σταυρωθῇ.	²⁵ᵇτὸν δὲ Ἰησοῦν παρέδωκεν τῷ θελήματι αὐτῶν.	¹⁶τότε οὖν παρέδωκεν αὐτὸν αὐτοῖς ἵνα σταυρωθῇ.
³:⁶οἱ δὲ λαβόντες τὸν κύριον	²⁷Τότε οἱ στρατιῶται τοῦ ἡγεμόνος παραλαβόντες τὸν Ἰησοῦν εἰς τὸ πραιτώριον συνήγαγον ἐπ' αὐτὸν ὅλην τὴν σπεῖραν.	¹⁶Οἱ δὲ στρατιῶται ἀπήγαγον αὐτὸν ἔσω τῆς αὐλῆς, ὅ ἐστιν πραιτώριον, καὶ συγκαλοῦσιν ὅλην τὴν σπεῖραν.		Παρέλαβον οὖν τὸν Ἰησοῦν
ὤθουν αὐτὸν τρέχοντες καὶ ἔλεγον· σύρωμεν τὸν υἱὸν τοῦ θεοῦ ἐξουσίαν αὐτοῦ				

GP 1:1–5:19	Matt 27	Mark 15	Luke 23	John 19
ἐσχηκότες.			¹¹ἐξουθενήσας δὲ αὐτὸν [καὶ] ὁ Ἡρῴδης σὺν τοῖς στρατεύμασιν αὐτοῦ καὶ ἐμπαίξας	
⁷καὶ πορφύραν αὐτὸν περιέβαλον	²⁸καὶ ἐκδύσαντες αὐτὸν χλαμύδα κοκκίνην περιέθηκαν αὐτῷ	¹⁷ᵃκαὶ ἐνδιδύσκουσιν αὐτὸν πορφύραν...	περιβαλὼν ἐσθῆτα λαμπρὰν ἀνέπεμψεν αὐτὸν τῷ Πιλάτῳ.	²ᵇκαὶ ἱμάτιον πορφυροῦν περιέβαλον αὐτόν
καὶ ἐκάθισαν αὐτὸν ἐπὶ καθέδραν κρίσεως				¹³ᵃὉ οὖν Πιλᾶτος ἀκούσας τῶν λόγων τούτων ἤγαγεν ἔξω τὸν Ἰησοῦν, καὶ ἐκάθισεν ἐπὶ βήματος
λέγοντες· δικαίως κρῖνε βασιλεῦ τοῦ Ἰσραήλ.	²⁹ᵇλέγοντες, Χαῖρε, βασιλεῦ τῶν Ἰουδαίων	¹⁸καὶ ἤρξαντο ἀσπάζεσθαι αὐτόν, Χαῖρε, βασιλεῦ τῶν Ἰουδαίων		³ᵃκαὶ ἤρχοντο πρὸς αὐτὸν καὶ ἔλεγον, Χαῖρε, ὁ βασιλεὺς τῶν Ἰουδαίων
⁸καί τις αὐτῶν ἐνεγκὼν στέφανον ἀκάνθινον ἔθηκεν ἐπὶ τῆς κεφαλῆς τοῦ κυρίου ⁹καὶ ἕτεροι ἑστῶτες ἐνέπτυον αὐτοῦ ταῖς ὄψεσι καὶ ἄλλοι τὰς σιαγόνας αὐτοῦ ἐράπισαν,	²⁹ᵃκαὶ πλέξαντες στέφανον ἐξ ἀκανθῶν ἐπέθηκαν ἐπὶ τῆς κεφαλῆς αὐτοῦ καὶ κάλαμον ἐν τῇ δεξιᾷ αὐτοῦ, καὶ γονυπετήσαντες ἔμπροσθεν αὐτοῦ ἐνέπαιξαν αὐτῷ... ³⁰καὶ	¹⁷ᵇκαὶ περιτιθέασιν αὐτῷ πλέξαντες ἀκάνθινον στέφανον ¹⁹καὶ ἔτυπτον αὐτοῦ τὴν κεφαλὴν καλάμῳ καὶ ἐνέπτυον αὐτῷ, καὶ τιθέντες τὰ γόνατα προσεκύνουν		²ᵃκαὶ οἱ στρατιῶται πλέξαντες στέφανον ἐξ ἀκανθῶν ἐπέθηκαν αὐτοῦ τῇ κεφαλῇ ³ᵇκαὶ ἐδίδοσαν αὐτῷ ῥαπίσματα.

GP 1:1–5:19	Matt 27	Mark 15	Luke 23	John 19
ἕτεροι καλάμῳ ἔνυσσον αὐτὸν καί τινες αὐτὸν ἐμάστιζον λέγοντες· ταύτῃ τῇ τιμῇ τιμήσωμεν τὸν υἱὸν τοῦ θεοῦ.	ἐμπτύσαντες εἰς αὐτὸν ἔλαβον τὸν κάλαμον καὶ ἔτυπτον εἰς τὴν κεφαλὴν αὐτοῦ.	αὐτῷ.		
⁴:¹⁰καὶ ἤνεγκον δύο κακούργους καὶ ἐσταύρωσαν ἀνὰ μέσον αὐτῶν τὸν κύριον. αὐτὸς δὲ ἐσιώπα ὡς μηδένα πόνον ἔχων.	³⁸Τότε σταυροῦνται σὺν αὐτῷ δύο λῃσταί, εἷς ἐκ δεξιῶν καὶ εἷς ἐξ εὐωνύμων.	²⁷Καὶ σὺν αὐτῷ σταυροῦσιν δύο λῃστάς, ἕνα ἐκ δεξιῶν καὶ ἕνα ἐξ εὐωνύμων αὐτοῦ.	³³ᵇἐκεῖ ἐσταύρωσαν αὐτὸν καὶ τοὺς κακούργους, ὃν μὲν ἐκ δεξιῶν ὃν δὲ ἐξ ἀριστερῶν.	¹⁸ὅπου αὐτὸν ἐσταύρωσαν, καὶ μετ' αὐτοῦ ἄλλους δύο ἐντεῦθεν καὶ ἐντεῦθεν, μέσον δὲ τὸν Ἰησοῦν.
¹¹καὶ ὅτε ὤρθωσαν τὸν σταυρόν, ἐπέγραψαν ὅτι οὗτός ἐστιν ὁ βασιλεὺς τοῦ Ἰσραήλ.	³⁷καὶ ἐπέθηκαν ἐπάνω τῆς κεφαλῆς αὐτοῦ τὴν αἰτίαν αὐτοῦ γεγραμμένην· Οὗτός ἐστιν Ἰησοῦς ὁ βασιλεὺς τῶν Ἰουδαίων.	²⁶καὶ ἦν ἡ ἐπιγραφὴ τῆς αἰτίας αὐτοῦ ἐπιγεγραμμένη - Ὁ βασιλεὺς τῶν Ἰουδαίων.	³⁸ἦν δὲ καὶ ἐπιγραφὴ ἐπ' αὐτῷ, Ὁ βασιλεὺς τῶν Ἰουδαίων οὗτος.	¹⁹ἔγραψεν δὲ καὶ τίτλον ὁ Πιλᾶτος καὶ ἔθηκεν ἐπὶ τοῦ σταυροῦ· ἦν δὲ γεγραμμένον, Ἰησοῦς ὁ Ναζωραῖος ὁ βασιλεὺς τῶν Ἰουδαίων.
¹²καὶ τεθεικότες τὰ ἐνδύματα ἔμπροσθεν αὐτοῦ διεμερίσαντο καὶ λαχμὸν ἔβαλον ἐπ᾽ αὐτοῖς.	³⁵σταυρώσαντες δὲ αὐτὸν διεμερίσαντο τὰ ἱμάτια αὐτοῦ βάλλοντες κλῆρον	²⁴καὶ σταυροῦσιν αὐτὸν καὶ διαμερίζονται τὰ ἱμάτια αὐτοῦ, βάλλοντες κλῆρον ἐπ' αὐτὰ τίς τί ἄρῃ.	³⁴ᵇδιαμεριζόμενοι δὲ τὰ ἱμάτια αὐτοῦ ἔβαλον κλήρους.	²³Οἱ οὖν στρατιῶται ὅτε ἐσταύρωσαν τὸν Ἰησοῦν ἔλαβον τὰ ἱμάτια αὐτοῦ καὶ ἐποίησαν τέσσαρα μέρη, ἑκάστῳ στρατιώτῃ μέρος, καὶ τὸν χιτῶνα. ἦν δὲ ὁ χιτὼν

GP 1:1–5:19	Matt 27	Mark 15	Luke 23	John 19
				ἄραφος, ἐκ τῶν ἄνωθεν ὑφαντὸς δι' ὅλου.
	⁴⁴τὸ δ' αὐτὸ καὶ οἱ λησταὶ οἱ συσταυρωθέντ ες σὺν αὐτῷ ὠνείδιζον αὐτόν.	³²ᵇκαὶ οἱ συνεσταυρω- μένοι σὺν αὐτῷ ὠνείδιζον αὐτόν.	³⁹Εἷς δὲ τῶν κρεμασθέντων κακούργων ἐβλασφήμει αὐτὸν λέγων, Οὐχὶ σὺ εἶ ὁ Χριστός; σῶσον σεαυτὸν καὶ ἡμᾶς. ⁴⁰ἀποκριθεὶς δὲ ὁ ἕτερος ἐπιτιμῶν αὐτῷ ἔφη, Οὐδὲ φοβῇ σὺ τὸν θεόν, ὅτι ἐν τῷ αὐτῷ κρίματι εἶ; ⁴¹καὶ ἡμεῖς μὲν δικαίως, ἄξια γὰρ ὧν ἐπράξαμεν ἀπολαμβάνο- μεν, οὗτος δὲ οὐδὲν ἄτοπον ἔπραξεν. ⁴²καὶ ἔλεγεν, Ἰησοῦ, μνήσθητί μου ὅταν ἔλθῃς εἰς τὴν βασιλείαν σου. ⁴³καὶ εἶπεν αὐτῷ, Ἀμήν σοι λέγω, σήμερον μετ' ἐμοῦ ἔσῃ ἐν τῷ παραδείσῳ.	
¹³εἷς δέ τις τῶν κακούργων ἐκείνων ὠνείδισεν αὐτοὺς λέγων· ἡμεῖς διὰ τὰ κακὰ ἃ ἐποιήσαμεν οὕτω πεπόνθαμεν οὗτος δὲ σωτὴρ γενόμενος τῶν ἀνθρώπων τί ἠδίκησεν ὑμᾶς;				
				³¹Οἱ οὖν Ἰουδαῖοι, ἐπεὶ παρασκευὴ ἦν, ἵνα μὴ μείνῃ ἐπὶ τοῦ

GP 1:1–5:19	Matt 27	Mark 15	Luke 23	John 19
				σταυροῦ τὰ σώματα ἐν τῷ σαββάτῳ, ἦν γὰρ μεγάλη ἡ ἡμέρα ἐκείνου τοῦ σαββάτου, ἠρώτησαν τὸν Πιλᾶτον ἵνα κατεαγῶσιν αὐτῶν τὰ σκέλη καὶ ἀρθῶσιν. ³²ἦλθον οὖν οἱ στρατιῶται, καὶ τοῦ μὲν πρώτου κατέαξαν τὰ σκέλη καὶ τοῦ ἄλλου τοῦ συσταυρωθέντ ος αὐτῷ· ³³ἐπὶ δὲ τὸν Ἰησοῦν ἐλθόντες, ὡς εἶδον ἤδη αὐτὸν τεθνηκότα, οὐ κατέαξαν αὐτοῦ τὰ σκέλη
¹⁴καὶ ἀγανακτήσαντες ἐπ᾽αὐτῷ ἐκέλευσαν ἵνα μὴ σκελοκοπηθῇ, ὅπως βασανιζόμενος ἀποθάνοι.				
⁵:¹⁵ἦν δὲ μεσημβρία καὶ σκότος κατέσχε πᾶσαν τὴν Ἰουδαίαν.	⁴⁵Ἀπὸ δὲ ἕκτης ὥρας σκότος ἐγένετο ἐπὶ πᾶσαν τὴν γῆν ἕως ὥρας ἐνάτης.	³³Καὶ γενομένης ὥρας ἕκτης σκότος ἐγένετο ἐφ᾽ ὅλην τὴν γῆν ἕως ὥρας ἐνάτης.	⁴⁴Καὶ ἦν ἤδη ὡσεὶ ὥρα ἕκτη καὶ σκότος ἐγένετο ἐφ᾽ ὅλην τὴν γῆν ἕως ὥρας ἐνάτης	
καὶ ἐθορυβοῦντο καὶ ἠγωνίων μήποτε ὁ ἥλιος ἔδυ, ἐπειδὴ ἔτι ἔζη· γέγραπται αὐτοῖς ἥλιον μὴ δῦναι ἐπὶ πεφονευμένῳ.				

GP 1:1–5:19	Matt 27	Mark 15	Luke 23	John 19
				²⁸Μετὰ τοῦτο εἰδὼς ὁ Ἰησοῦς ὅτι ἤδη πάντα τετέλεσται, ἵνα τελειωθῇ ἡ γραφή, λέγει, Διψῶ.
¹⁶καὶ τις αὐτῶν εῖπεν· ποτίσατε αὐτὸν χολὴν μετὰ ὄξους. καὶ κεράσαντες ἐπότισαν,	³⁴ἔδωκαν αὐτῷ πιεῖν οῖνον μετὰ χολῆς μεμιγμένον· καὶ γευσάμενος οὐκ ἠθέλησεν πιεῖν.	²³καὶ ἐδίδουν αὐτῷ ἐσμυρνισμένον οῖνον, ὃς δὲ οὐκ ἔλαβεν.		
		³⁶δραμὼν δέ τις [καὶ] γεμίσας σπόγγον ὄξους περιθεὶς καλάμῳ ἐπότιζεν αὐτόν, λέγων, Ἄφετε ἴδωμεν εἰ ἔρχεται Ἡλίας καθελεῖν αὐτόν.	³⁶ἐνέπαιξαν δὲ αὐτῷ καὶ οἱ στρατιῶται προσερχόμενοι ὄξος προσφέροντες αὐτῷ	²⁹σκεῦος ἔκειτο ὄξους μεστόν· σπόγγον οὖν μεστὸν τοῦ ὄξους ὑσσώπῳ περιθέντες προσήνεγκαν αὐτοῦ τῷ στόματι.
¹⁷καὶ ἐπλήρωσαν πάντα καὶ ἐτελείωσαν κατὰ τῆς κεφαλῆς αὐτῶν τὰ ἁμαρτήματα. ¹⁸περιήρχοντο δὲ πολλοὶ μετὰ λύχνων νομίζοντες ὅτι νύξ ἐστιν ἔπεσάν τε				
¹⁹καὶ ὁ κύριος ἀνεβόνσε λέγων·	⁴⁶περὶ δὲ τὴν ἐνάτην ὥραν ἀνεβόησεν ὁ	³⁴καὶ τῇ ἐνάτῃ ὥρᾳ ἐβόησεν ὁ Ἰησοῦς φωνῇ μεγάλῃ, Ελωι		

GP 1:1–5:19	Matt 27	Mark 15	Luke 23	John 19
ἡ δύναμις μου, ἡ δύναμις, κατέλειψάς με.	Ἰησοῦς φωνῇ μεγάλῃ λέγων, Ηλι ηλι λεμα σαβαχθανι; τοῦτ' ἔστιν, Θεέ μου θεέ μου, ἱνατί με ἐγκατέλιπες;	ελωι λεμα σαβαχθανι; ὅ ἐστιν μεθερμηνευόμε νον Ὁ Θεός μου ὁ θεός μου, εἰς τί ἐγκατέλιπές με;		
καὶ εἰπὼν ἀνελήφθη.	⁵⁰ὁ δὲ Ἰησοῦς πάλιν κράξας φωνῇ μεγάλῃ ἀφῆκεν τὸ πνεῦμα.	³⁷ὁ δὲ Ἰησοῦς ἀφεὶς φωνὴν μεγάλην ἐξέπνευσεν.	⁴⁶ᵇτοῦτο δὲ εἰπὼν ἐξέπνευσεν.	³⁰ᵇκαὶ κλίνας τὴν κεφαλὴν παρέδωκεν τὸ πνεῦμα.

The extant portion of GP opens with a proper sentence that apparently contrasts with something that preceded it, as indicated by the particle δέ (GP 1:1).[1] The scene appears to be the conclusion of a trial or some other legal proceeding involving Jesus. In this first verse we have a rough parallel to Matt 27:24–25, since in each gospel there is a reference to handwashing. Here GP states that "none of the Jews washed the hands," whereas in Matthew Pilate washes his hands while declaring his own innocence. In GP the Jews have no desire to wash their hands (καὶ μὴ βουληθέντων νίψασθαι), a phrase without parallel in the NT accounts. Herod the king orders that Jesus be taken away, declaring, "What I commanded you to do to him, do" (GP 1:2).[2] In each of the NT parallels, it is Pilate rather than Herod who hands over Jesus to be executed (Matt 27:26; Mark 15:15; Luke 23:24–25; John 19:16).

There is an abrupt shift in GP 2:3–5a, as Joseph asks Pilate that he be allowed to bury Jesus after the crucifixion.[3] While in GP this comes before the crucifixion, Joseph appears only after the death of Jesus in all of the canonical stories (Matt 27:57–58; Mark 15:42–45; Luke 23:50–52; John

---

[1] The Akhmîm manuscript is not damaged at this point, but it picks up the story in the middle of the gospel's narrative. This would seem to indicate that the scribe who composed it either 1) was working with an abbreviated exemplar that contained the same portion of GP as the Akhmîm text, or 2) made a choice to copy only this section of his exemplar manuscript. Minnen ("Akhmîm *Gospel of Peter*," 53–60) discusses these two options and provides his case for the latter.

[2] Swete (*Akhmîm Fragment*, 2) suggests that this statement from Herod alludes to an earlier portion of GP that included his instructions but which is not included in the extant text.

[3] This must certainly be understood as the same Joseph that each of the NT accounts identifies as Joseph of Arimathea (Matt 27:57; Mark 15:43; Luke 23:50–51; John 19:38).

19:38). Another significant difference is found in the reaction of Pilate to the request of Joseph. In the NT gospels Pilate himself grants the request, but in GP he must go to Herod and ask for the body. The Petrine evangelist adds the detail that not only is Joseph a friend of Jesus – something mentioned also in Matthew and John – he is also a friend of Pilate (GP 2:3). Herod and Pilate appear to be already on friendly terms in GP on the day of Jesus' crucifixion. In contrast, the Third Evangelist describes them becoming friends as a result of the circumstances surrounding Jesus' death (Luke 23:12). In GP, when Pilate asks Herod for Jesus' body, the reply from the Jewish leader indicates that he was planning to bury Jesus in accordance with the requirements of Torah. This bears some similarity to the Jewish legal sensibilities expressed in John 19:31.

In GP 2:5b Herod delivers Jesus "to the people before the first day of unleavened bread, their feast." That Jews are in mind is clear from the reference to the day of unleavened bread being "their feast." In contrast to Jesus being given to the Jewish people, the NT parallels state that Jesus is handed over to Roman soldiers (Matt 27:27; Mark 15:15–16; Luke 23:25, 36, 47; John 19:1–7, 23–25, 31–34). Chronologically, GP aligns with the Fourth Gospel in having the first day of Passover fall on the Sabbath and in the crucifixion preceding it.

Beginning in GP 3:6, the Jewish people inflict various abuses on Jesus, many of which are paralleled in the actions of the Roman soldiers in the canonical narratives. No NT account, however, includes the pushing of Jesus by his executioners as they run, nor does any include a statement about having power over the Son of God (GP 3:6).

Jesus is clothed in a purple robe (πορφύρα), set on a seat of judgment (καθέδρα κρίσεως), and told, "Judge righteously, King of Israel" (GP 3:7). Both Mark and John refer to Jesus being clothed in πορφύρα (Mark 15:17; John 19:2), while the seating of Jesus is potentially paralleled in John 19:13.[4] A crown of thorns is placed on the head of Jesus in GP 3:8, as also occurs in Matt 27:29; Mark 15:17; and John 19:2, 5.

Those abusing Jesus spit in his face, slap him on the cheeks, prick him with a reed, and scourge him before their mocking expression, "With this honor let us honor the Son of God" (GP 3:9). These acts are paralleled in the NT gospels. Spitting occurs in Matt 27:30 and Mark 15:19. The execu-

---

[4] John 19:13 begins ὁ οὖν Πιλᾶτος ἀκούσας τῶν λόγων τούτων ἤγαγεν ἔξω τὸν Ἰησοῦν καὶ ἐκάθισεν ἐπὶ βήματος. The point of contention in translating this is in determining whether ἐκάθισεν is transitive or intransitive here. In other words, is Pilate setting Jesus on the seat or is Pilate himself sitting on the seat? The merits of both sides of the argument are summarized in C. K. Barrett, *The Gospel according to St. John: An Introduction with Commentary and Notes on the Greek Text* (London: SPCK, 1955), 452–53. If the transitive understanding of John is correct, then we would have a parallel to GP, though in the Fourth Gospel Jesus is seated on a βῆμα rather than a καθέδρα.

tioners of Jesus slap him on the face in John 19:3, strike him with a reed in Mark 15:19, and scourge him in Matt 27:26; Mark 15:15; Luke 23:16, 22; and John 19:1. All four NT accounts include some form of mockery (Matt 27:29; Mark 15:20; Luke 23:11, 36; John 19:2–3), but none includes the "honor" statement from the executioners as in GP 3:9.

Jesus is then crucified between two malefactors, just as all of the NT evangelists describe (GP 4:10; Matt 27:38; Mark 15:27; Luke 23:33; John 19:18). The reference in GP 4:10 to Jesus' silence is unique to this gospel.[5] In GP 4:11 we find a reference to the title on the cross: οὗτός ἐστιν ὁ βασιλεὺς τοῦ Ἰσραήλ.[6] In contrast, all of the canonical gospels give the title as ὁ βασιλεὺς τῶν Ἰουδαίων (Matt 27:37; Mark 15:26; Luke 23:38; John 19:19). The Jewish executioners in GP divide Jesus' clothing and cast lots for them (GP 4:12), an act also found in all of the NT narratives (Matt 27:35; Mark 15:24; Luke 23:34; John 19:23–24).

In GP 4:13–14 we have a scene in which one of those being crucified with Jesus rebukes the executioners for killing "the saviour of men," who has done no wrong to them. Those carrying out the crucifixion become enraged at this and order that Jesus' legs not be broken, so that he will undergo more suffering. This reflects elements also found in the Lukan and Johannine stories. One of the crucified men in Luke's account reproaches the other for mocking Jesus, saying that Jesus has done no wrong while they are indeed guilty of the crimes for which they have been condemned (Luke 23:39–43). Luke is the only other gospel in which one of the male-factors expresses sympathy for Jesus. Similarly, only John mentions leg-breaking at the crucifixion (John 19:31–33). In the Fourth Gospel, the Jews ask Pilate to break the legs of all three of the crucified in order that they might die soon enough to be removed from the crosses before the Sabbath. However, because the soldiers in John discover that Jesus has already died, they do not actually break his legs.

GP 5:15 describes the onset of darkness over all Judea at midday. In response to this darkness, the executioners become fearful that the sun will set while Jesus is still alive. This verse then notes that Jewish law stipulates that the sun cannot set on one who has been put to death. All three

---

[5] Some have found in this statement an indication of GP's alleged docetic sympathies, as, for example, in Swete, *Akhmîm Fragment*, 6. However, the text of GP does not actually state that Jesus felt no pain; rather, it emphasizes his remaining silent during his suffering *as if* he did not feel pain (αὐτὸς δὲ ἐσιώπα ὡς μηδένα πόνον ἔχων) (GP 4:10b). The portrait is of a noble suffering martyr, not of one whose bodily appearance is only an illusion. This has been argued persuasively in Jerry W. McCant, "The Gospel of Peter: Docetism Reconsidered," *NTS* 30 (1984): 258–73; Peter M. Head, "On the Christology of the Gospel of Peter," *VC* 46 (1992): 209–24.

[6] The title "King of Israel" also appears earlier in GP 3:7 and is used there as a term of mockery.

Synoptic Gospels refer to darkness at noon (Matt 27:45; Mark 15:33; Luke 23:44). While GP states that this occurred throughout "all Judea," the canonical stories more generically recount that it happened in the whole "land" (γῆς).

As he hangs on the cross, Jesus is offered gall mixed with vinegar (χολὴ μετὰ ὄξους) to drink (GP 5:16). This bears some resemblance to what is found in Matthew and Mark. Both of these NT evangelists describe two separate drinks being offered to Jesus (Matt 27:34, 48; Mark 15:23, 36). The first drink is wine mixed with either gall (Matthew) or myrrh (Mark), the second is a sponge full of vinegar (Matthew and Mark). John 19:29–30 also speaks of an offer of vinegar to Jesus.[7] As Koester notes, the offering of gall mixed with vinegar in GP is appropriately followed by the statement that "they fulfilled everything" (GP 5:17).[8] However, as I will argue below, the fulfillment reference in GP does not appear to be to the gall/vinegar episode alone but rather to the entire series of acts that the executioners have carried out against Jesus. This is evidenced by the second half of GP 5:17, which states that they "filled the measure of sins upon their head." The Scriptures are fulfilled in everything that happens at the crucifixion. There are no parallels to GP 5:17 in any of the NT Passion Narratives. Similarly, GP 5:18 has nothing in common with the canonical material, as it describes the crucifiers going about with lamps because of the darkness and falling down in the process.

Jesus' only statement in GP comes in 5:19 with his exclamation from the cross: "My power, power, you have forsaken me." This is nearly identical to the final cry in Matthew and Mark: "My God, my God, why have you forsaken me?" (Matt 27:46; Mark 15:34). The most significant differences between GP and the canonical sayings are GP's use of δύναμις

---

[7] Psalm 69:22 likely lies behind GP 5:16 and the references to vinegar in the NT gospels. In evaluating the use of this verse by the gospel writers, Koester (*Ancient Christian Gospels*, 230) concludes, "No question, the *Gospel of Peter* has preserved the most original narrative version of the tradition of scriptural interpretation. In this instance, a dependence of the *Gospel of Peter* upon any of the canonical gospels is excluded. It is unlikely that such a dependence exists with respect to any other features of the passion narrative of this gospel."

In contrast, Brown (*Death of the Messiah*, 2:944) notes that it was common for second-century Christian writers to bring their texts into closer alignment with the OT texts, and he finds GP to be indicative of this practice. In the case of Ps 69:22, Brown cites as evidence *Barn.* 7:3 and Irenaeus, *Haer.* 4.33.12. Swete (*Akhmîm Fragment*, 8–9) adds other early examples as well.

[8] Koester, *Ancient Christian Gospels*, 230.

where Matthew and Mark have θεός, and the exclamation being in the form of a statement in GP and a question in the NT versions.[9]

2.2 GP 1:1–5:19: An Anti-Jewish Perspective

In this section I will review the numerous ways in which GP reflects a heightened anti-Jewish perspective as it relates to responsibility for the death of Jesus and, at the same time, moves toward exonerating Pilate for his role in the crucifixion. This will be accomplished through an examination of four items from GP 1:1–5:19.

2.2.1 "But None of the Jews Washed the Hands" (GP 1:1)

Perhaps it is not mere coincidence that the opening line of the Akhmîm text reads as it does (τῶν δὲ Ἰουδαίων οὐδεὶς ἐνίψατο τὰς χεῖρας), as it states in summary form one of the primary themes of the narrative that follows.[10] What precisely came before the opening line of the Akhmîm text is uncertain, but the particle δέ is likely contrastive here and probably

---

[9] Swete (*Akhmîm Fragment*, 10) claims to have found only one other instance in early Christian literature where the question in Matthew and Mark has been transformed into a statement (Ephrem the Syrian, *Serm. adv. Haer.* 56).

[10] Minnen ("The Akhmîm *Gospel of Peter*," 58–60) argues that the Akhmîm manuscript is a redacted version of the original text of GP, and that this redaction was driven largely by anti-Jewish motivations, either by the Akhmîm scribe himself or an earlier one. In support of this, he claims that the version of the *Apocalypse of Peter* that is included in the Akhmîm manuscript contains demonstrable anti-Jewish redactions of that work. If his contention about GP is true, it would make it nearly impossible to discern a more original text of GP than what is found in the Akhmîm edition, since any alleged anti-Jewish characteristics could be attributed to a later redactor. Minnen's claim, as he acknowledges, cannot be falsified without the discovery of further manuscripts of GP.

In response, I would note that portions of four works are included in the Akhmîm manuscript: GP, *Apocalypse of Peter*, *1 Enoch*, and *Martyrdom of Julian of Anazarbus*. Minnen detects noticeable and demonstrable anti-Jewish redaction in only one of these four writings – the *Apocalypse of Peter*. So while Minnen's proposal is possible, the current state of the evidence does not allow us to grant it a high degree of likelihood. Might it not be just as likely that GP originally was anti-Jewish and that the *Apocalypse of Peter* was selected for inclusion because it, too, carried the name "Peter," and upon being included it underwent editing to bring it into greater conformity with its gospel namesake? Or might it have been the case that of the four texts, the *Apocalypse of Peter* was the only one to have undergone such anti-Jewish redaction, possibly by an earlier scribe whose version of the apocalypse was the only one available or even known to the Akhmîm scribe? In light of the presently available evidence, these two alternative explanations would seem to be as likely as Minnen's suggestion. For this reason, I will operate with the assumption that the anti-Jewish traits of GP can generally be considered to represent something close to its "original" version rather than being the result of later scribal activity.

indicates that some other individual(s) was washing his hands previously. The persons mentioned in GP 1:1–2 are Herod, his judges, and Pilate, the first two being of "the Jews."[11] Hans von Schubert was confident enough to include in his edition of GP the following line prior to the actual Akhmîm text: πειλᾶτος ἐνίψατο τὰς χεῖρας ("Pilate washed his hands").[12] While I do not have the certainty to declare this to be the exact wording of the preceding text, Schubert is likely correct in proposing a previous reference to handwashing by Pilate. Because of what follows at the end of GP 1:1 (καὶ μὴ βουληθέντων νίψασθαι ἀνέστη πειλᾶτος), the best explanation is that indeed Pilate had washed his hands at some earlier point in the narrative.

Support for this inference can also be found in the tradition preserved in Matt 27:24. The author of GP was likely acquainted with the Matthean handwashing episode. Because of the desire to heighten the guilt of the Jews, the scene was reworked in GP for a specific polemical purpose: to present the Jews as remaining guilty for the death of Jesus.[13] What in Matthew was a means of portraying Pilate's innocence has now become much more in GP 1:1–2, because not only is the Petrine Pilate absolved of guilt but also, more importantly, the wickedness and guilt of the Jews are heightened by their lack of desire to absolve themselves (μὴ βουληθέντων νίψασθαι).[14] Perhaps this is even to indicate that they are proud of their role. It may also be said that at one level "all" of the Jews remain condemned in GP since "none" of them have washed their hands.

2.2.2 The Primacy of Herod (GP 1:2–2:5)

In GP 1:2 there is a further development regarding the role of the Jews and it entails the transformation of an episode involving Herod. As I mentioned in the synoptic analysis above, all of the NT accounts clearly present Pilate, despite his reticence, as the one who formally condemns Jesus to death. However, in GP it is Herod the king (ὁ βασιλεύς) who gives this pronouncement with his statement, ὅσα ἐκέλευσα ὑμῖν ποιῆσαι αὐτῷ ποιήσατε (GP 1:2). This is the second use of κελεύω in this verse; in the

---

[11] Tobias Nicklas ("Die 'Juden' im Petrusevangelium [PCair 10759]: Ein Testfall," *NTS* 46 [2000]: 213–14) provides a summary of the portrayal of the various individuals in this opening scene of GP.

[12] Schubert, *The Gospel of Peter: Synoptic Tables, with Translations and Critical Apparatus* (trans. John MacPherson; Edinburgh: T&T Clark, 1893), 4.

[13] Vaganay (*Évangile de Pierre*, 198–206) shares some of the same insights.

[14] The same idea is present in Melito's *Hom. on Pascha* 92: "But you [i.e., the Jews] cast the opposite vote against your Lord. For him whom the gentiles worshipped and uncircumcised men admired and foreigners glorified, over whom even Pilate washed his hands, you killed him at the great feast."

previous sentence Herod commands (κελεύει) Jesus to be taken away.[15] In Matthew's gospel, κελεύω is used when Pilate "order[s]" that Jesus' body be given to Joseph and again when the Jewish leaders ask Pilate to "command" that Jesus' tomb be made secure (Matt 27:58, 64). While Pilate is in command in Matthew's story, Herod the king of the Jews plays this role in GP. The Jewish ruler is now the principal authority responsible for the official death sentence of Jesus. From where has this idea come?

Luke is the only other NT evangelist to include Herod in the proceedings that lead to Jesus' death (Luke 23:7–12). In the reconstruction of Crossan, Luke has created his scene in order to "integrate the tradition about Antipas from the *Cross Gospel* with the tradition about Pilate from the Markan gospel."[16] In his estimation, the hypothetical Cross Gospel, itself an earlier version of GP, served as a source for Luke. I would suggest, rather, that it is the other way around. The Petrine evangelist rewrites the story by including the Lukan report of Herod's role in the condemnation of Jesus, and this is likely due to the fact that he is the most significant Jewish authority to appear in the Passion Narratives known to him.[17] The writer of GP, because of his focus on Jewish responsibility, employs Herod since he represents the presence of a Jewish political figure who could plausibly "command" people to carry out the crucifixion.[18] Therefore, Herod's prominence rose in direct correlation to the desire to reflect Jewish guilt for the death of Jesus.

The primacy of Herod is exemplified further in the subsequent scene (GP 2:3–5). Joseph, upon learning that Jesus is about to be crucified, goes to Pilate to request the body for burial. But Pilate himself cannot grant this request; he must send to Herod and ask for the body. Herod is thus the primary authority through whom all official decisions are made pertaining to the execution.

2.2.3 The Role of the Jewish People in the Mockery, Abuse, and Crucifixion

The Jewish people first appear in GP 2:5 and their role in carrying out the orders of Herod is in the forefront throughout the account of Jesus' execu-

---

[15] The verb κελεύω is defined as "to give a command, ordinarily of an official nature, command, order, urge" (BDAG, s.v., 538).

[16] Crossan, *Cross That Spoke*, 43.

[17] Vaganay (*Évangile de Pierre*, 198–201) argues along similar lines.

[18] Compare, for example, the story in *Acts Pet.* 8 in which Caiaphas condemns Jesus and hands him over to the Jewish crowd. Christians could employ others for this role when wishing to portray Jews as responsible for Jesus' death. However, the figure is typically one in authority, either politically or religiously.

tion.[19] Herod delivers Jesus "to the people" (τῷ λαῷ) and it is immediately clear that "the people" are the Jews, since this act takes place "before the first day of unleavened bread, *their* feast" (GP 2:5). The term "Jew(s)" does not appear again until GP 6:23, but it is apparent that the numerous third person pronouns in the intervening verses refer to Jews.[20] In describing the various ways in which Jesus is mistreated prior to the actual crucifixion, GP presents all of them as being carried out by the Jewish people in general. There is no participation by Pilate, Roman soldiers, or Jewish leaders. This stands in marked contrast to the Passion Narratives of the NT gospels, each of which leaves little or no ambiguity in stating that the Roman authorities oversee the actual crucifixion. What we find in GP, then, is a transfer of blame. Where the NT accounts assign varying degrees of guilt to both Romans and Jews, GP has placed virtually all of the responsibility onto Herod and the Jewish people.

An examination of the various acts against Jesus carried out by the Jews in GP 3:6–5:16 reveals that the author has not only gathered all of the blame to assign to the Jews, he has also compiled a wide array of the types of abuse and included them in his account. Numerous features are common to GP and multiple NT accounts (e.g., Jesus clothed in purple, crown of thorns, spitting, striking). GP also includes details unique to each of the NT gospels (excluding Mark).[21] Matthew and GP both mention gall in a drink offered to Jesus (Matt 27:34; GP 5:16). Luke and GP relate Jesus' death to Jerusalem's demise (Luke 23:28–31; GP 7:25). Jesus is slapped in both John and GP (John 19:3; GP 3:9). While GP includes many of the acts of abuse and mockery that are found in the canonical stories, it is more significant to note here the way in which the identity of the abusers is changed in GP.

The mistreatment of Jesus in GP 2:5–3:9 is done by Jews. This includes taking Jesus and pushing him, clothing him in purple, placing him on a

---

[19] Here again I follow some of the insights in Nicklas, "'Juden' im Petrusevangelium," 215–19.

[20] For example, in GP 5:15 the people become anxious that Jesus will not die before the setting of the sun, a clear allusion to the OT mandate that had been cited in GP 2:5 and which again is said to have been "written for *them*" (GP 5:15).

[21] As Brown (*Death of the Messiah*, 2:1327) notes, Mark, as the primary source for at least two of the other NT narratives, is to be removed from this discussion. This is true because if GP's author has knowledge of all four NT gospels, as I am proposing, we cannot determine – in those instances where Mark agrees with Matthew or Luke – whether GP is reflecting knowledge of Mark or of one of the gospels that used Mark as a source (i.e., Matthew or Luke). In Brown's judgment there are only two uniquely Markan items absent from all of the other NT Passion Narratives: the reference to crucifixion at the third hour (Mark 15:25), and Pilate's asking if Jesus is dead yet (Mark 15:44). That these two insignificant details are missing from both GP and the three NT gospels is not surprising.

seat and mocking him, setting a crown of thorns on his head, spitting in his face, slapping him on the cheeks, poking him with a reed, and scourging him. Most of these actions have a parallel in at least one NT gospel. More significantly, when it comes to the crucifixion itself, the Jews carry it out in GP (4:10). To depict Jews, rather than Romans, as the perpetrators of abuse, mockery, and crucifixion is to retell the story with purposes that are almost certainly polemical.

2.2.4 The Heightened Malevolency of the Jewish Actions (GP 4:10–14)

Not only are Jews in GP the sole group to condemn Jesus to death, to carry out all of the abuse and mockery toward him, and to crucify him, they are also at times even more malevolent in their actions than is the case in parallel accounts. Alan Kirk has compared the "Legs Not Broken" epi-sodes in John 19:31–36 and GP 4:10–14 and concludes that "Peter's ver-sion is a retelling of the Johannine pericope that embodies the 'social memory' of a second-century community, constructing this archetypal story in accordance with specific contours of its own social identity."[22] In his estimation, the social conflict between Christians and Jews was a key influence on the author of GP in his "retelling" of this pericope, as it af-forded him the opportunity to heighten the malevolency of the Jews in their behavior and attitude toward Jesus.

In John's gospel, the Jews are not overseeing the crucifixion events; in-stead, they must ask Pilate to break the legs of the crucified (John 19:31). Such is not the case in GP, since they, the ones carrying out the crucifix-ion, command that the legs not be broken (GP 4:14). The identity of the one whose legs are not to be broken is unclear in GP, since the Greek in 4:14 simply reads ἐκέλευσαν ἵνα μὴ σκελοκοπηθῇ. Whose legs are not to be broken? The clause indicates only that one individual is the referent. The second purpose clause also specifies by the use of a singular participle and verb that the lack of leg-breaking was in order that one person "might die in torment" (ὅπως βασανιζόμενος ἀποθάνοι).

---

[22] Kirk, "The Johannine Jesus in the Gospel of Peter: A Social Memory Approach," in *Jesus in Johannine Tradition* (ed. Robert T. Fortna and Tom Thatcher; Louisville: West-minster John Knox, 2001), 315. On the other hand, Mara sees in GP's reference to dying in torment an emphasis on prophetic fulfillment, specifically that of Jesus as the Suffer-ing Servant of Isa 50–53 (*Évangile de Pierre*, 122). Crossan (*Cross That Spoke*, 167–74) differs from both Kirk and Mara in concluding that "John 19:31–37 is a powerful redac-tional creation based on two separate units from the *Cross Gospel*" (169). The two units from GP to which he refers are the reed-poking from 3:9 and the leg-breaking of 4:14. In Crossan's judgment, "it is immediately clear that John has transferred the nonbreaking of the legs from the thief to Jesus himself, and that he sees in this the fulfilment [*sic*] of biblical prophecy" (168).

The question then is whether it is Jesus or the other malefactor (i.e., the one who reproaches the Jews) whom the Jews want to die in torment by not having his legs broken. Determination based solely on grammatical grounds is not possible. The English translation of Kraus and Nicklas seems to point toward the other malefactor as the one whose legs are not to be broken: "Then they were enraged at him and commanded that (his) legs should not be broken, so that he might die in torment" (GP 4:14).[23] Since the nearest antecedent in their translation is the crucified man who had reproached the Jews, this rendering implies that it was his legs that were not to be broken.[24] On the other hand, Kirk asserts without argument that Jesus is the referent and displays no awareness of the ambiguity.[25] Brown seems much more cognizant of the difficulties involved in making a firm judgment, eventually concluding that Jesus is the most likely referent.[26] I share this conclusion.

In my estimation the suggestion that GP 4:13–14 was formed as a result of an anti-Jewish sentiment offers a plausible explanation for the ways in which it differs from the accounts in John and Luke. GP links John's story of the leg-breaking with Luke's account of the sympathetic crucifixion victim. The primary purpose in doing so is to heighten the level of malevolence shown by the Jews against not only Jesus but also against those sympathetic to the Christian movement.

So, regardless of whether GP refers to Jesus or to the other malefactor as the one whose legs are not to be broken, the point is that anyone who sides with Jesus will face hostility from the Jews. The confession of the malefactor is significant: "We are suffering for the evil which we have committed. But this man, who has become the saviour of men, what wrong has he done to you?" (GP 4:13). To identify Jesus as the "saviour of men" is effectively a Christian proclamation, thus making the man crucified next to Jesus a representative of Christians. In the end, though, the subject of the one whose legs are not to be broken is best understood as Jesus, since in the immediately subsequent scene the Jews become fearful that the sun has set while "he was still alive" (GP 5:15). This is clearly a reference to Jesus and would make the previous referent best understood also as Jesus.

The identity of the one whose legs are not to be broken is of less import than is the motivation behind the Jewish actions in the narratives of John

---

[23] Kraus and Nicklas, *Petrusevangelium*, 50.

[24] At the time he wrote his commentary, Vaganay noted that the majority of critics were of the opinion that the other crucified man, rather than Jesus, was the object of wrath from the Jews here (*Évangile de Pierre*, 242). Crossan also identifies the referent in GP as the other man (*Cross That Spoke*, 165–69).

[25] Kirk, "Johannine Jesus in the Gospel of Peter," 317.

[26] Brown, *Death of the Messiah*, 2:1176, 1330.

and GP.[27] In John the concern behind the leg-breaking incident is related to Torah observance: "Since it was the day of Preparation, the Jews did not want the bodies left on the cross during the Sabbath, especially because that Sabbath was a day of great solemnity. So they asked Pilate to have the legs of the crucified men broken and the bodies removed" (John 19:31). The Jews in John's gospel want the legs of *all* the crucified men broken in order to hasten their death, not so that they will suffer more but so that their bodies can be removed from the crosses before sunset, a prescription outlined in Deut 21:22–23. Faithfulness to the Torah lies behind John's depiction of the Jews, a motive that is certainly good in itself.

Jewish motivations are markedly different in GP. The desire that the legs *not* be broken is driven by sheer sadism: ὅπως βασανιζόμενος ἀποθάνοι (GP 4:14). They wish to prolong the agony by keeping the crucified alive longer.[28] The desire to adhere to the requirements of Torah are not behind the motives in the leg-breaking episode, though they are present elsewhere in GP (e.g., 2:5; 5:15). Instead, it is the malevolency in the actions of Jews that is at work in the Petrine account. We see that our author has rewritten his story by incorporating Luke's sympathetic malefactor and John's leg-breaking episode. This has been done in a way that shows Jews to be hostile to Jesus (or possibly to those sympathetic to him) to the point that they wish to bring about greater torment for him rather than alleviating his suffering through the breaking of legs.

2.3 The Role of Scripture in GP's Portrayal of the Jews

From its inception as a small group of Jews, the early Christian movement claimed the Scriptures of Israel as their own. To understand these texts from the perspective of the first Christ-followers, we should recognize the way these Christians imagined Jesus' life, death, and resurrection. The Christian appropriation of the OT led to religious and consequently social conflict with other Jewish groups. Indeed, this disagreement between Christians and Jews was an argument over who held the role as the proper interpreters of shared sacred texts, a situation that was by no means new within Judaism. For centuries, various Jewish sects had disagreed about the proper understanding of the Scriptures, and even about which texts were

---

[27] Kirk, "Johannine Jesus in the Gospel of Peter," 317–18.

[28] This again holds true regardless of whether we conclude that it is Jesus or the other man whose legs are not to be broken. In the former instance, the hostility is directed against the leader of the Christian movement, whereas in the latter the violence is directed against his followers or those sympathetic to the movement.

authoritative.[29] The early Christians recognized their status as the much younger sect, but this did not stop them from criticizing Jews whose interpretations of OT texts differed from their own.

Scholars have long been aware of the OT background to much of the contents of GP. However, the role of the OT in GP has been understood in various ways. Swete conjectured that "perhaps the writer has been led by his anti-Judaic spirit to affect indifference to the Jewish Scriptures."[30] In this section, I will suggest that Swete is correct in noting the influence of an anti-Jewish *Tendenz* as it pertains to the use of the OT in GP, and I will identify several cases in which the author employs the Scriptures in specific ways that reinforce or heighten the negative portrayal of Jews, especially as it relates to their role in Jesus' death.

Martin Dibelius was prominent among those who first suggested that the earliest Passion Narrative developed as a result of Christian reflection on Scripture.[31] Though he considered GP to be later than the NT Passion Narratives and dependent upon them, Dibelius proposed that the use of the OT in GP preserved an earlier exegetical tradition as it relates to the role of Scripture in gospel literature. Later writers – including Denker, Crossan, and Koester – would follow Dibelius' proposal that GP preserves a more primitive use of the OT, but all of these more recent scholars have concluded that GP does not reflect any knowledge of the canonical works.[32]

Koester, for example, has taken a form-critical approach in evaluating the tradition history of GP and the role of the OT in it. He claims that, because the episode in GP 3:6–9 "has not yet split the mocking account into several scenes," it "is older than its various usages in the canonical gospels."[33] In his estimation the original form of the mocking scene that arose out of Christian reflection on the OT – specifically the scapegoat ritual of Lev 16 and other texts – was a single unified account that was later divided into multiple scenes like those in the parallel NT stories (e.g., Matt 26:67; 27:26–30; Mark 14:65; 15:16–20; John 19:1–5, 13).

---

[29] A summary of this issue can be found in the assorted essays in the first half of McDonald and Sanders, *Canon Debate*.

[30] Swete, *Akhmîm Fragment*, xxvi. It is not entirely clear what Swete means by the "indifference" of GP's author, since his subsequent discussion is brief. In my estimation, Swete might be meaning to say that the author is not careful to give verbatim quotations of any particular OT version. Rather, his OT background has come primarily via the anti-Jewish *testimonia* with which he was acquainted.

[31] As it relates to the use of Scripture in GP's Passion Narrative, see Dibelius, "Die alttestamentliche Motive in der Leidensgeschichte des Petrus- und Johannes-Evangeliums," BZAW 33 (1918): 125–50.

[32] Denker, *Theologiegeschichtliche Stellung*; Crossan, *Cross That Spoke*; Koester, *Ancient Christian Gospels*, 216–40. In the case of Crossan, the original version of GP (his Cross Gospel) reflected no knowledge of the NT accounts.

[33] Koester, *Ancient Christian Gospels*, 227.

A form-critical judgment in this area – that stories tend to go from the simple to the complex – has increasingly been called into question. Kirk has argued that recent research on orality and writing in ancient cultures "render[s] the form-critical canon of developmental tendencies in the oral tradition all but a dead letter."[34] He expresses similar sentiments about written texts as well. In evaluating the tradition history of gospel material, there are additional factors to be weighed that are at least as important as measuring the proximity of any given story to its hypothetical original form. One of these is the social context in which a story is told or written. Kirk again issues a helpful reminder when he states that "the morphology of tradition depends not upon developmental or de-pristinating tendencies but upon social variables impinging upon the different performance arenas in which a given tradition is enacted."[35]

Rather than gauging the degree to which the OT background to GP fits certain hypothetical forms, my study here will focus on how, at several points in GP, the OT is utilized in a manner that disparages Jews. This is exemplified in GP's use of the biblical texts in ways that show how the Jewish people have acted in violation of their Scriptures. Along the way, I will be indebted to the work of Thomas Hieke, whose conclusions align closely with my own.[36]

2.3.1 Handwashing (GP 1:1)

As I mentioned briefly above, the washing of hands in GP 1:1 symbolizes a declaration of innocence concerning responsibility for Jesus' execution. The clearest allusion in GP's handwashing scene is to Deut 21:1–9, which gives instructions to the Israelites for how to handle the discovery of a

---

[34] Kirk, "Tradition and Memory in the *Gospel of Peter*," in Kraus and Nicklas, *Evangelium nach Petrus*, 139. In contrast, Brown (*Death of the Messiah*, 2:944) finds in the tradition history "a tendency to gradually increase" scriptural allusions and echoes. While this might be a "tendency," there are exceptions to trends. The contexts in which traditions arise and develop, in addition to other factors such as genre and authorial preferences, may or may not lead to an increase of biblical references. One might cite Justin Martyr's two primary works as representative of this. He employs vastly more OT allusions and quotations in *Dialogue with Trypho* than in his *First Apology*.

[35] Kirk, "Tradition and Memory," 138. Denker (*Theologiegeschichtliche Stellung*, 78–87) also notes the importance of the polemical background to GP as central to understanding its use of the OT. As I discuss below, however, this leads him to conclusions that at times border on being reductionist, as, for instance, in his claim that the apologetic tendencies of GP are directed *solely* in response to disputes with Jewish opponents.

[36] Hieke, "Das Petrusevangelium vom Alten Testament her gelesen: Gewinnbringende Lektüre eines nicht-kanonischen Textes vom christlichen Kanon her," in Kraus and Nicklas, *Evangelium nach Petrus*, 91–115. He summarizes matters thus: "The use of the Holy Scriptures of Israel reveals the anti-Jewish tendency of GP" (94).

murder victim whose killer is unknown.[37] The primary indication that the ritual comes in response to a perceived murder, as opposed to an accidental death, comes in the reference in v. 1 to a person being "struck down" by another person. The Hebrew verb here is *nakah*, which can be used in contexts referring to either injury or death.[38]

In such an instance, the elders and judges (κριταί) from the nearest town are to oversee a ceremony in which they take a heifer to a nearby valley with flowing water.[39] When coming to the stream they are to break the neck of the animal. The ritual concludes with the elders and judges washing their hands over the dead heifer while making the following declaration: "Our hands did not shed this blood, nor were we witnesses to it. Absolve, O LORD, your people Israel, whom you redeemed; do not let the guilt of innocent blood remain in the midst of your people Israel" (Deut 21:7–8). In so doing this, they are released of any guilt and the innocent blood is purged from their community.

What we find in GP 1:1 is a reenactment of the Deuteronomic ritual, but now the Jewish κριταί refuse to wash their hands. Herod, the judges (κριταί), and all the other Jews fail to take the step of absolving themselves of guilt. None of the NT accounts includes κριταί in its Passion Narrative. GP's author, in my estimation, has added them to the present scene in order to strengthen the allusion to the ceremony of Deut 21, specifically in showing the failure of the Jewish κριταί to fulfill their responsibility in the case of Jesus.

This lack of washing on the part of the Jews is not out of ignorance, for their reason is clearly stated: μὴ βουληθέντων νίψασθαι (GP 1:1). The implication is that they have a full realization of the significance of washing, yet even armed with this knowledge they refuse to do so. Only Pilate, the non-Jew, cleanses himself of innocent blood. As important as the Deuteronomic handwashing act itself is the event that initiates it: a murder (Deut 21:1). By alluding to this ritual, GP is indicating that Jesus' death was on a par with murder; it was not a lawful execution but rather an un-

---

[37] So also Vaganay, *Évangile de Pierre*, 202; Crossan, *Cross That Spoke*, 96–98; Brown, *Death of the Messiah*, 1:834. Other OT texts mentioned as possibly being relevant are Exod 30:18–21; Ps 26:4–6; 73:13.

[38] See BDB, s.v., 645–47. This account describes an intentional act. The law pertaining to accidental death is given elsewhere – in Deut 19:4–5. Commentators seem to be in agreement on Deut 21:1–9 referring to intentional homicide. For instance, Moshe Weinfeld (*Deuteronomy and the Deuteronomic School* [Oxford: Clarendon Press, 1972], 210) identifies these verses as "the law of unsolved murder." Similarly, J. Gordon McConville (*Deuteronomy* [AOTC 5; Leicester: Apollos, 2002], 326–29) repeatedly refers to "murder" and "murderer" in his discussion and states that the ritual "deal[s] with the unsolved murder" (326).

[39] All Greek text of the OT is from the LXX, unless otherwise noted.

just killing.[40] Therefore, what follows in GP is, to use its own language, "the murder of the Lord."

Other handwashing texts in the OT further illustrate this same point and perhaps are being echoed in GP. Two examples are found in the Psalms:[41]

I do not sit with the worthless, nor do I consort with hypocrites; I hate the company of evildoers, and will not sit with the wicked. I wash my hands in innocence, and go around your altar, O LORD. (Ps 26:4–6)

All in vain I have kept my heart clean and washed my hands in innocence. (Ps 73:13)

Crossan is correct in saying that these psalms presuppose the ritual described in Deut 21 and clearly express its signification of innocence.[42] In GP 1:1 Pilate now plays the same role as the psalmist. The Roman governor "stood up" out of a desire not to remain seated among the "worthless" and "wicked" Jews who would condemn and murder Jesus (GP 1:1; Ps 26:4–5). The author of GP, in order to heighten the contrast between the parties, describes the standing of Pilate immediately after the Jews' refusal to wash. Furthermore, he indicates through the echo of the psalm that the Jews are among the wicked who remain seated.[43]

Matthew's handwashing account has been rewritten in an attempt to highlight Jewish guilt for shedding innocent blood and to indicate that it still remains upon them. This effort has been enhanced through further allusions to OT texts. By calling to mind these texts, GP also presents Jesus' death not as an execution but as the killing of one who is innocent.

---

[40] The use of πεφονευμένῳ ("murdered one") in GP 2:5; 5:15 is also significant in this regard and will be discussed in more detail below.

[41] These are treated as background to GP 1:1 in Crossan, *Cross That Spoke*, 97–100; Brown, *Death of the Messiah*, 1:834; Hieke, "Petrusevangelium vom Alten Testament," 94.

[42] Crossan, *Cross That Spoke*, 97.

[43] It is probable that the original Hebrew text of Ps 26:4–5, in using the verb *yashav*, conveyed the notion of "dwelling/living/being" with the worthless and wicked rather than actually "sitting" with them. However, lest it be thought that my suggestion regarding GP requires an overly literal understanding of the psalm, the LXX uses καθίζω to render *yashav* in both instances in Ps 26:4–5. While καθίζω can carry the connotation of "dwelling/living/being" (e.g., Luke 24:49; Acts 18:11), this usage for it is rare (see BDAG, s.v., 491–92). Far more often καθίζω refers to a literal "sitting/seating," so it seems that the LXX has rendered the psalm in a way that plausibly could have been understood in this fashion. In any case, I have found nothing to persuade me that GP's author had any knowledge of Hebrew. In my estimation, all of his knowledge of OT texts has come to him in Greek, be it through particular translations (e.g., LXX) or through Christian *testimonia*, or both. On the Greek of GP see Vaganay, *Évangile de Pierre*, 141–47; Stanley E. Porter, "The Greek of the Gospel of Peter," in Kraus and Nicklas, *Evangelium nach Petrus*, 77–90.

2.3.2 The Sun Should Not Set on One Who Has Been Murdered
(GP 2:5; 5:15)

In only two instances does GP make an explicit claim to be quoting Scripture, and on both occasions the same text – Deut 21:22–23 – is mentioned (GP 2:5; 5:15).[44] The first reference to these verses comes in Herod's reply to the request that Jesus' body be given to Joseph (GP 2:5). Herod alludes to this text when he informs Pilate that the Jews would have observed the legal requirement to give Jesus a proper burial before sundown. The second quotation appears after the Jewish people become enraged at Jesus during the crucifixion and command that his legs not be broken (GP 4:14–5:15). At this point darkness descends over the land, which leads the Jews to fear that they have violated their law. I quote here these two excerpts as they are commonly rendered in English translations:

And Herod said: "Brother Pilate, even if no one had asked for him, we would have buried him since the Sabbath draws on. For it is written in the law that *the sun should not set on one that has been put to death*" (ἥλιον μὴ δῦναι ἐπὶ πεφονευμένῳ). (GP 2:5)[45]

And they became anxious and in fear lest the sun had already set, since he was still alive. It is written for them that *the sun should not set on one that has been put to death* (ἥλιον μὴ δῦναι ἐπὶ πεφονευμένῳ). (GP 5:15)[46]

We may now also quote the relevant verses from Deuteronomy:

When someone is convicted of a crime punishable by death and is executed (ἐὰν δὲ γένηται ἔν τινι ἁμαρτία κρίμα θανάτου καὶ ἀποθάνῃ), and you hang him on a tree, his corpse must not remain all night upon the tree; you shall bury him that same day, for anyone hung on a tree is under God's curse. You must not defile the land that the LORD your God is giving you for possession. (Deut 21:22–23)

The instructions in Deuteronomy apply to someone who has committed a sin or crime worthy of death: ἐὰν δὲ γένηται ἔν τινι ἁμαρτία κρίμα θανάτου (Deut 21:22). They stipulate that when someone is convicted of a capital offense, he "is executed" (ἀποθάνῃ).[47] The Hebrew original of this

---

[44] Vaganay, *Évangile de Pierre*, 215–16; Mara, *Évangile de Pierre*, 86–87; Crossan, *Cross That Spoke*, 201–8; Brown, *Death of the Messiah*, 2:1339; Heike, "Petrusevangelium vom Alten Testament," 94–95.

[45] I have slightly revised the translation of Kraus and Nicklas (*Petrusevangelium*, 50) here. But compare their German translation: "Die Sonne nicht über einem Ermordeten untergehen solle" (*Petrusevangelium*, 33, 35). This German would translate best as, "The sun should not set on one who has been *murdered*." Brown (*Death of the Messiah*, 2:1318–19) gives these two renderings: 1) "The sun is not to set on one put to death" (2:5); 2) "Let not the sun set on one put to death (5:15).

[46] I have slightly revised the translation of Kraus and Nicklas (*Petrusevangelium*, 50) here.

[47] The verb ἀποθνήσκω alone indicates only death in general. However, the context makes clear that the verb is being used in regard to executions here. This is evidenced by

verse reads with the verb *mut* to carry the idea of killing that is part of a lawful taking of life.[48] The LXX has properly rendered the original Hebrew idea that this is an instance of capital punishment with its use of ἀποθνήσκω, a verb whose semantic range includes the notion of legal executions.[49]

Where Deuteronomy, both in its Hebrew and LXX forms, presents the legal instructions as pertaining to capital punishment, GP changes the context to one of unjustified killing. This occurs through its alteration of the verb from the original *mut*/ἀποθνήσκω idea of capital punishment to the term φονεύω and its connotations: ἥλιον μὴ δῦναι ἐπὶ πεφονευμένῳ (GP 2:5; 5:15). Φονεύω refers not to the lawful taking of life but to murder or unjustified killing.[50] The verb appears in the same form in both versions of the Decalogue: οὐ φονεύσεις (Exod 20:15; Deut 5:18). It is used a total of twelve times in the NT (Matt 5:21 [2X]; 19:18; 23:31, 35; Mark 10:19; Luke 18:20; Rom 13:9; Jas 2:11 [2X]; 4:2; 5:6). In all of these NT appearances, it refers unambiguously to murder.[51] Φόνος is the most common Greek term to signify "murder" in both the LXX and the NT, and φονεύς is what is most often used for "murderer."[52] It is highly significant that the Hebrew *mut* is never rendered with φονεύω anywhere in the LXX

---

the opening clause: "When someone is convicted of a crime punishable by death." Weinfeld (*Deuteronomy*, 51) points out that this verse is speaking of "the public exhibition of the executed bodies." So the rendering of the NRSV ("he is executed") is accurate.

[48] The Hebrew here is the Hophal perfect form of *mut*. BDB (s.v., 560) gives these definitions for the Hophal: "be killed, put to death: 1. by conspiracy. 2. by capital punishment ... 3. by divine infliction ... 4. die prematurely." BDB includes Deut 21:22 among the examples connoting "capital punishment."

[49] In HRCS (s.v. ἀποθνήσκω, 128–30), over 95% of the appearances of ἀποθνήσκω have the Hebrew *mut* behind them, so it is clear that the LXX has provided a typical reading of the Hebrew in Deut 21:22. Other instances of ἀποθνήσκω in contexts of capital punishment or justified killing can be found in, for example, Lev 10:6, 7, 9; 22:9; Num 1:51; 17:13; 18:32; Josh 1:18; 1 Kgs 21:10.

[50] BDAG (s.v., 1063) defines it as "murder, kill." In L&N (s.v., 238) it is defined as "to deprive a person of life by illegal, intentional killing – 'to murder, to commit murder.'" Of all the appearances of φονεύω in the LXX, there appears to be only one instance in which it is used in the context of capital punishment (Num 35:30). Other Greek verbs are typically used in the LXX to describe the instructions for legally executing a criminal (e.g., τελευτάω, θανατόω, ἀποκτείνω).

[51] In eight of these twelve NT occurrences, φονεύω appears in contexts where the writers are referring to the Hebrew Bible's injunction forbidding murder (Matt 5:21 [2X]; 19:18; Mark 10:19; Luke 18:20; Rom 13:9; Jas 2:11 [2X]).

[52] In Melito's extended homily on what he considers to be the murder of Jesus by the Jews, he uses the terms φονεύω, φόνος, and φονεύς to describe the occasion (see especially *Hom. on Pascha* 94–97). More on this below.

or any other known Greek version of Scripture.[53] This is a strong indication that the author of GP is not dependent upon any non-LXX version of Scripture for his use of φονεύω.[54]

In light of this alteration of verbs, it would be more accurate to translate the statements in GP 2:5 and 5:15 "the sun should not set on one who has been *murdered*."[55] Instead of the Deuteronomic law speaking of legally executed criminals, GP presents its burial requirements as pertaining to murder victims. This modification portrays the Jews not as rightful executioners of a condemned criminal but as murderers of an innocent man. We cannot know whether the author was aware that his choice of words here puts the Jews in direct violation of one of the chief commandments of the Decalogue – οὐ φονεύσεις. But it is certainly plausible to suppose that from his anti-Jewish perspective he was fully aware of the implications of his selection.

The second item of interest is that "the law" mentioned in our gospel "is written for *them*" (γέγραπται αὐτοῖς) (GP 2:5; 5:15).[56] While the writer of GP employs OT allusions to further his negative portrayal of Jews, he views the legal requirement of Deuteronomy as something that does not apply to him or, presumably, to other Christians.[57] The mandate is for Jews alone, who are considered in GP to be "the other": what is for "them" is not for "us." This may indicate that the demands of Torah were solely for Jews (them) but not for Christians (us) in the community of the author.

---

[53] According to HRCS (s.v. φονεύω, 1437), φονεύω translates four different Hebrew verbs: *harag, kharam, nakah, ratsakh*. This includes not only the LXX but other Greek versions as well.

[54] Swete (*Akhmîm Fragment*, 3) noted long ago the oddity of this verb here in GP, suggesting that we should expect to find κρεμάννυμι in place of φονεύω. He also makes a passing reference to the use of φονεύω comporting with the "anti-Judaic tone of the fragment" (ibid.), but he offers no further elaboration.

[55] Hieke ("Petrusevangelium vom Alten Testament," 94–95) comes to the same conclusion with his description of the Petrine Jesus as "ein Ermordeter" (a murder victim).

[56] The appearance of γράφω with the dative typically means "to them" (e.g., writing a letter to someone). However, it is not without precedent to find this arrangement carrying the meaning that something has been written "for" someone, the idea that I am proposing for GP 5:15. The LXX has several examples of this construction: Deut 17:18; 2 Kings 17:37; 1 Esd 4:47, 49; 3 Macc 6:41. Similar instances occur in the NT: "But Jesus said to them, 'Because of your hardness of heart *he* [i.e., Moses] *wrote this commandment for you* (ἔγραψεν ὑμῖν τὴν ἐντολὴν ταύτην)'" (Mark 10:5); "Teacher, Moses *wrote for us* (ἔγραψεν ἡμῖν) that if a man's brother dies, leaving a wife but no child, the man shall marry the widow and raise up children for his brother" (Mark 12:19; cf. Luke 20:28). It is interesting that the context in both of these NT examples is the exposition of pentateuchal laws, the very background of GP's instance.

[57] Brown (*Death of the Messiah*, 2:1340) notes that Deut 21:22–23 was also used in anti-Jewish apologetic in *Dialogue between Jason and Papiscus*. This lends further support to the function I am proposing for it in GP.

2.3.3 Running to Evil (GP 3:6)

In GP 3:6 we have a brief scene not found in any of the NT gospels: "But those who took the Lord pushed him as they ran (τρέχοντες) and said: 'Let us drag away the Son of God, because we have got power over him.'" The subject here is "the people" (i.e., the Jews). Herod has handed over Jesus to the Jewish people, who now push him as they run on the way to participating in further mockery and abuse. Hieke has suggested Prov 1:16 and Isa 59:7 as background texts for this episode:[58]

For their feet run (τρέχουσιν) to evil, and they hurry to shed blood. (Prov 1:16)

Their feet run (τρέχουσιν) to evil, and they rush to shed innocent blood; their thoughts are thoughts of iniquity, desolation and destruction are in their highways. (Isa 59:7)

The context of Prov 1:16 is that the wise person is not to be involved in the actions of sinners (cf. Prov 1:10), because in the end the evil that he plots will work against him (Prov 1:18–19). The Isaianic text is even more illuminating, as it connects in a single verse the same ideas as those dispersed throughout Prov 1:8–19. The prophetic message of Isaiah 59 warns that oppression and injustice will not go unpunished by God. Those whose feet run to evil in order to shed innocent blood will meet destruction.

In GP we find that the Jews are running to evil in order to shed the innocent blood of Jesus. Though Pilate has washed his hands of this blood, the Jews have refused to do so. In fact, they rush to be involved. Those who run to such evil in GP discover that judgment will come in response to their actions, as we read later that the destruction of Jerusalem occurs as a result of Jewish responsibility for Jesus' death: "Woe on our sins! Judgment has come close and the end of Jerusalem" (GP 7:25).[59] The Jews in GP fail to heed the wisdom of their Scriptures in their eagerness to spill innocent blood.

2.3.4 "Judge Righteously" (GP 3:7)

Immediately after the Jews run and push Jesus, they clothe him in a purple robe and seat him on the seat of judgment (GP 3:7). Upon doing so, they instruct him with the command δικαίως κρῖνε βασιλεῦ τοῦ Ἰσραήλ (GP 3:7). The concept of judging in a righteous manner is common in the OT.[60]

---

[58] Heike, "Petrusevangelium vom Alten Testament," 96. Isaiah 59:7 is cited by Mara, *Évangile de Pierre*, 89. Denker (*Theologiegeschichtliche Stellung*, 65–66) suggests Ps 118:13 (LXX 117:13) as another possible source for this allusion. However, Crossan (*Cross That Spoke*, 144) is skeptical that this psalm is relevant to the GP episode.

[59] I will discuss Christian apologetic use of Jerusalem's destruction in Chapter Three.

[60] The OT background to this statement in GP is discussed in Mara, *Évangile de Pierre*, 91–94; Hieke, "Petrusevangelium vom Alten Testament," 97–98. I follow much the same line as Hieke here.

Several OT texts have been cited as being significant for this section of GP:

He judges the world with righteousness; he judges the peoples with equity. (Ps 9:8)

He will judge the world with righteousness, and the peoples with his truth. (Ps 96:13)

Let the floods clap their hands; let the hills sing together for joy at the presence of the LORD, for he is coming to judge the earth. He will judge the world with righteousness, and the peoples with equity. (Ps 98:8–9)

Speak out, judge righteously, defend the rights of the poor and needy. (Prov 31:9)

His delight shall be in the fear of the LORD. He shall not judge by what his eyes see, or decide by what his ears hear; but with righteousness he shall judge the poor, and decide with equity for the meek of the earth; he shall strike the earth with the rod of his mouth, and with the breath of his lips he shall kill the wicked. (Isa 11:3–4)

Yet day after day they seek me and delight to know my ways, as if they were a nation that practiced righteousness and did not forsake the ordinance of their God; they ask of me righteous judgments, they delight to draw near to God. (Isa 58:2)

It was the LORD who made it known to me, and I knew; then you showed me their evil deeds. But I was like a gentle lamb led to the slaughter. And I did not know it was against me that they devised schemes, saying, "Let us destroy the tree with its fruit, let us cut him off from the land of the living, so that his name will no longer be remembered!" But you, O LORD of hosts, who judge righteously, who try the heart and the mind, let me see your retribution upon them, for to you I have committed my cause. Therefore thus says the LORD concerning the people of Anathoth, who seek your life, and say, "You shall not prophesy in the name of the LORD, or you will die by our hand" – therefore thus says the LORD of hosts: I am going to punish them; the young men shall die by the sword; their sons and their daughters shall die by famine; and not even a remnant shall be left of them. For I will bring disaster upon the people of Anathoth, the year of their punishment. (Jer 11:18–23)

Though Jesus is by all appearances powerless before his captors in GP, these OT texts allude to the traditional belief that divine righteousness will reign in the end.

In Isa 11 and Jer 11 righteous judgment includes the destruction of those who plot and pursue evil deeds. Hieke states that these two passages are "anti-texts to the narrative logic of GP."[61] The abusers of Jesus yet again act in violation of their Scriptures. Rather than being on the side of God's anointed, the Jews of GP work against him to the point of seeking his death. While the Jews call for Jesus to judge righteously, they themselves completely fail to do likewise. It is only later that they recognize the true identity of Jesus in their declaration, "If at his death these most mighty signs have come to pass, see how righteous he is" (GP 8:28). As warned in Isaiah and Jeremiah, those who fail to judge righteously await destruction.

---

[61] Hieke, "Petrusevangelium vom Alten Testament," 98.

The one who judges righteously has brought judgment on the Jewish people, and it is only after destruction has come upon them that they acknowledge Jesus as the righteous one of God.

The words of GP 3:7 have been cited as evidence of the author's familiarity with early Christian *testimonia* collections.[62] It is likely that GP's use of the OT has been filtered, in some cases, through such Christian exegesis and proof texts. The present verse is perhaps the best example. None of the NT gospels refers unambiguously to Jesus being placed on a seat.[63] However, Justin makes such a reference in *1 Apol.* 35: "And, as the Prophet said, they placed Him in mockery on the judgment seat, and said: 'Judge us.'" Earlier in *1 Apol.* 35, Justin cites a form of Isa 58:2 ("They now ask judgment from Me, and dare to approach God"), and he prefaces his description of Jesus' mockery on the judgment seat with "as the Prophet said." Skarsaune cites this as an example of the pattern: 1) non-LXX prophecy; 2) exposition; and 3) fulfillment report.[64] The combination of Jesus' placement on a seat with the instruction to judge is strikingly similar in GP and Justin. I concur with Skarsaune's judgment that these parallels "point to some kind of common tradition," the most likely candidate being a testimony source.[65] It should come as no surprise to find that a writer whose apologetic interests are as strong as those of the author of GP would be familiar with and utilize *testimonia* resources. Scholars from J. Rendel Harris to C. H. Dodd and Barnabas Lindars, though differing from one another in their overall methodology and conclusions, have noted that apologetic motivations underlie the origin and development of early Christian use of the OT and the employment of testimony sources.[66]

At first glance, it might be claimed that a significant difference between GP and Justin in the present instance is that GP does not include a fulfillment reference. As I will suggest below, however, the summary statement

---

[62] On the *testimonia* hypothesis, see Martin C. Albl, *"And Scripture Cannot Be Broken": The Form and Function of the Early Christian Testimonia Collections* (NovTSupp 96; Leiden: Brill, 1999). While Albl cites a few examples from GP as exhibiting signs of familiarity with *testimonia* traditions (e.g., the darkness of 5:15, and the gall and vinegar in 5:16), he does not include GP 3:7 among them. More significantly for the present issue, Oskar Skarsaune (*The Proof from Prophecy: A Study in Justin Martyr's Proof-Text Tradition: Text-type, Provenance, Theological Profile* [NovTSup 56; Leiden: Brill, 1987], 146–48) discusses GP 3:7 as evidence of its employment of *testimonia* sources.

[63] Yet note my earlier discussion in the Synoptic Analysis about this being a possible understanding of John 19:13.

[64] Skarsaune, *Proof from Prophecy*, 146.

[65] Ibid., 147.

[66] Harris, *Testimonies*; Dodd, *According to the Scriptures: The Sub-structure of New Testament Theology* (London: Nisbet, 1952); Lindars, *New Testament Apologetic: The Doctrinal Significance of the Old Testament Quotations* (Philadelphia: Westminster, 1961).

in GP 5:17 (ἐπλήρωσαν πάντα) should be viewed as one overarching fulfillment citation that covers all of the acts perpetrated against Jesus. In this sense, then, there is no major difference between Justin and GP. Both have likely used a testimony source in their effort to show the fulfillment of Scripture. GP has also gone to significant lengths to include the motif of Jewish culpability in this process.

2.3.5 Darkness at Noon (GP 5:15)

Darkness at midday is a common characteristic of Passion Narratives; three of the NT gospels refer to its occurrence around the time of the cruci-fixion (Matt 27:45; Mark 15:33; Luke 23:44). All of these NT accounts state that this happened at the sixth hour, and all use the same expression (i.e., a form of ὥρα ἕκτη). GP differs, however, in its reference to the time of the darkness: ἦν δὲ μεσημβρία καὶ σκότος κατέσχε πᾶσαν τὴν 'Ιουδαίαν (GP 5:15). I want to suggest that the use of μεσημβρία, when combined with other contextual clues, echoes OT texts in a manner that further disparages the portrait of Jews in GP.

The following OT verses provide examples of how darkness functions in the same way as in GP:[67]

The LORD will afflict you with madness, blindness, and confusion of mind; you shall grope about at noon (μεσημβρίας) as blind people grope in darkness, but you shall be unable to find your way; and you shall be continually abused and robbed, without anyone to help. (Deut 28:28–29)

Therefore justice is far from us, and righteousness does not reach us; we wait for light, and lo! there is darkness; and for brightness, but we walk in gloom. We grope like the blind along a wall, groping like those who have no eyes; we stumble at noon (μεσημβρία) as in the twilight, among the vigorous as though we were dead. (Isa 59:9–10)

On that day, says the Lord GOD, I will make the sun go down at noon (μεσημβρίας), and darken the earth in broad daylight. (Amos 8:9)

In all three texts there is a time reference to μεσημβρία – the same term that appears at GP 5:15 – and in each of them this noon indicator is linked to darkness. Furthermore, the darkness in each episode comes as a result of judgment from God (cf. Isa 59:15–18).

Turning to GP, we can see that the same motif is allowed to echo in the use of μεσημβρία in 5:15 and the consequent actions of the Jews, who "went about with lamps, because they thought it was night, and fell down" (GP 5:18). As in the OT texts, the darkness at μεσημβρία in GP's crucifix-ion scene symbolizes judgment that has come from God for the unright-

---

[67] Vaganay, *Évangile de Pierre*, 245–46; Mara, *Évangile de Pierre*, 125–26; Crossan, *Cross That Spoke*, 198–200; Hieke, "Petrusevangelium vom Alten Testament," 101–3.

eous acts committed against his son (cf. the "Son of God" title in GP 3:6, 9). As is also the case in the OT texts, the darkness in GP leads to stumbling or falling down by those under divine judgment. The darkness leads the Jews to think that it is night, a sign that they have allowed Jesus to remain hung on a tree in violation of the Torah. Despite carrying lamps in the darkness, they still fall down, thus indicating their association with those in Deut 28 and Isa 59 who were blind and groped in the darkness in an effort to find their way. The Jews once again are acting in direct violation of the will and commandments of God, behavior that results in divine judgment descending on Judea in the form of darkness.[68] They then stumble as though blinded by the darkness, a darkness that represents their misdeeds. GP depicts Jews as those who have not learned the lessons of their Scriptures and are in fact repeating even greater sins than those of their ancestors. This will lead to their downfall.

2.3.6 "They Fulfilled Everything" (GP 5:17)

The cumulative efforts of the Jewish people in GP are summarized in GP 5:17: ἐπλήρωσαν πάντα καὶ ἐτελείωσαν κατὰ τῆς κεφαλῆς αὐτῶν τὰ ἁμαρτήματα. It is noteworthy that when referring to the fulfillment of Scripture, the writer does so in association with the misdeeds of the Jewish people. This confirms the suggestion I have made concerning the specific function of the OT in GP, which is to point out the ways in which the Jews both violate and fulfill their Scriptures. In the estimation of some early Christians, Jewish ignorance leads them unknowingly to fulfill the Scriptures through their actions against Jesus. Disputes between Christians and Jews continued well into the second century and beyond, and Christians frequently accused Jews of having a role in the death of Jesus. GP does this by providing a narrative in which the various Jewish actors perform their roles as the perpetrators of this act. Christian application of biblical texts focuses in GP on the sins of the Jewish people and presents those failures as though they took place in fulfillment of the OT. We find here a generically different precursor to what we read in Melito's *Homily on Pascha*. What Melito tells in homiletic fashion, our gospel presents in the form of a Passion Narrative: Israel has simultaneously killed its Messiah and fulfilled its Scriptures.[69]

---

[68] In referring to the darkness at the time of the crucifixion, Irenaeus quotes Amos 8:9–10 as the prophecy which is fulfilled (*Haer.* 4.33.12). Tertullian does likewise (*Adv. Jud.* 10.17). Albl (*Form and Function*, 142–44) notes that later Christians included Amos 8:9–10 in their testimonies against the Jews. GP is an early example of this sort of practice.

[69] Melito, *Hom. on Pascha*, 74–77. Other similar early Christian sentiments are found in Matt 23:31–32; John 12:38–41; *Barn.* 5:11; 14:5. Mara (*Évangile de Pierre*, 129–32)

2.4 The Exoneration of Pilate and the Romans in GP 1:1–5:19

In GP Pilate is not responsible for condemning Jesus to death, as is the case in all of the canonical stories.[70] Instead, he refuses to participate in the events, leaving the Jews to carry out the execution. The Pilate of GP is not hostile to Jesus; in fact, he shows signs of a positive disposition toward the Christian movement. I will discuss here three items indicative of this *Tendenz* in GP: Pilate's handwashing, Jesus' condemnation by Herod, and Pilate's role as a friend of Joseph.

2.4.1 Pilate's Handwashing As Symbolic of Innocence

I stated in my previous discussion of Jewish responsibility that the opening scene of the extant portion of GP, by describing the failure of the Jews to wash their hands, implies that Pilate had washed his hands at an earlier point in the narrative. In GP 1:1 Pilate stands when the Jews "did not want to wash the hands" (μὴ βουληθέντων νίψασθαι). Pilate's rising marks the end of his role in the trial of Jesus; he has declared Jesus innocent and has washed his hands of anything that might be done against him. Further support for an earlier reference to Pilate's washing can be found by looking at a much later scene in GP.

When those guarding the tomb witness the resurrection, they report it to Pilate and declare that Jesus was the Son of God (GP 11:45). In Pilate's response to them he defends himself with the declaration ἐγὼ καθαρεύω τοῦ αἵματος τοῦ υἱοῦ τοῦ θεοῦ (GP 11:46). This statement seems to be an allusion to the earlier scene of Pilate's handwashing, because it is in this symbolic act that one becomes cleansed of blood. In Matthew, the handwashing and declaration of innocence from Pilate occur at the same time:

---

also reviews the ways in which Jews in GP fulfill Scripture. I will examine Melito's homily in further detail below.

[70] On the role of Pilate in GP see Heike Omerzu, "Die Pilatusgestalt im Petrusevangelium: Eine erzählanalytische Annäherung," in Kraus and Nicklas, *Evangelium nach Petrus*, 327–47. Denker (*Theologiegeschichtliche Stellung*, 58–77) identifies the OT background to GP's passion account, including Pilate's role, as the key to understanding the gospel's apologetic interests, which he considers to be directed entirely toward a Jewish audience. This is simplistic, in my estimation. One need not deny apologetics toward a non-Jewish audience in order to affirm the influence of concerns related to Jewish claims. For this reason Denker does not give the complete picture when he says that "it seems very doubtful to me whether the apologetic tendency in GP has the Romans as addressees" (78). Contrary to Denker, my present discussion of Pilate's role in GP should indicate that non-Jews, as well as Jews, likely were addressed in the apologetic tendencies of this gospel. Further examples throughout this project will also exemplify this.

"So when Pilate saw that he could do nothing, but rather that a riot was beginning, he took some water and washed his hands before the crowd, saying, 'I am innocent of this man's blood (ἀθῷός εἰμι ἀπὸ τοῦ αἵματος τούτου); see to it yourselves'" (Matt 27:24). In GP the handwashing and declaration of Pilate have been separated. The washing comes in GP 1:1, but the declaration comes much later.

In GP 11:46 we find the strongest evidence of pro-Roman apologetic in the gospel. This is evidenced in Pilate's statement that only the Jews have condemned Jesus ("I am clean …, but you have concluded this"). This reiterates what was implicit in the opening verses of GP: the Romans are not responsible for the death sentence. The Jews alone made such a judgment.

While the Matthean Pilate speaks only of the innocence of "this man," the Pilate of GP proclaims the innocence of "the Son of God" (GP 11:46). By affirming the title "Son of God," the Petrine Pilate displays a greater awareness of the identity of Jesus than does the Pilate of Matthew and the other NT accounts. The trend to exonerate Pilate in early Christian apologetics finds a representative in our author, who washes the Roman governor clean of the guilt of innocent blood and transforms him into one making the Christian profession of Jesus as the Son of God.

2.4.2 Condemned Not by Pilate but by Herod

Handwashing is the primary *Symbolhandlung* demonstrating innocence in both Matthew and GP. But in Matthew Pilate eventually condemns Jesus to death, even after this gesture, and his soldiers mock and abuse Jesus violently throughout the process (Matt 27:26–38). Something significantly different occurs in GP, which moves much further in an apologetic direction seeking to exonerate Pilate.

After Pilate has separated himself from the Jewish authorities through the washing of his hands and the act of standing, "Herod the king" commands that Jesus be taken away and crucified (GP 1:2). Nothing like this appears in the NT narratives, which have Pilate condemning Jesus to death (Matt 27:26; Mark 15:15; Luke 23:25; John 19:16). What is reflected in this shift is the twofold evolution of heightening Jewish responsibility and downplaying Roman participation.[71] In a social context where the Christian movement was looked upon with scorn and suspicion by Roman authorities, the depiction of Pilate in GP makes very good apologetic sense: a Roman official did not condemn Jesus, the Jewish king did. In fact, the Roman governor declared the founder of the Christian sect innocent and never cast a vote in favor of the execution.

---

[71] Omerzu, "Pilatusgestalt im Petrusevangelium," 333–37.

Another sign of Pilate's reduced stature is found in his deferring to Herod's jurisdiction when Joseph asks him for Jesus' body to bury (GP 2:3–5).[72] Pilate must go to Herod in order to grant Joseph's request, an indication that the Roman governor is not overseeing the details of the execution; that task belongs to Herod. Pilate's prominent role throughout GP indicates the fixed nature of his presence in the tradition history (see 1:1; 2:3–5; 8:29–31; 11:43–49). Christians knew that Pilate was somehow involved in Jesus' execution, so it was folly to deny the fact. Rather than denial, our evangelist resorted to revision by demoting the Roman governor.

2.4.3 Pilate the Friend of Joseph

The role of Joseph of Arimathea as the one responsible for burying Jesus is found in all of the NT gospels (Matt 27:57–60; Mark 15:43–46; Luke 23:50–53; John 19:38–42).[73] As is the case with many characters in the gospels, Joseph undergoes some degree of transformation in the tradition history.[74] In the earliest source he is merely "a respected member of the council, who was also himself waiting expectantly for the kingdom of God" (Mark 15:43). The Lukan Joseph is not only a member of the council waiting for the kingdom of God but also "a good and righteous man" who "had not agreed to their plan and action" (Luke 23:50–51). Matthew and John are similar to one another in that Joseph has now evolved in their stories to the point of becoming a "disciple of Jesus" (Matt 27:57; John 19:38).

GP continues this tradition of Joseph as the one who buries Jesus.[75] A uniquely Petrine detail is that Joseph is identified as ὁ φίλος Πειλάτου καὶ τοῦ κυρίου (GP 2:3). In none of the NT narratives is Joseph a friend of Pilate. Those texts state only that the Roman governor grants the request of Joseph. The result of portraying Joseph, a companion of Jesus, as a friend of Pilate, is that the Roman governor is linked more closely to those affiliated with the Christian movement. Pilate is a friend of this particular follower of Jesus.

To be sure, though, the Pilate of GP is not yet the Christian of whom later Christians would write.[76] The indication in our gospel is that Jesus' execution was religiously, not politically, motivated. Pilate is present

---

[72] Ibid., 336; Swete (*Akhmîm Fragment*, 2) makes the same point.

[73] The historicity of the core tradition of Joseph of Arimathea is likely, as, for example, Rudolf Bultmann (*History of the Synoptic Tradition* [trans. J. Marsh; rev. ed.; Peabody, Mass.: Hendrickson, 1963], 274) concludes.

[74] Brown (*Death of the Messiah*, 2:1213–34) surveys the traditions about Joseph in early Christianity.

[75] On the role of Joseph in GP see ibid., 2:1232–33.

[76] See below for examples.

because he is firmly entrenched in the tradition as the leading political authority associated with the trial of Jesus. Though Pilate does not condemn Jesus to death, he is not entirely on the side of Christians. For example, he supports the Jews in their request for a guard at the tomb (GP 8:29–31), and he is called "brother" by Herod, the leader of the Jews and the one responsible for Jesus' death (GP 2:5). Furthermore, Pilate is complicit with the Jews in their move to suppress the reporting of the resurrection (GP 11:43–49). While he has moved closer to becoming a full-fledged sympathizer, if not a proselyte, Pilate has not yet become such.

2.5 Early Christian Parallels

The emphasis on Jewish culpability for the death of Jesus is not a late development within the emerging Christian movement. Similarly, we can find indications that the role of Pilate was often downplayed by early Christians. In this section I will survey several examples from Christian literature that parallel the move in GP to blame the Jews while exonerating the Romans. Though the sources often reflect both features of blame and exoneration, I will first focus on the role of Jews and then more briefly on that of Pilate and the Romans. My goal in this is to show that GP fits very well within a particular segment of early Christianity that, as numerous texts indicate, took similar polemical and apologetic steps.

2.5.1 The Increased Role of the Jews

Christian writings of the first two centuries provide numerous references to Jewish culpability for the death of Jesus. In order to represent this, I will survey material from four significant Christian authors of this era: Paul, Luke, Justin Martyr, and Melito.[77] Rather than becoming a matter that died out with the passing of time, Christian polemic toward Jews for their alleged role in this act remained high throughout the first and second centuries, and beyond.

Ironically, what might be the earliest Christian document contains a clear attribution of guilt to Jews for having "killed" Jesus. First Thessalonians is considered by most Pauline scholars to be the earliest of the letters penned by the apostle and it is most frequently dated circa 50 C.E.[78] The following appears in this epistle:

---

[77] I should emphasize that the sources surveyed are representative, not exhaustive, and should be understood to represent the general stream of thought in which GP flowed, as opposed to claiming that GP is dependent on these sources, or vice versa.

[78] As, for example, in F. F. Bruce, *1 & 2 Thessalonians* (WBC 45; Waco: Word, 1982), xxxiv–xxxv.

And we also thank God constantly for this, that when you received the word of God which you heard from us, you accepted it not as the word of men but as what it really is, the word of God, which is at work in you believers. For you, brethren, became imitators of the churches of God in Christ Jesus which are in Judea; *for you suffered the same things from your own countrymen as they did from the Jews, who killed both the Lord Jesus and the prophets,* and drove us out, and displease God and oppose all men by hindering us from speaking to the Gentiles that they may be saved – so as always to fill up the measure of their sins. But God's wrath has come upon them at last! (1 Thess 2:13–16)[79]

Some have proposed that this in fact is not a genuine Pauline statement but rather a later interpolation.[80] However, there is no textual evidence whatsoever to support this conclusion.[81]

Three relevant items can be proposed regarding the present passage. First, Paul is linking the sufferings of his Thessalonian audience to those of Christians in the Judean churches.[82] The Thessalonian imitation of the Judeans lies in the experience of persecution from their fellow countrymen. Just as Judean Christians faced hardship at the hands of fellow Jews/Judeans, so the Thessalonian Christians are now experiencing trouble from other Macedonians.[83] Second, not only does Paul associate the Thessalonian sufferings with those of the Judeans, he ties both experiences to the sufferings and death of Jesus, and it is Jews who are said to be culpable for both the Judean persecution and the killing of Jesus. Third, Paul speaks of Jewish responsibility for Jesus' death in the same context in which he refers to them "fill[ing] up the measure of their sins" ($εἰς$ $τὸ$ $ἀναπληρῶσαι$ $αὐτῶν$ $τὰς$ $ἁμαρτίας$) (1 Thess 2:16). The measure of the Jews' sins here includes the killing of Jesus and the prophets, along with the expulsion and hindrance of Christian missionaries. Rejection of the

---

[79] On this passage and its relevance to Jewish-Christian polemics, see John C. Hurd, "Paul Ahead of His Time: 1 Thess. 2:13–16," in Peter Richardson and David Granskou, eds., *Anti-Judaism in Early Christianity,* vol. 1: *Paul and the Gospels* (SCJ 2; Waterloo: Wilfrid Laurier University Press, 1986), 1:21–36.

[80] Birger A. Pearson, "1 Thessalonians 2:13–16: A Deutero-Pauline Interpolation," *HTR* 64 (1971): 79–94. A key argument made in favor of the interpolation theory centers on the language of wrath having come upon the Jews (1 Thess 2:16), which is viewed as a specific reference to the fall of Jerusalem in 70 C.E. Pearson also argues that vv. 11–12 introduce an "apostolic parousia" that does not actually begin until v. 17, which is to say that Paul's flow of thought is more natural if vv. 13–16 are excised from the letter.

[81] The authenticity of these verses is defended in Jon A. Weatherly, "The Authenticity of 1 Thessalonians 2.13–16: Additional Evidence," *JSNT* 42 (1991): 79–98.

[82] I use "Paul" throughout this discussion to refer to the author of these verses, with the recognition that this very well may be a later interpolation.

[83] The specific nature of the conflict underlying this passage is discussed in Claudia J. Setzer, *Jewish Responses to Early Christians: History and Polemics, 30–150 C.E.* (Minneapolis: Fortress, 1994), 16–25. Setzer considers these verses to be a post-Pauline interpolation that arose prior to 140 C.E.

Christian message is tied to what is, in the eyes of Paul, the ultimate rejection of God's chosen – the crucifixion of Jesus.[84] Moreover, to hinder the work of Christian missionary efforts is to call to mind the original refusal to heed the message brought by Jesus.

Paul's comments in 1 Thessalonians, therefore, are the first in a long line of commentary that connects certain Jews to the death of Jesus.[85] The claim of Jewish responsibility for the crucifixion of Jesus was conveyed in the context of Christian reaction to conflict with Jews. In 1 Thess 2:13–16 we see the first example in the extant literature of Christians responding to real or perceived conflict with Jews by raising to the forefront the claim that it was Jews who brought about the death of Jesus.

Especially important to our discussion of GP is the reference in 1 Thess 2:16 to the filling up of sins on the part of Jews, since this very same association appears in GP 5:17.[86] After GP describes the many actions that the Jews perpetrate against Jesus (e.g., placing a crown of thorns on his head, spitting in his face, scourging him, and eventually crucifying him), it concludes by saying that "they fulfilled everything and *filled the measure of sins* upon their head" (GP 5:17).

Furthermore, Paul's final sentence in v. 16 also shares the same sentiments as those of GP. Immediately after speaking about the Jewish fulfillment of their sins, the apostle closes this section by saying, "But God's wrath has come upon them at last!" (1 Thess 2:16). In GP, there are several indications of divine wrath falling upon the Jews, the clearest and strongest

---

[84] This idea of filling up the measure of sins by rejecting Israel's prophets or Messiah finds a parallel in Matthew's gospel. Matthew 23:31–32 identifies the Jewish leadership as the "sons of those who murdered the prophets," who will fill up the measure of their fathers' sins by rejecting the message of Jesus. Robert H. Gundry (*Matthew: A Commentary on His Handbook for a Mixed Church under Persecution* [2d ed.; Grand Rapids: Eerdmans, 1994], 468) remarks that in these verses "Matthew indicates that the scribes and Pharisees ... were going to murder Jesus and his followers just as their fathers had murdered the prophets."

[85] Another possible indicator of Jewish responsibility for Jesus' death that is from the Pauline corpus is alleged by some to be found in 1 Cor 2:8, where it is said that "the rulers of this age" (οἱ ἄρχοντες τοῦ αἰῶνος τούτου) were responsible for crucifying Jesus. The term "rulers of this age," which also appears earlier in v. 6, has long vexed commentators and there is a wide range of conclusions that have been reached as to its exact meaning. Anthony C. Thiselton (*The First Epistle to the Corinthians* [NIGTC; Grand Rapids: Eerdmans, 2000], 233–39) provides a concise summary of the various positions. A key question surrounding the proper understanding of οἱ ἄρχοντες τοῦ αἰῶνος τούτου is whether the term refers to demonic/spiritual powers, earthly political rulers, or some combination thereof. Even if one were to conclude that political rulers are the referent, there is not enough in the term itself or in the surrounding literary context to indicate with any confidence that Paul had Jews specifically in mind when composing this letter.

[86] The same idea is also expressed in Acts 13:27–29; *Barn.* 5:11; 14:5.

of which is the destruction of Jerusalem. After the crucifixion, the Jews who have witnessed it lament and proclaim, "Woe on our sins! Judgment has come close and the end of Jerusalem" (GP 7:25). Retribution for their actions comes in the form of the destruction of their holy city. However, if 1 Thess 2:13–16 is authentic, it was written two decades before Jerusalem's fall and Paul therefore must have had in mind a different punishment.[87] On the issue of divine wrath, Paul and the author of GP are of one theological mind when it comes to seeing its arrival as a response to the Jews' killing of Jesus.

The book of Acts is another NT writing that contains references to Jewish participation in the execution of Jesus.[88] There are eight passages related to our subject: Acts 2:22–24; 3:13–17; 4:10, 27–28; 5:30; 7:52; 10:39; 13:27–29. These appear almost exclusively in the speeches. Ulrich Wilckens has concluded that the claim of Jewish responsibility for Jesus' death in Acts rose to prominence within an intra-Jewish context.[89] Specifically, according to Wilckens, it can be traced to those Hellenistic Jewish Christians who were expelled from Jerusalem.[90] Although this level of specificity is difficult to prove, we may be on surer ground in following Wilckens' more general proposal that the Christian emphasis on Jewish culpability arose and was transmitted in contexts of intra-Jewish polemics, especially if there is any level of historicity in the speeches of Acts.[91]

---

[87] The lack of a clear referent for wrath here – besides the events of 70 C.E. – is a strong argument against the authenticity of these verses. Bruce (*1 & 2 Thessalonians*, 48–49) mentions a few possible alternatives for the background to Paul's comment: 1) a massacre at the temple during the Passover of 49 C.E.; 2) the expulsion of the Jews from Rome in 49 C.E.; and 3) the general misfortunes of the Jews throughout the Roman Empire at the time Paul wrote the epistle.

If 1 Thess 2:13–16 is considered an interpolation, the parallels with GP that I am proposing still apply. Any interpolation here must have taken place no later than the second century, since by that time Paul's letters were in wide circulation and were being copied often. Therefore, any significant changes to the text of First Thessalonians very likely would have left traces if they were made after this point. If this is an early interpolation, it is best understood that the wrath of God is a reference to the destruction of Jerusalem, in which case it bears an even more striking similarity to GP.

[88] The most thorough recent study on this is Jon A. Weatherly, *Jewish Responsibility for the Death of Jesus in Luke-Acts* (JSNTSup 106; Sheffield: Sheffield Academic, 1994).

[89] Wilckens, *Die Missionsreden der Apostelgeschichte* (3d ed.; WMANT 5; Neukirchen-Vluyn: Neukirchner, 1973), 119–21.

[90] Ibid., 207.

[91] It would be difficult to deny this without saying that these texts contain no historicity whatsoever regarding either the content of the speeches or the contexts in which they are said to have occurred, or both. Though I have little doubt that the speeches have been shaped by the author of Acts, I think that in at least some instances there is a historical kernel to them, both in content and context.

Of the eight relevant texts in Acts, six are found in speeches addressed to Jewish audiences.[92] While the emphasis in these discourses is primarily on the Jewish leaders and their responsibility, in two instances it is the general Jewish population (at least of Judea) that is assigned guilt (Acts 3:17; 13:27). In Acts 3:17 the distinction is made between "you" (i.e., Jews near the Jerusalem temple) and "your rulers," though both parties are said to have acted in ignorance when they killed Jesus (Acts 3:13–15). Similarly, Acts 13:27 refers to both "those who live in Jerusalem" and "their rulers."

To summarize the material from Acts, there is a strong focus on the theme of Jewish responsibility for the death of Jesus. The most likely origin of this is the early Christian preaching that took place in Jewish contexts. Early Christians occasionally emphasized Jewish guilt for the death of their messiah as the climax of Israel's misdeeds, much as Paul has done in 1 Thess 2:13–16. Both Jewish leaders and laypeople are assigned blame in Acts, though the emphasis appears to be on parties in Judea or Jerusalem.[93] This provides a parallel to the general framework of GP's Passion Narrative. In GP, as in Acts, both the Jewish leadership and the general populace participate in the condemnation, abuse, and execution of Jesus.

Writing in the middle of the second century, Justin Martyr reveals in his *1 Apology* and *Dialogue with Trypho* some further examples of the developing traditions of Jewish culpability for Jesus' death.[94] Both works are apologetic, attempting in various ways to convince readers of the truthfulness and non-threatening nature of the Christian movement. There are many instances where Justin alludes to Jewish involvement in the death of

---

However, a total denial of any historicity in the speeches would still leave us with a situation in which a first-century Christian (the author of Acts) apparently believed that the earliest Christian Jews had disputes with other Jews and, in the course of such exchanges, raised the issue of Jewish responsibility for the death of Jesus.

[92] As follows: 1) Peter to "men of Judea and all who dwell in Jerusalem" (2:14); 2) Peter to "men of Israel" (3:12); 3) Peter to "rulers of the people and elders" in Jerusalem (4:10); 4) Peter and the apostles to the council and high priest (5:27); 5) Stephen before the council (6:12); 6) Paul in a synagogue at Pisidian Antioch to "Men of Israel and you who fear God" (13:16).

[93] This is a major tenet of Weatherly's work, whose conclusion goes so far as to claim that "among Jews Luke regards only the leaders of Jerusalem and the people of Jerusalem as responsible for the crucifixion of Jesus" (*Jewish Responsibility*, 271).

[94] Surveys of Justin and his thought appear in Leslie W. Barnard, *Justin Martyr: His Life and Thought* (London: Cambridge University Press, 1967); Eric F. Osborn, *Justin Martyr* (BHT 47; Tübingen: Mohr [Siebeck], 1973); Parvis and Foster, *Justin Martyr and His Worlds*.

Jesus.[95] Though Justin typically emphasizes Jewish culpability, he is clearly familiar with stories that implicate other parties. Most notably, his
statements in *1 Apol.* 40 link the fourfold role of Herod, Jews, Pilate, and
soldiers to the "prophecy" of Ps 2:1–2.[96] More commonly, however, he
speaks solely of Jews as the ones who carry out Jesus' crucifixion. For
example, he says that Jesus "was crucified by the Jews who contradicted
(ἀντιλεγόντων) him and denied that He was the Messiah" (*1 Apol.* 35). In
two other instances in the *First Apology* Justin states that Jesus "was crucified by them" (i.e., Jews) and that they "mistreated him" (*1 Apol.* 36, 49).

In *Dialogue with Trypho* Justin brings up Jewish guilt on at least four
occasions. He claims that Jews will recognize at "the second coming" the
one whom "they have crucified" (*Dial.* 14). Two brief chapters later he
tells his putative Jewish audience, "You have murdered (ἀπεκτείνατε) the
Just One, and His prophets before him" (*Dial.* 16). This is followed shortly
by another address to them: "For after you had crucified (μετὰ γὰρ τὸ
σταυρῶσαι ὑμᾶς) the only sinless and just Man ..." (*Dial.* 17). The final
example is found in *Dial.* 93: "You have shown yourselves always to be
idolaters and murderers of the just; in fact, you even did violence to Christ
himself ... he whom you crucified was the Christ." Justin's understanding
is that Jesus had been killed through a combination of Roman and Jewish
action, though he emphasizes that of Jews much more frequently. His
casting of guilt upon the Jews is a means of explaining what is, in his eyes,
the refusal of his Jewish contemporaries to acknowledge the identity of
Jesus as Israel's Messiah.

Melito, bishop of Sardis, provides further indication of the continued
Christian emphasis on Jews as the perpetrators of Jesus' execution.[97] His
Homily on Pascha is usually dated to 160–170 C.E. and it reflects perhaps
the most vehemently critical attitude toward Jews of any Christian work

---

[95] The most important passages are *1 Apol.* 35, 36, 40, 49; *Dial.* 14, 16, 17, 93. On the
anti-Jewish polemics in Justin's thought, consult Harold Remus, "Justin Martyr's Argument with Judaism," in Stephen G. Wilson, ed., *Anti-Judaism in Early Christianity*, vol.
2: *Separation and Polemic* (SCJ 3; Waterloo: Wilfrid Laurier University Press, 1986),
2:59–80.

[96] Skarsaune (*Proof from Prophecy*) focuses on the role of prophecy in Justin's works.

[97] A range of perspectives on Melito and his anti-Jewish tendencies can be found in
Stuart G. Hall, "Melito in the Light of the Passover Haggadah," *JTS* n.s. 22 (1971): 29–
46; Stephen G. Wilson, "Melito and Israel," in idem, *Anti-Judaism in Early Christianity*,
2:81–102; David Satran, "Anti-Jewish Polemic in the Peri Pascha of Melito of Sardis:
The Problem of Social Context," in *Contra Iudaeos: Ancient and Medieval Polemics
between Christians and Jews* (ed. Ora Limor and Guy G. Stroumsa; Tübingen: Mohr
[Siebeck], 1996), 49–58; Alistair Stewart-Sykes, "Melito's Anti-Judaism," *JECS* 5
(1997): 271–83.

from the first two centuries.[98] Of particular relevance is the fact that Sardis had a substantial Jewish population during Melito's time, and in reading his *Homily on Pascha* we may be catching a glimpse of the ongoing tensions between Christians and Jews in the city.[99] Aside from the NT gospels, no work has closer affinities with GP than does Melito's homily.[100]

Passages of relevance from Melito's work are too numerous to cite. Therefore, a few summary comments followed by two of the most important and illustrative quotations will serve to convey its general tone. In *Hom. on Pascha* 72–99 Melito makes repeated references to the misdeeds of "Israel" as they relate to the death (murder [φόνος], in Melito's estimation) of Jesus. According to Stephen G. Wilson, this section is noteworthy in that it is the first occasion in which a Christian writer makes "an unambiguous accusation of deicide" against the Jews.[101] The crimes of which Melito speaks are said to be perpetrated by "Israel," thereby making no distinction between Jewish leaders and laypeople or between Palestinian and Diaspora Jews. In his estimation, to be a Jew is to be in some sense guilty of killing Jesus. This hostility may be partly due to his experience of Jewish resistance to the Christian message in Sardis and, conversely, the sympathy that some Christians in the city may have had toward certain aspects of Judaism.[102] The clearest expression from Melito concerning Jewish guilt and the charge of deicide is seen in the following:

---

[98] Stuart G. Hall (*Melito of Sardis: On Pascha and Fragments* [Oxford Early Christian Texts; Oxford: Clarendon, 1979], xvii–xxii) addresses the issues involved in dating Melito's homily. He arrives at "a date between 160 and 170" (xxii).

[99] Judith M. Lieu (*Image and Reality: The Jews in the World of the Christians in the Second Century* [Edinburgh: T&T Clark, 1996], 199–208) discusses Jewish-Christian relations in Sardis at the time of Melito. A summary of the vast archaeological discoveries in the city, including one of the most prominent ancient synagogues of the Diaspora and other remnants of the Jewish community there, is provided in George M. A. Hanfmann, *Sardis from Prehistoric to Roman Times: Results of the Archaeological Exploration of Sardis, 1958–1975* (Cambridge, Mass.: Harvard University Press, 1983).

[100] A recent treatment of the relationship between Melito and GP appears in Thomas R. Karmann, "Melito von Sardes und das Petrusevangelium," in Kraus and Nicklas, *Evangelium nach Petrus*, 215–35.

[101] Wilson, "Melito and Israel," 91. Melito is convinced that Jesus had to suffer and die in order to fulfill the divine plan, but he states explicitly that it was not necessary that the Jews be the ones to carry out the death sentence. Cf. his statement that "He [Jesus] had to suffer, but not by you; he had to be dishonoured, but not by you; he had to be judged, but not by you; he had to be hung up; but not by you and your right hand" (*Hom. on Pascha* 75). He follows this by telling the Jews that they should have pleaded to God that his Son instead suffer and die at the hands of "foreigners" and "uncircumcised men" (*Hom. on Pascha* 76).

[102] Both Satran ("Anti-Jewish Polemic," 49–58) and Wilson ("Melito and Israel," 97–98) mention this as the possible background situation in Sardis.

Listen, all you families of the nations, and see! An unprecedented *murder* (φόνος) has occurred in the middle of Jerusalem, in the city of the law, in the city of the Hebrews, in the city of the prophets, in the city accounted just. And who *has been murdered* (πεφόνευται)? Who is the *murderer* (φονεύς)? I am ashamed to say and I am obliged to tell. For if the *murder* (φόνος) had occurred at night, or if he had been slain in a desert place, one might have had recourse to silence.

But now, in the middle of the street and in the middle of the city, at the middle of the day for all to see, has occurred a just man's unjust *murder* (φόνος). Just so he has been lifted up on a tall tree, and a notice has been attached to show who *has been murdered* (πεφονευμένον). Who is this? To say is hard, and not to say is too terrible.

Yet listen, trembling at him for whom the earth quaked. He who hung the earth is hanging; he who fixed the heavens has been fixed; he who fastened the universe has been fastened to a tree; the Sovereign has been insulted; the God *has been murdered* (πεφόνευται);[103] the King of Israel has been put to death by an Israelite right hand. (*Hom. on Pascha* 94–96; Hall 53–55)

Here we find a most emphatic description of Jewish culpability regarding the "murder" of Jesus. Melito's frequent use of words denoting murder (i.e., φονεύω, φόνος, and φονεύς) parallels the appearance of φονεύω in GP 2:5 and 5:15 and lends further support to my claim regarding its presence there being an indication of the belief on the part of GP's author that Jesus' death was indeed a murder.

As for the specific details of Jesus' execution, Melito mirrors GP in describing them as being carried out *exclusively* by Jews:

So then, you [Israel] set these things aside, and rushed to the slaying of the Lord. You prepared for him sharp nails and false witnesses and ropes and scourges and vinegar and gall and sword and forceful restraint as against a murderous robber. For you brought both scourges for his body and thorn for his head; and you bound his good hands, which formed you from earth; and that good mouth of his which fed you with life you fed with gall. And you killed your Lord at the great feast. (*Hom. on Pascha* 79; Hall 43)

The emphasis on Jews and their role in executing Jesus is the most significant thematic correlation between Melito and GP. A further parallel with GP in this regard may come in Melito's inference that the Jews did not wash their hands:

But you cast the opposite vote against your Lord. For him whom the gentiles worshipped and uncircumcised men admired and foreigners glorified, over whom even Pilate washed his hands, you killed him at the great feast. (*Hom. on Pascha* 92; Hall 51)

Melito takes the non-washing of hands to be indicative of a death sentence; by not washing they cast their vote against Jesus. This idea seems to be in the same vein as what we find in the opening verse of the extant portion of

---

[103] The Greek here reads ὁ θεὸς πεφόνευται. Hall includes the article in his translation ("the God"), which seems to lessen somewhat the implications of deicide in a monotheistic context. This sentence would more naturally be rendered "God has been murdered."

GP, and it might receive further confirmation in the immediately preceding scene that is missing from the Akhmîm text of the gospel.

In Melito – as in Paul, Acts, and Justin – the accusation against the Jews about their role in the death of Jesus has come in the context of Jewish-Christian polemics. In each instance as well, such charges downplay any Roman involvement, despite the fact that all of these writers certainly knew that, from a strictly historical perspective, the actual execution of Jesus was carried out by Romans rather than Jews. Might something similar be occurring in GP? Might it be that polemical motivations, possibly as a result of conflict with Jewish communities, have driven its author in the same direction as these other writers?

In order to reflect its widespread presence in the sources, I list here some further examples from second-century Christian texts that focus upon Jewish responsibility for the death of Jesus:[104]

For they will see him on that day, wearing a long scarlet robe about his body, and they will say, "Is this not the one whom we once crucified, insulting and piercing and spitting on him? Surely this was the man who said then that he was the Son of God!" (*Barn.* 7:9; Holmes 403)

And the persecution which he was to suffer, and the tortures with which the children of Israel were to afflict him. (*Mart. Ascen. Isa.* 3.13; *NTApoc*[2] 2:608)

And when he grew up he performed great signs and wonders in the land of Israel and in Jerusalem. And after this the adversary envied him and roused the children of Israel against him, not knowing who he was, and they delivered him to the king and crucified him, and he descended to the angel. (*Mart. Ascen. Isa.* 11.18–19; *NTApoc*[2] 2:618)

He was pierced by the Jews; and He died and was buried. (Aristides, *Apol.* 2; Harris 36–37)

Thou didst harden the heart of Herod and provoke Pharaoh, making him fight against Moses, the holy servant of God; thou didst give Caiaphas the boldness to hand over our Lord Jesus Christ to the cruel throng. (*Acts Pet.* 8; *NTApoc*[2] 2:295)

A shining light of knowledge shalt thou shine in Jacob, and as the sun shalt thou be to all the seed of Israel. And a blessing shall be given to thee, and to all thy seed, until the Lord shall visit all the heathen in the tender mercies of His Son, even for ever. Nevertheless thy sons shall lay hands upon Him to crucify Him; and therefore have counsel and understanding been given thee, that thou mightest instruct thy sons concerning Him, because he that blesseth Him shall be blessed, but they that curse Him shall perish. (*T. Levi* 4; *ANF* 8:13)

---

[104] A comprehensive list of noncanonical Christian sources up to the fourth century that depict Jewish involvement can be found in Walter Bauer, *Das Leben Jesu: Im Zeitalter der Neutestamentlichen Apokryphen* (Tübingen: Mohr, 1909; repr., Darmstadt: Wissenschaftliche Buchgesellschaft, 1967), 199–204.

For while they were thought to offer correctly so far as outward appearance went, they had in themselves jealousy like to Cain; therefore they slew the Just One, slighting the counsel of the Word, as did also Cain. (Irenaeus, *Haer.* 4.18.3; *ANF* 1:485)

For if He had not so come, it follows that these men could not have become the slayers of their Lord; and if He had not sent prophets to them, they certainly could not have killed them, nor the apostles either. (Irenaeus, *Haer.* 4.28.3; *ANF* 1:501)

Oh wickedness! Once did the Jews lay hands on Christ; these mangle His body daily. (Tertullian, *Idol.* 7; *ANF* 3:64)

For against Him did they wreak their fury after they had slain His prophets, even by affixing Him with nails to the cross. (Tertullian, *Marc.* 3.18; *ANF* 3:336–37)

That is, Christ, whom – after the slaughter of prophets – they slew, and exhausted their savagery by transfixing His sinews with nails. (Tertullian, *Adv. Jud.* 10; *ANF* 3:165)

In examining the focus on Jewish responsibility for Jesus' death in the Christian sources of the first two centuries, I have demonstrated that the belief was widespread and often included hostile rhetoric toward Jews. I have also shown that Christian reflection on Jewish culpability frequently occurred in contexts where conflict between the groups was present in the community of the author. Therefore, this tendency often appears to have been partly due to the social contexts of the people and groups composing them.

2.5.2 The Exoneration of Pilate and the Romans

We might say that most of the texts reviewed in the previous section, by highlighting almost exclusively the role of Jews in the death of Jesus, reflect an "exoneration through silence" as it relates to the role of Pilate and the Romans. Those authors who fail to include Pilate in their description of Jesus' death, while focusing solely on Jewish guilt, effectively eliminate the responsibility of the Romans. I will not revisit those instances here; instead, I will look at two texts that do not merely practice "exoneration through silence" but rather take specific measures to employ Pilate as an ally of the Christian movement. My goal in this very brief survey is to demonstrate the degree to which some Christians of the second century could go in their pro-Roman apologetic efforts.

Putatively addressing a Roman audience in the middle of the second century, Justin Martyr writes the following:

Concerning the prophecy that our Christ should cure all diseases and raise the dead to life, hear what was spoken. Here are the exact words of the prophecy: "At His coming the lame shall leap like a stag, and the tongue of the dumb shall be cleansed, and the dead shall rise and walk about." That Christ did perform such deeds you can learn from the Acts of Pontius Pilate. (*1 Apol.* 48; Falls 85)

Justin here may be under the impression that there existed the actual records of Pilate's political dealings.[105] The claim itself is dubious, but what is of import is the manner in which Justin employs Pilate as an ally. He is convinced that the Roman governor would have recorded the allegedly miraculous deeds of Jesus when compiling his account. Pilate, in Justin's estimation, is one who provides testimony about some of the central Christian claims concerning the life of Jesus.[106]

Writing around the end of the second century, Tertullian goes even further than Justin by transforming Pilate into a professing Christian. At one point in his *Apology*, Tertullian tells the passion story of Jesus in his own unique way and includes the role of Pilate as the executioner of Jesus. But he follows up this account with the following:

> All these things Pilate did to Christ; and now in fact a Christian in his own convictions, he sent word of Him to the reigning Caesar, who was at the time Tiberius. Yes, and the Caesars too would have believed on Christ, if either the Caesars had not been necessary for the world, or if Christians could have been Caesars. (*Apol.* 21; *ANF* 3:35)

In the section immediately preceding this, Tertullian had explained that Pilate acted on the basis of the tremendous outcry from the Jews. So while he recognizes Pilate's active role in executing Jesus, he partially excuses it. Most important, though, is that Pilate has undergone a post-crucifixion transformation, indicated in Tertullian's statement that the Roman governor is "now in fact a Christian in his own convictions." To be a Christian in one's convictions is to be anything but an enemy of the movement, an apologetic move that Tertullian also seeks to exploit elsewhere in his writings.[107] In this Christian apologist the conversion of Pilate is complete and the Roman executioner has become not only tolerant of the sect but has himself joined it. The seeds of this trend to exonerate Pilate, though finding full bloom in the expressions of Tertullian, have taken root in GP as well. When turning to GP we find a Pilate that has moved closer to the one expressed in the works of Justin and Tertullian than is the case with the four portraits of him in the NT Passion Narratives.

---

[105] Some, however, find in Justin's "Acts of Pontius Pilate" a reference not to Roman documents but to Christian texts, perhaps gospels. See, for example, Koester, *Ancient Christian Gospels*, 41–42; Charles E. Hill, "Was John's Gospel among Justin's *Apostolic Memoirs*?," in Parvis and Foster, *Justin Martyr and His Worlds*, 89–91. Justin is certainly not referring to the Christian text known as the *Acts of Pilate*.

[106] Justin also appeals to the records of Pilate in *1 Apol.* 35.

[107] This is best illustrated in *Apol.* 5, where Tertullian alleges the following: 1) Tiberius, when learning of Jesus, ruled in favor of Christ's divinity while the Roman Senate rejected it; 2) Tiberius threatened "wrath against all accusers of the Christians"; 3) Marcus Aurelius was a protector of Christians and persecutor of their opponents; and 4) Trajan forbade the persecution of Christians.

2.6 Apologetics and Polemics in GP 1:1–5:19

The issues involved in the study of the traditions that refer to the death of Jesus are complex and are often complicated by two millennia of subsequent history, most notably the horrific events of the WWII-era Holocaust. Disputes over the accounts of Jesus' death recently came to the forefront in popular culture with the release of Mel Gibson's 2004 film, *The Passion of the Christ*, which includes a highly graphic portrayal of the trial, abuse, mockery, and crucifixion of Jesus and presents certain Jews as heavily involved in many of these actions. Responses to the film's depiction have ranged from praise for its historical accuracy to condemnation for its blatant anti-Semitism.[108] Heated modern controversies, however, should not keep us from a sober evaluation of ancient texts and stories.

In seeking to understand GP's vilification of Jews, we must first recognize the social factors at work in the gradual separation of the Christian movement from its origins as a Jewish sect.[109] In the pre-Constantinian era, Jews generally held more social and political power than Christians in the larger Greco-Roman world.[110] As early Christian groups sought to distinguish themselves from other Jewish factions, conflict in the form of polemics often gave expression to the underlying issues. At a fundamental level there was competition for adherents to the various sects, since the Christian movement came to view itself as unique in relation to other Jewish groups. Conversely, the various Jewish sects eventually considered the Christian factions to be outside the pale of acceptable Jewish belief and praxis.

Christian self-identity included the firm belief that a proper understanding of Israel's Scriptures could take place only when viewed through the life, death, and resurrection of Jesus. Therefore, the polemical exchanges between Christians and other Jewish groups included not only the memory of Jesus' teachings and deeds but also, and especially, those events that

---

[108] A variety of responses from biblical scholars to the film appear in Kathleen E. Corley and Robert L. Webb, eds., *Jesus and Mel Gibson's Passion of the Christ: The Film, the Gospels and the Claims of History* (New York: Continuum, 2004).

[109] On this so-called parting of the ways during the period under discussion, see Stephen G. Wilson, *Related Strangers: Jews and Christians 70–170 C.E.* (Minneapolis: Fortress, 1995); Lieu, *Image and Reality*; James D. G. Dunn, *The Partings of the Ways: Between Christianity and Judaism and their Significance for the Character of Christianity* (2d ed.; London: SCM Press, 2006).

[110] See the treatment of this matter in Michael Grant, *The Jews in the Roman World* (New York: Scribner, 1973), 97–169; E. Mary Smallwood, *The Jews under Roman Rule: From Pompey to Diocletian, A Study in Political Relations* (2d ed.; Boston: Brill, 2001).

had come to be a part of the early Christian memory of his death.[111] To a large extent, the Christian focus on Jewish responsibility for the death of Jesus was a means of maintaining clear boundaries between themselves and those people and groups that had come to be understood as outsiders. Blame was then often cast on Jews who were unsympathetic to the Christian movement, who were thereby deemed to be outsiders. Social-memory theorists have shown us the significance that a community's present experience plays in their memory of its foundational narratives.[112] Kirk, one such proponent of the relevance of social memory, recognizes that in GP "the Passion narrative tradition is being brought into dramatic alignment with the social realities impinging upon this community."[113] Conflict between Jews and Christians, both socially and religiously, was a factor that likely contributed to the formation of GP's Passion Narrative. As we saw in Paul, Acts, Justin, and Melito, the move to blame Jews for the death of Jesus frequently occurred in such contexts.

One of the early Christian movement's most obvious self-defining characteristics was a marked devotion to Jesus.[114] As Christian devotion to Jesus distinguished the movement in its relationship to other sects within Judaism, and because of the significance assigned to his death by early Christ-followers, the circumstances surrounding his demise soon came to

---

[111] This point is emphasized in social-memory approaches to early Christian texts. As it relates to the death of Jesus in GP, see Kirk, "Tradition and Memory," 156–58.

[112] A relatively contemporary example might be found by comparing the "memory" of two different groups as it relates to their foundational narratives of the origins and early history of the United States of America. If we were to compare the Ku Klux Klan to the Black Panther Party in this area, we would most certainly find this phenomenon at work. The foundational narratives related to each group's understanding of the early history of the country would bear some resemblance to one another, but there would be vastly different emphases in many instances and outright contradictions between the "memories" of each group. The experiences of the members of each community play a part in their "memory" of distant history. This is the type of phenomenon reflected in social-memory approaches.

[113] Kirk, "Tradition and History," 156.

[114] The leading work in recent years in this area is now recognized as Larry W. Hurtado, *Lord Jesus Christ: Devotion to Jesus in Earliest Christianity* (Grand Rapids: Eerdmans, 2003). For an earlier representative, whose conclusions differ markedly from Hurtado's in key ways, see Wilhelm Bousset, *Kyrios Christos: Geschichte des Christglaubens von den Anfangen des Christentums bis Irenaeus* (Göttingen: Vandenhoeck & Ruprecht, 1913). While Bousset concluded that religious devotion to Jesus unfolded relatively slowly among Christian groups and did not become full-fledged worship until the sect moved from Jewish to pagan environments, Hurtado contends that the worship of Jesus took place much earlier and occurred even among the first Palestinian Jewish Christians.

be of the utmost importance.[115] The origins of the Christian sect's earliest accusations of guilt against fellow Jews for the death of Jesus may very well have proliferated in the earliest years of the movement through the traditional Jewish pattern of calling the nation of Israel to repentance for its disobedience and/or the rejection of its prophets (e.g., Neh 9:26; 2 Chr 36:14–16).[116] For the earliest Christians the death of Jesus was sometimes viewed as foremost among Israel's sins. To reject the nation's alleged messiah, or to be involved in any manner in the events leading to his death, is to invite a demand for repentance from the followers of that messiah. This pattern of assigning Jewish guilt for Jesus' death and linking it to a call for repentance is common in some of the speeches of the early chapters of Acts, though the level of historicity of these speeches remains uncertain (Acts 2:22–38; 3:12–26; 4:8–22; 5:29–32). Paul's First Letter to the Thessalonians makes the same connection between condemning Jews and noting their lack of repentance (1 Thess 2:13–16). It is at least plausible, if not probable, that this context of early Christian preaching to fellow Jews provided the earliest social situations in which Jewish culpability for the execution of Jesus was emphasized and increasingly became a point of bitterness between Jews devoted to Jesus and other Jewish groups.

Though this project is concerned primarily with the history and development of traditions and not with the historicity of the events themselves, a few comments on this subject are needed in order to lend clarity to my discussion. I concur with Crossan when he writes, "I take it as historical that Jesus was executed by some conjunction of Jewish and Roman authority."[117] While the early Christians were increasingly blaming Jews for their role in Jesus' death, the tendency seems to run in the opposite direction in their attitudes toward Pilate and the Roman authorities. The earliest Christian tradition/memory included Roman and Jewish cooperation in the death of Jesus and this reflects my own judgment concerning the question of historicity. In the subsequent tradition history, however, Christians would emphasize the role of each party to varying degrees. What tended to occur is similar to the dividing of a whole. If 100% of the guilt must be assigned, some accounts tended to divide it relatively evenly while others appeared to be much closer to total guilt/innocence. When the latter occurred it was nearly always in the direction of Jewish guilt/Roman innocence. Hence,

---

[115] See the various contributions in Richardson and Granskou, *Anti-Judaism in Early Christianity,* vol. 1; Wilson, *Anti-Judaism in Early Christianity,* vol. 2; Craig A. Evans and Donald A. Hagner, eds., *Anti-Semitism and Early Christianity: Issues of Polemic and Faith* (Minneapolis: Fortress, 1993).

[116] Wilckens, *Missionsreden der Apostelgeschichte,* 109–37; Stephen G. Wilson, "The Jews and the Death of Jesus in Acts," in Richardson and Granskou, *Anti-Judaism in Early Christianity,* 1:155–64.

[117] Crossan, *Who Killed Jesus?*, 147.

much of what I have said about Jewish participation in Jesus' execution must be kept in mind in the discussion of the exoneration of Pilate.

Pilate's role as the one who condemns Jesus generally diminishes in later Christian sources.[118] Paul Winter has proposed the following explanation for this: "There is a definite connection between two facts: the more Christians are persecuted by the Roman State, the more generous becomes the description of Pontius Pilate as a witness to Jesus' innocence."[119] This trend, according to Winter, was entirely apologetic in nature and it had a pre-Christian precedent, ironically enough, in Jewish apologetics. For example, Philo appealed to Emperor Caligula and reminded him of the many privileges that previous emperors had granted to Jews. He made such petitions in response to measures the emperor was about to enforce that were considered offensive by Jews.[120]

In Winter's estimation, when Christians faced persecution by Roman authorities they occasionally resorted to presenting Pilate as an ally of the movement's founder. He examines Christian depictions of Pilate and claims that this positive imagery ends in the fourth century with the arrival of Constantine and the establishment of Christianity as a *religio licita*.[121] The Edict of Milan made it so that Christians no longer needed an ally in the form of a Roman government official, according to Winter. Constantine and his successors were living, breathing emperors whose stature greatly overshadowed that of a long deceased Roman governor.[122] Winter's claim that Christians sought an ally in the form of a government official, which led them to depict Pilate as such, is not entirely wrong, but it emphasizes only half of the story. While Winter focuses on the need *to have an advocate* in the form of a Roman official, I think that it was just as

---

[118] Again, I am not suggesting that this trend is chronologically consistent, as if we could estimate the degree to which Pilate is exonerated in a given text simply by dating it. There are exceptions to trends. On Pilate in early Christian tradition see Paul Winter, *On the Trial of Jesus* (rev. & ed. T. A. Burkill and Geza Vermes; 2d ed.; SJ 1; Berlin: de Gruyter, 1974), 70–89; Brown, *Death of the Messiah*, 1:693–705; Helen K. Bond, *Pontius Pilate in History and Interpretation* (SNTSMS 100; Cambridge: Cambridge University Press, 1998).

[119] Winter, *Trial of Jesus*, 85.

[120] Ibid. See Philo, *Embassy* 28–31; Josephus, *Ant.* 18.8.

[121] Ibid., 88.

[122] Winter (ibid., 88–89) overstates the abruptness with which the positive depictions of Pilate end after the ascendency of Constantine. He cites the *Gospel of Nicodemus* as the sole representative of a post-Constantinian work that reflects the earlier emphasis. Brown (*Death of the Messiah*: 1:696), however, provides numerous examples of later Christians esteeming Pilate, including Augustine's classification of Pilate as a prophet of the kingdom of God, Ethiopic homilies from the 5th–6th centuries describing Pilate as a Christian martyr, Coptic use of "Pilate" as a baptismal name in the 6th–7th centuries, and a Latin apocryphon that describes Pilate's death at the hands of the emperor.

significant for Christians of the first two centuries *not to have an enemy* in the form of a Roman official. This is really to speak of two sides of the same coin, but I would like to focus on the side which Winter neglects. I wish to suggest that Pilate's role in Jesus' death was occasionally suppressed in order to downplay a particular aspect of the Christian movement's origins.

There was an inherent skepticism surrounding new religious movements in the Greco-Roman world in which Christianity developed, so that novel sects could expect to face severe scrutiny from political authorities. Early sources from those outside the Christian movement are especially helpful for gaining a sense of the attitude that was prevalent among government officials toward the sect. Three different Roman writers in the second century, each of whom at one time served as a government official, refer to emerging Christianity as a *superstitio*.[123] Robert L. Wilken defines it as follows:

In its most common and familiar sense, the term *superstition* referred to beliefs and practices that were foreign and strange to the Romans. What was foreign and strange, of course, was defined by whoever was making the judgment, but to a Roman senator, or to members of the ruling classes of Rome, *superstition* designated the kinds of practices and beliefs associated with the cults that had penetrated the Roman world from surrounding lands.[124]

A brief look at a passage from one of these early writers is needed so that we might understand better the Roman attitudes to the Christian movement during this era.

The first known significant conflict between Roman officials and Christians came in 64 C.E. in the aftermath of the great fire in Rome.[125] In order to squelch the rumor that Nero had ordered the fire set, the emperor cast

---

[123] The three writers are Pliny, Tacitus, and Suetonius. On Roman views of *superstitio* as it relates to early Christianity see Robert L. Wilken, *The Christians as the Romans Saw Them* (2d ed.; New Haven: Yale University Press, 2003), 48–67.

[124] Wilken, *Christians as the Romans Saw Them*, 50.

[125] There were earlier incidents involving Christians before Roman government officials (e.g., Paul's trial). The Roman fire, though, is the first instance in which Christians seem to be targeted as a class of people that is either distinct from Judaism or recognized as an identifiable sect within Judaism, though the former seems most likely. However, Dunn (*Partings of the Ways*, 315) argues that even as late as the second century, Greco-Roman writers, including Tacitus, did not clearly recognize Christians as a group separate from Jews. He suggests that in Tacitus' description of the Neronian persecution we have an author who "thought of these 'Christians' as Jews" (ibid.). This is doubtful, though, since Tacitus in other places could identify "Jews" as a separate and equally despised class of people (see esp. Book 5 of his *Histories*). That Tacitus can refer to the Christians as "a class of men" indicates that he viewed them as distinct from Jews, though it may have been the case that the class known to him as "Christians" was comprised of ethnic Gentiles as well as ethnic Jews.

blame on the Christians of Rome. The Roman historian Tacitus, himself a former provincial governor and friend of Pliny, gives this account:

> But neither human help, nor imperial munificence, nor all the modes of placating Heaven, could stifle scandal or dispel the belief that the fire had taken place by order. Therefore, to scotch the rumour, Nero substituted as culprits, and punished with the utmost refinements of cruelty, a class of men, loathed for their vices, whom the crowd styled Christians. Christus, the founder of the name, had undergone the death penalty in the reign of Tiberius, by sentence of the procurator Pontius Pilatus, and the pernicious superstition was checked for a moment, only to break out once more, not merely in Judaea, the home of the disease, but in the capital itself, where all things horrible or shameful in the world collect and find a vogue. First, then, the confessed members of the sect were arrested; next, on their disclosures, vast numbers were convicted, not so much on the count of arson as for hatred of the human race. And derision accompanied their end: they were covered with wild beasts' skins and torn to death by dogs; or they were fastened on crosses, and, when daylight failed were burned to serve as lamps by night. Nero had offered his Gardens for the spectacle, and gave an exhibition in his Circus, mixing with the crowd in the habit of a charioteer, or mounted on his car. Hence, in spite of a guilt which had earned the most exemplary punishment, there arose a sentiment of pity, due to the impression that they were being sacrificed not for the welfare of the state but to the ferocity of a single man. (*Ann.* 15.44; Jackson, LCL 4:283–85)

This passage is not useful primarily for understanding Roman attitudes of the 60s C.E., nor will I gauge its historical accuracy.[126] Instead, this resource, which is typically dated circa 115 C.E., provides an excellent opportunity to learn about views of Christianity in the early part of the second century. I will highlight four features from Tacitus that shed light on Christian motivation for exonerating Pilate.

First, the Romans were well aware that Jesus, the founder of the Christian movement and the one after whom his followers were named, was crucified at the hands of a Roman procurator. Aside from any other knowledge of the sect, this likely was enough to bring about a great deal of skepticism from those in authority. Second, Tacitus considers Christianity to be a "pernicious superstition," one that has spread from Judea to Rome. It is very likely that knowledge of Jesus' execution at the hands of the Roman government was one of the primary reasons for skepticism, especially when we combine this with the fact that it was a new religious movement.

Third, Christians are known for their "hatred of the human race," a description that is indicative of what outsiders considered to be their antisocial behavior. This was exemplified in Christian avoidance of certain

---

[126] As is true of all historians, Tacitus is no unbiased reporter of facts. His dislike of Nero is apparent, as is his desire to attribute many of Rome's misfortunes to the degeneracy and misguided leadership of this particular emperor. On this point, see Mark Morford, "Tacitus' Historical Methods in the Neronian Books of the 'Annals,'" *ANRW* 33.2:1582–627.

practices, such as participation in the emperor cult. Wilken proposes that it was Christian religious exclusivism – the claim that their beliefs and praxis alone were valid – that led to labels such as this.[127] Fourth, and lastly, the comments of Tacitus indicate that for various reasons Christians were "loathed for their vices." His words here and elsewhere in this passage demonstrate the tremendously steep hill that Christians of the second century were climbing in order to gain acceptance in the eyes of Roman outsiders. Their movement was associated with one who had been executed at the hands of a previous administrator, was known as a *superstitio*, and was often hated by the general populace for its anti-social behavior.

Classical historian Michael Grant has remarked that during the middle decades of the second century C.E. "Christianity was well on the way to replacing Judaism, in popular estimation, as the enemy of the Roman regime."[128] Justin provides an example of the lengths to which Christians would go to demonstrate the innocence of their sect and its loyalty to the emperor:

As we have been instructed by Him [i.e., Jesus], we, before all others, try everywhere to pay your appointed officials the ordinary and special taxes. For in His time some people came to Him and asked if it were necessary to pay tribute to Caesar, and He replied: "Tell Me, whose likeness does this coin bear?" They said: "Caesar's." And He again replied: "Render therefore to Caesar the things that are Caesar's, and to God, the things that are God's." Wherefore, only God do we worship, but in other things we joyfully obey you, acknowledging you as the kings and rulers of men, and praying that you may be found to have, besides royal power, sound judgment. (*1 Apol.* 17; Falls 52)

Robert M. Grant has contended that one of the reasons for the eventual success of Christianity in the Roman Empire is that, despite being persecuted at times, Christians insisted that they posed no threat to those in authority and were devoted to the welfare of the empire.[129] We catch a glimpse of this effort in the way GP has recast Pilate.

Emerging Christianity was in an awkward position since the founder of the sect had been executed by a Roman government official in the relatively recent past, thus meaning that any attention given to the crucifixion would call to mind Roman responsibility for it. This was a firm part of Christian memory and tradition. However, if Christians wished to see their

---

[127] Wilken, *Christians as the Romans Saw Them*, 63. He quotes without citation some early martyr traditions to support this notion. However, his larger discussion of second-century Roman thought concerning the role of religion as a function for the public good gives credence to his claim that Christian belief and praxis did not foster the Roman ideal in this arena.

[128] Grant, *Jews in the Roman World*, 265.

[129] Grant, *Augustus to Constantine: The Thrust of the Christian Movement into the Roman World* (New York: Harper & Row, 1970); idem, *Early Christianity and Society: Seven Studies* (San Francisco: Harper & Row, 1977), 13–43.

movement survive and thrive they could not be expected to emphasize Roman involvement in Jesus' death. To do so would be to invite even more suspicion in their direction. If the traditions present in the Christian movement included stories of both Jewish and Roman culpability, it should scarcely surprise us to discover a greater emphasis on the former than the latter, perhaps even to the extent that one party is vilified while the other is virtually exonerated.

The shift of blame from Pilate and the Romans to the Jews sometimes served Christian apologetic interests. The more that Jesus' execution was attributed to Roman authorities, the greater the likelihood that government officials would be negatively disposed toward the movement bearing his name. By exonerating the Roman procurator Christians could declare Jesus innocent of the charge of sedition. Furthermore, by downplaying the role of Pilate Christians could possibly lessen the degree of skepticism directed toward them for their loyalty to one condemned as a political troublemaker.

In GP we find this exoneration of Pilate on display. Whether this is due to a strong pro-Roman – or at least non-"anti-Roman" – sentiment on the part of its author is not possible to determine on the grounds of Pilate's portrayal alone, though it appears plausible. In subsequent chapters I hope to give further examples of apologetics in GP that appear to be directed toward Roman or Gentile audiences and claims. In this way I am claiming that a cumulative case examination of GP will show that Pilate's depiction is part of the author's apologetic efforts to rewrite his story in response to both Jewish and non-Jewish dialogue partners. And as I argued earlier in this chapter, the anti-Jewish perspective is very strong, such that the question of Roman vs. Jewish responsibility for Jesus' death in GP appears to be more a case of blaming the Jews than exonerating the Romans, although I do not want to exclude the latter. Our author, had he wished still to cast blame on the Romans, could have presented a joint effort on the part of Jews and Romans in the execution of Jesus. Yet we find something different, which seems to point toward the idea that there is some degree of interest in excusing the Romans.

2.7 Conclusions

The opening synoptic analysis showed that there are many features in common between GP 1:1–5:19 and each of the four NT gospels. For example, GP resembles Matthew in its handwashing scene, Mark in the general plot of its Passion Narrative, Luke in the inclusion of Herod as an important Jewish figure who condemns Jesus, and John in the account of leg-breaking at the crucifixion. In my estimation, our evangelist is familiar with all of these gospels.

Acquaintance with earlier texts, however, does not confine the author of GP to simple copying of his sources in a cut-and-paste fashion. He completely reworks them in order to form his own version of Jesus' death, as I argued in the second section of the chapter. This is not unlike the manner in which the author of a rewritten Bible text from the Second Temple period – the Qumram *Temple Scroll* – gathers and reorganizes portions of Exodus, Leviticus, Numbers, and Deuteronomy in writing his own work.

The primary area of GP's Passion Narrative that I explored is the shift to blame Jews as the sole party responsible for killing Jesus. In addition to the plot itself, I reviewed the ways in which OT texts are employed in ways that discredit or disparage Jews. In GP, Jews simultaneously are ignorant of their Scriptures yet unknowingly fulfill them through their actions against Jesus. I contended that at the same time Jews are made culpable for Jesus' death, the Romans are exonerated in the person of Pilate, who refuses to condemn Jesus.

The early Christian parallels to this twofold trend were reviewed in the writings of Paul, Acts, Justin, and Melito, each of whom depicts Christian accusations on this matter as occurring in contexts of disputes with Jews. I suggested that this might also provide part of the background to the creation of GP. Similarly, I provided additional texts that reflect the move by Christians to "Christianize" Pilate, that is, to make him an ally of the movement. This, I suggested, may play a small role in GP as well.

In the final section of the chapter I offered some explanations for better understanding the polemical nature of GP's attitude toward Jews, in addition to its general pro-Roman posture. Religious proximity to and competition with other Jewish sects contributed to Christian attitudes toward Jews. Likewise, the significance of Jesus' death in early Christian theology made it a point of emphasis. Concerning the depiction of Pilate, because of the Christian sect's status as a new religious movement, it would have been looked upon suspiciously by outsiders. This is more so when it was known that its leader had been executed by Roman officials. Christians thus understandably sought to downplay this aspect of their group's origins. This first section of GP, therefore, is a rewriting of earlier Passion Narratives that has been influenced by polemical and apologetic interests related to the parties responsible for the death of Jesus.

Chapter 3

Rewritten Signs: GP 5:20–8:28

In this chapter I will examine the reworking of earlier gospel texts and traditions about the signs present at the crucifixion of Jesus. First, I will provide a synoptic analysis of GP 5:20–8:28 and its NT parallels. This will be followed by an examination of the ways in which the author depicts divine judgment falling on the Jews and is reflected in four visible signs. I will then survey early Christian parallels to these portents. Following this, I will summarize the role that apologetics and polemics played in the early Christian portrayals of judgment on the Jews for their role in the death of Jesus.

3.1 Synoptic Analysis of GP 5:20–8:28

GP 5:20–8:28	Matt 27	Mark 15	Luke 23	John 19
^{5:20}καὶ αὐτῆς ὥρας διεράγη τὸ καταπέτασμα τοῦ ναοῦ τῆς Ἰερουσαλὴμ εἰς δύο.	⁵¹Καὶ ἰδοὺ τὸ καταπέτασμα τοῦ ναοῦ ἐσχίσθη ἀπ' ἄνωθεν ἕως κάτω εἰς δύο,	³⁸Καὶ τὸ καταπέτασμα τοῦ ναοῦ ἐσχίσθη εἰς δύο ἀπ' ἄνωθεν ἕως κάτω.	^{45b}ἐσχίσθη δὲ τὸ καταπέτασμα τοῦ ναοῦ μέσον.	
^{6:21}καὶ τότε ἀπέσπασαν τοὺς ἥλους ἀπὸ τῶν χειρῶν τοῦ κυρίου καὶ ἔθηκαν αὐτὸν ἐπὶ τῆς γῆς· καὶ ἡ γῆ πᾶσα ἐσείσθη	καὶ ἡ γῆ ἐσείσθη, καὶ αἱ πέτραι ἐσχίσθησαν		^{53a}καὶ καθελὼν ἐνετύλιξεν αὐτὸ σινδόνι	³⁸Μετὰ δὲ ταῦτα ἠρώτησεν τὸν Πιλᾶτον Ἰωσὴφ [ὁ] ἀπὸ Ἀριμαθαίας... ἦλθεν οὖν καὶ ἦρεν τὸ σῶμα αὐτοῦ.
	⁵⁴Ὁ δὲ ἑκατόνταρχος καὶ οἱ μετ' αὐτοῦ τηροῦντες τὸν			

GP 5:20–8:28	Matt 27	Mark 15	Luke 23	John 19
καὶ φόβος μέγας ἐγένετο.	Ἰησοῦν ἰδόντες τὸν σεισμὸν καὶ τὰ γενόμενα ἐφοβήθησαν σφόδρα			
²²τότε ἥλιος ἔλαμψε καὶ εὑρέθη ὥρα ἐνάτη.	⁴⁵Ἀπὸ δὲ ἕκτης ὥρας σκότος ἐγένετο ἐπὶ πᾶσαν τὴν γῆν ἕως ὥρας ἐνάτης.	³³Καὶ γενομένης ὥρας ἕκτης σκότος ἐγένετο ἐφ' ὅλην τὴν γῆν ἕως ὥρας ἐνάτης.	⁴⁴Καὶ ἦν ἤδη ὡσεὶ ὥρα ἕκτη καὶ σκότος ἐγένετο ἐφ' ὅλην τὴν γῆν ἕως ὥρας ἐνάτης.	
²³ἐχάρησαν δὲ οἱ Ἰουδαῖοι				
		⁴³ἐλθὼν Ἰωσὴφ [ὁ] ἀπὸ Ἁριμαθαίας... εἰσῆλθεν πρὸς τὸν Πιλᾶτον καὶ ᾐτήσατο τὸ σῶμα τοῦ Ἰησοῦ.		³⁸...ἠρώτησεν τὸν Πιλᾶτον Ἰωσὴφ [ὁ] ἀπὸ Ἁριμαθαίας...
	⁵⁸οὗτος προσελθὼν τῷ Πιλάτῳ ᾐτήσατο τὸ σῶμα τοῦ Ἰησοῦ.		⁵²οὗτος προσελθὼν τῷ Πιλάτῳ ᾐτήσατο τὸ σῶμα τοῦ Ἰησοῦ.	ἵνα ἄρῃ τὸ σῶμα τοῦ Ἰησοῦ καὶ
καὶ δεδώκασι τῷ Ἰωσὴφ τὸ σῶμα αὐτοῦ ἵνα αὐτὸ θάψῃ,	τότε ὁ Πιλᾶτος ἐκέλευσεν ἀποδοθῆναι.	⁴⁵καὶ γνοὺς ἀπὸ τοῦ κεντυρίωνος ἐδωρήσατο τὸ πτῶμα τῷ Ἰωσήφ.		ἐπέτρεψεν ὁ Πιλᾶτος. ἦλθεν οὖν καὶ ἦρεν τὸ σῶμα αὐτοῦ.
			⁵⁰Καὶ ἰδοὺ ἀνὴρ ὀνόματι Ἰωσὴφ βουλευτὴς ὑπάρχων [καὶ] ἀνὴρ ἀγαθὸς καὶ δίκαιος	
	⁵⁷Ὀψίας δὲ γενομένης ἦλθεν ἄνθρωπος πλούσιος ἀπὸ Ἁριμαθαίας, τοὔνομα Ἰωσήφ, ὃς καὶ αὐτὸς ἐμαθητεύθη τῷ	⁴³ᵃἐλθὼν Ἰωσὴφ [ὁ] ἀπὸ Ἁριμαθαίας εὐσχήμων βουλευτής, ὃς καὶ αὐτὸς ἦν προσδεχόμεν-ος τὴν βασιλείαν τοῦ	⁵¹οὗτος οὐκ ἦν συγκατατεθειμ ένος τῇ βουλῇ καὶ τῇ πράξει αὐτῶν ἀπὸ Ἁριμαθαίας πόλεως τῶν Ἰουδαίων, ὃς προσεδέχετο τὴν βασιλείαν	³⁸...Ἰωσὴφ [ὁ] ἀπὸ Ἁριμαθαίας, ὢν μαθητὴς τοῦ Ἰησοῦ κεκρυμμένος δὲ διὰ τὸν φόβον τῶν
ἐπειδὴ θεασάμενος ἦν ὅσα ἀγαθὰ				

GP 5:20–8:28	Matt 27	Mark 15	Luke 23	John 19
ἐποίησεν.	Ἰησοῦ	θεοῦ	τοῦ θεοῦ	Ἰουδαίων… [39]ἦλθεν δὲ καὶ Νικόδημος, ὁ ἐλθὼν πρὸς αὐτὸν νυκτὸς τὸ πρῶτον, φέρων μίγμα σμύρνης καὶ ἀλόης ὡς λίτρας ἑκατόν.
[24]λαβὼν δὲ τὸν κύριον ἔλουσε καὶ εἵλησε σινδόνι	[59]καὶ λαβὼν τὸ σῶμα ὁ Ἰωσὴφ ἐνετύλιξεν αὐτὸ [ἐν] σινδόνι καθαρᾷ	[46a]καὶ ἀγοράσας σινδόνα καθελὼν αὐτὸν ἐνείλησεν τῇ σινδόνι	[53]καὶ καθελὼν ἐνετύλιξεν αὐτὸ σινδόνι,	[40]ἔλαβον οὖν τὸ σῶμα τοῦ Ἰησοῦ καὶ ἔδησαν αὐτὸ ὀθονίοις μετὰ τῶν ἀρωμάτων, καθὼς ἔθος ἐστὶν τοῖς Ἰουδαίοις ἐνταφιάζειν.
καὶ εἰσήγαγεν εἰς ἴδιον τάφον καλούμενον Κῆπον Ἰωσήφ.	[60a]καὶ ἔθηκεν αὐτὸ ἐν τῷ καινῷ αὐτοῦ μνημείῳ ὃ ἐλατόμησεν ἐν τῇ πέτρᾳ,	καὶ ἔθηκεν αὐτὸν ἐν μνημείῳ ὃ ἦν λελατομημένον ἐκ πέτρας,	καὶ ἔθηκεν αὐτὸν ἐν μνήματι λαξευτῷ οὗ οὐκ ἦν οὐδεὶς οὔπω κείμενος.	[41]ἦν δὲ ἐν τῷ τόπῳ ὅπου ἐσταυρώθη κῆπος, καὶ ἐν τῷ κήπῳ μνημεῖον καινὸν ἐν ᾧ οὐδέπω οὐδεὶς ἦν τεθειμένος· [42]ἐκεῖ οὖν διὰ τὴν παρασκευὴν τῶν Ἰουδαίων, ὅτι ἐγγὺς ἦν τὸ μνημεῖον, ἔθηκαν τὸν Ἰησοῦν.
[7:25]τότε οἱ Ἰουδαῖοι καὶ οἱ πρεσβύτεροι καὶ οἱ ἱερεῖς γνόντες, οἷον κακὸν ἑαυτοῖς ἐποίησαν,				

GP 5:20–8:28	Matt 27	Mark 15	Luke 23	John 19
ἤρχαντο κόπτεσθαι καὶ λέγειν· οὐαί, ταῖς ἁμαρτίαις ἡμῶν· ἤγγισεν ἡ κρίσις καὶ τὸ τέλος Ἰερουσαλήμ. ²⁶ἐγὼ δὲ μετὰ τῶν ἑταίρων μου ἐλυπούμην καὶ τετρωμένοι κατὰ διάνοιαν ἐκρυβόμεθα. ἐζητούμεθα γὰρ ὑπ' αὐτῶν ὡς κακοῦργοι καὶ ὡς τὸν ναὸν θέλοντες ἐμπρῆσαι.	²⁶:⁵⁶ᵇΤότε οἱ μαθηταὶ πάντες ἀφέντες αὐτὸν ἔφυγον.	¹⁴:⁵⁰καὶ ἀφέντες αὐτὸν ἔφυγον πάντες.		²⁰:¹⁹ᵃΟὔσης οὖν ὀψίας τῇ ἡμέρᾳ ἐκείνῃ τῇ μιᾷ σαββάτων, καὶ τῶν θυρῶν κεκλεισμένων ὅπου ἦσαν οἱ μαθηταὶ διὰ τὸν φόβον τῶν Ἰουδαίων, ἦλθεν ὁ Ἰησοῦς καὶ ἔστη εἰς τὸ μέσον
²⁷ἐπὶ δὲ τούτοις πᾶσιν ἐνηστεύομεν, καὶ ἐκαθεζόμεθα πενθοῦντες καὶ κλαίοντες νυκτὸς καὶ ἡμέρας ἕως τοῦ σαββάτου. ⁸:²⁸συναχθέντες δὲ οἱ γραμματεῖς καὶ Φαρισαῖοι καὶ πρεσβύτεροι πρὸς ἀλλήλους ἀκούσαντες ὅτι ὁ λαὸς ἅπας γογγύζει καὶ κόπτεται τὰ στήθη λέγοντες ὅτι εἰ τῷ θανάτῳ		[Later addition] ¹⁶:¹⁰ἐκείνη πορευθεῖσα ἀπήγγειλεν τοῖς μετ' αὐτοῦ γενομένοις πενθοῦσι καὶ κλαίουσιν	⁴⁸καὶ πάντες οἱ συμπαραγενόμενοι ὄχλοι ἐπὶ τὴν θεωρίαν ταύτην, θεωρήσαντες τὰ γενόμενα, τύπτοντες τὰ στήθη ὑπέστρεφον.	

GP 5:20–8:28	Matt 27	Mark 15	Luke 23	John 19
αὐτοῦ ταῦτα τὰ μέγιστα σημεῖα γέγονεν, ἴδετε ὅτι πόσον δίκαιός ἐστιν.				

The preceding section of GP concluded with the final cry from "the Lord" just before he was "taken up" (ἀνελήφθη), an apparent euphemism for death (GP 5:19).[1] In the next verse, the veil of the Jerusalem temple is torn in two "at the same hour" (GP 5:20).[2] All three of the Synoptic Gospels include a similar reference to the tearing of the temple veil and use the same term as GP in identifying the curtain: καταπέτασμα (Matt 27:51; Mark 15:38; Luke 23:45; GP 5:20). Mark and Matthew, like GP, mention the torn curtain immediately after Jesus dies, but Luke refers to it just prior to Jesus' last breath.

While the three NT gospels use the verb σχίζω when describing the curtain tear (Matt 27:51; Mark 15:38; Luke 23:45), GP 5:20 has διαρρήγνυμι.[3] This follows the tendency in GP not to have close verbal parallels with any of the NT gospels while it maintains many of the same ideas.[4] The appearance of διεράγη here should, as is also true of ἐσχίσθη

---

[1] Jesus is also "taken up" (ἀνελήμφθη) in Acts 1:2, though this scene carries a different connotation than the one in GP 5:19.

[2] Swete (*Akhmîm Fragment*, 10) was among the first to suggest that GP's reference to the temple being in Jerusalem "is one of several indications that the fragment was written outside Palestine, or at all events for non-Palestinian readers." Although he does not expound on this point, I take him to be suggesting that Palestinian readers would not have needed the descriptor "in Jerusalem" when referring to the temple. Those outside Palestine, however, would be more likely to speak of "the temple *in Jerusalem*."

[3] The term διαρρήγνυμι is most often used in the LXX in association with the tearing of clothes (see HRCS, s.v., 309), an act which typically expresses anger, grief, or, mourning (e.g., Gen 37:29; Num 14:6; Josh 7:6; 2 Sam 1:11–12; 1 Kgs 21:27). In the NT, διαρρήγνυμι appears when the high priest tears his clothes upon hearing what he considers to be a blasphemous statement from Jesus (Matt 26:65; Mark 14:63).

[4] The entire matter of GP's lack of verbal agreements with the NT texts is addressed in Martha K. Stillman, "The Gospel of Peter: A Case for Oral-Only Dependency?" *ETL* 73 (1997): 114–20. Stillman operates from the usual paradigm in which GP is viewed as "dependent" on the NT gospels. She summarizes her conclusion: "GP is dependent on the canonical gospels through oral but not written transmission" (115). As I claim throughout this project, the conventional idea of dependency may not be the best category through which to view GP, since dependency is generally conceived in terms that involve the maintenance of close verbal parallels with sources. The author of GP, on the other hand, freely and liberally "rewrites" the antecedent texts.

in the Synoptics, be understood as a divine passive: God is the agent through whom the rending of the veil takes place.

In GP 6:21 the Jews remove the nails from Jesus' hands and place his body on the ground. Subsequently, there is an earthquake that causes great fear among those present. The only NT evangelist to refer to nails is John, though the statement appears after the resurrection rather than at the crucifixion (John 20:25).[5] Matthew is the only NT gospel to mention an earthquake at the time of the crucifixion and, like GP, it refers to fear as a response to the event (Matt 27:51–54). Likewise, among the NT gospels Matthew alone includes darkness, the veil, and an earthquake in his Passion Narrative, a trait shared with GP.

The sun again shines in GP 6:22 and the occasion is marked by a reference to the ninth hour, thus placing GP's chronology in alignment with that of Matt 27:45, Mark 15:33, and Luke 23:44. While the Synoptics give the timing of the darkness in a single statement, GP has separated the onset of the darkness from the return of the sun by several verses (GP 5:15; 6:22). It should be kept in mind throughout this discussion that GP includes three allusions to the darkness (5:15, 18; 6:22).

In GP 6:23–24 the burial of Jesus is briefly described. Jesus' body had been requested from Pilate prior to the crucifixion (GP 2:3–5). This differs from all the canonical stories, which state that the request comes after Jesus has died (Matt 27:57–58; Mark 15:42–45; Luke 23:50–52; John 19:38).[6] The Jews give Jesus' body to Joseph for burial (GP 6:23).[7] This is

---

Similarly, Brown proposes a model of GP's oral dependency on the NT gospels, stating that "a literary dependence of *GPet* on all or three of the canonical Gospels really does not explain" the available evidence (*Death of the Messiah*, 2:1333). He continues by contending that all of GP's frequent "switchings" of canonical material cannot be understood as "redactional preferences by the *GPet* author who was deliberately changing the written Gospels before him" (2:1334). But Brown does not state why such deliberate changes could not have been made to the written sources. If the author of GP saw fit to alter drastically the overall plot of the stories known to him by depicting, for example, Jews as the sole executioners of Jesus, or the enemies of Jesus as the first witnesses of the resurrection, then it seems quite plausible, if not likely, that he would have had no difficulty "deliberately changing" many of the minor details along the way.

[5] Swete (*Akhmîm Fragment*, 11) notes that in both GP and John it is only hands, and not feet, that are mentioned in regard to the nails.

[6] Crossan (*Cross That Spoke*, 20–23) views the burial story of GP 6:23–24 not as part of the original version of GP (his "Cross Gospel") but as belonging to the "intracanonical stratum" of GP. By this he means that GP 6:23–24 is a later interpolation. Koester (*Ancient Christian Gospels*, 231) counters by claiming that Mark 15:42–47 and John 19:38–42 are two independent witnesses to a common source that was used in the composition of Mark, John, and GP. He concludes that "[t]he episode of Joseph requesting the body from Pilate was relocated in the Gospel of Peter to a position before the scene of the mocking of Jesus" (ibid.). In the case of GP, I find it unnecessary to follow Koester in positing a common pre-Markan/pre-Johannine/pre-Petrine source used by all three writ-

presumably to be understood as the same person as the Joseph (of Arimathea) who buries Jesus in all four of the intracanonical gospels (Matt 27:57–60; Mark 15:43–46; Luke 23:50–53; John 19:38–42). The statement of GP 6:23 that Joseph "had seen what good deeds [Jesus] had done" is likely an allusion to Joseph's status as a disciple or follower of Jesus, a claim made also in Matt 27:57 and John 19:38.[8] Joseph buries Jesus by wrapping him in linen and placing him in his own tomb (GP 6:24).[9] The material in which Jesus is wrapped in GP is σινδών, the same as in Matt 27:59; Mark 15:46; and Luke 23:53.[10] GP 6:24 shares with Matthew the unique detail that Jesus was buried in Joseph's own tomb and agrees with John on the tomb's location in a garden (Matt 27:60; John 19:41). Concerning the garden, the Fourth Evangelist states plainly that where he was crucified there was a garden, and that "in the garden there was a new tomb in which no one had ever been laid" (John 19:41). In GP 6:24 this locale is given the name Κῆπος Ἰωσήφ.[11]

The Jews, the elders, and the priests soon recognize the evil that they have done to themselves (γνόντες, οἷον κακὸν ἑαυτοῖς ἐποίησαν) (GP

---

ers, since GP's author knew both Mark and John and at numerous points felt free not to follow them when composing his own gospel.

[7] In the reconstruction of Crossan, burial by Jesus' enemies is "taken for granted throughout the *Cross Gospel*," and this reflects the earliest burial tradition (*Cross That Spoke*, 237). It is Mark who later "created the motif of Jesus' burial by his friends" (ibid., 238). As I will discuss in Chapter Four, I find it more plausible to suggest that the burial story originally involved burial by friends but was later changed to portray enemies in the role.

[8] Alternatives on the rationale behind the statement, "since he had seen what good deeds he had done," can be found in Swete, *Akhmîm Fragment*, 11; Vaganay, *Évangile de Pierre*, 266; Mara, *Évangile de Pierre*, 147–48. Swete holds that this expression "must be taken as a jeer" from the Jews and is part of their "heartless banter at the expense of Joseph" (*Akhmîm Fragment*, 11). But this is not clear. It seems, rather, that the expression is being presented as a sincere rationale from the Jews for their offer to give the body to Joseph.

[9] Mara (*Évangile de Pierre*, 149–53) sees in the burial in Joseph's own tomb an allusion to 1 Kgs 13:29–31, where the prophet of Bethel buries the man of God in his own tomb. This suggestion is questionable, though.

[10] John differs by stating that Jesus' body was wrapped in ὀθόνιον rather than σινδών (John 19:40; 20:5–7). Σινδών has two definitions in BDAG (s.v., 924): 1) fabric made from linen, linen cloth; and 2) a light piece of clothing like a chemise, shirt. The synoptic texts and GP 6:24 are listed in BDAG under the first definition. That the intended meaning here is a fabric – and not a garment – is indicated by the fact that the body is "wrapped" (ἐντυλίσσω in Matt 27:59 and Luke 23:53; ἐνειλέω in Mark 15:46; εἰλέω in GP 6:24) in the material.

[11] Swete (*Akhmîm Fragment*, 12) quotes without citation an interesting question posed by Harnack concerning the reference to the Garden of Joseph in GP: "War der κῆπος Ἰ. zur Zeit des Verfassers etwa eine bekannte Localität?" (Was the Garden of Joseph perhaps a known location in the time of the author?).

7:25). Upon this realization they declare, "Judgment has come close and the end of Jerusalem" (ἤγγισεν ἡ κρίσις καὶ τὸ τέλος 'Ιερουσαλήμ). The closest NT parallel to what we find here is the behavior of some of those gathered at the crucifixion in the Third Gospel: "And when all the crowds who had gathered there for this spectacle saw what had taken place, they returned home, beating their breasts" (Luke 23:48). The beating of chests signifies sorrow or mourning at what they have witnessed in the death of Jesus.[12]

There is an important development in the textual tradition of Luke 23:48 that is relevant to GP. Tatian's *Diatessaron* apparently included material very close to what is found in GP 7:25, as did an old Latin version of Luke.[13] I quote here the relevant texts:

Then, as the Jews and the elders and the priests perceived what evil they had done to themselves, they began to lament and to say: "Woe on our sins! Judgment has come close and the end of Jerusalem." (GP 7:25)

And all the multitudes who assembled to see the sight, when they saw what had taken place, returned home beating their breasts. (Luke 23:48)

...saying, "Woe to us on account of our sins that we have committed this day! For the desolation of Jerusalem has drawn near." (Conclusion of Luke 23:48 in Old Latin manuscript it^g)[14]

"Woe was it, woe was it to us; this was the Son of God" ... "Behold, they have come, the judgments of the desolation of Jerusalem have arrived!" (Ephrem, *Comm. Diat.* 20.28)[15]

William L. Petersen cites various proposals that have been made as to the origin of this material, including GP itself, Tatian, or a common source such as an early version of Luke, an *Urevangelium*, or a Jewish-Christian gospel.[16] He locates its source as a Jewish-Christian gospel. This is possible, although oral tradition is also a possibility.

---

[12] GP, however, places the chest beating a few verses later in GP 8:28. Other examples of this act as an expression of sorrow or mourning are found in Luke 18:13; Josephus, *Ant.* 7.10.5.

[13] Bruce M. Metzger (*A Textual Commentary on the Greek New Testament* [2d ed.; Stuttgart: Deutsche Bibelgesellschaft, 1994], 155–56) includes GP, Ephrem's commentary on the *Diatessaron*, and an Old Latin manuscript (it^g) in his treatment of the textual tradition of Luke 23:48.

[14] ET in ibid., 155.

[15] ET in ibid., 156. Harris (*Popular Account*, 75–81) was among the first to note this connection between GP and the *Diatessaron*. A more recent treatment of this question as it relates to the *Diatessaron* is found in William L. Petersen, *Tatian's Diatessaron: Its Creation, Dissemination, Significance, and History in Scholarship* (VCSup 25; New York: Brill, 1994), 414–20.

[16] Petersen, *Tatian's Diatessaron*, 419–20.

The scene in GP shifts dramatically in 7:26–27 as the disciples are in hiding because they fear that they are being sought by the Jews for wanting to set fire to the temple. While concealed, they fast, mourn, and weep until the Sabbath. Though differing in the details, some of the NT gospels include similar references to the actions of the disciples. Matthew and Mark state that at the time of Jesus' arrest, "all the disciples deserted him and fled" (Matt 26:56; Mark 14:50). In John, Jesus tells those arresting him to "let these men go" (John 18:8). After denying Jesus three times, Peter goes out and weeps (Matt 26:75; Mark 14:72; Luke 22:62). One of the later additions to the end of Mark's gospel includes the detail that Mary Magdalene "went out and told those who had been with him, *while they were mourning and weeping* (πενθοῦσι καὶ κλαίουσιν)" (Mark 16:10), which resembles the statement in GP 7:27 that the disciples "fasted and sat *mourning and weeping* (πενθοῦντες καὶ κλαίοντες)."

In regard to the enigmatic reference to the disciples wanting to set fire to the temple (GP 7:26), the false witnesses at Jesus' trial in Matthew testify that Jesus claimed to be able to destroy the temple and rebuild it in three days (Matt 26:61).[17] The closest parallel to GP 7:26–27 comes in John 20:19, where the disciples are hiding in a locked house "for fear of the Jews" after Mary Magdalene has told them that she has seen the risen Jesus. John, however, differs significantly from GP in having Jesus appear to the disciples in this scene. Earlier in the Fourth Gospel, Joseph of Arimathea is a secret disciple of Jesus "because of his fear of the Jews" (John 19:38), a description also bearing some similarity to GP. In GP 8:28 the author returns to the motif of Jewish reaction to the death of Jesus by drawing a distinction between the Jewish religious leaders and Jewish laypeople. Here the scribes, Pharisees, and elders witness the "whole people" beating their breasts and proclaiming, "If at his death these most mighty signs have come to pass, see how righteous he is" (GP 8:28). As mentioned above, Luke 23:48 bears some resemblance to this.[18] Crossan notes that Luke's scene of onlookers at the crucifixion entails a distinction between the Jewish authorities and the Jewish people in their response to

---

[17] In Luke 9:54 the disciples James and John ask Jesus if they should "command fire to come down from heaven and consume them (i.e., a Samaritan village)." Later in Luke's gospel Jesus says, "I came to bring fire to the earth, and how I wish it were already kindled" (Luke 12:49).

[18] On the parallel between GP 8:28 and Luke 23:48, see Swete, *Akhmîm Fragment*, 14; Mara, *Évangile de Pierre*, 165–66; Crossan, *Cross That Spoke*, 257–61. Swete judges GP to be combining Luke's confession of the centurion with other signs that accompanied the crucifixion. According to Crossan, Luke has combined GP 7:25 and 8:28 in his account.

the event, which is what is found in GP 8:28.[19] The parallel with Luke 23:48 can therefore be seen in GP 7:25 and 8:28.

3.2 GP 5:20–8:28: Signs of Judgment on the Jews

In this section I will suggest that GP's author includes signs at the death of Jesus as indications of judgment against the Jewish people. In order to introduce this subject we need to look first at the closing verse of this unit, where the Jewish leaders witness the people expressing sorrow over the crucifixion of Jesus as the crowd declares that at his death "these most mighty signs have come to pass" (ταῦτα τὰ μέγιστα σημεῖα γέγονεν) (GP 8:28). The question naturally must be asked: what are the specific μέγιστα σημεῖα that have appeared prior to this point and of which the Jewish people have been witnesses? Swete identifies ταῦτα τὰ μέγιστα σημεῖα with "the phaenomena that attended the Crucifixion."[20] I would follow him on this point by suggesting four particular events as candidates for μέγιστα σημεῖα: 1) darkness (GP 5:15, 18; 6:22); 2) the torn veil (GP 5:20); 3) an earthquake (GP 6:21); and 4) Jerusalem's destruction (GP 7:25). Three of these signs – darkness, earthquake, and the fall of Jerusalam – draw reactions from the Jewish people, a good initial reason to propose them.

A second introductory matter concerns my claim that these events should be taken to signify retribution against the Jews. At this point I offer GP 7:25 as support for this, since here the entire company of Jewish people, including the elders and the priests, expresses lament over their sins while proclaiming that judgment has come (ἤγγισεν ἡ κρίσις). This occurs in the context of a statement about Jerusalem's destruction, though, as I will suggest, judgment accompanies the other signs as well.

3.2.1 Darkness (GP 5:15, 18; 6:22)

Chronologically, the darkness during the crucifixion is the first sign of judgment in GP. It initially comes in GP 5:15 at noon, and is alluded to in 5:18 and again in the reappearance of the sun in 6:22. All three of the Synoptics include the darkness, though only GP separates its onset from the return of the sun. In the NT stories it is unclear what the darkness

---

[19] Crossan, *Cross That Spoke*, 257–61. Crossan suggests that "'the people' are in no way responsible for the Passion of Jesus" in Luke's gospel and that the scene "allows the multitudes involved in the Crucifixion of Jesus to respond to the miracles at his death ... with repentance" (260).

[20] Swete (*Akhmîm Fragment*, 14). However, he does not specify the particular signs that he has in mind.

connotes. In GP, however, the darkness is clearly understood by the Jewish characters; they respond to it in fear (GP 5:15). This recognition of its meaning points toward it being among the μέγιστα σημεῖα.

The darkness does not appear to be a naturally occurring event but rather a supernatural sign. Crossan cites several biblical texts in which it accompanies revelatory events (Exod 10:22; Isa 13:9–10; 50:3; Joel 2:1–10; Amos 8:9–10).[21] As I argued in Chapter Two, the OT background to the darkness in GP is noteworthy since our gospel appears to be echoing biblical texts that describe scenes of judgment. Included among these in my earlier discussion were Deut 28:28–29; Isa 59:9–10; and Amos 8:9, all of which have the darkness come as a result of divine wrath. We appear on firm ground, then, in including this phenomenon among those μέγιστα σημεῖα portending retribution from God for the death of Jesus.

3.2.2 Torn Veil (GP 5:20)

The second sign of judgment is the tearing of the temple veil (GP 5:20). Commentators often debate whether the NT writers are speaking of the innermost veil separating the holy of holies from the rest of the temple or the outer curtain covering the temple entrance itself.[22] However, Vaganay is correct in saying of GP that "it is too far from the events, in time and in geographical distance, to be interested in a detail of this type."[23] GP's author knows only that the torn veil episode is among those events thought to have occurred around the time of Jesus' death.

The accounts of the torn veil in the NT gospels have been understood in diverse ways in recent scholarship: as opening the door to Gentile inclusion in the kingdom of God; as making God more accessible to humans; as demonstrating the fulfillment of prophecy, either from Jesus or the OT; as a foreshadowing of the events of 70 C.E.; as punishment for the death of Jesus; and many others.[24] That the tearing is meant to carry symbolism is certain, but none of the NT evangelists describes its particular significance. The book of Hebrews also utilizes καταπέτασμα language for theological purposes: Jesus makes accessible through his death the atonement that once was provided in the old covenant only behind the curtain of the temple's holy of holies (Heb 6:19–20; 9:1–10; 10:19–22).

This diversity of understanding concerning the temple veil and the lack of an explicit statement explaining its meaning in GP has led Crossan to

---

[21] Crossan, *Cross That Spoke*, 198–200.

[22] The matter is summarized in Brown, *Death of the Messiah*, 2:1109–13.

[23] Vaganay, *Évangile de Pierre*, 258.

[24] See the wide array of views concerning just Matthew's veil pericope that have recently been summarized in Daniel M. Gurtner, *The Torn Veil: Matthew's Exposition of the Death of Jesus* (SNTSMS 139; Cambridge: Cambridge University Press, 2007), 1–24.

judge of GP's torn veil that "any interpretation from context is even more difficult than in the case of the synoptic writers."[25] While it is far from certain, I find it likely that the torn curtain should be included among the divine signs of judgment in GP.[26] The reference to the tearing of the veil "at the same hour" as Jesus' death signifies the connection between the two events.[27] None of the NT accounts includes such a time indicator; therefore, the inclusion of this phrase in GP makes more explicit the connection implied in the synoptic parallels between Jesus' death and the *vellum scissum*.[28] We are told in GP 7:25 that the retribution is against the Jews: "Woe on *our* sins!" That Jews are the only ones to join in the crucifixion also points toward them as the sole recipients of divine wrath. And the temple, as a centerpiece of Jewish religious praxis, would have been a natural target of God's disfavor. In some sense, then, the veil incident is to be linked directly to the death of Jesus and I would propose that, in light of the later statements about signs and judgment, we take this event as the second sign to the Jews.[29]

3.2.3 Earthquake (GP 6:21)

The earthquake of GP 6:21 is the third of the portents. Matthew is the only NT evangelist to mention an earthquake at the time of the crucifixion (Matt 27:51).[30] In the Hebrew Bible earthquakes are a common indicator of divine wrath (e.g., Isa 5:25; 24:18; Jer 4:23–24; Ezek 38:19–20; Joel 2:10). In some of these instances, darkness and earthquakes appear together in contexts where retribution comes from God (e.g., Jer 4:23–24; Joel 2:10).

---

[25] Crossan, *Cross That Spoke*, 226–27.

[26] This is also the interpretation of GP's veil in Marinus de Jonge, "Matthew 27:51 in Early Christian Exegesis," *HTR* 79 (1986): 73–74.

[27] The Akhmîm manuscript at this point actually reads "αυτοϛωρας," one of its many grammatical and spelling errors. Kraus and Nicklas (*Petrusevangelium*, 32–48) provide an inventory of such cases and proposed solutions; their own reconstruction in the present instance is αὐτῆς ὥρας (36–37). Their English translation of this phrase is followed by most other translators as well, rendering αὐτός as an identical adjective, even though it is anarthrous and not in agreement with the noun it modifies: "at the same hour" (cf. Luke 13:31).

[28] Crossan (*Cross That Spoke*, 225) also judges that the inclusion of "at the same hour" is to emphasize the link between the torn veil and Jesus' death.

[29] It was also common in second-century Christianity to interpret the veil episode as symbolizing judgment. See below.

[30] Matthew's gospel includes two earthquakes, the first coming at the crucifixion and the second when the women come to the tomb on the first day of the week (Matt 27:51–54; 28:2).

Unlike the Matthean earthquake, the tremors in GP come as a result of Jesus' body being placed on the earth.[31]

The reaction of the Jewish executioners to the earthquake is also telling, because it is part of a recurring motif of fear in this gospel (GP 6:21).[32] The fright expressed by them is likely due to their recognition that the earthquake is a sign of wrath, and of course fear is the expected response of those facing divine retribution. We see, then, that two of the proposed signs – darkness and the earthquake – have included reactions of fear from the Jews (GP 5:15; 6:21).

The three phenomena discussed to this point are all paralleled in one or more of the NT gospels, though they are not primarily indicators of judgment in those stories. Among the NT gospels Matthew is the only one to mention darkness, the veil, and an earthquake in his Passion Narrative, a trait shared with GP. Furthermore, both GP and Matthew give these in the same order: 1) darkness (GP 5:15; Matt 27:45); 2) torn veil (GP 5:20; Matt 27:51); 3) earthquake (GP 6:21; Matt 27:54). Brown has suggested that the pre-Matthean tradition continued to evolve after the composition of Matthew's gospel, and that it is from these later developments that GP has occasionally drawn.[33]

In the synoptic accounts these occurrences appear to reflect the great importance of the occasion or to confirm the identity of Jesus. They lead the centurion to declare Jesus to be Son of God (Matthew and Mark), or to judge him innocent/righteous (δίκαιος in Luke 23:47).[34] It is difficult to find the theme of judgment at the forefront of any of the NT accounts. Though the darkness, torn veil, and earthquake did not operate primarily as symbols of retribution in some or all of these NT stories, GP's author has employed them in just such a manner. He has taken these traditions and

---

[31] That Jesus' body triggers the earthquake indicates its power, a characteristic that does not support a docetic reading of GP. In recent decades, the scholarly tide has turned away from the earlier consensus that GP is docetic, a view that can be traced to Serapion in the second century and that was subsequently followed by nearly all scholars in the immediate wake of GP's rediscovery at the end of the 19th century. Many have noted the import of GP 6:21 for a non-docetic reading of this gospel; see McCant, "Docetism Reconsidered," 258–73; Head, "Christology of the Gospel of Peter," 209–24.

[32] Matthew's earthquake at the crucifixion draws a response of fear as well, though it comes from the Roman soldiers overseeing the crucifixion (Matt 27:54).

[33] Brown, *Death of the Messiah*, 2:1136–37. While I do not wish to dismiss Brown's suggestion out of hand, it may not be necessary to posit GP's use of such post-Matthean traditions. Rather, it is perhaps more likely that GP's author is rearranging the Matthean stories in order to serve his own purpose, which in this case is to present the phenomena at the crucifixion as signs to the Jews.

[34] In GP 8:28 the Jewish crowd, after seeing the signs at the crucifixion, exclaims that Jesus was δίκαιος.

presented them as signs against the Jews. This is reflected to a certain degree in the fearful reactions of the Jews.

3.2.4 The Destruction of Jerusalem (GP 7:25)

After these first three signs the Jews finally realize the great sin they have committed: "Then, as the Jews and the elders and the priests perceived what evil they had done to themselves, they began to lament and to say: 'Woe on our sins! Judgment has come close and the end of Jerusalem'" (GP 7:25). This verse clearly indicates that judgment is a key idea in this section and that the events discussed to this point are indeed among those acts of divine wrath. Here the Jews, the elders, and the priests recognize that their actions against Jesus were evil and that by their involvement they have brought judgment upon themselves.

In response to their recognition they declare, "Judgment has come close and the end of Jerusalem" (ἤγγισεν ἡ κρίσις καὶ τὸ τέλος Ἰερουσαλήμ). As I stated in the synoptic analysis above, there is no explicit NT parallel to this statement.[35] While a cursory reading of this verse would seem to require a post-70 C.E. setting for it, Crossan claims that there is "nothing in *Gospel of Peter* 7:25 that demands a date after the fall of Jerusalem or an experience of the destruction."[36] He concedes that a statement which appears to allude to Jerusalem's destruction (e.g., Matt 24:1–28; Luke 19:41–44; 21:5–24; 1 Thess 2:16) is typically a *vaticinium ex eventu*, but in the case of GP 7:25 he contends that the background lies in Ezek 9:1 and Isa 41:21. For further support, he notes a Qumran pesher text (4Q169) that predates the fall of Jerusalem and yet refers to the city's eventual destruction by foreigners.[37] This argument, however, carries little merit. When considering GP in its entirety, it is more likely that it represents a development to be placed later than the intracanonical

---

[35] As Swete (*Akhmîm Fragment*, 12–13) suggests, however, Amos 8:10 and Isa 3:9 may lie in the background of GP 7:25: "I will turn your feasts into mourning, and all your songs into lamentation; I will bring sackcloth on all loins, and baldness on every head; I will make it like the mourning for an only son, and the end of it like a bitter day" (Amos 8:10); "The look on their faces bears witness against them; they proclaim their sin like Sodom, they do not hide it. Woe to them! For they have brought evil on themselves" (Isa 3:9). Crossan charts a similar course (*Cross That Spoke*, 252–57). GP may very well be alluding to these verses.

[36] Crossan, *Cross That Spoke*, 257.

[37] Ibid. The Qumran text is a commentary on Nahum, and Crossan quotes the passage as follows: "[God did not surrender Jerusalem into] the hands of the kings of Greece from Antiochus until the rise of the power of the rulers of the Kittim; but afterwards [the city] shall be trodden down" (4QpNah 1:3; square brackets original).

gospels.[38] Moreover, Crossan's appeal to 4Q169 looks like special plead-
ing when we consider that it would open up the possibility that most apparent *vaticinia ex eventu* are actually legitimate prophecies/predictions, an
implication that Crossan himself likely would reject in other instances.

The best explanation is that GP's author has added the destruction of Jerusalem to the intracanonical traditions of darkness, torn veil, and earthquake because it could and was so easily understood by many early Christians as punishment on the Jews. In fact, for GP's author the events of 70
C.E. were the culmination of God's retribution against the Jews for their
role in the crucifixion of Jesus. In GP 7:25 the Jews become aware of this
reality, although there is a clear anachronism in depicting an event that
happened forty years after the crucifixion as a sign to those who killed
Jesus. Such telescoping of events is not uncommon among early Christians.[39] It is as if we have in this verse a Christian projection of what the
proper Jewish response should be at the time GP was composed. In the
eyes of some early Christians, Jews should lament over their role in the
death of Jesus and acknowledge that God has judged their nation in the
destruction of their capital and temple by the Romans.

After the interlude in GP 7:26–27 that describes the activities of the disciples at the time of the crucifixion, the story returns to the Jewish reaction
to the crucifixion events (GP 8:28). There is a split here between the Jewish authorities and laypeople, as the common folk profess that the μέγιστα
σημεῖα they have witnessed testify to the fact that Jesus is righteous
(δίκαιος). This causes the leaders to take measures to squelch any report
of the resurrection (GP 8:29–11:49). In the expression "If at his death these
most mighty signs have come to pass," the connection is clear between the
μέγιστα σημεῖα and Jesus' death. The signs accompany his death. Judgment has progressed from the onset of darkness, to the veil and earthquake,
and reached its culmination in the eventual fall of Jerusalem. This has led
to an awareness by some Jews that they have committed a great sin in
crucifying the righteous Jesus. This final sign is not only an indicator of
judgment; it also confirms the identity of the crucified one, a function
similar to that of the signs in the NT parallels. GP's author again appears
to be presenting an ideal situation for the Jews of his day: confess Jesus as
righteous and acknowledge the signs that God has given you, both in the
events at the death of Jesus and in those that took place forty years later in
your nation.

---

[38] When it comes to issues of dating, the most persuasive arguments are based not on
a single datum but on the accumulation of evidence that leads to a particular conclusion.
See below for further points that count against Crossan's thesis here.

[39] See the example below.

3.3 Early Christian Parallels

Outside the NT gospels we find numerous instances in which early Christian writers use the darkness, torn veil, and earthquake at the time of the crucifixion, along with the later fall of Jerusalem, as signs of divine judgment against the Jews. In this section I will survey parallels from the first two centuries. In doing so, I plan to show that GP is not unique in what I am claiming for it, but rather that such sentiments were relatively frequent in the early Christian movement.

The strongest parallel to what I have proposed above for GP comes in a work from Melito of Sardis.[40] In his *Homily on Pascha,* he frequently emphasizes the punishments that God has brought upon the Jews, and he employs all four signs found in GP in the following words:

O unprecedented murder! Unprecedented crime! The Sovereign has been made unrecognizable by his naked body, and is not even allowed a garment to keep him from view. *That is why the luminaries turned away, and the day was darkened,* so that he might hide the one stripped bare upon the tree, darkening not the body of the Lord but the eyes of men.

For when the people did not tremble, the earth quaked; when the people were not terrified, the heavens were terrified; when the people did not tear their clothes, the angel tore his; when the people did not lament, the Lord thundered out of heaven and the Highest gave voice.

Therefore, O Israel, you did not quake in the presence of the Lord, so you quaked at the assault of foes; you were not terrified in the presence of the Lord, < .... > [text missing] you did not lament over the Lord, so you lamented over your firstborn; you did not tear your clothes when the Lord was hung, so you tore them over those who were slain; you forsook the Lord, you were not found by him; you did not accept the Lord, you were not pitied by him; *you dashed down the Lord, you were dashed to the ground.* (*Hom. on Pascha* 97–99; Hall 55, 57, emphasis added)

Melito is tying all of these things to the death of "the Lord." They have happened because of the "murder" of Jesus, as indicated by the opening line quoted: "O unprecedented murder! Unprecedented crime!" (*Hom. on Pascha* 97). He contrasts the attitude of the Jews with the mighty signs that were shown to them. Their failure to acknowledge the true identity of Jesus is what leads to the destruction of their nation in *Hom. on Pascha* 99.

The first parallel to GP comes in the statement that the luminaries (i.e., sun and stars) "turned away" because of the crucifixion of the naked Jesus in order that God might hide the one hung upon the tree (*Hom. on Pascha* 97). Though the subject of the verb is lacking in the phrase "so that he might hide" (ὅπως κρύψῃ), the purpose indicator ὅπως along with the active verb implies some type of personal agency, the most likely being a

---

[40] These phenomena in Melito are discussed in Brown, *Death of the Messiah*, 2:1115, 1119–20.

divine agent. This suggestion receives support in *Hom. on Pascha* 98, where "the Lord (κύριος) thundered out of heaven and the Highest (ὕψιστος) gave voice" in response to the failure of the people to lament over their misdeeds. The divine references "Lord" and "Highest" in connection with these signs demonstrate that God is probably also to be understood as the one responsible for hiding the man stripped bare earlier in *Hom. on Pascha* 97. There is potentially a further allusion to the darkness at the crucifixion in the statement that "the heavens were terrified" when the people were not terrified (*Hom. on Pascha* 98). The terror of the heavens manifested itself through the sun's disappearance.

The second connection to GP is found in this line: "For when the people did not tremble, the earth quaked" (*Hom. on Pascha* 98). By referring to a lack of trembling by the people, Melito emphasizes their lack of recognition of what they had done in crucifying Jesus and their failure to repent for these actions. Had they truly known the great sin they had committed, they would have trembled before God in fear, but because they did not do so, God sent an earthquake. I find it probable that by referring to the Lord, the Highest, thundering from the heavens, Melito is expressing divine agency for the earthquake, too.

While Melito's references to the darkness and shaking of the earth are typical of the standard collection of signs of judgment, his allusion to the torn veil is less so. This has not kept Campbell Bonner from claiming that "there can be no doubt that Melito thought of the veil of the temple as if it were the garment of the angel who dwelt there, rent in grief at the death of the Lord."[41] The line in question from Melito's homily is this one: "when the people did not tear their clothes, the angel tore his" (*Hom. on Pascha* 98). Bonner appears correct in finding a reference to the torn veil here. This would then link the three signs – earthquake, darkness, veil – to a lack of proper response by the Jewish people. In each case the failure of the Jews in *Hom. on Pascha* 98 brings a divine reply: 1) the failure to tremble leads to the earthquake; 2) the lack of fear brings about the darkness; and 3) by not tearing their own clothes, an angel, a messenger from God, is forced to tear the temple veil.[42]

As for the fourth proposed sign – the destruction of Jerusalem – almost all of *Hom. on Pascha* 99 alludes to that event. Melito again sets up the matter in a cause-and-effect structure: because Israel did not quake in the

---

[41] Bonner, *The Homily on the Passion by Melito Bishop of Sardis and Some Fragments of the Apocryphal Ezekiel* (SD 12; Philadelphia: University of Pennsylvania Press, 1940), 41.

[42] I do not intend to imply that Melito is dependent upon GP, or vice versa. In the case of the first three phenomena it is just as likely that Melito is modeling his homily after Matthew's gospel.

presence of the Lord, they quaked "at the assault of foes"; because the Jews dashed down the Lord, they were dashed to the ground, and so forth. The homilist considers the incredible events that overtook the Jewish nation in 70 C.E. to be punishment for their rejection and crucifixion of Jesus forty years earlier.[43] Melito therefore provides a highly noteworthy parallel for understanding the motives underlying the composition of GP. Melito and GP narrate the four signs in the same order: 1) darkness; 2) torn veil; 3) earthquake; 4) destruction of Jerusalem. Both authors understand the phenomena accompanying the crucifixion, as described in the gospel stories, to be indications of punishment or judgment on those who carried out the act. Moreover, GP and Melito both interpret the Jerusalem events of 70 C.E. in a similar manner. GP tells in story form what Melito expresses in a homily.

The second-century apologist Justin Martyr frequently employs the military, economic, and social misfortunes of the Jews in his arguments. Quite often he cites the fall of Jerusalem in such contexts.[44] At one point in his *Dialogue with Trypho*, he describes various afflictions suffered by the Jews, including the desolation of their land, the burning of their cities, and their eventual banishment from Jerusalem. After this he writes, "Therefore, the above-mentioned tribulations were justly imposed upon you, for you have murdered the Just One, and His prophets before Him" (*Dial.* 16). Little doubt lies in Justin's mind as to the reason for these calamities – they are due to Jewish responsibility for the death of Jesus. In this regard he is in agreement with GP.

The *Gospel of Bartholomew* was composed possibly as early as the end of the second century.[45] This gospel provides an interesting parallel to the references to the veil in both GP and Melito:

---

[43] Karmann ("Melito von Sardes," 228–29) summarizes the similarities between GP and Melito as it concerns the fall of Jerusalem as punishment. The language of judgment in *Hom. on Pascha* 99 may not be intended to refer only to the happenings of 70 C.E. It might be that the later calamities that befell the Jews, including those during the Bar-Kochba revolt in 132–135 C.E., are also behind Melito's words. In studies of early Christianity and Judaism, the events of 70 C.E. often overshadow those of 132–135 C.E., perhaps in part because the sources are more numerous and reliable in the case of the former. However, the destruction brought upon the Jews by the Romans in the Bar-Kochba rebellion was in fact greater and more widespread than the events of six decades prior. On this point, see Smallwood, *Jews under Roman Rule*, 428–66.

[44] *1 Apol.* 47; *Dial.* 16, 52, 108, 110. As was also possibly true of Melito, Justin does not limit Israel's tragedies to those of 70 C.E. but instead includes those of later times as well, including the Bar-Kochba era.

[45] It is dated to the third century in Felix Scheidweiler and Wilhelm Schneemelcher, "The Gospel of Bartholomew," in *NTApoc*[2] 1:542. They also discuss the question of patristic references to "The Gospel of Bartholomew" and whether this gospel is to be identified with the extant work identified as "The Questions of Bartholomew" (1:537–

But one of the angels, greater than the others, would not go up. He had in his hand a fiery sword and looked at you. And all the angels besought him to go up with them; but he would not. But when you commanded him, I saw a flame issuing out of his hands, which reached as far as the city of Jerusalem. And Jesus said to him: Blessed are you, Bartholomew, my beloved, because you saw these mysteries. This was one of the avenging angels, who stand before my Father's throne. He sent this angel to me. And for this reason he would not go up, because he wished to destroy the power of the world. But when I commanded him to go up, a flame issued from his hand, and after he had rent the veil of the Temple, he divided it into two parts as a testimony to the children of Israel for my passion, because they crucified me. (*Gos. Bart.* 1.24–27; *NTApoc*[2] 1:542–43)

The final section of this passage is most relevant, as it describes an angel who tears the temple curtain so that it might be a testimony to the Jewish people for their crucifixion of Jesus. We have here an unambiguous case in which the *vellum scissum* is intended as a sign of divine judgment on the Jews, the very same suggestion that has been proposed for the veil in GP.

The Pseudo-Clementine literature is a vast and complex subject of study.[46] Sections of the Pseudo-Clementines, particularly the *Recognitions*, are thought to reflect early Jewish-Christian traditions.[47] Graham Stanton has suggested that the source behind a lengthy section of *Recognitions* (1.27–71) is to be identified as "an apologia for Jewish believers in Jesus" and that this *apologia* dates to around the middle of the second century.[48] Within this part of the *Recognitions* there appears a reference to events at the crucifixion:

And the mountains were shattered, and the graves were opened, and the veil of the temple was torn so that it was lamenting as if in mourning over the destruction of the place that was imminent. (Ps-Clem. *Rec.* 1.41.3)[49]

F. Stanley Jones has compared this statement and other material from *Rec.* 1.27–72 to parallels in GP and concludes that "the Jewish Christian author of *Recognitions* ... knew and used the *Gospel of Peter*."[50] Setting aside the question of whether Jones is correct on this question, we may take notice of the interpretation of the veil episode. For the writer of *Recognitions,* the

---

40). For the sake of simplicity, I will refer to the text I quote as the *Gospel of Bartholomew*.

[46] Background on introductory matters can be found in Johannes Irmscher and Georg Strecker, "The Pseudo-Clementines," in *NTApoc*[2] 2:483–493.

[47] See, for example, Georg Strecker, *Das Judenchristentum in den Pseudoklementinen* (2d ed.; TU 70; Berlin: Akademie, 1981); Stanton, "Jewish Christian Elements in the Pseudo-Clementine Writings," in *Jewish Believers in Jesus: The Early Centuries* (ed. Oskar Skarsaune and Reidar Hvalvik; Peabody, Mass.: Hendrickson, 2007), 305–24.

[48] Stanton, "Jewish Christian Elements," 317–23.

[49] ET in F. Stanley Jones, "The Gospel of Peter in Pseudo-Clementine Recognitions 1,27–71," in Kraus and Nicklas, *Evangelium nach Petrus*, 239. Jones dates this material to "around 200 C.E." (ibid., 237).

[50] Ibid., 243.

torn curtain was a prelude to the eventual destruction of the temple; it marked the imminence of what was to take place. Something similar is implied in GP's veil episode.

We have in the *Testament of Levi* another instance in which the torn curtain anticipates the later destruction that would befall the temple and the Jewish people. The hands of a Christian redactor are evident in these words:

I am clear from all your ungodliness and transgression which ye will do in the end of the ages against the Saviour of the world, acting ungodly, deceiving Israel, and raising up against it great evils from the Lord. And ye will deal lawlessly with Israel, so that Jerusalem shall not endure your wickedness; but the veil of the temple shall be rent, so as not to cover your shame. And ye shall be scattered as captives among the heathen, and shall be for a reproach and for a curse, and for a trampling under foot. (*T. Levi* 10; *ANF* 8:15)[51]

The chronology here is that the rending of the temple veil will be followed by the scattering of Jews among the Gentiles (Romans), where the latter will trample the former. Though the temple's destruction is not described, the fate of Jerusalem and the Jewish people in the aftermath of their war with Rome is clear enough. These calamities come in response to their actions against "the Saviour of the world."

Celsus, the second-century critic of the Christian movement, gives us further evidence in this area.[52] His major work, *True Doctrine*, was originally composed in the 170s C.E. but is no longer extant.[53] Fortunately, thanks in large measure to quotations preserved in Origen's *Contra Celsum*, much of Celsus' text has been reconstructed.[54] By the time of Celsus, even those outside of Christian and Jewish sects recognized that Christians were claiming that the events of 70 C.E. had come upon the Jews

---

[51] A recent summary of Christian interpolations in the *Testaments of the Twelve Patriarchs* appears in Torleif Elgvin, "Jewish Christian Editing of the Old Testament Pseudepigrapha," in Skarsaune and Hvalvik, *Jewish Believers in Jesus*, 286–92. See already James H. Charlesworth, "Christian and Jewish Self-Definition in Light of the Christian Additions to the Apocryphal Writings," in *Aspects of Judaism in the Graeco-Roman Period* (ed. E. P. Sanders, A. I. Baumgarten, and A. Mendelson; Philadelphia: Fortress, 1981), 27–55.

[52] Overviews of Celsus and his thought are found in Pierre de Labriolle, *La réaction païenne: Étude sur la polémique antichrétienne du Ier zu VIe siècle* (2d ed.; Paris: Artisan du Livre, 1948), 111–69; Carl Andresen, *Logos und Nomos: Die Polemik des Kelsos wider das Christentum* (ArbKir 30; Berlin: de Gruyter, 1955); Stephen Benko, "Pagan Criticism of Christianity during the First Two Centuries A.D.," *ANRW* 23.2:1101–8; Wilken, *Christians as the Romans Saw Them*, 94–125.

[53] On the dating of *True Doctrine*, see Henry Chadwick, *Origen: Contra Celsum* (Cambridge: Cambridge University Press, 1953), xxiv–xxviii.

[54] Stanton (*Jesus and Gospel*, 149) estimates that 70% of Celsus' now lost work has been recovered through quotations in Origen and elsewhere.

as a consequence of their rejection of Jesus. Origen preserves the words of Celsus here:

> Christians also add certain doctrines to those maintained by the Jews, and assert that the Son of God has already come on account of the sins of the Jews, and that because the Jews punished Jesus and gave him gall to drink they drew down upon themselves the bitter anger of God. (*Cels.* 4.22; Chadwick 198)

For someone who is not a participant in the Jewish-Christian debates of the second century, Celsus is particularly well informed. In reply to the comments of Celsus, Origen reiterates the Christian claims in this regard:

> I challenge anyone to prove my statement untrue if I say that the entire Jewish nation was destroyed less than one whole generation later on account of these sufferings which they inflicted upon Jesus. For it was, I believe, forty-two years from the time when they crucified Jesus to the destruction of Jerusalem. Indeed, ever since the Jews existed, it has not been recorded in history that they were ejected for so long a time from their sacred ritual and worship, after they had been conquered by some more powerful people.... Accordingly, one of the facts which show that Jesus was some divine and sacred person is just that on his account such great and fearful calamities have now for a long time befallen the Jews. (*Cels.* 4.22; Chadwick 198–99)

There is little doubt in the mind of Origen that there is a direct connection between Jewish rejection of Jesus, including their involvement in his death, and the calamities that befell them.

Tertullian's argument against Marcion's exclusion of the OT provides our final parallel. At one point he writes this:

> At noon the veil of the temple was rent by the escape of the cherubim, which "left the daughter of Sion as a cottage in a vineyard, as a lodge in a garden of cucumbers." (*Marc.* 4.42; *ANF* 3:421)

The apologist is citing Isa 1:8, though he does not quote the final clause of the verse: "like a besieged city." The first two similes were apparently enough to convey the idea that would have been fulfilled in the actual siege of Jerusalem in 70 C.E. For Tertullian the torn veil was a precursor of the later and more severe divine punishment that would be meted out to the Jews.[55]

---

[55] Tertullian has lengthy discussions of divine retribution on the Jews for their rejection of Jesus in *Marc.* 3.23; *Adv. Jud.* 3; 13. Other third- and fourth-century writers express similar sentiments in their work, and the practice continued in later Christians as well. See, for example, Hippolytus, *Adv. Jud.* 6–7. Hippolytus writes of the eyes of the Jews being darkened, their stumbling, and the destruction of the temple, all on account of their rejection of Jesus. Ps.-Gregory of Nyssa's *Testimonies against the Jews* includes a chapter entitled "Concerning the cross and the darkness that occurred" (ch. 7). OT texts quoted in regard to darkness during the crucifixion are Amos 8:9; Jer 15:9; Zech 14:6–7. Greek text and ET in Martin C. Albl, *Pseudo-Gregory of Nyssa: Testimonies against the Jews* (SBLWGRW 8; Atlanta: Society of Biblical Literature, 2004).

3.4 Apologetics and Polemics in GP 5:20–8:28

If the author of GP has used his knowledge of other gospel material for his own composition, what has influenced him to rewrite those stories in order to depict judgment on the Jews? First and foremost, he was driven by a desire to have the actions of the Jews condemned by God. He also wished to show that God was on the side of Christians in their claims about Jesus. There was an apologetic move to show the superiority of the Christian movement over against Jewish groups. Since Jews were the sole party responsible for the death of Jesus in GP, it is fitting that divine wrath should come only against them. GP's author found in the NT gospels, and likely elsewhere as well, three events that could be depicted as signs of judgment: darkness, earthquake, and the torn temple veil.

When it comes to the inclusion of Jerusalem's fall, the author of GP represents a segment of early Christianity that viewed the event as divine retribution on the Jews for the rejection of Jesus or their role in his death.[56] There is a causal connection between the two events in GP. It is likely that the culmination of God's response, in the estimation of GP's author, came in the defeat of the Jewish nation by the Romans. God had both judged those who rejected Jesus and vindicated those who had remained loyal to the crucified one.

The forty or so years that separated the crucifixion and the fall of Jerusalem did not prevent early Christians from drawing a close link between the two events. Brown notes that it became characteristic of many early Christian writers to blur the line between Jesus' crucifixion in 30 C.E. and the events of 70 C.E.[57] He cites three possible reasons for this: 1) some early Christians encountered references in Jewish texts that referred to

---

[56] There is a thorough survey of early Christian understandings of the events of 70 C.E. in G. W. H. Lampe, "A.D. 70 in Christian Reflection," in *Jesus and the Politics of His Day* (ed. Ernst Bammel and C. F. D. Moule; Cambridge: Cambridge University Press, 1984), 153–71. Some have concluded that it was Jesus himself who warned in advance that tragedy would befall the Jewish people if they rejected him and his message, as, for example, N. T. Wright, has done in *Jesus and the Victory of God* (Minneapolis: Fortress, 1996), 320–68. Wright notes that if his reconstruction is near the mark, then Jesus belongs in the line of earlier prophetic critics who stood within Judaism in their criticisms and call to the people (322–26). If true, this would potentially push the origin of Christian belief about the fate of Jerusalem to a point *before* it actually happened. However, even if Wright's position about Jesus is granted – a conclusion that itself is questionable – what we find in GP, Melito, and other second-century Christian sources is something much different from critique from within. These Christian writers stand firmly outside Judaism and its traditions.

[57] Brown, *Death of the Messiah*, 2:1116–17. Brown's discussion focuses on Jerome's role in the development of the veil tradition but is informative also for the larger issue in early Christianity.

events at the temple that took place four decades before its destruction and then linked these events to the destruction itself; 2) many Christians held the belief that the temple's demise was divine retribution for the death of Jesus; and 3) it was thought by some Christians that Jesus had foretold the temple's destruction, an event whose precursor was the tearing of the veil at the time of the crucifixion.[58] GP fits squarely into Brown's second category. What we find in GP is a fusing of events that are thought to be part of God's judgment. The author is looking back at the events of 30 C.E. through the lens of Jerusalem's destruction and this provides him with further material he can use in his anti-Jewish narrative.

Highly significant historical events have often led some religious people to offer theological explanations for them, and this is true of both the early Christians and others. Josephus, writing as an eyewitness to many of the events, provides an example of a Jew who viewed the result of the Jewish-Roman war as divine punishment of the Jews for what he considered to be their greatest misdeeds. Included among these are the proliferation of messianic claimants and the zealot movement. Josephus thought that God's authority was present in the Romans and that the Jewish refusal to submit to this authority had led to their demise.[59]

For some early Christians, one of the greatest sins was the killing of their leader. In the previous chapter I described how early Christian memory often assigned blame for this event solely to Jews. Likewise, the Christian understanding of divine retribution frequently emphasized the misfortunes of the Jewish people and assigned divine agency or, at the very least, divine permission, to those difficulties and calamities. If a particular group of people were associated with the death of the leader of the Christian movement, and if a brief time later that group were to suffer a terrible tragedy, it is not surprising that people prone to looking for theological explanations on such occasions would connect the dots in a way that viewed the group's earlier misdeeds as the cause of later troubles. This is what Josephus did, and it is also what the author of GP has done by

---

[58] Ibid., 2:1116. Many have noted the role that Jerusalem's fall played in early Christian understandings of OT prophecy. Other early Christians viewed the event as a means of authenticating the church's status as true Israel, the rightful heir of God's promises. Gurtner (*Torn Veil*, 72–96) provides a survey of Jewish views on the temple veil during the Second Temple period. He notes that the veil came to be understood in diverse ways: it symbolized the temple itself (Sir. 50:5), was associated in some sense with "heaven" (Josephus), and during the rabbinic period its removal depicted "the revelation of biblical truths" (ibid., 96).

[59] See, for example, Josephus, *J.W.* 2.254–266; 5.288–309, 366–367, 378; *Ant.* 20.164–166. The sentiments of Josephus are well exemplified in the words of Jesus, son of Ananus, who allegedly began warning the inhabitants of Jerusalem of their impending doom four years before the start of the war with the Romans (Josephus, *J.W.* 5.300–309).

including Jerusalem's destruction as the fourth and climactic sign against the Jews.

The apologetics and polemics of GP 5:20–8:28 are manifested in the depiction of Jews as perpetrators of a great sin, in the divine symbols and acts of judgment of which they are recipients, in their fearful response to these signs, and in the vindication of Christian claims about Jesus. The apologetic move to place God on the side of Christians and in opposition to the Jews is present in GP and other texts. Melito does this very thing in his homily – employing among his signs the four I have identified in GP – in order to show that God has both judged the Jews and communicated his displeasure through specific events. GP seems to allow for the possibility of Jewish repentance, as indicated in the recognition of Jesus' righteousness by some Jews. What we find in GP 5:20–8:28, then, is part of the larger dispute between emerging Christianity and contemporary Jewish groups, as each sought to claim Israel's God as its own, often to the exclusion of those competing sects.

3.5 Conclusions

In the synoptic analysis of GP 5:20–8:28 I set out the parallels between this section and the material in the NT gospels. I noted details in GP that are unique to only one other gospel in the cases of Matthew, Luke, and John. For example, GP shares with Matthew the earthquake at the time of the crucifixion and Jesus' burial in a tomb belonging to Joseph. Both GP and Luke refer to the beating of chests and the lamentation of the Jewish people at the crucifixion. John parallels GP in the location of Jesus' tomb in a garden and in the description of the disciples in hiding after the crucifixion. These parallels are best explained as reflecting knowledge of the NT gospels, although their stories have been reworked in GP. As I mentioned in my discussion of the Passion Narrative in Chapter Two, this is the same practice that is reflected in the Qumran *Temple Scroll*'s handling of the Pentateuch.

Conversely, GP contains details without known parallels, including the request for Jesus' body coming *before* the crucifixion, separate references to the disappearance and reappearance of the sun, and the Jewish reactions of fear to some of the events accompanying the crucifixion. These differences are best accounted for by positing a free use of sources on the part of the Petrine evangelist, a use that is indicative not so much of simple "dependence" as of a free rewriting of earlier traditions in order to serve a particular purpose.

In the second section of this chapter I suggested that an important purpose in the reworking of earlier gospel traditions was the desire to include
signs of judgment against the Jews for their role in Jesus' death. I proposed
four such signs: darkness, torn veil, earthquake, and the fall of Jerusalem.
In the course of expounding on this claim I noted some specific reasons
that they should be taken in the manner suggested.

I then reviewed early Christian parallels to my proposed understanding
of the phenomena accompanying the crucifixion and showed that Melito's
Homily on Pascha provides the strongest affinities with GP. In order to
demonstrate further the plausibility of my suggestion, I surveyed several
other early Christian texts that interpreted the four symbols in the way
suggested for GP. Included among these were Justin Martyr's *Dialogue
with Trypho*, the *Gospel of Bartholomew*, the Pseudo-Clementine *Recognitions*, *Testament of Levi*, and excerpts from Tertullian.

I concluded that the apologetic interest to show God on the side of
Christians over against Jews was the key factor in the rewriting of earlier
gospels. The desire to have divine wrath come upon the Jews led to the
portrayal of these four phenomena as symbols of God's disfavor toward
them for their role in the death of Jesus. The culmination of this judgment
came in the events of 70 C.E., thus vindicating the Christian claim in the
eyes of our author.

Chapter 4

Rewritten Guard Story: GP 8:29–9:34

This chapter concerns the first portion of the guard account, which appears in GP 8:29–9:34. I will argue that the author of this gospel has used the Matthean guard story as the primary source for his own retelling. First, I will address the general similarities between GP and Matthew in the opening synoptic analysis. In the second portion of the chapter, I will discuss seven specific ways in which GP differs from Matthew and claim that these alterations function to assure the reader that the tomb was secure, thereby making less likely the possibility that the disciples could have stolen the body of Jesus. Following this, a review of early Christian references to the guard at the tomb will be provided. The chapter concludes with a discussion of the role that criticisms of the Christian resurrection claim have played in the tradition history of GP's guard story.

4.1 Synoptic Analysis of GP 8:29–9:34

GP 8:29–9:34	Matt 27	Mark 15	Luke	John
[8:29]ἐφοβήθησαν οἱ πρεσβύτεροι καὶ ἦλθον πρὸς Πειλᾶτον δεόμενοι αὐτοῦ καὶ λέγοντες·	[62]Τῇ δὲ ἐπαύριον, ἥτις ἐστὶν μετὰ τὴν παρασκευήν, συνήχθησαν οἱ ἀρχιερεῖς καὶ οἱ Φαρισαῖοι πρὸς Πιλᾶτον [63]λέγοντες, Κύριε, ἐμνήσθημεν ὅτι ἐκεῖνος ὁ πλάνος εἶπεν ἔτι ζῶν, Μετὰ τρεῖς ἡμέρας ἐγείρομαι.			
[30]παράδος ἡμῖν στρατιώτας	[64]κέλευσον οὖν ἀσφαλισθῆναι τὸν τάφον ἕως			

GP 8:29–9:34	Matt 27	Mark 15	Luke	John
ἵνα φυλάξω[μεν] τὸ μνῆμα αὐτοῦ ἐπὶ τρεῖς ἡμέρας, μήποτε ἐλθόντες οἱ μαθηταὶ αὐτοῦ κλέψωσιν αὐτὸν καὶ ὑπολάβῃ ὁ λαὸς ὅτι ἐκ νεκρῶν ἀνέστη, καὶ ποιήσωσιν ἡμῖν κακά.	τῆς τρίτης ἡμέρας, μήποτε ἐλθόντες οἱ μαθηταὶ αὐτοῦ κλέψωσιν αὐτὸν καὶ εἴπωσιν τῷ λαῷ, Ἠγέρθη ἀπὸ τῶν νεκρῶν, καὶ ἔσται ἡ ἐσχάτη πλάνη χείρων τῆς πρώτης.			
³¹ὁ δὲ Πειλᾶτος παραδέδωκεν αὐτοῖς Πετρώνιον τὸν κεντυρίωνα μετὰ στρατιωτῶν φυλάσσειν τὸν τάφον. καὶ σὺν αὐτοῖς ἦλθον πρεσβύτεροι καὶ γραμματεῖς ἐπὶ τὸ μνῆμα.	⁶⁵ἔφη αὐτοῖς ὁ Πιλᾶτος, Ἔχετε κουστωδίαν· ὑπάγετε ἀσφαλίσασθε ὡς οἴδατε.			
³²καὶ κυλίσαντες λίθον μέγαν μετὰ τοῦ κεντυρίωνος καὶ τῶν στρατιωτῶν ὁμοῦ πάντες οἱ ὄντες ἐκεῖ ἔθηκαν ἐπὶ τῇ θύρᾳ τοῦ μνήματος.	⁶⁰ᵇκαὶ [Ἰωσήφ] προσκυλίσας λίθον μέγαν τῇ θύρᾳ τοῦ μνημείου ἀπῆλθεν.	⁴⁶ᵇκαὶ [Ἰωσήφ] προσεκύλισεν λίθον ἐπὶ τὴν θύραν τοῦ μνημείου.		
³³καὶ ἐπέχρισαν ἑπτὰ σφραγῖδας καὶ	⁶⁶οἱ δὲ πορευθέντες ἠσφαλίσαντο τὸν τάφον			

GP 8:29–9:34	Matt 27	Mark 15	Luke	John
σκηνὴν ἐκεῖ πήξαντες ἐφύλαξαν. ⁹·³⁴πρωΐας δὲ ἐπιφώσκοντος τοῦ σαββάτου ἦλθεν ὄχλος ἀπὸ Ἰερουσαλὴμ καὶ τῆς περιχώρου ἵνα ἴδωσι τὸ μνημεῖον ἐσφραγισμένον	σφραγίσαντες τὸν λίθον μετὰ τῆς κουστωδίας.			

At the conclusion of the previous section of GP, some of the Jewish people come to acknowledge Jesus as righteous, and this happens largely as a result of the signs they have witnessed at the crucifixion. In response to this, the Jewish leaders become afraid and approach Pilate to ask him for a contingent of soldiers to guard the tomb of Jesus (GP 8:29–30). Only one of the NT gospels – Matthew – includes an account of soldiers at the tomb (Matt 27:62–66). Because of this, our synoptic analysis will focus almost exclusively on a comparison of GP and Matthew.[1] To be more specific, I will be concerned in the present chapter primarily with the pre-resurrection portion of the guard episode. Matthew's full account of the guard is scattered in Matt 27:62–66; 28:4, 11–15, and in the extra-canonical gospel it appears consecutively in GP 8:29–11:49. The pre-resurrection sections include Matt 27:62–66 and GP 8:29–9:34. The fact that the guard episode in GP is one consecutive account has been used by some to argue that it

---

[1] Among treatments of the Matthean guard story, Brown's is one of the most thorough (*Death of the Messiah*, 2:1284–1313). Regarding the sources of Matthew, Brown concludes that a "consecutive story about the guard at the sepulcher came to Matt from the same collection of popular tradition that he tapped for previous additions he made to Mark's PN" (2:1287). In his estimation, GP is a later development than Matthew in which "the author of *GPet* drew not only on Matt but on an independent form of the guard-at-the-sepulcher story" to form his own account (ibid.). As I have been contending in this study, and as I will do for the guard stories, it may not be necessary to follow Brown in positing the Petrine evangelist's knowledge of any other account besides that of Matthew as his source here.

preserves a more original form than Matthew, or that the Petrine evangelist must have used another source in addition to Matthew.[2]

The burial in GP takes place a few verses before the opening scene of the guard episode (GP 6:23–24; 8:29–9:34), a characteristic that differs from Matthew's uninterrupted narrative which runs directly from the burial (Matt 27:57–61) to the story about the guard (Matt 27:62–66). As I mentioned in the previous chapter, GP 7:25–8:28 allows for a description of the various responses and actions of the different parties in the aftermath of the crucifixion and burial. This interlude is not of present concern, as our focus will be on the burial and, to a greater extent, the guarding of the tomb. Both GP and Matthew seem to use the terms μνημεῖον and τάφος interchangeably to refer to the burial site.[3] There is thus no significance to

---

[2] The form-critical arguments that the consecutive nature of GP's guard story is indicative of it being more primitive than Matthew's version can be found in Johnson, "Empty Tomb Tradition"; Koester, "Apocryphal and Canonical Gospels," 126–30; idem, *Ancient Christian Gospels*, 231–40.

Though he does not judge GP to be more primitive than Matthew, Brown uses as one of his primary arguments the claim that the consecutive nature of GP's guard story is unexplainable if his only source is Matthew's already broken up account (cf. *Death of the Messiah*, 2:1306–9). This assumes that GP's author must have had a *form* of the story after which he modeled his own, a claim that I find unpersuasive. It also ignores the fact that in other instances GP does not follow the same form as its predecessors, as Brown himself seems to acknowledge. For example, Joseph's request for the body of Jesus is moved much earlier in GP, to a point before the crucifixion (GP 2:3–5). Therefore the consecutive scenes with Joseph that are found in the NT gospels (Matt 27:57–61; Mark 15:42–47; Luke 23:50–56; John 19:38–42) are divided into two separate episodes in GP (2:3–5; 6:23–24). Yet Brown never posits a noncanonical source to explain GP in the case of Joseph (cf. ibid., 2:1232–33). So it appears unnecessary to do so in the case of the guard story. If the author of GP could divide what was unified in the accounts of Joseph, then is it not plausible to suggest that he could have unified what was divided in the Matthean guard scenes?

Susan E. Schaeffer, Brown's student, poses a question similar to my own when she asks, "In the case of the guard story, is it not possible that the elements of the legend in Matthew may have been reshaped in the retelling to become a fully-formed and unified epiphany story in the *GosPet* – precisely because of the storyteller's interest in the miraculous per se?" (Schaeffer, "The Guard at the Tomb [Gos. Pet. 8:28–11:49 and Matt 27:62–66; 28:2–4, 11–16]: A Case of Intertextuality?" *SBL Seminar Papers, 1991* [ed. E. H. Lovering; SBLSP 30; Atlanta: Scholars Press, 1991], 502). Where Schaeffer suggests interest in the miraculous as an influence on GP's author and the form of his guard story, I will claim apologetic interests are at work. The two factors are not necessarily mutually exclusive, as Schaeffer herself acknowledges in subsequent comments. As a further counterexample to the form-critical argument and Brown's claim, Schaeffer notes the nearly perfect chiastic form of Matt 27:26–31 where the earlier gospel, Mark 15:15–19, is less formally structured ("Guard at the Tomb," 501–2).

[3] μνημεῖον is used in Matt 27:60; 28:8; GP 9:34; 12:51, 53. τάφος appears in Matt 27:61, 64, 66; 28:1; GP 6:24; 8:31; 9:36, 37; 10:39; 11:45; 13:55 (2X). GP also includes the synonymous μνῆμα at several points: GP 8:30, 31, 32; 11:44; 12:50, 52.

be found in the differences in terminology at any given point in their stories.

In Matthew it is the "chief priests and the Pharisees" who go to Pilate with their request for a guard, while in GP it is "elders" who do so (Matt 27:62; GP 8:29).[4] The Jewish leaders in Matthew are not said to be afraid as they are in GP, but they are at least concerned enough to approach Pilate for a favor. Both stories give the same rationale for the petition to post the guard: to prevent the disciples from stealing the body and claiming that Jesus had risen from the dead (Matt 27:63–64; GP 8:30).[5]

A comparison of the two requests for a guard will allow for a closer examination of the similarities and differences:

"Sir, we remember what that impostor said while he was still alive, 'After three days I will rise again.' Therefore command the tomb to be made secure until the third day; otherwise his disciples may go and steal him away, and tell the people, 'He has been raised from the dead,' and the last deception would be worse than the first." (Matt 27:63–64)

"Give us soldiers, so that we may have his sepulcher guarded for three days, lest his disciples come and steal him away, and the people believe that he has risen from the dead, and they do us evil." (GP 8:30)

In the First Gospel, the Jewish leaders echo the prediction of Jesus that he would rise after three days. This is presumably an allusion to the scene in Matt 12:38–42, where Jesus, in an encounter with the scribes and Pharisees, says that the Son of Man will be in the heart of the earth for three days and three nights (Matt 12:40). The request in Matt 27:63–64 indicates that the scribes and Pharisees have recalled this prediction, and they are now taking measures to prevent its fulfillment. Their concern is that the followers of Jesus will steal the body and then tell "the people" (λαός) that

---

[4] Crossan (*Cross That Spoke*, 270) supposes that Matthew has added the Pharisees to his scene, since they are the primary enemies of Jesus in his gospel. In his estimation, GP 8:28, which includes "the scribes and Pharisees and elders," is part of the redactional stratum of the gospel (i.e., it was added to the original version), while GP 8:29, which mentions only elders, is original. Koester (*Ancient Christian Gospels*, 235) also concludes that "the best solution is to assume that the original story mentioned only the elders." However, Koester's summary table is misleading in giving the impression that in GP the scribes, Pharisees, and elders all go to Pilate with the request (ibid., 234–35). While the three groups are mentioned in GP 8:28 as convening in response to the reaction of the Jewish people, GP 8:29 specifies only "the elders" as the ones who are afraid and beseech the Roman governor.

[5] GP 8:30 uses the active form of ἀνίστημι for its resurrection language (cf. GP 13:56), while Matt 27:64 has a passive form of ἐγείρω (cf. Matt 11:5; 14:2; 17:23; 20:19; 27:52, 63; 28:6, 7). GP does not include any uses of ἐγείρω, and Matthew never employs ἀνίστημι in contexts involving resurrection. What we likely have are differing authorial preferences for resurrection terminology.

he has been raised from the dead. In GP, there is no resurrection prediction, but the concern is still that the disciples will steal the body, which
would lead "the people" (λαός) to think that Jesus had risen. We can see
that "the people" and their response to the Christian resurrection claim are
of central import in both gospels.

The English translations of Matt 27:64 and GP 8:30 quoted above blur
the fact that we have here the longest verbatim agreement between GP and
any known gospel. The eight-word Greek phrase μήποτε ἐλθόντες οἱ
μαθηταὶ αὐτοῦ κλέψωσιν αὐτὸν καί appears in both gospels. An agreement of this length poses some difficulty to those who reject any literary
relationship between the two gospels.[6] If, however, GP's author has rewritten earlier stories and is well acquainted with them, we should not be
surprised to find an instance such as this where there is identical wording.

The Jewish leaders ask Pilate to give them στρατιῶται (GP 8:30). That
the soldiers are Roman is clear from GP 8:31, as here Pilate grants the task
to Petronius the κεντυρίων and his στρατιῶται.[7] In contrast, the scene in
Matthew is ambiguous as to whether the soldiers are Roman or Jewish.[8]
When the Jews ask Pilate to guard the tomb, the procurator responds, ἔχετε
κουστωδία (Matt 27:65).[9] Pilate's response has been understood in vari-

---

[6] Brown seeks to downplay this verbal agreement in saying, "While I think that the
author of *GPet* was familiar with Matthean phrasing, too much should not be deduced
about literary dependence from this clause" (*Death of the Messiah* 2:1292 n. 16). Not
surprisingly, Vaganay and Crossan provide exactly the opposite explanation from one
another on this point. Vaganay (*Évangile de Pierre*, 282) argues that GP's author has
copied Matthew, while Crossan (*Cross That Spoke*, 271) claims that Matthew has copied
GP.

[7] The Greek κεντυρίων is a Latin loanword (*centurio*) and is synonymous with
ἑκατοντάρχης/ος. See BDAG, s.v. "ἑκατοντάρχης/ος," 298–99; ibid., s.v.
"κεντυρίων," 540. The terms refer to a Roman officer in command of approximately 100
soldiers. Swete (*Akhmîm Fragment*, 15) notes that Petronius was a common name of the
period. But I am not convinced of his proposal that its appearance here "may have been
suggested by the similarity in sound of Πετρώνιος and Πέτρος" (ibid.). Vaganay
(*Évangile de Pierre*, 284) finds in the name the Christianization of the centurion: "it
signifies 'disciple of Peter.'" This, too, is questionable. Bruce M. Metzger ("Names for
the Nameless in the New Testament: A Study in the Growth of Christian Tradition," in
Kyriakon: Festschrift Johannes Quasten [ed. Patrick Granfield and Josef A. Jungmann; 2
vols.; Münster: Aschendorff, 1970], 1:79–99) demonstrates that many early Christians, at
least from the second century onward, frequently assigned names to characters who were
left unnamed in the NT gospels, and he includes GP's centurion as an example of this
tendency.

[8] Matthew writes, at a later point in his own account, that the στρατιῶται – a term
used frequently throughout GP – are bribed by the Jewish leaders (Matt 28:12).

[9] All three NT uses of κουστωδία appear in Matthew's guard story (Matt 27:65–66;
28:11). This term, like κεντυρίων, is a Latin loanword (*custodia*). Brown (*Death of the
Messiah*, 2:1295) uses the appearance of κουστωδία as an argument for viewing the

ous ways. Is he, in effect, saying that the Jews themselves already have a Jewish κουστωδία at their disposal and that they have his permission to employ them in securing the burial site? Or does Matthew's account indicate that Pilate is granting their request by giving them Roman guards for the task?[10] Any lack of clarity in Matthew is gone in GP's story. While the Roman soldiers are prominent throughout Matthew's earlier account of the crucifixion (Matt 27:27–37), their appearance in GP comes for the very first time here in the protection of the tomb. In both GP and Matthew the Jewish leaders accompany the guard to the tomb (Matt 27:66; GP 8:31).

Matthew and GP differ in their accounts of the stone being rolled in front of the tomb. Each gives the same description of the stone: λίθος μέγας (Matt 27:60; GP 8:32). The Petrine version has the centurion and his soldiers, along with the Jewish elders and scribes, arrive at the sepulcher with the stone not yet placed before the entrance. This is implied by the fact that it is they who actually roll the stone. In contrast, the stone in Matthew has already been set before the tomb by Joseph of Arimathea at the time he performed the burial (Matt 27:60–61).

In GP 8:33 the Roman and Jewish authorities, upon rolling the stone to block access to the burial place, seal it by affixing seven σφραγῖδες. This securing of the tomb is mentioned again in GP 9:34, when a crowd comes the next morning in order to see "the sealed sepulcher" (τὸ μνημεῖον ἐσφραγισμένον). The Matthean story also includes a sealing of the tomb, and this is expressed with the verb σφραγίζω (Matt 27:66). Unlike GP, no crowd comes to the burial location in the First Gospel.

In this brief synoptic analysis we have looked at some of the similarities between the guard stories in Matthew and GP. Their general plots bear a strong resemblance to one another. Each has Jewish individuals approach Pilate with a request that the tomb of Jesus be protected so that his disci-

---

Matthean guard as Roman rather than Jewish, since such a Latinism comports best with this understanding.

[10] The key grammatical question is whether ἔχετε should be taken as imperative or indicative. In the former instance, a Roman guard would be implied ("Take a guard!"); in the latter, a Jewish referent would be intended ("You [already] have a guard"). Arguments in favor of viewing this as a Roman guard appear in Crossan, *Cross That Spoke*, 271–72; William D. Davies and Dale C. Allison, Jr., *A Critical and Exegetical Commentary on the Gospel according to Saint Matthew* (2 vols.; ICC; Edinburgh: T&T Clark, 1988–1991), 2:655; Brown, *Death of the Messiah*, 2:1294–96; Gundry, *Matthew*, 584; Donald A. Hagner, *Matthew 14–28* (Word Biblical Commentary 33B; Nashville: Thomas Nelson, 1995), 863. Examples of ἔχω being used in the imperatival sense of "take" or "request granted" can be found in Kevin Smyth, "The Guard at the Tomb," *HeyJ* 2 (1961): 157–59. Proponents of the view that a Jewish guard is intended include William L. Craig, "The Guard at the Tomb" *NTS* 30 (1984): 273–81. Similarly, Koester (*Ancient Christian Gospels*, 235) claims that "it is clearly a Jewish guard" that is bribed in Matt 28:11–15.

ples are not able to steal the body. A guard is granted, and together the soldiers and the Jewish authorities make the tomb secure. Despite this general agreement between the two stories, however, there are also key differences that may hold potential significance. It is to these that we now turn.

4.2 GP 8:29–9:34: A More Secure Tomb

Bultmann identifies the guard story in Matthew as an "apologetic legend" whose primary purpose is to enhance the evidence for the resurrection of Jesus.[11] In what follows I will propose that the parallel account in GP moves further in the direction proposed by Bultmann. The Petrine version provides an even stronger apologetic proof for the security of the tomb than what we find in the First Gospel. Though the alterations to Matthew by GP's author are in most instances minor, together they serve to enhance the impression of the preservation of the tomb's integrity and to reduce the possibility that the disciples could steal the body, which is the primary motive behind the need for protective measures (GP 8:30). To this end, I will examine seven features of GP that, when compared with Matthew, are indicative of this: the chronology of the guard's deployment, the timing of the placement of the stone, the identity of those who move the stone, the sealing of the tomb, an alibi for the disciples, the diligence of those guarding the tomb, and the visit of a crowd from Jerusalem. The cumulative effect of these changes to Matthew's earlier account is significant, as they reveal the apologetic motives of the author.

4.2.1 The Chronology of the Guard's Deployment

The first detail to notice is the timing of the various events related to the securing of the tomb. In Matthew we find the following chronology: 1) Jesus is buried on Friday evening (Matt 27:57–61); 2) the chief priests and the Pharisees go to Pilate "the next day, that is, after the day of Preparation" to request the placement of the guard (Matt 27:62); 3) the guards are dispatched to the site sometime on Saturday (Matt 27:65–66). The terminology used in Matt 27:57 regarding the time of burial on Friday is ὀψίας γενομένης, and it is probable that Matthew has taken this time reference from Mark 15:42. The adjective ὄψιος most often functions as a substantive in early Christian literature, as it does here, in which cases it typically

---

[11] Bultmann, *History of the Synoptic Tradition*, 281–82. For Bultmann, "apologetic legend" is primarily a form-critical classification, although he also concludes against the historicity of this legend.

signifies the period between late afternoon and the onset of darkness.[12] Matthew, then, is probably envisioning a burial that occurs in the early evening hours (i.e., before sunset), so as not to violate the Sabbath.

The First Evangelist is explicit in stating that the chief priests and Pharisees do not visit Pilate to request a guard until "the next day" (ἐπαύριον) (Matt 27:62). Matthew does not specify when on Saturday the meeting with Pilate takes place, but even if he intends it to be very early in the day, the tomb has been left unguarded from Friday evening until Saturday morning. The Matthean account implies that those sent to secure the grave arrive at a tomb that has been unattended for no less than twelve hours, most of which were during darkness when theft is most likely to have taken place.

The Petrine author has changed the timing of the events in a way that tightens this chronological gap in Matthew, the time when the tomb was left unprotected.[13] Although GP occasionally includes unclear time indicators, I will contend that its chronology is to be understood as follows: 1) Jesus is buried on Friday afternoon (GP 6:21–24); 2) the elders go to Pilate on Friday afternoon/evening asking for soldiers (GP 8:29–30); 3) the soldiers are immediately sent to the burial place on Friday afternoon/evening (GP 8:31).[14] GP specifies that Jesus died no later than the ninth hour (i.e., Friday afternoon). This is deduced from noticing that Jesus dies in GP 5:19 while it is yet dark, before the sun reappears in GP 6:22 at the ninth hour. After receiving the body from the Jews, Joseph buries Jesus in the mid- or late afternoon. The impression left by GP 6:21–24 is that the burial takes place very soon after Jesus' removal from the cross, that is, during the mid-afternoon hours.

Concerning my second claim regarding GP's timeline (i.e., the request for the guard occurring on Friday), we need to remember that GP 7:26–27 is an interlude that breaks up the narrative chronology. These two verses

---

[12] BDAG, s.v. "ὄψιος," 746.

[13] Schaeffer offers a line of argument similar to my own on the significance of GP's chronology, both in her dissertation ("Gospel of Peter," 226–28) and essay ("Guard at the Tomb," 505–6).

[14] Brown claims that the chronological variation between Matthew and GP is likely due to there being "no precise time indication" in the original guard story known to both authors (*Death of the Messiah*, 2:1288–89). While this is possible, it cannot be demonstrated. In addition, according to Brown's own theory, GP's author knows Matthew's report, which means that the Petrine evangelist is familiar with the chronology (Brown's "precise time indication") of at least one earlier guard story. When looking at the cumulative differences between the guard stories in Matthew and GP, as I will present them here, I find more compelling the suggestion that the Petrine evangelist has consciously chosen to alter the timing of the events in order to make less credible the claim that the disciples stole the body. In other words, it is not a mere coincidence that GP's chronology differs from Matthew's in the way that it does.

serve to describe the actions of the disciples during the period presumably from the arrest of Jesus until the day after the crucifixion, and as such, we should not take the reference to the Sabbath (Saturday) in GP 7:27 as a time indicator that is relevant to the actions of the Jews in GP 7:25 and 8:28–30. That GP 8:28 picks up the narrative from 7:25 is made clear by the reason given for the meeting of the scribes, Pharisees, and elders: they had heard the people murmuring and lamenting over Jesus' death and the signs which accompanied it (GP 8:28). This is certainly referring back to the mourning that took place in GP 7:25.

Granted this alone, we would be led to view the petition for a guard as taking place on Friday. However, there are two further and clearer indicators that GP is describing a Friday meeting. When the Jewish group makes its request to Pilate in GP 8:30, they ask for the soldiers "so that we may have his sepulcher guarded *for three days*" (ἐπὶ τρεῖς ἡμέρας). In GP, as in Matthew and the other NT gospels, the resurrection takes place on Sunday. This is found in GP in the expression ἡ κυριακή, which, by the second century, had become a common term for Sunday.[15] So by referring to the need to have a guard for "three days," the request from the Jews is best understood as occurring on Friday, in which case the three days would entail Friday, Saturday, and Sunday. By way of comparison, the Jews in Matthew also know that the resurrection is expected on Sunday and, in making their request, they specify that the guard be kept until the third day: "Therefore command the tomb to be made secure *until the third day*" (ἕως τῆς τρίτης ἡμέρας) (Matt 27:64). The third day here would, of course, be measured from the day of death, since that is the context of the prediction that the Jewish leaders are recalling.

Finally, GP 9:34 states that a crowd from Jerusalem comes to the tomb as the Sabbath morning dawns. This takes place after the soldiers have come to the tomb, sealed it, and pitched a tent in order to keep watch. The only way to understand this chronological marker is to view the posting of the guard as occurring sometime *before* Saturday.

In light of these three indicators, it appears certain that in GP Pilate dispatches the soldiers to accompany the Jewish leaders to the sepulcher immediately after a Friday meeting. Therefore, the tomb is guarded very soon after the burial. We can see that the substantial time gap that was present between the burial and the posting of the guard in Matthew has

---

[15] On two occasions, GP marks the day of the resurrection as ἡ κυριακή (GP 9:35; 12:50). This use of the term appears in Rev 1:10 and becomes more frequent from the second century onward (e.g., *Did.* 14:1; Ign. *Magn.* 9:1). On this development in the early Christian movement, see Bauckham, "The Lord's Day," in *From Sabbath to Lord's Day: A Biblical, Historical, and Theological Investigation* (ed. D. A. Carson; Grand Rapids: Zondervan, 1982), 197–220.

been drastically reduced, if not all but eliminated, in GP. By rewriting the chronology of this episode, the author of GP has rendered it far less likely that any theft of Jesus' corpse could have taken place.[16]

4.2.2 The Timing of the Placement of the Stone (GP 8:32)

Closely related to the chronology of the guard is the timing of the placement of the stone at the tomb. The final step in ancient burial in a cave or tomb was to place an object before its entrance in order to keep out scavenging birds or animals, or to make tampering with the contents of the tomb more difficult. In his detailed study of burial practices in ancient Palestine, Byron R. McCane notes that in most instances the rocks that covered entrances to Jewish tombs were not round but rather square or rectangular.[17] Round stones, which could be rolled, were rare and appear to have been used almost exclusively at the burial sites of the wealthy.[18] All of the NT gospels state that a rock was at the entrance of Jesus' tomb (Matt 27:60; Mark 15:46; Luke 24:2; John 20:1), and three of these describe the rock rolling either before or after the resurrection (Matt 27:60; Mark 15:46; Luke 24:2). Similarly, the Petrine gospel includes a rock that rolls (GP 8:32; 9:37).

In two of the canonical stories – Matthew and Mark – the placement of the stone at burial is described as the final step in the burial process (Matt 27:60; Mark 15:46). This occurs in these two stories on Friday evening. GP, however, has a different timeframe. When Joseph performs the burial

---

[16] Brown, being unconvinced by this sort of argument, "doubt[s] that better apologetics caused the author [of GP] to move the sealing story up to Friday afternoon. That dating is related to another motive for sealing the tomb, namely, a reaction to what the people were saying in response to Jesus' death that had just taken place (8:28–29)" (*Death of the Messiah*, 2:1309 n. 53). But this is not entirely persuasive, since the reaction of the people has nothing to do with resurrection, tomb sealing, or grave robbery. Rather, it comes from their recognition of the divine judgment that has come upon them. The motive for the guard and tomb sealing is the same in GP as it is in Matthew: to prevent the disciples from stealing the body (GP 8:30; Matt 27:64). I also would not wish to use Brown's term "better apologetics" to describe what is happening in GP's guard story. Both Matthew and the Petrine evangelist are driven to a certain degree by apologetics, but each is telling his own tale with an awareness of antecedent stories. As Matthew likely formed his account with knowledge of earlier versions, GP's author did likewise. The very fact that Matthew is motivated by a desire to refute the allegation that the disciples stole the body, but yet leaves a large time gap between burial and guarding, seems to indicate this. As Hagner (*Matthew 14–28*, 863) writes, "If Matthew created this story *ex nihilo*, … it is more likely that he would have had the guard posted immediately after the interment."

[17] McCane, *Roll Back the Stone: Death and Burial in the World of Jesus* (Harrisburg, Pa.: Trinity Press International, 2003), 33.

[18] Ibid.

in GP 6:23–24, nothing is stated about a rock at the tomb. The placing of the stone does not occur until the Roman soldiers and Jewish leaders arrive at the site a brief time later: "And having rolled a large stone, all who were there, together with the centurion and the soldiers, set it at the door of the sepulcher" (GP 8:32).[19] At first glance, this appears to make theft from the tomb more likely, as it is left open from the time of burial until the guards and Jewish leaders arrive to close it. As I will suggest in the next section, though, this may actually be a means by which the charge of theft by the disciples is made far less plausible.

4.2.3 The Identity of Those Who Move the Stone (GP 8:32)

All of the NT gospels and GP depict Joseph (of Arimathea) as the individual primarily responsible for the burial. In the four canonical stories, a person or persons sympathetic to Jesus sets a rock at the entrance to the tomb. In the two gospels that explicitly describe the placement of the stone, Joseph performs this act (Matt 27:60; Mark 15:46). The implication in the Third Gospel is that Joseph does so, but it is not stated outright (Luke 23:53; 24:2). Similarly, John implies that Joseph and Nicodemus move a rock to the tomb's entrance (John 19:41–42; 20:1). In contrast to all of the canonical accounts, where *one or two people* who are *sympathetic* to Jesus place the stone, GP finds a *large group of people* who are *unsympathetic*, if not hostile, towards Jesus in this role (GP 8:32). Why might this be?

Swete, Vaganay, and many later commentators have argued that this change in GP is to reflect the strength that would have been required to

---

[19] I have slightly altered the translation of Kraus and Nicklas (*Petrusevangelium*, 51), which is lacking grammatically: "And all who were there rolled a large stone together with the centurion and the soldiers, set it at the door of the sepulcher."

There is also a textual issue here. Behind the English "together with the centurion and the soldiers" lies the Greek κατὰ τοῦ κεντυρίωνος καὶ τῶν στρατιωτῶν in the Akhmîm manuscript. This would, of course, mean something like "*against* the centurion and the soldiers," which seems to make little sense contextually. Herbert W. Smyth (*Greek Grammar* [rev. ed.; Cambridge, Mass.: Harvard University Press, 1956], 380) summarizes the range of meanings for κατά with the genitive, the first being a local sense (e.g., "down from, down toward, under"), the second – though very rare – is a temporal sense (e.g., duration), and other senses connoting such things as "against" or "by." Swete (*Akhmîm Fragment*, 15) takes κατά as the intended word in GP, resulting in the translation "to exclude the Centurion and soldiers." He understands this to indicate that the Romans might be bribed to hand over Jesus' body to the disciples. Swete's explanation is not convincing. I find more compelling the suggestion of others, going back to Harnack, who have argued that κατά is a scribal error where we should read μετά, thus providing the more coherent meaning of "together with the centurion and the soldiers." See, for example, Vaganay, *Évangile de Pierre*, 285; Crossan, *Cross That Spoke*, 272–73.

move a λίθος μέγας (Matt 27:60; GP 8:32).[20] "How large a stone was it, if one man could move it?" might have been the question from skeptics hearing Matthew or the other canonical stories, which all depict Joseph (and perhaps Nicodemus) setting the rock at the burial entrance. To indicate the strength needed to place the stone at the tomb, GP 8:32 states that "all who were there, together with the centurion and the soldiers" rolled the large stone. In this scene – with Jewish leaders and Roman soldiers – we are probably to envision something close to the group of twenty individuals mentioned in the variant reading of Luke 23:53. This is a strong argument, and I think it has a good deal of merit when it comes to explaining one difference between GP and Matthew (and the other NT gospels). While it accounts for the increased number of people involved in moving the stone, thus emphasizing its great size, this explanation does not address the other significant difference between Matthew and GP: placement by friends vs. placement by enemies. I wish to suggest a possible reason for this.

In my judgment, thinking apologetically might assist us in this endeavor, since we need to bear in mind once again the motive behind the guard story in both Matthew and GP: to refute the claim that the disciples made off with the body. In Matthew, we have a tomb with a stone at its entrance that has been left unattended overnight, which would be for at least twelve hours. The guards arrive at the burial site the next day and seal it. Might a doubter not wonder if the guard ever moved the stone to check that the body was still inside, in which case they would have been protecting a tomb whose body had already been stolen?[21] This may sound trite, but at

---

[20] Swete, *Akhmîm Fragment*, 15; Vaganay, *Évangile de Pierre*, 285. In support of this understanding of GP, they note a variant reading of Luke 23:53 in the fifth–century manuscript Codex Bezae Cantabrigiensis: "And after he (Jesus) had been placed [there], he (Joseph of Arimathea) set at the tomb a stone that twenty men could hardly roll" (καὶ θέντος αὐτοῦ ἐπέθηκεν τῷ μνημείῳ λίθον ὃν μόγις εἴκοσι ἐκύλιον). This reading also appears in other manuscripts and in some Coptic and Sahidic versions. The hyperbole in these readings of Luke 23:53 is obvious, and it is certainly possible that such apologetic also lies behind GP's account.

[21] Brown (*Death of the Messiah*, 2:1309 n. 53) finds this reading of Matthew unconvincing: "If the authorities were smart enough to remember and understand a statement of Jesus about resurrection made long ago, they were scarcely so naive as to guard an empty tomb." What Brown says is certainly true if we are speaking of sympathetic readers or hearers of Matthew, but for those not favorable to the Christian movement any holes in the story could be exploited. Brown seems to reveal as much in his next comment, "We are left to assume that the Jewish authorities would have taken the elementary caution to have the sepulcher checked to see that the body was still there before they sealed it on Saturday" (ibid.). An author concerned to refute the claim that the disciples stole the body, and who is rewriting earlier sources, as Brown himself contends for GP, may not be prone to "assuming" a generous reading of Matthew like the one Brown proposes. Writers with apologetic motives respond to objections – real, perceived, or potential – in formulating their responses. If an objection was conceived, perhaps similar

the level of story those who would wish to make it absolutely certain that Jesus' body was not stolen may have entertained such real or potential objections. It is easier for the soldiers to check whether a body is still in the tomb if there is not a λίθος μέγας already covering its entrance when they arrive on the scene.

More significantly, Joseph of Arimathea, who is a *disciple* of Jesus in both Matt 27:57 and GP 6:23, is not the person to carry out one of the most important steps in securing the tomb if an author is attempting to refute the claim of theft *by the disciples!* The stone is an important measure in ensuring that grave robbery does not occur. Therefore, it makes little apologetic sense to have one of the prime persons under suspicion cast in the role of security administrator. To do so is counter to the entire purpose of the guard episode. It is here, I would suggest, that we may find a more specific reason for the altered identity of the stone movers in GP. Because the stone was part of the apologetic to counter the idea that Jesus' friends stole his corpse, and because GP is retelling the guard story, it improves upon Matthew in this area by having enemies of Jesus carry out the act of ensuring the security of the grave site. This understanding provides a fuller reading of GP's version than does the suggestion of Swete and Vaganay alone. For example, if the only concern of GP is to have a greater number of people perform the stone placement in order to signify the size of the boulder, this could have easily been accomplished by introducing other characters allied with Joseph. But to choose enemies of Jesus for this task, when this specification is not found in any earlier gospel, seems to call for an explanation. The one I have suggested fits well.[22]

4.2.4 Sealing the Tomb (GP 8:33)

The sealing of the stone at the tomb, like the stone itself, is one of the means of preventing theft. Among the NT gospels, only Matthew mentions it: οἱ δὲ πορευθέντες ἠσφαλίσαντο τὸν τάφον σφραγίσαντες τὸν λίθον μετὰ τῆς κουστωδίας (Matt 27:66). A question has sometimes been raised about the proper rendering of this verse.[23] It is grammatically

---

to the one I mentioned about the guard arriving at a tomb with the stone already in place, then an author retelling the story may simply change this detail to avoid a potential problem.

[22] One of the central suppositions of Crossan's reconstruction is that the earliest version of GP (the Cross Gospel) "seems to take it so absolutely for granted that Jesus' burial was under the total control of those who had crucified him that it was not necessary to state that fact explicitly or describe it exactly" (*Cross That Spoke*, 237). Later gospel writers (i.e., NT evangelists), according to Crossan, change burial by enemies to burial by friends. This is nearly the reverse of what I have been arguing.

[23] See the discussion in Hagner, *Matthew 14–28*, 863.

possible to translate it so that it carries a metaphorical meaning: "And they went and made the tomb secure by sealing the stone with a guard."[24] In this view, then, the guard functions symbolically as a seal would, protecting the tomb from intruders. There is no actual seal placed on the stone. But this rendering is not generally favored.

Most English translations instead translate σφραγίσαντες τὸν λίθον to indicate a literal sealing of the tomb. In this understanding Matthew is describing a process whereby wax is placed on the stone in such a way that any movement of the rock would result in the wax breaking, thus indicating a breach.[25] If the stone and the guard are the first two lines of defense, the seal is the third means of ensuring the integrity of the burial site. This is the case in Matthew and, as we will see, it is also true of GP. But in what way does the author of GP retell the sealing incident?

We notice two references to the seal in GP. The first is when the Roman soldiers and Jewish leaders affix seven seals (ἑπτὰ σφραγῖδες) to the tomb (GP 8:33). Some have found in this an allusion to various OT texts. Zechariah 3:9 is often included among these: "For on the stone that I have set before Joshua, on a single stone with seven facets, I will engrave its inscription, says the LORD of hosts, and I will remove the guilt of this land in a single day."[26] Vaganay, on the other hand, dismisses this OT background as unwarranted.[27] Instead, he suggests that they symbolize "the perfect sealing of the tomb that God alone can open."[28] This is perhaps similar to the scene in Rev 5, in which a scroll is sealed with seven seals and "no one in heaven or on earth or under the earth was able to open the scroll" except for the lamb who had been slain (Rev 5:1–10). I find Vaganay's suggestion persuasive, and I would like to supplement it with some further thoughts. But in order to do that, some comments about GP's second reference to the seal are necessary.

On the morning after the guard is posted, a crowd from Jerusalem comes to the site in order "that they might see the sealed sepulcher" (ἵνα ἴδωσι τὸ μνημεῖον ἐσφραγισμένον) (GP 9:34). The circumstantial participial phrase τὸ μνημεῖον ἐσφραγισμένον might more literally be rendered "the tomb in-its-having-been-sealed-state," which emphasizes its

---

[24] This is listed as a possible understanding of Matt 27:66 in BDAG, s.v. σφραγίζω, 637. The verb conveys a similar metaphorical sense in John 3:33.

[25] Brown, *Death of the Messiah*, 2:1296. Hagner (*Matthew 14–28*, 863) mentions Dan 6:17 as reflecting this same practice: "A stone was brought and laid on the mouth of the den, and the king sealed it with his own signet and with the signet of his lords, so that nothing might be changed concerning Daniel" (Dan 6:17).

[26] Swete (*Akhmîm Fragment*, 15–16) surmises that this verse may have been in view. Mara (*Évangile de Pierre*, 169–70) claims that GP echoes Dan 6:17.

[27] Vaganay, *Évangile de Pierre*, 286.

[28] Ibid.

sealed nature. By including the ἵνα clause, the author makes apparent his concern for the security of the tomb. It is sealed by the guard on Friday and is still intact on Saturday. These twin references to the seal indicate a heightened emphasis on this aspect of the burial. Where Matthew makes only a general, and possibly even only metaphorical, reference using the verb σφραγίζω, GP removes any ambiguity by referring to the affixing of seven seals. And where Matthew has only a single reference, GP includes two statements about the seal, one of which is quite specific. In my estimation, the Petrine author has rewritten this aspect of Matthew's earlier guard story in order to highlight further this issue.

4.2.5 An Alibi for the Disciples (GP 7:26–27)

Commentators have offered a range of explanations for the description of the disciples' actions in the aftermath of Jesus' arrest and crucifixion in GP 7:26–27:

But I mourned with my companions, and having been wounded in heart, we concealed ourselves. For we were being sought after by them as malefactors, and as persons who wanted to set fire to the temple. Because of all these things we fasted and sat mourning and weeping night and day until the Sabbath.[29]

Vaganay mentions the piety of their actions in fasting, and claims that it is indicative of their exemplary conduct during the passion.[30] He, along with Mara, also proposes that this is likely a reflection of second-century debates among Christians concerning the pre-Paschal fast and other guidelines for the practice of fasting.[31] Crossan includes these two verses among the redactional insertions that were not part of the original version of GP but were added later "to prepare for the later insertion of another scene from the intracanonical tradition, namely, an apparition to the disciples by the Sea of Galilee in 14:60, based on John 21."[32] Their demeanor – mourning, being wounded in heart, fasting, and weeping – signifies the proper response to the fate of Jesus, according to Crossan.[33] These suggestions may very well lie behind GP 7:26–27, but Schaeffer has offered an addi-

---

[29] I have provided my own translation "having been wounded in heart" where Kraus and Nicklas (*Petrusevangelium*, 51) have "with disturbed senses." Their translation, in my judgment, lacks the proper connotation of the Greek τετωμένοι κατὰ διάνοιαν. By referring to the mourning and weeping, GP focuses on the emotional state of the disciples, a sense better captured with my more literal "having been wounded in heart." The phrase is intended to convey sorrow.

[30] Vaganay, *Évangile de Pierre*, 271–75.

[31] Ibid., 273–75; Mara, *Évangile de Pierre*, 156–60.

[32] Crossan, *Cross That Spoke*, 265.

[33] Ibid., 266–67.

tional explanation of the description of the disciples in these verses: an alibi for those who were alleged to have stolen the body.[34]

The disciples could not have stolen the body, according to GP, because they were nowhere near the tomb. Instead, they were in hiding "night and day until the Sabbath" in order to mourn properly the death of their Lord (GP 7:27).[35] Those alleged to have removed the corpse were not involved in theft but rather were acting piously during the time in question. This might be contrasted with the silence in Matthew concerning the disciples' whereabouts after the crucifixion. The First Evangelist says nothing of the matter, thus leaving open the question in the minds of potential skeptics. The storyteller of GP does not allow for this; he states explicitly what the disciples were doing during the time they could have stolen the body.

4.2.6 The Diligence of Those Guarding the Tomb

The competence of those protecting the tomb in Matthew is less than impressive. The little we are told of their activities does not bring to mind images of excellence in the execution of guard duties. Nothing beyond the stationing of the guards in Matt 27:66 is said concerning their work, that is, until they grow so fearful as to tremble and become like dead men (Matt 28:4).

In GP, we find soldiers with a much greater level of proficiency than their Matthean counterparts. Having secured the tomb with a stone and sealed it seven times, those responsible for protecting the burial place in GP "pitched a tent there and kept watch" (σκηνὴν ἐκεῖ πήξαντες ἐφύλαξαν) (GP 8:33). The pitching of a tent indicates that the Roman soldiers were diligent in carrying out their assignment of ensuring the integrity of the grave.[36] As a place of shelter, the σκηνή also shows their fixed presence at the tomb for the duration of the task. This point is reiterated in GP 9:35, where the soldiers are keeping guard two by two at their post, a further sign of the attention they have paid to their assignment.

The author of GP seems to be painting a picture that does not allow for anyone to claim that the guard was incompetent. Perhaps the account of the guards in Matthew left some readers with the impression that those responsible for securing the tomb were anything but diligent. How reliable could such soldiers be if they "trembled and became like dead men" at the ap-

---

[34] Schaeffer, "Guard at the Tomb," 506.

[35] There has been some debate about the meaning of "until the Sabbath." Is this the day after the crucifixion or is it eight days later? Crossan (*Cross That Spoke*, 266) suggests the latter. Swete (*Akhmîm Fragment*, 13–14) also discusses the alternatives. Regardless of one's judgment on this question, the disciples have an alibi at least until a point in time well after the guard is in position at the gravesite.

[36] Vaganay, *Évangile de Pierre*, 286.

pearance of an angel at the tomb (Matt 28:2–4)? Those guarding the tomb in GP express no such fear. The details I have just cited from GP – the building of a tent, and the references to "two by two" and "at their post" – have no Matthean counterparts. Their presence in GP is best explained as an effort to improve upon Matthew's portrayal of the competency of those protecting the site. A closer comparison of the vocabulary in Matthew and GP will reveal more in this regard.

The primary verb used to describe the actions of the guards in Matthew is ἀσφαλίζω. It appears three times in Matthew's story: 1) in the request from the Jews to have the tomb secured (Matt 27:64); 2) in Pilate's reply granting the guards (Matt 27:65); and 3) in the pursuant action of the guards (Matt 27:66). GP uses a different verb, φυλάσσω, in all of its three parallels to Matthew: 1) in the request from the Jews to have the tomb guarded (GP 8:30);[37] 2) in Pilate's reply granting the soldiers (GP 8:31); and 3) in the pursuant action of the soldiers (GP 8:33). Is there a connotative difference between Matthew's ἀσφαλίζω and GP's φυλάσσω? Perhaps.

While I do not wish to put too much weight on the appearance of φυλάσσω in GP, it may have been chosen for a reason.[38] Matthew's verb ἀσφαλίζω normally signifies "to fortify" or "to secure."[39] Louw and Nida define it as "to cause something to be secure in the sense of something which could not be tampered with or opened."[40] Outside of Matthew, it appears in the NT only in Acts 16:24, describing feet being fastened in stocks.[41]

The term used by the Petrine author, φυλάσσω, very often connotes protection from outsiders. BDAG gives three primary definitions: 1) "to

---

[37] The Akhmîm manuscript reads φυλάξω ("*I* might guard") at GP 8:30, which is clearly in error. Commentators have been divided as to whether this should read φυλάξωμεν ("*we* might guard") or φυλάξωσιν ("*they* might guard"). Crossan supports φυλάξωμεν "because the general picture in [GP] … is that the Jewish authorities remain in charge of the proceedings" (*Cross That Spoke*, 270–71). The translation of Kraus and Nicklas also adopts this reading (*Petrusevangelium*, 38, 51). On the other hand, Vaganay (*Évangile de Pierre*, 282) argues for φυλάξωσιν as original, claiming that the Roman soldiers are the principal guardians of the tomb in the following scene and therefore would make a better subject for this verb. Little hinges on this determination, but I lean toward Vaganay's judgment.

[38] The two verbs under discussion are unique to the guard story of each evangelist, which is to say that Matthew never uses φυλάσσω in his account of the guards (the word appears only once in the entire gospel, at Matt 19:20), and the Petrine evangelist does not use ἀσφαλίζω.

[39] These are the first two definitions given in LSJ, s.v. "ἀσφαλίζω," 266.

[40] L&N, s.v. "ἀσφαλίζω," 240.

[41] The verb also appears in Codex Bezae Cantabrigiensis at Acts 16:30 in the same context and scene as its use in Acts 16:24.

carry out sentinel functions"; 2) "to protect by taking careful measures"; and 3) "to be on one's guard against."[42] According to TDNT, the verb φυλάσσω "comes from φύλαξ 'watchman' and denotes the activity or office of a watchman whose job is 'to protect' those who are asleep from harm during the night."[43] We can see this emphasis on protection from outside threats represented in the following uses of φυλάσσω:

He drove out the man; and at the east of the garden of Eden he placed the cherubim, and a sword flaming and turning to guard (φυλάσσειν) the way to the tree of life. (Gen 3:24)

I am going to send an angel in front of you, to guard (φυλάξῃ) you on the way and to bring you to the place that I have prepared. (Exod 23:20)

In that region there were shepherds living in the fields, keeping watch over (φυλάσσοντες) their flock by night. (Luke 2:8)

When a strong man, fully armed, guards (φυλάσσῃ) his castle, his property is safe. (Luke 11:21)

But the Lord is faithful; he will strengthen you and guard (φυλάξει) you from the evil one. (1 Thess 3:3)

These my brethren hated me, and the Lord loved me: they wished to slay me, and the God of my fathers guarded (ἐφύλαξεν) me. (*T. Jos.* 1; *ANF* 8:32)

These examples represent the connotation that I am suggesting for the appearance of this verb in GP.

In light of this brief review of the two verbs in question, it may be possible to suggest that φυλάσσω was chosen because it carried stronger connotations of protection from outsiders, which is the very impetus behind the threat that leads to the need for a guard in the gospel stories. The disciples are the outsiders who were alleged to have plotted to rob the tomb of Jesus' corpse. It is perhaps the case that φυλάσσω better represents the actions of well-trained, proficient Roman soldiers working to prevent such a theft. While the Matthean ἀσφαλίζω signifies an effort to make the tomb secure, the term appears to be more inwardly focused on the tomb itself. In contrast, by using φυλάσσω GP highlights the outward alertness of the guard to any potential threat.

A further indication that GP emphasizes the protection of the tomb more than Matthew does can be found in the sheer volume of references to this act. As I stated above, GP's first three uses of φυλάσσω very neatly parallel the three appearances of ἀσφαλίζω in Matthew: GP 8:30=Matt 27:64; GP 8:31=Matt 27:65; GP 8:33=Matt 27:66. However, where Matthew has no further mention of guarding the grave, GP includes three additional references to the act, in each instance using the preferred verb φυλάσσω.

---

[42] BDAG, s.v. "φυλάσσω," 1068.

[43] G. Bertram, "φυλάσσω, φυλακή," *TDNT* 9:236–44. The quotation here is on 9:236.

The first comes in GP 9:35. The soldiers are keeping guard (φυλασσόντων) two by two at their post early on Sunday morning as the resurrection is about to take place. That the guarding is still diligently being carried out on Sunday morning serves to confirm again the strength of the security present at the burial site and renders improbable any theft. Then again in GP 10:38 we read that not only the Roman soldiers, but also the centurion and elders, are present guarding (φυλάσσοντες) the tomb. This is a joint effort between the Roman and Jewish authorities. The sixth and final appearance comes in GP 11:45, and in this instance the reference is to "the tomb which they were guarding" (τὸν τάφον ὅν ἐφύλασσον). The repeated use of φυλάσσω undoubtedly indicates the assurance that soldiers were constantly present, protecting the grave from any threat that might have come from would-be thieves. This occurs in GP to a degree significantly beyond what we find in Matthew's account.

4.2.7 The Crowd from Jerusalem (GP 9:34)

There remains the need to explore one final detail of GP not present in Matthew. On the morning after the guards in GP come to the tomb, seal it, and set up camp at the site, "a crowd from Jerusalem and the region round about came that they might see the sealed sepulcher" (GP 9:34). This crowd scene serves as a further testimony to the protected state of the grave. The point of this statement is revealed by the conjunction ἵνα, which indicates purpose: they came "in order that" they could see the sealed grave.[44] In this brief episode a group of people "sees" (ἴδωσι[ν]) the tomb in its sealed state on Saturday.[45] The inclusion of the verb ὁράω points toward language used to describe witnesses.[46] In seeing the sealed grave, these particular individuals serve as witnesses to the integrity of the burial site. In much the same way that Paul appeals in 1 Cor 15:6 to five hundred witnesses who had seen the post-mortem Jesus in order to bolster his claim that Jesus had been raised, GP includes this crowd from Jerusa-

---

[44] While ἵνα does not always indicate purpose, that is its most common function and clearly its role here.

[45] Crossan concludes that the narrative logic of GP is that "the authorities want the tomb guarded *so that the people will have time to visit it and see that Jesus is dead and buried, gone and finished, once and for all.* . . . Once the crowd has seen the sealed tomb, it will be too late for the disciples to do anything" (*Cross That Spoke*, 280 [emphasis original]). In Crossan's estimation, there is at this point in GP a divide between the Jewish authorities and laypeople; the former are attempting to dissuade the people from joining the Christian movement.

[46] Beginning as early as the Pauline literature, ὁράω was used of witnesses to the risen Jesus, who "was seen" by his followers (1 Cor 15:5–8). The NT gospels also use this verb frequently in emphasizing the witnesses to the resurrection (Matt 28:7, 10; Mark 16:7; Luke 24:34; John 20:8, 18, 25, 29).

lem in an effort to have further support for the claim that the tomb was safe, secure, and sealed. Not only do the Roman soldiers, a centurion, Jewish elders, and scribes – all authorities of one sort or another – testify to the Christian claim of tomb security, but a group of Jewish laypeople does likewise. GP has included this crowd to add yet one more layer to its effort to refute the notion that the disciples had any possible means of stealing the body of Jesus.

4.3 Early Christian Parallels

Several early Christian texts refer to the guard at the tomb. As the following survey will demonstrate, these parallels most often appear to be referring to the Matthean account. For this reason we cannot say with certainty that any of them reflect a familiarity with GP, though there are a few texts that share details that are unique to GP rather than Matthew. My goal here is to demonstrate its lasting significance for some Christians of the first few centuries, especially in the area of apologetics and polemics.

The *Gospel of Nicodemus* includes an extended account of the guards that seems to be based largely on Matthew's version. It is the fullest extant guard account from the pre-Nicene era outside GP. In this gospel the Jews arrest Joseph of Arimathea for his association with Jesus and his desire to provide a proper burial (*Gos. Nic.* 12.1). While the Jewish leaders are determining the fate of Joseph, "there came some of the guard which the Jews had asked from Pilate to guard the tomb of Jesus, lest his disciples should come and steal him" (*Gos. Nic.* 13.1). The soldiers tell the religious authorities that they saw an angel descend from heaven, roll away the stone at the tomb, and sit upon it. The Jews begin questioning the actions of the guards by asking them what the women at the tomb said, what time the angel descended, and why they did not apprehend the women (*Gos. Nic.* 13.2). In their own defense, the soldiers reply, "We were like dead men through fear, and gave up hope of seeing the light of day; how could we then have seized them?" (*Gos. Nic.* 13.2). At the conclusion of the exchange the Jewish figures "feared greatly and said: '(Take heed) lest this report be heard and all incline to Jesus'" (*Gos. Nic.* 13.2).

After the Jews receive further confirmation of Jesus' resurrection they become even more fearful, and we read the following:

But Annas and Caiaphas said: "Why are you troubled? Why do you weep? Do you not know that his disciples gave much money to the guards of the tomb, took away his body and taught them to say that an angel descended from heaven and rolled away the stone from the door of the tomb?" But the priests and the elders replied: "Let it be that his disciples stole his body. But how did the soul enter again into the body, so that Jesus now waits in Galilee?" (*Gos. Nic.* 14.3; *NTApoc*[2] 1:516)

There is an interesting twist in the *Gospel of Nicodemus* in the statement of
Annas and Caiphas that the *disciples* paid the guard in order to succeed in
their crime. This is a significantly different retelling of the Matthean account in which the *Jews* bribe the guard to say that the disciples stole the
body (Matt 28:11–15). This revisionism that we find in the *Gospel of
Nicodemus* bears a resemblance to what happens throughout GP. No brib-
ery occurs in GP, primarily because it is unnecessary since the Jewish
leaders and the Romans are present as witnesses of and participants in the
burial, guard, and resurrection events.

The guarding of the tomb in the *Gospel of Nicodemus* provides several
other points of comparison with GP and Matthew. This text presents the
guard as Roman rather than Jewish, since they are those "which the Jews
had asked from Pilate" (*Gos. Nic.* 13.1). The reason that a guard is needed
is expressed in the same language as in GP and Matthew: "lest his disciples should come and steal him (and)" (*Gos. Nic.* 13.1). These are the same
consecutive eight Greek words found in Matt 27:64 and GP 8:30: μήποτε
ἐλθόντες οἱ μαθηταὶ αὐτοῦ κλέψωσιν αὐτὸν καί.[47] The level of competence of those responsible for protecting the tomb is not high in this
gospel. They justify their ineptitude by appealing to the overwhelming fear
they experienced, a feature that has much more in common with Matthew's
depiction than with that of GP. None of the other references to the guard
that I will survey below contains a level of detail as great as the version in
the *Gospel of Nicodemus*, but the various features of these other accounts
are worth exploring.

There is a Jewish-Christian gospel that contains an intriguing detail that
may have relevance to our examination of GP. Jerome states in his *Lives of
Illustrious Men* that he had recently translated into Greek and Latin a
gospel that Origen had frequently used, which was called "according to the
Hebrews."[48] Jerome quotes the following from this gospel, a scene that he
says comes after the resurrection:

> But the Lord, after he had given his grave clothes to the servant of the priest, appeared to
> James. (*Vir. ill.* 2; *NPNF*[2] 3:362)

Although this gospel proceeds to describe the appearance of Jesus to
James, the incidental reference to Jesus giving his clothes to the servant of

---

[47] Greek text of the *Gospel of Nicodemus* in Constantin von Tischendorf, *Evangelia
Apocrypha* (2d ed.; Leipzig: Mendelssohn, 1876; repr., Hildesheim: Georg Olms, 1966),
210–332.

[48] On Jewish-Christian gospels and the possible relationship between the *Gospel of
the Hebrews*, the *Gospel of the Nazarenes*, and the *Gospel of the Ebionites*, see A. F. J.
Klijn, *Jewish-Christian Gospel Tradition* (VCSup 17; Leiden: Brill, 1992); Craig A.
Evans, "The Jewish Christian Gospel Tradition," in Skarsaune and Hvalvik, *Jewish
Believers in Jesus*, 241–77.

the priest seems to point toward the presence of Jewish authorities, particularly priests, at the tomb of Jesus when the resurrection takes place.[49] This would parallel the presence of such figures at the grave in GP. While priests are not specifically mentioned in this Petrine story, they are included in the immediately preceding scene of GP 7:25.

In the Pseudo-Clementine *Recognitions* we find two statements related to the story about the guards:

For some of them [i.e., wicked men], watching the place with all care, when they could not prevent His rising again, said that He was a magician; others pretended that he was stolen away. (Ps-Clem. *Rec.* 1.42; *ANF* 8:88)

And their [i.e., the Jews'] fear grows all the greater, because they know that, as soon as they fixed Him on the cross, the whole world showed sympathy with Him; and that His body, although they guarded it with strict care, could nowhere be found; and that innumerable multitudes are attaching themselves to His faith. (Ps-Clem. *Rec.* 1.53; *ANF* 8:91)

In contrast to the *Gospel of Nicodemus*, the Pseudo-Clementine author gives the impression that Jews are among those guarding the tomb. We also see again that the guard is mentioned in relation to the charge of a stolen body, though the disciples are not explicitly identified as the perpetrators of this act. These passages reflect anti-Jewish polemic, the desire to depict the Jews in a negative light and to rebut their allegations. The charge that Jesus was a magician is coupled with the claim of theft by the disciples.

The Christianized version of the *Martyrdom and Ascension of Isaiah* includes a passing mention of the guard:

For Beliar harboured great wrath against Isaiah on account of the vision and of the exposure with which he had exposed Sammael, and because through him the coming forth of the Beloved from the seventh heaven had been revealed, and his transformation, … and that the twelve who were with him would be offended because of him, and the watch of the guards of the grave. (*Mart. Ascen. Isa.* 3.13–14; *NTApoc*[2] 2:608)

Little can be deduced from such a brief reference, in my estimation, but Crossan is among those who have argued from the surrounding literary context that this passage is independent from GP and the canonical gospels.[50] Of course, it is true that the original version of the *Martyrdom and Ascension of Isaiah* is probably independent of both Matthew and GP, and in fact predates the Christian era. But the later Christian interpolations often seem to be based on details found in Christian gospels, canonical or

---

[49] Vaganay, *Évangile de Pierre*, 286.
[50] Crossan, *Cross That Spoke*, 276, 341–45, 368–73.

otherwise. Therefore, Crossan's claim that this is an independent witness to the guard at the tomb seems to go beyond the available evidence.[51]

Tertullian, writing at the end of the second century, gives us a glimpse at a slightly more extended parallel account:

> Then, when His body was taken down from the cross and placed in a sepulchre, the Jews in their eager watchfulness surrounded it with a large military guard, lest, as He had predicted His resurrection from the dead on the third day, His disciples might remove by stealth His body, and deceive even the incredulous. But, lo, on the third day there was a sudden shock of earthquake, and the stone which sealed the sepulchre was rolled away, and the guard fled off in terror: without a single disciple near, the grave was found empty of all but the clothes of the buried One. But nevertheless, the leaders of the Jews, whom it nearly concerned both to spread abroad a lie, and keep back a people tributary and submissive to them from the faith, gave it out that the body of Christ had been stolen by His followers. (*Apol.* 21; *ANF* 3:35)

As in the Pseudo-Clementine text, Tertullian presents the guard as comprised of Jews. The apologist here follows Matthew in linking Jesus' prediction of his own resurrection to the disciples' plan to steal the body. As we have seen in other literature, the competence of the guard is low in Tertullian's account: they flee in terror. Lastly, the Jewish leaders discourage Jews from joining the Christian movement by continuing to promote the idea that the resurrection was a hoax.

Writing a few decades after Tertullian, Origen describes the actions taken by certain Jews to refute Christian claims about Jesus. In the following passage he provides this comparison of their work:

> Their action was akin to that of those who won over the soldiers of the guard at the tomb who were eyewitnesses of his resurrection from the dead and reported it, and persuaded them by giving them money and saying to them: "Say that his disciples stole him by night while we slept. And if this comes to the governor's ears we will persuade him and rid you of care." (*Cels.* 1.51; Chadwick 48)

One potentially significant detail appears in Origen's statement: that those protecting the tomb "were eyewitnesses of his resurrection from the dead." This would fit much better with the story in GP than it would in Matthew, since in the canonical version the guards appear to be witnesses only of the

---

[51] Scholars are divided on the question as to whether this text is a composite of two or three original works, at least one of which is Jewish and pre-Christian in nature, or whether it is a unified whole that was composed by Christians. An argument for this being a composite work appears in R. H. Charles, *The Apocrypha and Pseudepigrapha of the Old Testament in English: With Introduction and Critical and Explanatory Notes to the Several Books* (2 vols.; Oxford: Clarendon, 1913), 2:155–58. For two proposals supporting the unity of the text, see Bauckham, "The Ascension of Isaiah: Genre, Unity, and Date," in idem, *The Fate of the Dead: Studies on the Jewish and Christian Apocalypses* (NovTSup 93; Leiden: Brill, 1998), 363–90; Elgvin, "Jewish Christian Editing," 292–95.

descent of the angel. It certainly is not true that they are said to observe the resurrection. In contrast, those guarding the grave in GP do see the resurrection. In all other regards, Origen appears to be dependent on Matthew's gospel. For this reason, it may be that his description of the guards as eyewitnesses is intended to be understood in a looser sense: they saw the events that accompanied the resurrection. As has been true of several other texts, the guards appear in Origen along with a reference to the stealing of the body.[52]

These parallels indicate the continuing understanding of the episode about the guard in some circles. When alluding to this account, early Christian authors appear to be most familiar with the Matthean version, though there is some indication of familiarity with non-Matthean details. In reviewing these parallels, we have found nothing analogous to GP in its extended effort to retell the guard account, except for what is found in the *Gospel of Nicodemus*. One reason for this perhaps lies in the respective genres of these texts. The nature of a guard story is such that an extended discussion of details would most likely appear in a narrative genre, especially a gospel, and such burial and resurrection narratives are scarce in early Christian literature.

4.4 Apologetics and Polemics in GP 8:29–9:34

In light of the differences between the stories in Matthew and GP, how are we to explain the details in the extra-canonical version that have been discussed in this chapter? As I stated previously, the guard episode is to be included among the early Christian defenses and proclamations of the reality of the resurrection of Jesus. Any such defense requires that there be another side to the matter under dispute; an offense, we might say. The Christian use of the guard at the tomb was primarily a means of attempting

---

[52] Lactantius is one further example of a writer with apologetic interests who employs the guard story in his works. His *Divine Institutes* was composed early in the fourth century, and in it he retells the burial and resurrection episodes, staying very close to the details found in the canonical gospels: "But since He had foretold that on the third day He should rise again from the dead, fearing lest, the body having been stolen by the disciples, and removed, all should believe that He had risen, and there should be a much greater disturbance among the people, they took Him down from the cross, and having shut Him up in a tomb, they securely surrounded it with a guard of soldiers. But on the third day, before light, there was an earthquake, and the sepulchre was suddenly opened; and the guard, who were astonished and stupefied with fear, seeing nothing, He came forth uninjured and alive from the sepulchre, and went into Galilee to seek His disciples: but nothing was found in the sepulchre except the grave-clothes in which they had enclosed and wrapt His body." (*Inst.* 4.19; *ANF* 7:122)

to refute a particular claim being made by opponents. In this case, the opposing claim was that the body of Jesus had been stolen from its burial place – taken, in fact, by his own followers in order to perpetuate their claim that he had been raised from the dead. We are seeing in narrative form an instance of resurrection apologetics. The author of GP has been heavily influenced by competing claims from outsiders in his rewriting of the guard episode. One response to objections to any story is to change the story, either through the addition, alteration, or subtraction of details. The attempt to rebut the claims of Jews, who seem to be behind the earliest counterclaims refuting the Christian resurrection proclamation, falls under the general category of anti-Jewish polemics. As we have seen in previous chapters, this is a trait that is exemplified in much of GP. The guard story thus exemplifies both resurrection apologetics and anti-Jewish polemics.

In a short essay on early objections to the resurrection of Jesus, Stanton provides three reasons why astute historians and theologians should listen to the voices of "outsiders" when it comes to this issue:

(1) Criticisms of early Christian claims concerning the resurrection of Jesus give us some limited insights into the variety of ancient attitudes to life after death. (2) They help us to appreciate more keenly the ways Christian proclamation of the resurrection was understood or misunderstood by both Jews and pagans. (3) By paying attention to early criticisms we may be able to trace more readily the points at which early Christian traditions about the resurrection have been shaped by apologetic concerns.[53]

It is Stanton's third point that in my judgment is central for understanding GP and, for the present purpose, its account of the guard at the tomb. The guard story in GP almost certainly has been shaped by apologetic concerns that have arisen in response to criticism of earlier versions of it.

Great significance was assigned to the resurrection of Jesus in early Christian communities, and apologetic interests are detectable even in the earliest sources that treat the issue. In 1 Cor 15 Paul gives a detailed defense of his position on both the past resurrection of Jesus and the future resurrection of Christians. This comes in response to the claim by some in Corinth that there is no resurrection of the dead (1 Cor 15:12–19).[54] As I will discuss more thoroughly in the next chapter, Paul's inclusion of an appearance of Jesus "to more than five hundred brothers and sisters, most of whom are still alive" is likely driven by apologetics (1 Cor 15:6). But what might be said about the objections from those *outside* the Christian movement as it relates specifically to the guard at the tomb?

In nearly every early Christian text that includes a reference to the guard, there is also mention of the disciples stealing the body. The two

---

[53] Stanton, *Jesus and Gospel*, 148.

[54] For a summary of the various reconstructions of the Corinthian view of resurrection, see Thiselton, *First Epistle to the Corinthians*, 1172–76.

claims – guard at the tomb and theft of the body – seem inextricably linked in the sources. Most have concluded that the rise of the guard story came in response to the charge of theft. Regardless of judgments about the historicity of the guard, there has been a general consensus on the development of the exchange between Christians and outsiders. Reginald H. Fuller, in his study on the formation of the resurrection narratives, comments that the guard episode assumes several earlier developments in the tradition history: 1) the earliest resurrection kerygma of the resurrection of Jesus from the dead on the third day; 2) the story of the burial and empty tomb in its Marcan form; 3) the Jewish polemic against that story.[55] According to Fuller, it was in response to Jewish criticisms of the empty tomb account – particularly the allegation that the tomb became empty as a result of the disciples' theft – that the guard story arose as an apologetic legend to refute the Jewish counterclaim.

N. T. Wright has argued for a similar understanding of the tradition history of the guard, though he goes much further than Fuller in claiming that the Matthean version may have a significant degree of historicity.[56] Most importantly, he finds it implausible to conclude that Christians would have invented the charge of theft by the disciples. This conclusion appears on firm ground even if we doubt his judgment about the historicity of the guard itself. Like Fuller, Wright alleges that the guard story presupposes the criticism from outsiders, which itself presumes the Christian claim of an empty tomb. In other words, the criticisms of those outside the Christian movement appear to provide the key for unlocking the explanation for the inclusion of the guard scene. When both Christians and critics assumed the tomb to have been empty, each group provided a competing explanation for it.[57] Christians proclaimed the resurrection as the cause, while some others explained it by alleging grave robbery.[58]

---

[55] Fuller, *The Formation of the Resurrection Narratives* (2d ed.; Philadelphia: Fortress, 1980), 73.

[56] Wright, *The Resurrection of the Son of God* (Minneapolis: Fortress, 2003), 636–40.

[57] This is not to argue for or against the historicity of the empty tomb; I am speaking solely of the competing *claims* being made by first-century people and groups. Furthermore, I am not attempting to assign a date to the claims with any more precision than to say that they must have predated the writing of Matthew's gospel, probably by at least several years. At the conclusion of the guard episode in Matthew, the author adds his explanatory note about the accusation of theft by the disciples, "And this story is still told among the Jews to this day" (Matt 28:15). It is not likely that Matthew has invented this scene in its entirety, and he seems to be under the impression that the Jewish counterclaim has been in circulation for some time.

Some wish to place the Christian empty tomb claim to a time only a few days after the death of Jesus, while others contend that such a claim was invented decades later by the author of Mark's gospel. In the former instance, alternative explanations for the empty tomb claim could have arisen immediately in the days and weeks after the alleged resur-

The charge of theft by the disciples apparently continued to be used by some critics of early Christian claims well into the second century and beyond. Justin is still sensitive to the objection that the disciples took the body, and he claims that the Jews of his day had sent out counter-missionaries to spread this story:

[Y]et you not only refused to repent after you learned that He arose from the dead, but, as I stated, you chose certain men and commissioned them to travel throughout the whole civilized world and announce: "A godless and lawless sect has been started by an impostor, a certain Jesus of Galilee, whom we nailed to the cross, but whose body, after it was taken from the cross, was stolen at night from the tomb by His disciples, who now try to deceive men by affirming that He has arisen from the dead and has ascended into Heaven." (*Dial.* 108; Falls 315–16)

While Justin is clearly exaggerating by claiming that such travels have gone "throughout the whole civilized world," there is very likely a kernel of truth to his claim.[59] At another point in his *Dialogue with Trypho* he refers again to this Jewish counter-mission:

After you had crucified the only sinless and just Man ... you not only failed to feel remorse for your evil deed, but you even dispatched certain picked men from Jerusalem to every land, to report the outbreak of the godless heresy of the Christians and to spread

---

rection, while in the latter scenario the rebuttals would have obviously postdated Mark. These are not the only options, either. The empty tomb claim, along with criticisms of it, theoretically could have arisen at any period between the two extremes I have mentioned.

[58] Some have appealed to the so-called Nazareth inscription as having possible relevance to the specific charge that Jesus' body was stolen. This inscription appears on a marble slab, bears the title Διάταγμα Καίσαρος, and has been dated anywhere from the first century B.C.E. to the second century C.E. Its twenty-two lines of text issue a stern warning against the theft of corpses from burial places and other disturbances of gravesites. It closes by stating that violators are subject to capital punishment. The *editio princeps* of this archaeological find appears in Franz Cumont, "Un rescrit impérial sur la violation de sépulture," *RevHist* 163 (1930): 241–66. Cumont himself concluded that the inscription likely predated the death of Jesus, though he allowed for the remote possibility that the conflict between Christians and Jews over Jesus' alleged resurrection led Pilate to inquire of Tiberius, and that the emperor's response is found in the inscription. Metzger ("The Nazareth Inscription Once Again," in *Jesus und Paulus: Festschrift für Werner Georg Kümmel zum 70. Geburtstag* [ed. E. Earle Ellis and Erich Gräßer; Göttingen: Vandenhoeck & Ruprecht, 1975], 221–38) has revisited the potential significance of this inscription and provides an English translation of it. Metzger concludes, correctly in my opinion, that "all attempts to identify the emperor and to determine the date and occasion of the inscription end in conjectures that neutralize one another" (236). For this reason, the most we can claim is not a lot: stealing corpses from tombs was a serious violation in the ancient Greco-Roman world.

[59] On the alleged Jewish activities of which Justin writes, see Stanton, "Aspects of Early Christian-Jewish Polemic and Apologetic," *NTS* 31 (1985): 377–92, esp. 379–84; Setzer, *Jewish Responses*, 139–40.

those ugly rumors against us which are repeated by those who do not know us. (*Dial.* 17; Falls 173)[60]

Stanton has argued persuasively that these excerpts reflect "what Justin *felt* to be the heart of Jewish arguments against Christianity."[61] Whether perception was reality in this instance is not significant. What we can state with confidence is that in the middle of the second century, probably within a few decades of the writing of GP, a Christian with strong apologetic interests was still concerned to rebut critics of the resurrection claim who were explaining the empty tomb by alleging a conspiracy on the part of Jesus' followers.

Christian apologists after Justin reflect a similar concern about the counterclaims of skeptics. At the end of the second century, Tertullian provides these comments:

"This is He whom His disciples secretly stole away, that it might be said He had risen again, or the gardener abstracted, that his lettuces might come to no harm from the crowd of visitants!" What quaestor or priest in his munificence will bestow on you the favour of seeing and exulting in such things as these? (*Spect.* 30; *ANF* 3:91)

[T]here were given to Him both "the wicked for His burial," even those who had strenuously maintained that His corpse had been stolen, "and the rich for His death," even those who had redeemed Him from the treachery of Judas, as well as from the lying report of the soldiers that His body had been taken away. (*Marc.* 3.23; *ANF* 3:341–42)

In the first reference Tertullian is sarcastically echoing the claims of the critics. He includes the allegation that the actions of a gardener near the tomb of Jesus may have led to the mistaken claim of resurrection. By including this charge, which is probably based on John 20:15, Tertullian is most likely echoing criticisms that were still being made in his day rather than simply repeating what is found in early Christian texts known to him.

In the post-Constantinian era, it is difficult to ascertain how popular this line of argumentation was among critics of Christianity. But the claim that the disciples stole the corpse of Jesus was resurrected in the 18th century by Hermann Reimarus.[62] The actions of the disciples, according to Reimarus, were motivated by the transformation of their beliefs about Jesus. Before his death, they believed that he would end Roman domination and establish himself as Israel's Messiah. This conviction came to an abrupt end at the crucifixion, and led them instead to claim a new view of Jesus in which he dies for the sins of the world, rises from the dead, and

---

[60] There may also be a further allusion to the Jewish counter-mission in *Dial.* 117.

[61] Stanton, "Aspects," 379 (emphasis original).

[62] The title of the work was *Apologie oder Schutzschrift für die vernünftigen Verehrer Gottes*, though Reimarus himself never published it. After his death, G. E. Lessing published excerpts from it in *Fragmente des Wolfenbüttelschen Ungennanten: Ein Anhang zu dem Fragment vom Zweck Jesu und seiner Jünger* (Berlin: Wever, 1784).

will soon return to establish the earthly messianic kingdom. In order to "prove" that Jesus had risen from the dead, they stole his body and kept it hidden until it was no longer identifiable. The stream of Christian apologetic responses to arguments against the resurrection has seemed to swell into a mighty rushing torrent in recent years.[63]

Much like Matthew, Justin, Tertullian, and modern apologists, the Petrine evangelist was influenced by the criticisms of Christian claims. His knowledge of the charge of theft is apparent by its inclusion in the story (GP 8:30). Where modern apologists would never consider altering the canonical stories to enhance their arguments, the author of GP was apparently under no such compunction. His familiarity with the Matthean account of the guard, and perhaps other traditions related to it, led him to retell the episode in ways that make certain objections to the Christian resurrection claim much less convincing.

4.5 Conclusions

In the opening portion of this chapter I reviewed the parallels between the guard accounts in Matthew and GP. As the only text to include the guard story and to predate GP, my comparison with GP looked almost exclusively at this particular gospel. In the course of the analysis, I suggested that it may not be necessary to posit as sources for GP any other accounts beyond Matthew's.

In the second section I noted seven characteristics of GP that differ from Matthew in an effort to counter the claim that the disciples of Jesus stole his body from its burial place. While the tale of the guards may have initially arisen to refute this charge, it seems that it continued to evolve as both proponents and critics reflected upon it. The seven features illustrate this. First, GP's timeline of the deployment of the guards is significantly different from that of Matthew, a change that does not leave the tomb unguarded during the first night after burial, a prime time for would-be thieves. Second, while the timing of the placement of the stone in GP would seem to make the tomb less secure, it allows for the third feature – the identity of the stone movers – to have a prominent role in ensuring the

---

[63] Among the apologetic responses to Reimarus was William Paley, *A View of the Evidences of Christianity* (London: Faulder, 1794). In recent decades, a sampling of attempted defenses of the historicity of the bodily resurrection can be found in Stephen T. Davis, *Risen Indeed: Making Sense of the Resurrection* (Grand Rapids: Eerdmans, 1993); Wright, *Resurrection of the Son of God*; Robert B. Stewart, ed., *The Resurrection of Jesus: John Dominic Crossan and N. T. Wright in Dialogue* (Minneapolis: Fortress, 2006).

security of the tomb, whereas in Matthew's story this important act was carried out by one of those suspected of conspiring to steal the body. Removing the prime suspects from security roles is one small way to reduce the plausibility of the claim that a theft had occurred.

Fourth, while Matthew may not be describing an actual sealing of the tomb, or, if he is, he provides no detail, GP makes twin references to a very specific act of sealing. By including seven seals, there is little doubt that any tampering with the tomb would have been detectable. Fifth, in GP the disciples have an alibi for the charge that they stole the body, while their location and actions during the window of opportunity are left unstated in Matthew. Prior to the posting of the guard in the Petrine version, the disciples are in hiding, mourning the death of Jesus, and nowhere near the tomb. Sixth, the competence of the soldiers in GP is vastly superior to that of their Matthean counterparts, thus making the likelihood remote that a band of eleven Galilean peasants could successfully steal the body. Lastly, by describing a visit from a crowd of onlookers on Saturday, the author of GP provides further witnesses to the secure nature of the burial place.

In surveying early Christian references to the guard at the tomb, we found that in nearly every instance they appear together with a charge of theft. While this may be a remnant of their being linked in Matthew, these parallels indicate the continued significance of the guard story among many early Christians. The final section of the chapter demonstrated the role of both resurrection apologetics and anti-Jewish polemics in the formation of GP's guard story. Examples from Second Temple rewritten Bible texts resemble GP's handling of the NT gospels. Just as the Petrine evangelist has altered the Matthean story to counter ongoing claims that the disciples did or could have stolen Jesus' body, so the author of *Jubilees* altered stories from Genesis and Exodus in his effort to show that the heroes of Genesis practiced pentateuchal laws long before the time of Moses. Likewise, where the writer of the *Genesis Apocryphon* adds a name to one of the Egyptian princes in the story of Abraham and Sarah, GP assigns the name Petronius to the centurion who is left unnamed in the NT stories.

Chapter 5

Rewritten Resurrection: GP 9:35–11:49

The present chapter explores the ways in which the author of GP reworks the earlier accounts of the resurrection in order to provide a more persuasive demonstration of the event.[1] I analyze the few direct NT parallels to GP 9:35–11:49 before showing how the latter describes the resurrection itself, emphasizes the witnessing of the event by those present,

---

[1] Throughout this chapter I am presupposing that my use of the term "resurrection," as it relates to the ancient texts and individuals under review, should be understood to refer to the belief that Jesus was raised bodily from the dead. In the estimation of the authors of the gospels (GP and NT), the resurrection was an event in history. This is not to say that there were no early Christians who denied a physical, bodily resurrection, or some who may have conceived of "resurrection" in non-physical terms. I mean only to clarify that when the term "resurrection" appears in this chapter, it refers to physical, bodily resurrection. Many contemporary theologians would follow Bultmann ("New Testament and Mythology," in *Kerygma and Myth: A Theological Debate* [ed. Hans Werner Bartsch; trans. Reginald H. Fuller; New York: Harper & Row, 1961], 41) in claiming that resurrection can be understood in ways other than being historical, physical, and bodily, and thereby conclude that "faith in the resurrection is really the same thing as faith in the saving efficacy of the cross." Arguments for understanding the resurrection in terms that do not involve the transformation of Jesus' physical body are found, for example, in Stephen J. Patterson, "Why Did Christians Say: 'God Raised Jesus from the Dead'?" *Forum* 10 (1994): 135–60; Gerd Lüdemann, *What Really Happened to Jesus?: A Historical Approach to the Resurrection* (Louisville: Westminster John Knox, 1995); Michael Goulder, "The Baseless Fabric of a Vision," in *Resurrection Reconsidered* (ed. Gavin D'Costa; Rockport, Mass.: Oneworld, 1996), 48–61. However, as Bultmann himself acknowledged, the empty tomb and appearances in the gospels are intended to operate as apologetic proofs for the historicity of a bodily resurrection ("New Testament and Mythology," 39).

In this way, the arguments of Patterson ("Why Did Christians Say," 135–60) – who concludes that the earliest understanding of resurrection assumed only the martyrdom of a righteous person pursuing a divine cause – are not germane to my discussion, which concerns the nature of resurrection in the gospels. The NT gospels and GP do not depict resurrection solely in the terms proposed by Patterson. Instead, resurrection in these stories includes something happening to the body of Jesus, though it may also entail such things as the vindication of his cause or mission.

Similarly, the attempt by Wright (*Resurrection of the Son of God*, 685–738) and others to show that the earliest belief about Jesus' resurrection was that he had been raised in bodily form is also irrelevant to the present topic. I am not concerned with the earliest Christian beliefs, but with the depictions in the stories of GP and the NT gospels.

and alters the identity of these first witnesses. Following this, I examine two early Christian parallels – the *Martyrdom and Ascension of Isaiah* and a textual variant in Codex Bobbiensis – that bear a much stronger resemblance to the resurrection story of GP than does any NT version. I then briefly review the role of resurrection apologetics in the *Epistula Apostolorum* in order to offer an analogy for the motives at work in GP. The chapter concludes with some proposals as to why the writer of GP has retold the story of the resurrection in a way that differs from previous authors.

5.1 Synoptic Analysis of GP 9:35–11:49

GP 9:35–11:49	Matt 28	Mark 16	Luke 24	John 20
		¹Καὶ διαγενομένου τοῦ σαββάτου Μαρία ἡ Μαγδαληνὴ καὶ Μαρία ἡ [τοῦ] Ἰακώβου καὶ Σαλώμη ἠγόρασαν ἀρώματα ἵνα ἐλθοῦσαι ἀλείψωσιν αὐτόν.			
⁹:³⁵τῇ δὲ νυκτὶ ἐπέφωσκεν ἡ κυριακὴ φυλασσόντων τῶν στρατιωτῶν ἀνὰ δύο δύο κατὰ φρουράν, μεγάλη φωνὴ ἐγένετο ἐν τῷ οὐρανῷ	¹Ὀψὲ δὲ σαββάτων, τῇ ἐπιφωσκούσῃ εἰς μίαν σαββάτων, ἦλθεν Μαριὰμ ἡ Μαγδαληνὴ καὶ ἡ ἄλλη Μαρία θεωρῆσαι τὸν τάφον.	²καὶ λίαν πρωῒ τῇ μιᾷ τῶν σαββάτων ἔρχονται ἐπὶ τὸ μνημεῖον ἀνατείλαντος τοῦ ἡλίου.	¹τῇ δὲ μιᾷ τῶν σαββάτων ὄρθρου βαθέως ἐπὶ τὸ μνῆμα ἦλθον φέρουσαι ἃ ἡτοίμασαν ἀρώματα.	¹ᵃΤῇ δὲ μιᾷ τῶν σαββάτων Μαρία ἡ Μαγδαληνὴ ἔρχεται πρωῒ σκοτίας ἔτι οὔσης εἰς τὸ μνημεῖον
³⁶καὶ εἶδον ἀνοιχθέντας τοὺς οὐράνους καὶ δύο ἄνδρας κατελθόντας ἐκεῖθε πολὺ φέγγος	²καὶ ἰδοὺ σεισμὸς ἐγένετο μέγας· ἄγγελος γὰρ κυρίου καταβὰς ἐξ οὐρανοῦ καὶ προσελθὼν	⁵καὶ εἰσελθοῦσαι εἰς τὸ μνημεῖον εἶδον νεανίσκον καθήμενον ἐν τοῖς δεξιοῖς περιβεβλημέ-	⁴καὶ ἐγένετο ἐν τῷ ἀπορεῖσθαι αὐτὰς περὶ τούτου καὶ ἰδοὺ ἄνδρες δύο ἐπέστησαν αὐταῖς ἐν ἐσθῆτι	¹²καὶ θεωρεῖ δύο ἀγγέλους ἐν λευκοῖς καθεζομένους, ἕνα πρὸς τῇ κεφαλῇ καὶ ἕνα πρὸς τοῖς ποσίν, ὅπου

GP 9:35–11:49	Matt 28	Mark 16	Luke 24	John 20
ἔχοντας καὶ ἐγγίσαντας τῷ τάφῳ [37]ὁ δὲ λίθος ἐκεῖνος ὁ βεβλημένος ἐπὶ τῇ θύρᾳ ἀφ᾽ἑαυτοῦ κυλισθεὶς ἐπεχώρησε παρὰ μέρος καὶ ὁ τάφος ἠνοίγη καὶ ἀμφότεροι οἱ νεανίσκοι εἰσῆλθον. [10:38]ἰδόντες οὖν οἱ στρατιῶται ἐκεῖνοι ἐξύπνισαν τὸν κεντυρίωνα καὶ τοὺς πρεσβυτέρους· παρῆσαν γὰρ καὶ αὐτοὶ φυλάσσοντες· [39]καὶ ἐξηγουμένων αὐτῶν ἃ εἶδον πάλιν ὁρῶσιν ἐξελθόντας ἀπὸ τοῦ τάφου τρεῖς ἄνδρας καὶ τοὺς δύο τὸν ἕνα ὑπορθοῦντας καὶ σταυρὸν ἀκολουθοῦντα αὐτοῖς [40]καὶ τῶν μὲν δύο τὴν κεφαλὴν χωροῦσαν μέχρι τοῦ οὐρανοῦ, τοῦ δὲ χειραγωγουμέ-	ἀπεκύλισεν τὸν λίθον καὶ ἐκάθητο ἐπάνω αὐτοῦ. [3]ἦν δὲ ἡ εἰδέα αὐτοῦ ὡς ἀστραπὴ καὶ τὸ ἔνδυμα αὐτοῦ λευκὸν ὡς χιών. [4]ἀπὸ δὲ τοῦ φόβου αὐτοῦ ἐσείσθησαν οἱ τηροῦντες καὶ ἐγενήθησαν ὡς νεκροί.	νον στολὴν λευκήν, καὶ ἐξεθαμβήθησαν.	ἀστραπτούσῃ.	ἔκειτο τὸ σῶμα τοῦ Ἰησοῦ.

GP 9:35–11:49	Matt 28	Mark 16	Luke 24	John 20
νου ὑπ᾽αὐτῶν ὑπερβαίνου- σαν τοὺς οὐρανούς. ⁴¹καὶ φωνῆς ἤκουον ἐκ τῶν οὐρανῶν λεγούσης· ἐκήρυξας τοῖς κοιμωμένοις; ⁴²καὶ ὑπακοὴ ἠκούετο ἀπὸ τοῦ σταυροῦ [ὅ]τι ναί.	²⁷:⁵²καὶ τὰ μνημεῖα ἀνεῴχθησαν καὶ πολλὰ σώματα τῶν κεκοιμημένων ἁγίων ἠγέρθησαν, ²⁷:⁵³καὶ ἐξελθόντες ἐκ τῶν μνημείων μετὰ τὴν ἔγερσιν αὐτοῦ εἰσῆλθον εἰς τὴν ἁγίαν πόλιν καὶ ἐνεφανίσθησαν πολλοῖς.			
¹¹:⁴³συνεσκέπ- τοντο οὖν ἀλλήλοις ἐκεῖνοι ἀπελθεῖν καὶ ἐνφανίσαι ταῦτα τῷ Πειλάτῳ ⁴⁴καὶ ἔτι διανοουμένων αὐτῶν φαίνονται πάλιν ἀνοιχθέντες οἱ οὐρανοὶ καὶ ἄνθρωπός τις κατελθὼν καὶ εἰσελθὼν εἰς τὸ μνῆμα.	²⁸:²ᵇἄγγελος γὰρ κυρίου καταβὰς ἐξ οὐρανοῦ καὶ προσελθὼν ἀπεκύλισεν τὸν λίθον καὶ ἐκάθητο ἐπάνω αὐτοῦ.			
⁴⁵ταῦτα ἰδόντες οἱ περὶ τὸν κεντυρίωνα νυκτὸς ἔσπευσαν πρὸς	¹¹Πορευομένω ν δὲ αὐτῶν ἰδού τινες τῆς κουστωδίας ἐλθόντες εἰς τὴν πόλιν			

GP 9:35–11:49	Matt 28	Mark 16	Luke 24	John 20
Πειλᾶτον ἀφέντες τὸν τάφον ὃν ἐφύλασσον καὶ ἐξηγήσαντο πάντα ἅπερ εἶδον	ἀπήγγειλαν τοῖς ἀρχιερεῦσιν ἅπαντα τὰ γενόμενα.			
	27:54Ὁ δὲ ἑκατόνταρχος καὶ οἱ μετ' αὐτοῦ τηροῦντες τὸν Ἰησοῦν ἰδόντες τὸν σεισμὸν καὶ τὰ γενόμενα	15:39Ἰδὼν δὲ ὁ κεντυρίων ὁ παρεστηκὼς ἐξ ἐναντίας αὐτοῦ ὅτι οὕτως ἐξέπνευσεν εἶπεν,		
ἀγωνιῶντες μεγάλως καὶ λέγοντες· ἀληθῶς υἱὸς ἦν θεοῦ.	ἐφοβήθησαν σφόδρα, λέγοντες, Ἀληθῶς θεοῦ υἱὸς ἦν οὗτος.	Ἀληθῶς οὗτος ὁ ἄνθρωπος υἱὸς θεοῦ ἦν.		
46ἀποκριθεὶς ὁ Πειλᾶτος ἔφη· ἐγὼ καθαρεύω τοῦ αἵματος τοῦ υἱοῦ τοῦ θεοῦ· ὑμῖν δὲ τοῦτο ἔδοξεν.	27:24ἰδὼν δὲ ὁ Πιλᾶτος... λέγων, Ἀθῷός εἰμι ἀπὸ τοῦ αἵματος τούτου· ὑμεῖς ὄψεσθε.			
47εἶτα προσελθόντες πάντες ἐδέοντο αὐτοῦ καὶ παρεκάλουν κελεῦσαι τῷ κεντυρίωνι καὶ τοῖς στρατιώταις μηδὲν εἰπεῖν ἃ εἶδον.	28:12καὶ συναχθέντες μετὰ τῶν πρεσβυτέρων συμβούλιόν τε λαβόντες ἀργύρια ἱκανὰ ἔδωκαν τοῖς στρατιώταις 13λέγοντες, Εἴπατε ὅτι Οἱ μαθηταὶ αὐτοῦ νυκτὸς ἐλθόντες ἔκλεψαν αὐτὸν ἡμῶν κοιμωμένων.			
48σθμφέρει				

GP 9:35–11:49	Matt 28	Mark 16	Luke 24	John 20
γάρ, φασίν, ἡμῖν ὀφλῆσαι μεγίστην ἁμαρτίαν ἔμπροσθεν τοῦ θεοῦ καὶ μὴ ἐμπεσεῖν εἰς χεῖρας τοῦ λαοῦ τῶν Ἰουδαίων καὶ λιθασθῆναι. ⁴⁹ἐκέλευσεν οὖν ὁ Πειλᾶτος τῷ κεντυρίωνι καὶ τοῖς στρατιώταις μηδὲν εἰπεῖν.	¹⁴καὶ ἐὰν ἀκουσθῇ τοῦτο ἐπὶ τοῦ ἡγεμόνος, ἡμεῖς πείσομεν [αὐτὸν] καὶ ὑμᾶς ἀμερίμνους ποιήσομεν. ¹⁵οἱ δὲ λαβόντες τὰ ἀργύρια ἐποίησαν ὡς ἐδιδάχθησαν. Καὶ διεφημίσθη ὁ λόγος οὗτος παρὰ Ἰουδαίοις μέχρι τῆς σήμερον [ἡμέρας].			

The preceding section of GP concluded with the crowd from Jerusalem coming out to see the sealed tomb on Saturday (the Sabbath) morning. A time indicator in GP 9:35 – "in the night in which the Lord's day dawned" – marks the beginning of a new scene. The next such marker comes in GP 12:50: "At dawn of the Lord's day." The entire intervening episode thus narrates the things that happened "in the night" and before the dawn visit to the tomb by women followers of Jesus. For this reason, there are few parallels with the NT gospels, which, except for Matthew, tell us very little about the period between burial and the Sunday morning visit by female disciples.[2] The chronological references in Mark 16:2, Luke 24:1, and John 20:1 clearly refer to this occasion, while Matt 28:1 requires further examination, which will be given below. Therefore, the material in GP 9:35–11:49 is without direct parallel in Mark, Luke, and John, though there will be a few points of comparison. Our synoptic analysis will focus heavily on Matthew, since it is the lone antecedent text to include both the guard story and an account of what occurs between the burial and the discovery of the empty tomb. The description of the guard that had begun in GP 8:29 continues in GP 9:35–11:49 and includes numerous events that precede the discovery of the empty tomb.

Crossan and Koester conclude that the guard and appearance stories of GP 9:35–11:49 are more primitive versions of their Matthean counterparts. They argue that the chronological reference in Matt 28:1 ("After the Sabbath, as the first day of the week was dawning") indicates that the First Evangelist is "conflating two sources in his account of the angel and the guards."[3] The awkward combination of "after the Sabbath" with "as the first day of the week was dawning" reflects the two sources employed by Matthew, in their estimation. These two earlier texts, in Crossan's judgment, are Mark and the *Cross Gospel*. According to Koester, they are Mark and GP's unknown epiphany source.[4] It is far from certain, though, that this conclusion can be drawn from the confused chronological statement of Matt 28:1. It is equally likely that Matthew has clumsily combined the two time references of Mark: "when the Sabbath was over" (διαγενομένου τοῦ σαββάτου) (Mark 16:1); and "very early on the first day of the week, when the sun had risen" (λίαν πρωῒ τῇ μιᾷ τῶν σαββάτων ... ἀνατείλαντος τοῦ ἡλίου) (Mark 16:2). Therefore, there is no compelling reason to think that there is any source other than Mark behind the chronological indicator of Matt 28:1. Furthermore, to my mind, the use of κυριακή in GP 9:35 (cf. 12:50) indicates a later development in comparison with μία σαββάτων of Matt 28:1, despite the two terms being synonymous.[5] This poses a difficulty to the claim of Koester and Crossan that

---

[2] Mark 16:1 states that on Saturday night the women buy spices for anointing. In Luke 23:56 the women prepare spices and ointments on Friday and then rest on the Sabbath. John tells nothing of what happens between Friday's burial and Sunday morning.

[3] Crossan, *Cross That Spoke*, 352; quoted with approval in Koester, *Ancient Christian Gospels*, 236.

[4] Koester, *Ancient Christian Gospels*, 235–38.

[5] So Brown, *Death of the Messiah*, 2:1297. All four NT gospels include a form of μία σαββάτων to refer to the day of the resurrection (Matt 28:1; Mark 16:2; Luke 24:1; John 20:1), whereas GP never uses that expression but instead prefers κυριακή (GP 9:35; 12:50). On the rise of κυριακή as a reference to the first day of the week in early Christianity, see Bauckham, "The Lord's Day." This shift in terminology for Sunday is yet

GP 9:35–11:49 preserves an earlier form of the story than Matthew. What is clear concerning Matthew, although English translations frequently soften its force, is that he has moved the timing of his scene to an earlier point than that of his Markan source.[6]

The chronology of GP 9:35 is merely making explicit that the events of 9:35–11:49 happen before those of 12:50–13:57. The second half of GP 9:35 describes the soldiers still being on guard when there is a great voice in heaven. No such voice is present in Matthew or the other NT gospels.

Those at the tomb in GP see the heavens open and two men descend in great brightness and approach the sepulcher (GP 9:36).[7] This bears some resemblance to Matthew, in which "an angel of the Lord, descending from heaven, came and rolled back the stone and sat on it" (Matt 28:2). Moreover, the image of the Matthean angel is "like lightning, and his clothing white as snow" (Matt 28:3). We can see that although GP differs from Matthew in some ways, there are similarities in the descent from heaven, approaching the tomb, and brightness.

The stone at the tomb rolls of its own accord in GP 9:37. This is found in the expression ἀφ' ἑαυτοῦ κυλισθείς. Three of the canonical stories simply state that the stone had been moved, leaving unstated the actual means by which this occurs (Mark 16:4; Luke 24:2; John 20:1).[8] Matthew alone portrays the occasion: an angel descends from heaven and rolls it away (Matt 28:2). The self-rolling stone of GP is without parallel.

Having come down from heaven and approached the tomb, the two men enter it (GP 9:37). The single angel of Matt 28 does not enter the tomb but rather sits upon the stone he has just moved. The Petrine guards witness what has taken place and awaken the centurion and the elders (GP 10:38). In contrast, when those protecting the tomb in Matthew see the angelic

---

another argument for GP postdating the canonical gospels. So already Swete (*Akhmîm Fragment*, xliii) and Vaganay (*Évangile de Pierre*, 292).

[6] There is a detailed redaction-critical discussion of Matthean vs. Markan chronology in Gundry, *Matthew*, 585–86. According to Gundry, much of Matthew's redactional work in this area is done in order to make the evidence for the resurrection "more impressive" (586).

[7] Some have attempted to identify the two heavenly beings as Moses and Elijah, or the archangels Gabriel and Michael. See the summary in Vaganay, *Évangile de Pierre*, 294. GP is not consistent with the language it uses for the figures from heaven, which are best understood as angels both in the present instance and in the subsequent empty tomb scene. The two who appear in GP 9:36–10:42 are identified as ἄνδρες (9:36; 10:39). The lone figure who descends in the later empty tomb account is called both an ἄνθρωπος (11:44) and a νεανίσκος (13:55). In Mark 16:5 the figure is identified as νεανίσκος. In Matt 28:2 the heavenly being is an/the ἄγγελος κυρίου.

[8] It is uncertain whether we should follow Brown's conclusion: "Mark, Luke, and perhaps John imply that the angel(s) who appear in/at the tomb" performed this act (*Death of the Messiah*, 2:1274 n. 78).

appearance, they become so fearful as to shake and become like dead men (Matt 28:4).

The contents of GP 10:39–42 are unparalleled in any NT gospel. As the guards begin to relay to their superior what has transpired, they see three men exiting the tomb. The implication is clear: the third person is the one who had been buried, Jesus. The two angelic escorts support the risen one as they come out of the sepulcher, and a cross follows them.[9] All three are enormously tall, as the heads of the heavenly beings reach to the skies and that of Jesus exceeds them.[10]

While the words of the earlier heavenly voice in GP 9:35 are not specified, the one in GP 10:41 asks, "Have you preached to those who sleep?" (ἐκήρθξας τοῖς κοιμωμένοις;). The cross replies in the affirmative. A vaguely similar scene is found in Matt 27:52–53:

> The tombs also were opened, and many bodies of the saints who had fallen asleep (τῶν κεκοιμημένων) were raised. After his resurrection they came out of the tombs and entered the holy city and appeared to many.

Aside from referring to saints who have passed away, there is little in common between the two episodes.[11] In GP, Jesus preaches to those asleep during the time after his burial on Friday. In Matthew, Jesus does not preach to them; in fact, those who are asleep are raised before the burial of Jesus on Friday. The similarities are too remote to indicate dependence or even a common source, in my estimation.

Upon witnessing the talking cross and the three figures leaving the tomb, those who had been guarding the site decide to go to Pilate to tell him what they have witnessed, but before they can do so, yet another incredible occurrence takes place. The heavens open again, and a man descends and enters the sepulcher (GP 11:44).[12] When those at the grave see this they rush to Pilate and report everything, saying to the governor, "In truth he was the Son of God" (ἀληθῶς υἱὸς ἦν θεοῦ) (GP 11:45). This confession is identical to the exclamation of the Roman centurion and those with him at the crucifixion in Matthew: ἀληθῶς υἱὸς ἦν θεοῦ (Matt

---

[9] On similar symbolic functions of the cross in early Christian texts, see Mara, *Évangile de Pierre*, 188–89; Crossan, *Cross That Spoke*, 381–88.

[10] Other examples of heavenly figures of great size in early Christian literature appear in Rev 10:1–2; Herm. *Sim.* 9.6; 9.12.

[11] Crossan (Cross That Spoke, 391) notes that the same identification of the "fallen asleep" appears in Justin, *Dial.* 72; Irenaeus, *Haer.* 3.20.4; 4.22.1; 4.33.1; 4.33.12; 5.31.1; and *Epid.* 78.

[12] GP thus includes both the two figures of Luke and John, and the one figure of Matthew and Mark. Swete (*Akhmîm Fragment*, 20) remarks that in the *Diatessaron* Tatian also incorporates both incidents, but places them in the reverse order from what is in GP.

27:54).[13] The title υἱὸς θεοῦ is common in GP (3:6, 9; 11:45, 46). However, both words are articular in the other three occurrences of the expression: 3:6, 9; 11:46. The fact that it is anarthrous only here in GP 11:45 might be an indication that it is dependent on Matthew in this particular instance.[14] It is possible that the writer of GP has transferred the Matthean saying from the crucifixion scene to the present one because the statement is associated with a Roman centurion and no such figure is at GP's crucifixion. But since one is now present, he puts the statement on the lips of this centurion.[15] Both Jewish authorities and Roman soldiers are among those who have come to the governor. In contrast to GP, the guard in Matthew reports to the chief priests, rather than to Pilate, after seeing what happens at the tomb (Matt 28:11).

In the extra-canonical account, Pilate hears those who have come from the tomb declaring Jesus to be the Son of God, and he responds by proclaiming his own innocence: "I am clean from the blood of the Son of God; but you have concluded this" (GP 11:46). As I argued above in Chapter Two, this is a relocation of the profession Pilate makes in Matthew when he is seemingly forced to condemn Jesus to death: "I am innocent of this man's blood; see to it yourselves" (Matt 27:24).[16] The Petrine evangelist has moved the saying of Pilate (GP 11:46), just as he has done with the proclamation of Jesus as "Son of God." He has taken sayings from two entirely different scenes in Matthew, only to combine them in the same scene in his own gospel. This is not unlike what he does by merging the leg-breaking from John with the penitent crucified from Luke (GP 4:13–14).[17]

After Pilate's self-defensive reply, those present beg him to command the guard to say nothing of what they have seen (GP 11:47). This request must come from the Jewish authorities, who then state that it would be better for them to be guilty of the greatest sin before God than to be stoned by the Jewish people (GP 11:48). Pilate grants their wish and orders the

---

[13] At the Markan crucifixion the centurion alone makes a similar expression: ἀληθῶς οὗτος ὁ ἄνθρωπος υἱὸς θεοῦ ἦν (Mark 15:39).

[14] Crossan, on the other hand, presumes that "the author makes no particular distinction between the arthrous and anarthrous use of the title 'Son of God'" (*Cross That Spoke*, 59).

[15] In Crossan's reconstruction, GP 11:45 reflects the most primitive tradition of the confession of the centurion. Mark, using the *Cross Gospel* as a source, relocates it from the resurrection to the crucifixion, and Matt 27:54 "is a perfect combination of both his sources" (i.e., the Cross Gospel and Mark) (*Cross That Spoke*, 349).

[16] Another Matthean saying may also lie behind the last part of GP 11:46. The inclusion of "but you have concluded this" (ὑμῖν δὲ τοῦτο ἔδοξεν) in GP 11:46 echoes the question from the high priest to his fellow Jews concerning the fate of Jesus in Matt 26:66: τί ὑμῖν δοκεῖ;

[17] See Chapter Two above.

centurion and soldiers to say nothing (GP 11:49). In the Matthean story, the chief priests meet with the elders and devise a plan to bribe the soldiers and instruct them to say that the disciples came during the night and stole the body while they slept. The Jewish authorities give reassurances to the guard that if Pilate should hear of their failure, no trouble will find them (Matt 28:12–14). Money is exchanged and the soldiers do as they are told (Matt 28:15).

5.2 GP 9:35–11:49: Reimagining the Resurrection

François Bovon has made the following summary remarks about the portion of GP currently under review:

> It is the sole resurrection narrative that has come down to us with any pretense to objectivity. For the first time, the resurrection itself is recounted (the canonical Gospels only tell two results of the resurrection, in the empty tomb and the later appearances), and the witnesses to this resurrection are not Jesus' disciples, but the guards who stand watch about the tomb.[18]

What Bovon has encapsulated in two sentences, I plan to examine in detail in the remainder of this chapter. The synoptic analysis above shows the general lack of direct parallels between GP 9:35–11:49 and the NT gospels. Because of this, our present discussion will focus upon the unique features of GP. How has its author rewritten the story of Jesus' resurrection, a story that each previous evangelist has already told in his own unique manner? My treatment will be divided into three broad categories: the description of the resurrection itself, the references to seeing and hearing, and the characteristics of the first witnesses of the resurrection. Together, these three components reflect the unique nature of the resurrection story in GP.

5.2.1 Describing the Resurrection

None of the NT gospels describes the actual resurrection of Jesus. It is merely inferred to varying degrees in each of the accounts. The two most important demonstrations of the resurrection in these stories are the empty tomb and the post-mortem appearances of Jesus.[19] Mark is explicit in stat-

---

[18] Bovon, *The Last Days of Jesus* (trans. Kristin Hennessy; 2d ed.; Louisville: Westminster John Knox, 2006), 17.

[19] Other signs of the resurrection include the angelic announcement of the event (Matt 28:6–7; Mark 16:6), the testimony of the disciples (Luke 24:34), the statement of an evangelist (John 20:9), and possibly the raising of the saints from their tombs (Matt 27:52–53).

ing that Jesus' body is no longer in the tomb when the women arrive on Sunday morning (Mark 16:4–6). When it comes to appearances of the risen Jesus, Mark apparently knows of such stories but does not include them (Mark 14:28; 16:7).[20] In this gospel nobody sees Jesus after his burial.

In the other three NT gospels, both the empty tomb and appearances are narrated.[21] Matthew follows Mark's empty tomb account by having an angelic messenger tell the women that the tomb is empty (Matt 28:6). But where Mark ends his gospel before Jesus appears to anyone, Matthew includes two appearances of Jesus – first to the women and then to the male disciples (Matt 28:9–10, 16–20).

Luke includes a variation of the Markan empty tomb story, as the women discover that Jesus' body is no longer in the grave (Luke 24:3, 12). The Third Gospel also has multiple appearances of Jesus, though they differ from the two in Matthew. While walking to the village of Emmaus, two disciples encounter Jesus (Luke 24:13–32). A separate appearance to Peter is then inferred in Luke 24:34. After this, Jesus is seen yet again by the disciples and others in Jerusalem (Luke 24:36–53).

The Fourth Evangelist, like the synoptic authors, tells of the initial arrival at the tomb on Sunday morning by Mary Magdalene, who rushes to tell the news to Peter and the beloved disciple (John 20:1–2). The two men then run to the burial site and confirm that the body of Jesus is no longer there (John 20:3–10). In the Fourth Gospel, Jesus first appears to Mary Magdalene (John 20:14–17), then on two occasions to those of his inner circle of twelve disciples (John 20:19–29).[22]

The NT evangelists interpret the empty tomb and the post-mortem sightings of Jesus as indications that Jesus has been raised and, according to these writers, this is the only way to account for these events.[23] In Mark,

---

[20] This is the case if Mark 16:8 is the original ending to the gospel. Perhaps the ending has been lost, in which case Mark may have included epiphany stories (cf. Mark 14:28; 16:7). On the question of Mark's ending, see the summaries in Paul L. Danove, *The End of Mark's Story: A Methodological Study* (BibInt 3; Leiden: Brill, 1993), 119–31; Michael W. Holmes, "To Be Continued … The Many Endings of the Gospel of Mark," *BRev* 17, no. 4 (August 2001): 12–23, 48–50.

[21] A chart summarizing the various details of the empty tomb story in each of the NT gospels is provided in Pheme Perkins, *Resurrection: New Testament Witness and Contemporary Reflection* (Garden City, N.Y.: Doubleday, 1984), 91–93. A detailed study of the tradition history of the appearance stories is found in John E. Alsup, *The Post-Resurrection Appearance Stories of the Gospel Tradition: A History-of-Tradition Analysis, with Text-Synopsis* (CTM A5; Stuttgart: Calwer, 1975).

[22] John 21 is in all likelihood a later addendum to the gospel. For this reason, I will not be including it in my discussion of John's resurrection narrative.

[23] Of course there are also predictions that Jesus will be raised, which occur at earlier points in the Synoptics (i.e., Matt 16:21; 17:22–23; 20:18–19; Mark 8:31; 9:31; 10:33–

the white-robed messenger in the tomb confirms this when he states outright, "He has been raised" (ἠγέρθη) (Mark 16:6). Matthew includes two
statements of the angel at the tomb verifying the resurrection: 1) "He has
been raised" (ἠγέρθη) (Matt 28:6); and 2) the subsequent instruction to the
women to tell the disciples that "he has been raised from the dead"
(ἠγέρθη ἀπὸ τῶν νεκρῶν) (Matt 28:7). In the Third Gospel the disciples
make the resurrection proclamation "The Lord has risen indeed" (ὄντως
ἠγέρθη ὁ κύριος) (Luke 24:34).[24] The Fourth Evangelist indicates that a
resurrection has occurred through his statement that the Scriptures teach
that Jesus "must rise from the dead" (δεῖ αὐτὸν ἐκ νεκρῶν ἀναστῆναι)
(John 20:9).

It should be noticed that in the NT gospels the resurrection is expressed
through some combination of the empty tomb, post-mortem appearances,
and at least one statement from reliable individuals that it is proper to
conclude that Jesus has been raised from the dead. But there is no description of the resurrection itself.[25] How did it happen? Was anyone at the
burial site when it took place? What did it look like? These types of questions are not answered by Mark, Luke, or John, and are only indirectly
addressed by Matthew.

In marked contrast, GP goes into great detail in depicting exactly what
the resurrection looked like. GP contains an image of what the NT gospels
leave unstated. There are still the empty tomb and later appearances in GP
12:50–14:60. Yet no interpretation is required to lead to the understanding
that a resurrection has taken place, since the Petrine evangelist goes into
great detail describing the event.

This narration of the resurrection is centered in GP 9:37–10:42, where
numerous details are given. The stone moves, two men enter the tomb, and
three emerge, followed by a cross.[26] A voice from heaven asks, "Have you

---

34; 14:28; Luke 9:22; 18:32–33). Presently, I address only those statements after Jesus'
death that confirm he has been raised.

[24] It is possible that previously, in Luke 24:5, the two men at the tomb make a proclamation very similar to their counterparts in Matthew and Mark, but there is a text-
critical question there. Many manuscripts include their statement οὐκ ἔστιν ὧδε, ἀλλὰ
ἠγέρθη ("He is not here, but has risen"). Despite the UBS committee assigning a {B}
rating to this reading, to signify that it is likely original, the NRSV translators exclude it
from their translation. If original, this would be another resurrection statement in Luke.
On the text-critical issue in this verse, see Metzger, *Textual Commentary*, 157.

[25] Some might argue that Matt 28:2–3 does give an account of the resurrection. Even
if this is conceded, it is still true that no one observes the resurrection in this gospel.
Matthew is nearest to GP in the move to describe what happens at the raising of Jesus,
but it does not come close to the noncanonical account in terms of particular details.

[26] The two are "supporting" (ὑπορθόω) Jesus. Swete (*Akhmîm Fragment*, 18) notes
that this word is very rare. *PGL* (s.v., 1453) lists three appearances of it in early Christian
literature: *Acts Thom.* 37; Gregory of Nyssa, *Mart.* 1.1; Macarius Magnes, *Hom.* 16.6.

preached to those who sleep?" (ἐκήρυξας τοῖς κοιμωμένοις;) (GP 10:41).[27] No reply comes directly from Jesus. Instead, the cross responds on his behalf by confirming that Jesus has indeed preached to those who sleep.[28] This is a further development in Christian reflection on the work of Jesus during the time between his burial and resurrection. The question "What did Jesus do between Friday evening and Sunday morning?" is answered.

Where the NT gospels leave readers pondering the specific nature of the resurrection itself, GP provides a description of the occasion. No longer are such things left to the imagination; the retelling of the story has filled in what was previously left unstated. There is no need to infer that Jesus has been raised from the dead simply on the basis of an empty tomb, an appearance, or the testimony of someone. Mere inferences are replaced by vivid descriptions.

5.2.2 Seeing and Hearing

Although the inclusion of an account of the actual resurrection would seem to diminish the need for testimony to support the Christian claim that Jesus had been raised, GP still places a strong emphasis on witness language. It is not sufficient merely to state what occurred; the writer of our gospel makes it clear that people see and hear what is transpiring. Dependence on the testimony of witnesses to the resurrection is a characteristic of early

---

None of these uses appears in relation to Jesus' resurrection. BDAG (s.v., 1040) lists GP 10:39 as the only instance of it in early Christian texts.

[27] The singular ἐκήρυξας indicates that the question is directed only to Jesus, and not to those accompanying him.

[28] The notion of Jesus preaching to the dead is of course found elsewhere in early Christian literature. The earliest such examples may be those in 1 Pet 3:18–20; 4:6. The interpretive issues surrounding these two passages of 1 Peter are complex and will not be resolved here. For a summary of the history of interpretation and the maze of questions surrounding these verses and the idea of Jesus preaching to the dead, see William J. Dalton, *Christ's Proclamation to the Spirits: A Study of 1 Peter 3:18–4:6* (AnBib 23; Rome: Pontifical Biblical Institute, 1965); Harold W. Attridge, "Liberating Death's Captives: Reconsideration of an Early Christian Myth," in *Gnosticism and the Early Christian World: In Honor of James M. Robinson* (ed. James E. Goehring et al.; ForFasc 2; Sonoma, Calif.: Polebridge, 1990), 103–15; Rémi Gounelle, *La descente du Christ aux enfers: Institutionnalisation d'une croyance* (SerAnt 162; Paris: Institut d'Études Augustiniennes, 2000). Other relevant early Christian texts on the descent into Hades are Eph 4:8–10; Ign. *Magn.* 9:2; Justin, *Dial.* 72; Irenaeus, *Haer.* 3.20.4; 4.22.1; 4.33.1; 4.33.12; 5.31.1; *Sib. Or.* 1:376–382; 8:310–317; *Odes Sol.* 17:9–16; 22:1–10; 42:3–20; *Mart. Ascen. Isa.* 4.21; 9.7–18.

Christianity, one that can be seen in the earliest text to discuss the occasion in any detail (1 Cor 15).[29]

The greatest attention in the area of witnesses regards their "seeing" those things that accompany the resurrection and, more importantly, having visionary experiences of the risen Jesus. The most common verb for vision in Matt 28, Mark 16, Luke 24, and John 20 is ὁράω, and the NT gospels exhibit an increasing interest in seeing the signs of the resurrection.[30]

The focus on "seeing" the resurrection is even more pronounced in GP than in the canonical stories. This is all the more noteworthy when we remember that the Akhmîm text of GP ends before Jesus begins appearing to his followers. As the following analysis will suggest, it is probable that the now lost conclusion to the gospel had many more references to seeing the risen Jesus.

The verb ὁράω is a favorite of the Petrine evangelist. It appears thirteen times in the extant portion of the gospel, and at least nine of these occurrences relate directly to witnessing the resurrection.[31] The first occasion is when the guards see the heavens open and two men descend and come to the tomb (GP 9:36). Second, the soldiers see the stone roll from the tomb and the two men enter it (GP 10:38). The third use of ὁράω occurs when the soldiers tell the centurion and elders "what they *had seen*" (GP 10:39). As they are relating their experience, they see "three men coming out of the tomb, and two of them supporting one, and a cross following them, and the head of the two reaching to heaven, but that of the one who was led by them overpassing the heavens" (GP 10:39–40). These first four instances form a recurrence of including ὁράω with everything that has happened thus far in the resurrection scene: the heavens open, two men come down,

---

[29] The literature on 1 Cor 15 is voluminous. For a review of the various positions that have been staked out on the nature of these appearances, see Thiselton, *First Epistle to the Corinthians*, 1197–1203.

[30] Mark 16 includes only two uses of ὁράω, though neither is of an actual vision of the risen Jesus. In Mark 16:5 the women see a young man in the tomb, and in Mark 16:7 the young man tells the women that they will see the risen Jesus. There is also one use of θεωρέω at Mark 16:4. Matthew 28 has four uses of ὁράω (vv. 6, 7, 10, 17), and one of θεωρέω (v. 1). Luke 24 has five occurrences of ὁράω (vv. 23, 24, 34, 39 [2X]), two of θεωρέω (vv. 37, 39), and one of βλέπω (v. 12). The resurrection narrative of the latest gospel, John 20, places the greatest emphasis on seeing, with eight uses of ὁράω (vv. 8, 18, 20, 25 [2X], 27, 29 [2X]), three of θεωρέω (vv. 6, 12, 14), and two of βλέπω (vv. 1, 5).

[31] A tenth use of the verb that is related to the resurrection occurs in GP 9:34, where the crowd from Jerusalem comes out to see the sealed tomb. This detail, as I argued in Chapter Four above, is also apologetic in that it serves as further proof of the security of the burial site. The three uses of ὁράω that are unrelated to the resurrection occur in GP 8:28; 12:52, 54.

and the guards see it; the stone rolls away, the men enter, and the guards see it; the soldiers then relay all that they have seen and, as they are doing so, they see three figures emerge from the tomb. That there is an attempt to emphasize the witnessing of all these occurrences is obvious.

After Jesus rises, the heavens open again and a lone man descends in order to enter the grave (GP 11:44). As we might expect, this is immediately followed by the notice that "those who were with the centurion *saw* this" (GP 11:45). This leads to the witnesses providing our sixth example when they rush to Pilate in order to report "everything that they *had seen*" (GP 11:45).[32] This statement is noteworthy insofar as it has a relevant parallel in Matthew. When the guards in Matthew report to the chief priests, they tell "everything that had happened" (Matt 28:11). The two complete phrases are as follows:

ἀπήγγειλαν τοῖς ἀρχιερεῦσιν ἅπαντα τὰ γενόμενα
[They] told the high priests everything that had happened. (Matt 28:11)

ἐξηγήσαντο πάντα ἅπερ εἶδον
They reported everything that they had seen. (GP 11:45)

Where Matthew is content to say that they tell what happened, the author of GP specifies that they report what they themselves have *seen*. Matthew gives the impression that the guards do not see anything after they quake and become as dead men upon seeing the angel descend and roll back the stone (Matt 28:2–4). Therefore, we are uncertain as to precisely what is included in their relaying "everything that happened" (Matt 28:11). Whether they ever see Jesus is uncertain, and Matthew appears reticent to say that they did witness anything at the tomb after Matt 28:4. On the other hand, GP could not be any clearer in its description of what the soldiers have seen. Because of this, the reader knows what they are reporting in GP 11:45 when they inform Pilate of "everything that they had seen."

---

[32] The two terms used to characterize the guards reporting to Pilate are ἐμφανίζω (GP 11:43) and ἐξηγέομαι (GP 11:45). Swete (*Akhmîm Fragment*, 20) defines ἐμφανίζω here as "to make an official report." BDAG (s.v. "ἐμφανίζω," 325–26) defines it as "to convey a formal report about a judicial matter, present evidence, bring charges" and includes GP 11:43 under this meaning. For comparable uses of this verb, see Acts 23:15, 22; 24:1; 25:2, 15. Similarly, BDAG (s.v. "ἐξηγέομαι," 349) classifies the use of ἐξηγέομαι in GP 11:45 under the definition, "to relate in detail, tell, report, describe." Other NT examples are in Luke 24:35; Acts 10:8; 15:12, 14; 21:19. The connotation in GP is that those reporting to Pilate carefully relate all the minutiae of their experience at the burial site. Matthew, on the other hand, uses the more general ἀπαγγέλλω for the guards' report to Pilate (Matt 28:11). He seems far less concerned with the details. Therefore, there is a discernible difference between the two gospels in the nature of the account given to Pilate, and GP is better suited to serve apologetic interests.

Those who come to Pilate beg him "to command the centurion and the soldiers to say nothing of the things they *had seen*" (GP 11:47), and this serves as the seventh instance of ὁράω. This request that the soldiers say "nothing" of what they have seen stands in stark contrast to the "everything" they have witnessed in GP 11:45. In the Matthean parallel, the priests make no reference to what the guard has seen (Matt 28:12–15).

Though they fall outside the main portion of GP currently under review (GP 9:35–11:49), the final two uses of ὁράω are directly related to witnessing the resurrection. When the women discover the empty grave on Sunday morning, they witness "a young man sitting in the middle of the tomb, beautiful and clothed with a brightly shining robe" (GP 13:55).[33] Lastly, the messenger in the tomb invites the women to "*see* the place where he lay" (GP 13:56), a line that finds a parallel in Matt 28:6.[34] The recurrence of ὁράω throughout the resurrection scene (GP 9:35–10:42), the report to Pilate (GP 11:43–49), and the women's visit to the empty tomb (GP 12:50–13:57) suggests that it has been deliberately chosen by our author and has not simply been inherited from source material. This choice, I contend, was motivated by the desire to emphasize that many individuals saw the events at the resurrection.

As important as "seeing" is in GP, it is also relevant to note that the author twice refers to those at the tomb *hearing* the things of which they are witnesses. They hear the voice from heaven that asks Jesus if he has preached to those who sleep, and they also hear the reply from the cross (GP 10:41–42). Just as the Petrine evangelist follows each visible detail from the resurrection with a reference to its having been seen, so he also includes mention of hearing the audible phenomena.[35] Unlike the NT gospels, which do not refer to the hearing of anything in their respective resurrection accounts, GP probably includes this detail because it reinforces the claim that the witnesses perceived what was taking place.[36]

5.2.3 The Characteristics of the First Witnesses

Having reviewed the frequent references to seeing the resurrection and hearing the events accompanying it, we can recognize the prominence of

---

[33] This is one of the few places where GP is closest to Mark. As the women enter the tomb in Mark 16:5, they see "a young man, dressed in a white robe, sitting on the right side." I will address this further in Chapter Six below.

[34] GP 13:56: ἴδετε τὸν τόπον ἔνθα ἔκειτο; Matt 28:6: ἴδετε τὸν τόπον ὅπου ἔκειτο.

[35] An exception to this is that there is no reference to hearing the voice of GP 9:35.

[36] A potential instance of hearing appears in Matt 28:14, but this is not related to the resurrection itself. It concerns the chance that Pilate might "hear" of the plot between the guard and the Jewish leaders.

witnesses in this gospel. I have not yet addressed are the differences between the first witnesses of the resurrection in the NT gospels and those in
GP. What again should be remembered is that GP 9:35–11:49 is one large
block of material that does not find a direct parallel in Mark, Luke, or
John, and is present in Matthew only in fragmentary form. So, for example, everything in GP 9:35–11:49 takes place between Mark 16:1 and Mark
16:2, or between Luke 23:56 and Luke 24:1, or between John 19:42 and
John 20:1. It is only beginning with GP 12:50 that we find direct parallels
in Mark 16:2; Luke 24:1; and John 20:1.

In particular, I want to address three differences between the characteristics of the first witnesses in the canonical gospels and those in GP: 1)
friends vs. enemies; 2) women vs. men; and 3) doubt vs. certainty. These
shifts have profound effects. Collectively, these three traits result in a
different foundation on which apologetic arguments for the resurrection
can be built.

5.2.3.1 Friends in the NT Gospels, Enemies in GP

In all four NT accounts the first witnesses of the initial sign of the resurrection – the empty tomb – are followers of Jesus. Mark identifies the first
visitors as Mary Magdalene, Mary the mother of James, and Salome (Mark
16:1).[37] Earlier in Mark these same three people are present at the crucifixion, and Mark adds the comment there that they "used to follow him and
provided for him when he was in Galilee" (Mark 15:40–41). Mary Magdalene and Mary the mother of Joses are also present at the burial and see
where Jesus' body is laid (Mark 15:47), an indication that they will know
where to go on the return visit. On Sunday morning, the three individuals
enter the tomb and a white-robed young man announces to them that Jesus
is not there because he has risen, and that they should go tell his disciples
that Jesus will appear to them in Galilee (Mark 16:5–7).

Luke tells a similar story, referring to the first visitors to the empty
tomb as "the women who had come with him from Galilee" (Luke 23:55).
The Third Evangelist later identifies them as "Mary Magdalene, Joanna,
Mary the mother of James, and the other women with them" (Luke 24:10).
Mary Magdalene and Joanna are named among the followers of Jesus
earlier, in Luke 8:1–3. As in Mark, these are clearly friends of Jesus. When

---

[37] I am following the NRSV in identifying the second individual as "Mary the mother
of James." The Greek is Μαρία ἡ Ἰακώβου, which could be taken to mean either the
mother, wife, or daughter of James. The same issue is present in Mark 15:40, 47; Luke
24:10. See the treatment of this by Vincent Taylor (*The Gospel according to St. Mark:
The Greek Text with Introduction, Notes, and Indexes* [2d ed.; London: Macmillan,
1966], 598, 602–3), who includes a discussion of the manifold textual variants.

they find the tomb empty, they are informed by two men that Jesus has risen and is not there (Luke 24:2–6).

The Fourth Gospel identifies Mary Magdalene as the first visitor to the empty tomb (John 20:1). In the Johannine crucifixion scene she accompanies the mother of Jesus and the aunt of Jesus at the cross (John 19:25). Again, there is no doubt that, as in Mark and Luke, Mary Magdalene is a friend or follower of Jesus.

The question of the first witnesses in Matthew is more complex. Initially, it may appear as though the guards have this role. However, a closer examination of Matthew shows that while the soldiers see the descent of the heavenly messenger and the rolling back of the stone, they do not receive the angelic message of the resurrection given to the women in Matt 28:5–6.[38] At most, then, the guards in Matthew may be witnesses of a portion of the resurrection events, but they do not receive the full experience as the followers of Jesus do. Matthew identifies them as "Mary Magdalene and the other Mary" (Matt 28:1), and their status as followers of Jesus is established by their earlier presence at the crucifixion and burial (Matt 27:55, 61). In Matthew the friends of Jesus see and experience more than the guards and so become the central witnesses to the resurrection in this gospel.

Since nobody sees the actual resurrection in any of the four NT gospels, the first to see evidence of it are those who find the tomb empty, and this role belongs to friends and followers of Jesus. They are witnesses of the first sign that Jesus has been raised. This is not the case in our extra-canonical gospel. That role belongs to the soldiers, the centurion, and the Jewish elders, all of whom are understood to be enemies of Jesus (GP 9:35–11:49). It is these individuals who twice see the heavens open, revealing one or two divine messengers descending to the burial site. They watch as the stone rolls away from the entrance to the tomb. The very enemies of Jesus witness his departure from the grave as he is led by the angelic figures. They hear the voice from heaven and the reply from the cross. None of the followers of Jesus is included in the witnessing of anything that happens in GP 9:35–11:49; this task belongs solely to his opponents, the ones who would wish to prevent the resurrection if they had their way. The ones responsible for taking Jesus' life see him return from the dead.

---

[38] I am in agreement with Hagner (*Matthew 14–28*, 870) when he writes, "The angel [in Matthew] has not opened the tomb so that Jesus may come out. No one, indeed, saw Jesus come out of the tomb." The angel rolls back the stone so that the women might see that the tomb is empty. The Matthean guards witness only the angelic descent and the removal of the stone.

5.2.3.2 Women in the NT Gospels, Men in GP

The preceding discussion may serve as support for the claim that women are the first witnesses to the empty tomb in the four NT accounts.[39] Moreover, it is the testimony of these women that is supposed to convince the male disciples that Jesus has been raised.[40] In all four NT gospels, either the women are told to send word to the male disciples about what has taken place (Matt 28:7–8; Mark 16:7), or they do so of their own accord (Luke 24:8–9; John 20:2). Of the three gospels that include appearance stories, two have Jesus appear first to women (Matt 28:9–10; John 20:14–17). The primacy of women as those who first see the evidence for the resurrection in the NT accounts is undeniable.

Turning to GP, Setzer has claimed that its author "seems to suppress the women's role in the drama even more than the canonical Gospels."[41] In her

---

[39] Some have suggested that all of the NT evangelists attempt to downplay the role of women as the first witnesses. So while the women were not eliminated from the stories – likely because their involvement was well known in early Christian communities – it is claimed by some that the gospel writers had no desire to emphasize their status as witnesses. See, for example, Setzer, "Excellent Women: Female Witnesses to the Resurrection" *JBL* 116 (1997): 259–72. For a completely different perspective, Bauckham (*Gospel Women: Studies of the Named Women in the Gospels* [Grand Rapids: Eerdmans, 2002], 295–304) has argued that the women are included in the NT accounts because they "acted as apostolic eyewitness guarantors of the traditions about Jesus, especially his resurrection," and "their witness ... implies that it can never have been regarded as superseded or unimportant" (295) by the NT writers. Curiously, in the later development of his thesis regarding eyewitness testimony in the gospels, Bauckham (*Jesus and the Eyewitnesses*) does not include the women's roles in the resurrection accounts in his discussion.

[40] To go back even further in the NT stories, the women also attend the burial and thus serve as witnesses of that occasion in each of the Synoptics (Matt 27:61; Mark 15:47; Luke 23:55). This anticipates their later role as anointers of Jesus' body. Moreover, if the burial story is pre-Markan, the Second Evangelist's comment in Mark 15:47 that the women "saw where the body was laid" might be an apologetic reaction to the claim that they went to the wrong tomb on Sunday morning. Brown (*Death of the Messiah*, 2:1016) provides a table summarizing which women are present at the crucifixion, burial, and empty tomb in each of the four NT gospels.

[41] Setzer, "Excellent Women," 269–70. She goes further in speculating that behind GP "may be a Jewish complaint that this group, the Christians, defines itself on the basis of a tall tale reported by an unreliable woman" (ibid., 270). Studies on women in GP are found in Ann Graham Brock, "Peter, Paul, and Mary: Canonical vs. Non-Canonical Portrayals of Apostolic Witnesses," *SBL Seminar Papers, 1999* (SBLSP 38; Atlanta: Society of Biblical Literature, 1999), 173–202; Erika Mohri, *Maria Magdalena: Frauenbilder in Evangelientexten des 1. bis 3. Jahrhunderts* (MTSt 63; Marburg: Elwert, 2000), 71–89; Joseph Verheyden, "Silent Witnesses: Mary Magdalene and the Women at the Tomb in the Gospel of Peter," in *Resurrection in the New Testament: Festschrift J. Lambrecht* (ed. R. Bieringer, V. Koperski, and B. Lataire; BETL 165; Leuven: Leuven University Press, 2002), 457–82. Mara (*Évangile de Pierre*, 198–200) concludes that the

estimation, GP "is a more extreme example of the same discomfort that surfaced in the canonical Gospels over the crucial role of the women as resurrection witnesses."[42] On these points, I am in general agreement. The women are not present either at the burial or, more importantly, as the first witnesses of the resurrection. Joseph alone buries Jesus in his own tomb after the Jews hand over the body (GP 6:23–24). Unlike the Synoptic Gospels, where women are specifically named as being present at the burial, GP makes no reference to them in this context.

Even in the later empty tomb scene, the testimony of the women is not nearly as central in GP as it is in the NT parallels.[43] The empty tomb story of GP 12:50–13:57 is utterly anti-climactic because of its placement after the epiphany. Where the NT gospels have not yet indicated that Jesus has risen when the women come to visit, GP has already given a detailed account of what has caused the tomb to be empty.

Furthermore, in GP the women are no longer the real or supposed messengers to the male disciples. Mary Magdalene and "her friends" still arrive at the tomb on Sunday morning and find a young man inside who tells them that Jesus has risen and is no longer there, a scene with strong parallels in the NT gospels (GP 12:50–13:57; Matt 28:1–8; Mark 16:1–8; Luke 24:1–9; John 20:1, 11–13). But in GP the young man at the tomb does not tell the women to inform the disciples that Jesus has risen, as in Matthew and Mark, nor do the women take it upon themselves to apprise the male followers of what has happened, such as occurs in Luke and John. There is no contact between female and male disciples in GP. The role of the women as intermediaries who carry the news of the empty tomb is absent from this gospel, a sharp difference from the NT texts. GP represents a sizable shift from female to male witnesses, though the presence of women in the tradition is firmly fixed to the point that they are not entirely removed from the resurrection account.

5.2.3.3 Doubt in the NT Gospels, Certainty in GP

In the NT gospels there is some degree of skepticism about the nature and reality of the resurrection. When the male disciples in Matthew finally see

---

women are portrayed positively in GP. Similarly, Mohri (*Maria Magdalena*, 89) finds the depiction of the women to be "thoroughly positive." In contrast, Brock ("Peter, Paul, and Mary," 199) and Verheyden ("Silent Witnesses," 466–82) are in agreement with the judgment of Setzer that the role of women is minimized in GP to a degree beyond what we find in the NT gospels.

[42] Setzer, "Excellent Women," 270.

[43] Some of my discussion in the remainder of this chapter will address material from the final portion of GP (12:50–14:60) that pertains to resurrection, while in Chapter Six I will be discussing issues other than resurrection.

the risen Jesus, some (all?) doubt (Matt 28:17). Being fearful, the Markan women flee from the tomb, trembling in amazement and saying nothing to anyone (Mark 16:8). In Luke the male disciples refuse to believe the testimony of the women, thinking it to be a fanciful tale (Luke 24:11). Later, when Jesus appears among the disciples, they think him to be a ghost and Jesus rebukes them for having such doubts (Luke 24:37–38). Even after Jesus shows them his hands and feet, the disciples are unconvinced that he has risen (Luke 24:41).

The witnesses in the Fourth Gospel are not immune to doubt, either. Neither of the two effects of the resurrection – the empty tomb and appearances – initially convinces Mary Magdalene that Jesus has risen. Her interpretation of the empty tomb is that someone has moved the body to an unknown location (John 20:13), and she supposes Jesus to be the gardener when he appears to her (John 20:14–15). No more famous a scene of resurrection doubt can be found than the one in John 20:24–29. Thomas, who is not present when Jesus first appears to the disciples, tells the others that he will not believe that Jesus has been raised unless he sees for himself the crucifixion marks on the body of Jesus. His wish is granted eight days later.

When we turn to the resurrection witnesses in GP, we detect no such doubts about what has happened. While there is some level of distress upon seeing this amazing spectacle, the unease of the witnesses is the result of their recognition that Jesus has been raised (GP 11:45). None of those at the burial site who see Jesus come out of the tomb doubts what they are observing. During their report to Pilate they are theologically keen enough to know that the resurrection indicates that Jesus is the Son of God (GP 11:45). It seems that the resurrection functions primarily in GP as a way to bring outsiders into the movement. Such is the power of the event.

The importance of the resurrection in GP may be further indicated by the statement of the Jews who report the occurrence to Pilate: "For it is better for us to make ourselves guilty of the greatest sin before God than to fall into the hands of the people of the Jews and be stoned" (GP 11:48). Commentators have been puzzled by this comment. Swete, following Harnack, supposes that the author has forgotten that he began with συμφέρει ("it is better") and instead meant to say "to have incurred a grievous sin is enough, without being stoned besides."[44] These scholars understand "greatest sin" to be referring to the killing of Jesus. The Jews are lamenting their murder of the Son of God.

Vaganay has offered a different solution to this enigmatic verse.[45] The religious authorities prefer to admit their crime rather than to risk their

---

[44] Swete, *Akhmîm Fragment*, 21.
[45] Vaganay, *Évangile de Pierre*, 313.

lives if the people ever were to learn of the resurrection. If the Jewish people were to hear of the resurrection, and consequently the true identity of Jesus as the Son of God, they would surely stone their leaders. This is the motivation for begging that the Roman soldiers say nothing about what they have seen. The significance of the resurrection is shown by the strong desire that the people be kept from knowledge of it. The "greatest sin" is more about suppressing news of the resurrection than killing Jesus. To know that Jesus has been raised is to know that the Christian claims about him are true, and in GP there is no doubt about whether the resurrection actually happened and what its meaning is.

5.3 Early Christian Parallels

Outside of Matthew, there are few parallels to the scene in GP 9:35–11:49. Early Christian texts frequently recount appearances of the risen Jesus or dialogues between him and the disciples in post-resurrection contexts.[46] But it is rare to find accounts of the actual occasion on which Jesus leaves the tomb. In this regard GP has few siblings. There are, however, two noteworthy parallels that I will briefly review in order to show the uniqueness of GP's version and its emphasis on witnessing Jesus rising from the dead. In addition, I will provide an example of another second-century text that, although it does not have a direct correlation with the details of GP, also reflects apologetic interests related to the resurrection and thereby serves as a point of comparison with our gospel.

There is an intriguing parallel to GP 9:35–10:42 within the textual tradition of Mark's gospel. Codex Bobbiensis (it[k]), dating to the fourth/fifth century, is one of the earliest Latin manuscripts of the New Testament. Furthermore, most critics have concluded that it preserves an even earlier textual tradition. Kurt and Barbara Aland state that it "was copied from an exemplar of the period before Cyprian and presents a text whose Greek base is thought by some to be traceable to the second century."[47] It testi-

---

[46] A brief introduction to early Christian dialogues and the difficulties involved in defining the genre are provided in Schneemelcher, "Dialogues of the Redeemer," in *NTA-poc*[2] 1:228–31.

[47] Kurt Aland and Barbara Aland, *The Text of the New Testament: An Introduction to the Critical Editions and to the Theory and Practice of Modern Textual Criticism* (trans. Erroll F. Rhodes; 2d ed.; Grand Rapids: Eerdmans, 1989), 187. Aland and Aland do not identify any of those who trace the exemplar to the second century. However, E. A. Lowe is mentioned as an advocate of this view in Bruce M. Metzger and Bart D. Ehrman, *The Text of the New Testament: Its Transmission, Corruption, and Restoration* (4th ed.; New York: Oxford University Press, 2005), 102. Metzger and Ehrman echo the conclusion that the text of Codex Bobbiensis agrees very closely with the quotations of Cyprian

fies, then, to ideas that were likely circulating a few centuries prior. At Mark 16:4 of this manuscript the following appears:

But suddenly at the third hour of the day there was darkness over the whole circle of the earth, and angels descended from the heavens, and as [the Lord] was rising in the glory of the living God, at the same time they ascended with him; and immediately it was light.[48]

This fascinating anomaly in the textual history of Mark preserves an early attempt to describe the resurrection and ascension.

A second parallel to the resurrection account of GP is found in the *Martyrdom and Ascension of Isaiah*. After recounting the events from Jesus' life, this text then tells of his death and resurrection as revealed in the vision of Isaiah:

For Beliar harboured great wrath against Isaiah ... because through him the coming forth of the Beloved from the seventh heaven had been revealed, ... and that the twelve who were with him would be offended because of him, and the watch of the guards of the grave, and the descent of the angel of the church which is in the heavens, whom he will summon in the last days; and that the angel of the Holy Spirit and Michael, the chief of the holy angels, would open his grave on the third day, and that the Beloved, sitting on their shoulders, will come forth and send out his twelve disciples, and that they will teach to all the nations and every tongue the resurrection of the Beloved, and that those who believe on his cross will be saved, and in his ascension to the seventh heaven, whence he came. (*Mart. Ascen. Isa.* 3.13–18; *NTApoc*[2] 2:608)

There are similarities between the details in this passage, Codex Bobbiensis, and GP that call for further examination. Divergent judgments have been made about the nature of the relationship between these texts. According to Mara, Harnack estimated that GP was the source of the story in Codex Bobbiensis.[49] On the other hand, Crossan finds "no reason to presume any direct literary relationship" between the two.[50]

Vaganay surveys the parallels between GP and the *Martyrdom and Ascension of Isaiah* and concludes that "the alleged relation between the *Ascension of Isaiah* and GP does not rest on any reliable foundation."[51]

(ibid.). See the summary of the features of this manuscript in Metzger, *The Early Versions of the New Testament: Their Origin, Transmission and Limitations* (Oxford: Clarendon, 1977), 315–16.

[48] ET in Metzger, *Textual Commentary*, 102. See below for more on questions about the certainty of this translation.

[49] Mara, *Évangile de Pierre*, 181.

[50] Crossan, *Cross That Spoke*, 344.

[51] Vaganay, *Évangile de Pierre*, 184. I take him here to be claiming that there is no literary dependence between the two texts. Noteworthy is his review of the common vocabulary in GP and *Mart. Ascen. Isa.* 2.4–4.4 (ibid., 183). But this is insufficient to prove literary dependence in either direction and can be attributed to common subject matter, as Vaganay himself judges.

Similarly, Swete and Crossan find no compelling reason to suppose literary dependence.[52] The majority of scholars have judged that the best explanation for the similarities between GP, Codex Bobbiensis, and the *Martyrdom and Ascension of Isaiah* is that a common tradition lies behind all of them, and GP provides the fullest version.[53]

Crossan has created a chart summarizing the parallels in the three texts:

Literary Motifs	GP 9:35–10:42	*Mart. Ascen. Isa.* 3.16-17	Mark 16:4 in Codex Bobbiensis
Heavenly Beings	Two men	Two angels	Angels
Beings' Actions	Descend		Descend
		Open tomb	
	Enter tomb		
	Assist Jesus	Assist(?) Jesus	Accompany Jesus
	[Ascend?]		Ascend
Special Phenomena	Voice		
	Darkness		Darkness
	Brightness		Brightness[54]

The identity of those who come to the tomb is nearly the same in the three sources. The "men" of GP are not described as mere humans; they are messengers from heaven, that is, angels. In both parallels, too, these figures are clearly identified as angels. Codex Bobbiensis does not specify the number of angels, other than to say that there is a plurality, though some have claimed that two are indicated.[55] In GP and the *Martyrdom and Ascension of Isaiah* there are two who come from heaven. So the three stories agree in having multiple angels.

The actions of the heavenly visitors have similarities in the three versions as well, the angelic escort of Jesus from the tomb to the heavens

---

[52] Swete (*Akhmîm Fragment*, xxxvii) mentions, without explanation, that "a connexion has been supposed to exist between the Petrine Gospel and the *Ascension of Isaiah*, but the coincidence is one of ideas only and does not extend to the literary form."

[53] Crossan (*Cross That Spoke*, 344) states this unequivocally as his own conclusion. Vaganay is less specific in outlining his own position, other than to reject literary dependence.

[54] Adapted from Crossan, *Cross That Spoke*, 345.

[55] See the discussion in Metzger, *Textual Commentary*, 101–2. Metzger remarks that in "one or two places the text of the gloss does not appear to be sound, and various emendations have been proposed" (ibid., 101). A possible correction is to read *viri duo* ("two men") for *vivi Dei* ("living God") in the clause "as [the Lord] was rising in the glory of the living God." Metzger rejects this and other suggested emendations as unnecessary.

being the most prominent feature in common. As for the special phenomena, darkness is implied in GP by the reference to it being "in the night" (GP 9:35). In sum, the *Martyrdom and Ascension of Isaiah* 3.16–17 gives the story in abbreviated form, which is typical of what we find throughout that entire portion of this text. Codex Bobbiensis provides a slightly fuller account, and GP presents the most elaborate version.

If these three accounts are indeed dependent on a common tradition for the core of their stories, then we have another example of the Petrine evangelist supplementing the NT accounts with oral tradition or other legendary material. This time it involves an account of Jesus' departure from the tomb, a story without parallel in the NT gospels.

Most significantly, when GP's author retells this, he is careful to integrate his frequent commentary that those at the tomb see and hear what is taking place (GP 9:36; 10:38, 39–40, 41, 42). This element is absent from Codex Bobbiensis and the *Martyrdom and Ascension of Isaiah*. I grant that it is speculative to suggest this, but I find it very likely that the common tradition from which these three authors drew did not include repeated references to the witnessing of the resurrection events by those at the grave. In my judgment, while it is impossible to know a great deal more about the source from which GP drew, the Petrine evangelist has added the elements of seeing and hearing to his own version of the story. This reflects his apologetic interest: to have witnesses for every aspect of the resurrection so that there might be no doubt about its occurrence.

Another second-century text that reflects a similar apologetic interest to that of GP is the *Epistula Apostolorum*.[56] Müller classifies this work as "anti-gnostic."[57] One way in which this *Tendenz* is manifested is in the attempt to demonstrate the bodily nature of Jesus' resurrection, a theme that is most prominent in *Ep. Apost.* 9–12. Hills states that there are two types of proof at work in this section of the text: "proof of the identity of the risen one, and proof of his resurrection."[58] When Mary, the daughter of Martha, and Mary Magdalene discover the empty tomb, the story continues:

But as [the women] were mourning and weeping, the Lord appeared to them and said to them, "For whom are you weeping? Now do not weep; I am he whom you seek. But let one of you go to your brothers and say, "Come, the Master has risen from the dead. Martha came and told it to us. We said to her, "What do you want with us, O woman? He

---

[56] Introductory matters related to this text are summarized in C. Detlef G. Müller, "Epistula Apostolorum," in *NTApoc*[2] 1:249–51. Numerous similarities between GP and the *Epistula Apostolorum* are cited in Julian V. Hills, *Tradition and Composition in the Epistula Apostolorum* (exp. ed.; HTS 57; Cambridge, Mass.: Harvard University Press, 2008), esp. 67–95.

[57] Müller, "Epistula Apostolorum," 1:251.

[58] Hills, *Tradition and Composition*, 70.

who has died is buried, and could it be possible for him to live?" We did not believe her, that the Saviour had risen from the dead. Then she went back to the Lord and said to him, "None of them believed me that you are alive." He said, "Let another one of you go to them saying this again to them." Mary came and told us again, and we did not believe her. She returned to the Lord and she also told it to him.

Then the Lord said to Mary and also to her sisters, "Let us go to them." And he came and found us inside, veiled. He called us out. But we thought it was a ghost, and we did not believe it was the Lord. Then he said to us, "Come, do not be afraid. I am your master whom you, Peter, denied three times; and now do you deny again?" But we went to him, doubting in our hearts whether it was possibly he. Then he said to us, "Why do you still doubt and are you not believing? I am he who spoke to you concerning my flesh, my death, and my resurrection. That you may know that it is I, put your finger, Peter, in the nailprints of my hands; and you, Thomas, put your finger in the spear-wounds of my side; but you, Andrew, look at my feet and see if they do not touch the ground. For it is written in the prophet, "The foot of a ghost or a demon does not join the ground."

But we touched him that we might truly know whether he had risen in the flesh, and we fell on our faces confessing our sin, that we had been unbelieving. Then the Lord our redeemer said, "Rise up, and I will reveal to you what is above heaven and what is in heaven, and your rest that is in the kingdom of heaven. For my Father has given me the power to take up you and those who believe in me." (*Ep. Apost.* 10–12; *NTApoc*[2] 2:255–56)[59]

Unlike GP, the *Epistula Apostolorum* does not describe the emergence of Jesus from the tomb. This resembles the NT gospels in having the women's discovery of the empty tomb and an appearance to them as the first signs of the resurrection. But where the two extra-canonical texts do resonate with one another is in their emphasis on seeing the risen Jesus, and this firsthand witness serves to prove the reality of the bodily resurrection. In the *Epistula Apostolorum*, one woman, Martha, first tells the male disciples that Jesus has risen, to which they respond with disbelief. Next, Mary brings the news and receives the same skeptical reaction from the men. Jesus himself then accompanies the women on the third visit, and the disciples still do not believe at first sight. Ever patient, Jesus instructs Peter, Thomas, and Andrew to confirm that it is his own flesh and that he is not a phantom. It is when they finally touch him that they believe that he has truly risen from the dead. It is thus not merely seeing the risen Jesus that convinces the disciples; they must actually touch him or, in the case of Andrew, see that Jesus leaves footprints. The entire story is one prolonged attempt to prove both that it was Jesus in their presence and that he really had been raised.

Demonstrating the resurrection is the goal of the authors of GP and the *Epistula Apostolorum*, and each pursues this by different means. The *Epistula Apostolorum* appears concerned primarily with intra-Christian issues

---

[59] The text is extant in both Coptic and Ethiopic, with variations between the two. I have followed the Coptic in *NTApoc*[2].

such as refuting non-bodily understandings of the resurrection or confirming apostolic witnesses. As I will argue in the final section of this chapter, the Petrine evangelist is retelling the resurrection story with an eye toward extra-Christian objections and criticisms; those outside of the Christian movement have influenced him.

5.4 Apologetics and Polemics in GP 9:35–11:49

Regardless of one's judgment concerning the historicity of the empty tomb and epiphany stories in the NT, it cannot be denied that they are meant to function apologetically as demonstrations of the resurrection. And in turn, the resurrection proves the uniquely exalted status of Jesus, according to these writers. Witnesses to the empty tomb and appearances are integral to authenticating the event. The earliest list of resurrection witnesses, 1 Cor 15:5–8, is considered by most to be, at least in part, an attempt to prove the resurrection.[60] Similarly, the NT gospels reserve a prized place for those who discover the empty tomb and see the risen Jesus. Thus far in this chapter we have seen *how* GP retells the resurrection story – by describing Jesus rising in the presence of witnesses, and by having these first witnesses be male enemies rather than female friends of Jesus. We have also noticed the great emphasis placed on observing the event.

What I hope to do now is to offer an explanation as to *why* our author has rewritten his account in the manner he did. Following the pattern of my earlier discussion, I will attempt to answer three questions: 1) Why does GP include the scene of Jesus rising from the grave? 2) Why are enemies among the first witnesses of the resurrection? and 3) Why is the testimony of the women insignificant? In answering each of these, I will suggest that the voices of those outside the Christian movement provide insight for understanding the revised story. In my estimation, it is their criticisms and objections that have influenced our evangelist. Clearly, this is not the only factor influencing our author and his handling of earlier texts, but it is a relevant one for the present subject matter. After offering my proposals concerning these three questions, I will conclude with a brief excursus in which I explore another potential example of how the criticisms of earlier

---

[60] As in commentators as diverse as Bultmann ("New Testament and Mythology," 39), who puts it, "There is however one passage where St Paul tries to prove the miracle of the resurrection by adducing a list of eye-witnesses (1 Cor. 15.3–8)," and Wright (*Resurrection of the Son of God*, 322), who remarks, "But it is not enough for Paul, or the early tradition, simply to declare that the Messiah was in fact raised. Witnesses must come forward."

Christian gospels may have influenced our evangelist, although this final case does not relate directly to proving the resurrection.

Why does GP include the scene of Jesus rising from the grave? Beyond the vague kerygmatic expression "Jesus has been raised" that is prevalent throughout early Christian literature, there are relatively few attempts to report what happened on Easter Sunday in texts that antedate GP.[61] References to the resurrection are widespread, but rarely are any features such as people, places, times, or other details included. The earliest extant example is, of course, 1 Cor 15, whose meaning is widely debated.[62] When the sources are limited to those that very likely predate GP, the NT gospels are the leading candidates for further examples that purport to give a historical report of the resurrection.

People today often operate with the assumption that those in the ancient world were naïve about claims of the miraculous, as if those who lived two thousand years ago would believe any and every report about someone returning from the dead.[63] But this is not the case. Perkins has shown in her review of early Christian apologists that they often attempted to refute the claim from non-Christians that resurrection was not only undesirable but impossible.[64] The people of late antiquity were frequently sympathetic to the idea of some type of spiritual immortality (e.g., of the soul), but certainly not to the notion of bodily resurrection. Post-Enlightenment Western cultures were certainly not the first to be skeptical of such beliefs.[65]

Celsus, the second-century critic of the Christian movement, frequently expresses his disdain for the idea of a physical, bodily resurrection. While Celsus is obviously personally familiar with certain segments of Christi-

---

[61] The diversity of beliefs about resurrection in Second Temple Judaism and early Christianity is reviewed in Perkins, *Resurrection*; Setzer, *Resurrection of the Body in Early Judaism and Early Christianity: Doctrine, Community, and Self-Definition* (Boston: Brill, 2004); George W. E. Nickelsburg, *Resurrection, Immortality, and Eternal Life in Intertestamental Judaism and Early Christianity* (exp. ed.; HTS 56; Cambridge, Mass.: Harvard University Press, 2006).

[62] Various representative conclusions are found in Hans Conzelmann, *1 Corinthians: A Commentary on the First Epistle to the Corinthians* (trans. James W. Leitch; Hermeneia; Philadelphia: Fortress, 1975), 248–93; Thiselton, *First Epistle to the Corinthians*, 1169–1313.

[63] Beliefs about the nature of the afterlife were, of course, highly diverse in the ancient world. I will note again that my discussion of "resurrection" here refers to a returning from the dead into some kind of life such as humans experience in a body.

[64] Perkins, *Resurrection*, 348–55, 372–77. She cites examples from Justin, Tatian, Athenagoras, Theophilus, and Origen. The opponents of these apologists vary, ranging from Christian gnostics, to non-Christian gnostics, Platonists, and Jews.

[65] On the general and widespread disbelief in the idea of resurrection among non-Jews of the early Christian period, see Wright, *Resurrection of the Son of God*, 32–38.

anity, he also attributes some of his claims to an unnamed Jew.[66] Ernst Bammel and others have concluded that the ideas from this Jewish source can be traced back to the early second century.[67] So although Celsus almost certainly wrote his work after GP was composed, he often preserves ideas from a much earlier period (100–120 C.E. or earlier). Therefore, these objections would have been circulating very near the time, if not before, GP was written. I do not want to claim that there is any type of direct connection between GP and the Jewish source of Celsus, as if GP is responding specifically to the objections from the source used by Celsus. My goal is more modest: to suggest that Celsus and his Jewish source represent the types of criticisms and objections that would have been known to the writer of GP and to which his retelling of the resurrection is a reaction.

There are several points at which Celsus conveys his incredulity about resurrection, but this statement captures his general sentiment:

> The fact that this doctrine is not shared by some of you [Jews] and by some Christians shows its utter repulsiveness, and that it is both revolting and impossible.... As for the flesh, which is full of things which it is not even nice to mention, God would neither desire nor be able to make it everlasting contrary to reason. For He Himself is the reason of everything that exists; therefore He is not able to do anything contrary to reason or to His own character. (*Cels.* 5.14; Chadwick 274–75)

Origen later comments that Celsus frequently rebuts Christian claims regarding the resurrection (*Cels.* 8.49).[68] This aversion also shows up in the first-century Acts of the Apostles, when some of those in Athens scoff at the idea of resurrection after hearing about it from Paul (Acts 17:32). Ramsay MacMullen summarizes matters thus when speaking of the situation during the first few centuries of the Common Era, "Resurrection in the flesh appeared a startling, distasteful idea, at odds with everything that

---

[66] John Granger Cook (*The Interpretation of the New Testament in Greco-Roman Paganism* [STAC 3; Tübingen: Mohr Siebeck, 2000; repr. Peabody, Mass.: Hendrickson, 2002], 27–28) suggests that, while Celsus presents his source as a real person, this may simply be a rhetorical device. He may be familiar with Jewish texts, too, or with Christian texts responding to Jewish claims.

[67] Bammel, "Der Jude des Celsus," in *Judaica* (ed. idem; 2 vols; WUNT 37/91; Tübingen: Mohr, 1986–1997), 1:265–83. Stanton (*Jesus and Gospel*, 150) finds that "it is impossible to say just how early they [i.e., the ideas in his Jewish source] are, but their value as evidence for the views of Jewish opponents of Jesus and his followers can hardly be overestimated." Many of the claims that Celsus alleges to have come from his Jewish source comport with early second-century data from elsewhere.

[68] Another example of Celsus' perspective comes in one of the conclusions to his anti-resurrection arguments: "And it follows from this that Jesus could not have risen with his body; for God would not have received back the spirit which he gave after it had been defiled by the nature of the body" (*Cels.* 6.72).

passed for wisdom among the educated."[69] Christians who desired to convince others that Jesus had been raised often faced the obstacle presented
by Celsus and others: skeptics simply did not find such a notion compre-
hensible.

The most well-known stories (i.e., those in the NT gospels) based their
resurrection claims on an empty tomb and some later post-mortem appearances to a few followers. However, skeptics could and did present alternative explanations of the empty tomb and epiphanies.[70] One of the earliest
and most prevalent alternative explanations for the empty tomb was that
the disciples stole the body, a point that was addressed in Chapter Four.
Not surprisingly, critics also accounted for the appearances through means
other than the one presented by Christians.

Celsus explains the supposed appearances of the risen Jesus by suggesting that they were not actual visions of a living person but rather dreams or
hallucinations:

Someone dreamt in a certain state of mind or through wishful thinking had a hallucina-
tion due to some mistaken notion (an experience ... which has happened to thousands).
(*Cels.* 2.60; Chadwick 112)

He knows many instances in Greek literature, and perhaps through
firsthand experience, in which people supposed that they had seen someone or something that, in reality, they had only dreamed about or imagined
to have seen while hallucinating. This is one possible explanation for the
appearances of Jesus, though as we will see later, Celsus finds it equally or
more likely that some type of fraud or deception lies behind the alleged
appearances.

Given the assumption of ancient critics that resurrections do not happen,
and the NT gospels' evidence resting on only what must be inferred primarily from the empty tomb and appearances, it is natural to suppose that a
writer intent on proving the resurrection would enhance the story by including a report of the actual emergence of Jesus from the tomb. While no
amount of eyewitness testimony will typically overcome philosophical
presuppositions when it comes to judging a claim that someone has returned from the dead, the version of the resurrection story in GP is a more
compelling apologetic demonstration than what is found in the NT accounts. For those open to the chance, however remote, that resurrections

---

[69] MacMullen, *Christianizing the Roman Empire: A.D. 100–400* (New Haven: Yale
University Press, 1984), 12.

[70] As is clear from the entirety of his work, Celsus is very familiar with the NT gospels, or at least with the traditions and stories preserved in them. Therefore, his objections to the Christian resurrection claim appear to be based almost exclusively on those
texts. On Celsus' familiarity with the NT gospels, see Cook, *Interpretation of the New
Testament*, 26–61.

really happen, the story in GP 9:35–10:42 is far more convincing. This is one potential reason why GP includes the account of Jesus rising from the grave. If the story is granted any credibility, there would appear to be little opportunity for claiming that Jesus was not raised. Our author wanted to provide a convincing demonstration of the resurrection and thus left no room whatsoever for any objections to his claims. For this reason, I turn now to my second question.

Why are enemies among the first witnesses of the resurrection? As I argued above in Chapter Four, the shift from burial by friends of Jesus alone (NT gospels) to a burial that is overseen and completed by enemies (GP), is partly due to the fact that the NT gospels unwittingly fuel the charge that there was a conspiracy among followers of Jesus to steal his body in order to give the impression that he had been raised. Something very similar is behind the apologetic motives related to the resurrection witnesses as well. If only the followers of Jesus saw him, then what is to say that they were not conspiring amongst themselves not only to steal the body but then later to claim that they saw him alive? This story is not persuasive to skeptics.

It is this very doubt that is expressed by Celsus, who finds that, because Jesus appears only to those who supported him, the NT accounts are thoroughly unpersuasive:

If Jesus really wanted to show forth divine power, he ought to have appeared to the very men who treated him despitefully and to the man who condemned him and to everyone everywhere. (*Cels.* 2.63; Chadwick 114)[71]

This line of thought was prominent among early opponents of the Christian movement. The greatest figure in this regard was Porphyry, a third-century philosopher whom Wilken has called "the most learned critic of all."[72] He may have made a similar objection when he asks:

Why, after he had suffered and resurrected, did Jesus not appear before Pilate and claim he did nothing worthy of death; or to King Herod of the Jews; or to the high priest of the Jewish race; or to many credible men; and particularly to the Senate and people of Rome? (Macarius Magnes, *Apocrit.* 2.14; Berchman 195)[73]

---

[71] This comes immediately after his argument that the appearances were actually dreams or hallucinations. It is clear that a conspiracy by the followers of Jesus is in view. Origen includes Celsus' identical statement again in *Cels.* 2.67, after he has responded to it.

[72] Wilken, *Christians as the Romans Saw Them*, 126. Summaries of Porphyry's thought, with specific reference to his refutations of Christian claims, are in Labriolle, *Réaction païenne*, 223–96; Wilken, *Christians as the Romans Saw Them*, 126–63; Robert M. Berchman, *Porphyry against the Christians* (SPNP 1; Leiden: Brill, 2005).

[73] This excerpt is from the fourth-century Christian apologist Macarius Magnes. While confidence is high when reconstructing Celsus' work, the same cannot be said for the writings of Porphyry. Much of the evidence for Porphyry's view of Christianity has been based on statements in *Apocriticus*. It once was commonly believed that Macarius

For real proof of his resurrection and power, Jesus should have appeared not just to those who admired him but to his opponents – in particular, to those who condemned and crucified him!

GP has precisely the version of the resurrection demanded here by the skeptics. Jesus does appear to those who mocked, abused, and crucified him. Not only does he appear to his enemies, he does so even before he is seen by his own followers. In this way, the witnesses to the resurrection include those who are hostile to the Christian message. Both friends and enemies now know the truth of what happened on Easter morning; the question becomes what to do with this knowledge. The Jewish leaders attempt to suppress it (GP 11:47–49). We have here the answer to the question as to why GP includes enemies as the first witnesses to the resurrection. There remains one final query to address.

Why is the testimony of the women insignificant in GP? The simplest explanation is that they did not make for persuasive witnesses in the ancient world.[74] There is evidence for this reticence in Christian texts. When the women in Luke tell the disciples about the empty tomb, the men suppose it to be an "idle tale" (λῆρος) (Luke 24:11). This Greek word might even be translated "nonsense."[75] We noticed a similar reaction to the women's multiple resurrection reports in the *Epistula Apostolorum*. Even stronger sentiments in this area are found in non-Christian writers.

In her study of pagan views of early Christian women, Margaret Y. MacDonald has shown that many Greco-Roman critics of the Christian movement used the prominent role of women in the sect itself and its foundational texts as an argument against Christian claims.[76] Lucian of Samosata and Celsus are among those in the second century who write disparagingly of Christian women. Lucian belittles certain women on

---

was preserving and responding to the work of Porphyry, but this view has been challenged in recent decades. See Wilken, *Christians as the Romans Saw Them*, 135–37; Berchman, *Porphyry*, 1–6.

[74] This has been suggested as a reason for Paul's omission of women as witnesses to the resurrection in 1 Cor 15. Bauckham (*Gospel Women*, 304–10) includes a summary of the diverse explanations that have been offered for the absence of women in 1 Cor 15. Fuller (*Formation of the Resurrection Narratives*, 78) implies that either Paul did not know such a tradition or it had not yet arisen.

[75] BDAG, s.v. λῆρος, 594. The full definition provided is "that which is totally devoid of anything worthwhile, idle talk, nonsense, humbug." The NRSV's "idle tale" renders the single Greek word λῆρος.

[76] MacDonald, *Early Christian Women and Pagan Opinion: The Power of the Hysterical Woman* (Cambridge: Cambridge University Press, 1996). MacDonald shares my conclusion that GP has muted the role of women as resurrection witnesses (ibid., 105–6).

account of their gullibility for following a charlatan masquerading as an itinerant Christian preacher.[77]

Celsus' criticisms of Christian women are more wide ranging in scope. At several points he mocks the women in the gospels, including particularly their role as the primary witnesses to the resurrection.[78] Citing his Jewish source, Celsus compares Jesus to other Greek miracle workers before making this objection:

> While [Jesus] was still alive he did not help himself, but after death he rose again and showed the marks of his punishment and how his hands had been pierced. But who saw this? A hysterical female, as you say, and perhaps some other one of those who were deluded by the same sorcery, who either dreamt in a certain state of mind and through wishful thinking had a hallucination due to some mistaken notion (an experience which has happened to thousands), or, which is more likely, wanted to impress the others by telling this fantastic tale, and so by this cock-and-bull story to provide a chance for other beggars. (*Cels.* 2.55; Chadwick 109)

For Celsus, the origin of the Christian resurrection claim is a hysterical woman – probably Mary Magdalene, since she is most prominent in the gospels. Celsus offers three alternatives: 1) Mary dreamed that she saw Jesus; 2) she hallucinated; and 3) she concocted the story to impress the rest of her rogue band. He finds the third option to be the most likely. In any case, the identification of the primary witness as a "hysterical female," when combined with his other remarks criticizing Christian women, makes apparent that he finds their testimony wholly lacking in credibility.

In GP the witness of the women is not central for proving the reality the resurrection. Not only are men the eyewitnesses to this event, but the women in GP do not even act as intermediary witnesses to the male disciples as they do (or should do) in the NT gospels. The testimony of men, in the form of a Roman centurion, soldiers, and Jewish leaders, certainly is more reliable than the chattering of idle tales by hysterical women, in the estimation of ancient skeptics.[79]

---

[77] Lucian, *The Passing of Peregrinus* 12–13; see the commentary in MacDonald, *Early Christian Women,* 73–82.

[78] MacDonald (ibid., 94–120) surveys several other places where Celsus disparages the fact that women played a prominent role in Christian origins.

[79] It is sometimes alleged that the testimony of women in the ancient Jewish world was worthless. Some base this on the statement of Josephus that the Mosaic law prohibited women from acting as legal witnesses due to their "lightness and presumption" (διὰ κουφότητα καὶ θράσος) (*Ant.* 4.219). However, it is not the case that women could not testify or that their testimony was worthless. It is more accurate to follow the conclusion of Carolyn Osiek ("The Women at the Tomb: What Are They Doing There?" *ExAud* 9 [1993]: 97–107), who summarizes matters by saying that there was a "general reluctance in ancient Mediterranean society to see women as public spokespersons or officeholders" (104). See also the treatment of this issue in Moshe Meiselman, *Jewish Woman in Jewish Law* (New York: KTAV, 1978), 73–80; Judith Romney Wegner, *Chattel or Person? The*

The NT gospels were familiar to some opponents of the emerging Christian movement, and the resurrection stories were among their regular targets of criticism. What we have in GP is a rewriting of the resurrection account, a revision that is largely inspired by the desire to develop a stronger proof of the event. Several of the objections that were being made against the NT gospels are rendered ineffective by the new story in GP. It offers more persuasive proof that Jesus truly was raised from the dead.

5.4.1 Excursus: The Stone at the Tomb (GP 9:37)

Since we are in the realm of early objections to the claims of the NT resurrection stories, I wish to make one brief suggestion about another possible way in which the Petrine evangelist may have taken into account the questions and criticisms of outsiders. Matthew is the only NT writer to specify how the stone is moved away from the entrance to the tomb: an angel does it (Matt 28:2).[80] The other gospels state only that the stone had been removed, not how or by whom. Lest it be thought that naysayers could ever run out of criticisms, Celsus finds a flaw in this angelic removal of the stone. At one point, he concedes, for the sake of argument, that Jesus might be special in some sense, perhaps comparable to an angel. But he then immediately criticizes an apparent weakness of Jesus:

For the Son of God could not himself, as it seems, open the tomb, but needed the help of another to roll away the stone. (*Cels.* 5.52; Chadwick 305)

Jesus is inferior to other divine figures because of his need to have someone else open his tomb, or so the argument goes.

GP tells the story differently. On the morning of the resurrection, after the heavens open and two men descend to the tomb, we read the following:

But that stone which laid at the entrance started of itself (ἀφ᾽ ἑαυτοῦ) to roll and move sidewards, and the tomb was opened and both young men entered. (GP 9:37)

In his study of the miraculous in GP, David F. Wright remarks about the self-rolling stone that "a rationale for *EvP*'s version is elusive."[81] Indeed it is. Wright suggests that Jesus should be understood as the one who rolls the stone. Just as "the Lord" was responsible for the tearing of the temple veil (GP 5:20), and the placement of the body of "the Lord" on the ground

---

Status of Women in the Mishnah (New York: Oxford University Press, 1988), 120–26, 188–89.

[80] The angels also open the grave in *Mart. Ascen. Isa.* 3.16.

[81] Wright, "Apologetic and Apocalyptic: The Miraculous in the *Gospel of Peter*," in *Gospel Perspectives,* vol. 6: *The Miracles of Jesus* (ed. David Wenham and Craig Blomberg; Sheffield: JSOT Press, 1986), 411.

caused an earthquake (GP 6:21), so he is the one who also causes the stone to move from the entrance.

Regardless of whether Wright is correct in proposing Jesus as the agent here, the point is that Jesus needs no assistance from another in order to move the stone. According to this line of thought, then, the Petrine evangelist chose to take away the role of the angel(s) as mover(s) of the stone in order to avoid the charge that Jesus was somehow dependent on someone else for this act. Another detail from Matthew has been altered in order to avoid the objections of critics.

5.6 Conclusions

My synoptic analysis showed that Matthew is the only NT gospel that has any substantive material in common with GP 9:35–11:49. In the second section of this chapter I looked at the ways in which the resurrection story is retold, focusing on three aspects of GP's account: the description of the resurrection itself, the references to seeing and hearing, and the characteristics of the first witnesses of the resurrection. By depicting Jesus rising from the dead, GP does not base its resurrection claim merely on the effects of the resurrection (i.e., empty tomb, appearances, angelic pronouncement), as is true of the NT versions. This apologetic preoccupation to fill in gaps existing in earlier stories is also found in Rewritten Bible Texts from the Second Temple literature. For example, the *Genesis Apocryphon* answers the question of how Pharaoh learned of Sarah's identity, and it does this by saying that Lot informed the ruler of this.

The extra-canonical gospel also places a strong emphasis on both seeing and hearing what happens at the resurrection, to a point of repetitiveness at each step. In GP, the primary witnesses are male enemies of Jesus who have no doubts about what they see, which stands in contrast to the female followers of Jesus in the NT accounts, who are skeptical of their experiences of the empty tomb and appearances. Together, these three distinct features of GP make for a more compelling demonstration of Jesus rising from the dead than what is in the NT gospels.

I then argued that a common tradition lies behind the stories in GP, the *Martyrdom and Ascension of Isaiah*, and Codex Bobbiensis. More importantly, I noted that the Petrine author very likely added the element of seeing and hearing at several points, and that this reveals his interest in demonstrating the event and thus the true identity of Jesus as the Son of God. The second-century *Epistula Apostolorum* was then briefly compared to GP in order to show the apologetic motives common to both. The final section of the chapter has some specific proposals as to why GP's version of the resurrection differs from those in the other gospels, and I suggested that criticisms of those earlier stories influenced our author's rewriting of the account. In particular, I proposed that the objections of those outside the Christian movement led him to include the report of Jesus emerging from the tomb and to portray enemies and men as the primary witnesses to the event.

Chapter 6

Rewritten Empty Tomb and Appearance Stories: GP 12:50–14:60

In this chapter I review the final two pericopes of GP, looking first at the emphasis on the women's fear of the Jews during their visit to the tomb and then at the way Peter serves as an apostolic witness throughout this text. The synoptic analysis reviews the similarities between the empty tomb stories of Mark 16:1–8 and GP 12:50–13:57, and the possible relationship between the appearances of Jesus in John 21:1–14 and GP 14:58–60. In the second section, I suggest that, while GP relies on the structure of Mark for its empty tomb account, it has imported the motif of fearing the Jews from John. I then note the ways that Peter acts as the first-person narrator in two sections of GP. Following this, I summarize some examples of early Christian texts that reflect these two traits: a fear of hostility from the Jews, and the purported apostolic testimony behind the text. Lastly, I review the role of anti-Jewish polemic in GP's repeated statements about Christian fear of Jews, and the ways that early Christians appealed to apostolic authority to lend support to their claims and texts.

6.1 Synoptic Analysis of GP 12:50–14:60

GP 12:50–14:60	Matt 28	Mark 16	Luke 24	John 20
		¹Καὶ διαγενομένου τοῦ σαββάτου Μαρία ἡ Μαγδαληνὴ καὶ Μαρία ἡ [τοῦ] Ἰακώβου καὶ Σαλώμη ἠγόρασαν ἀρώματα ἵνα ἐλθοῦσαι ἀλείψωσιν αὐτόν.	²³:⁵⁶ὑποστρέψασαι δὲ ἡτοίμασαν ἀρώματα καὶ μύρα. Καὶ τὸ μὲν σάββατον ἡσύχασαν κατὰ τὴν ἐντολήν	
¹²:⁵⁰ὄρθου δὲ	¹ᵃ᾿Οψὲ δὲ	²ᵃκαὶ λίαν	²⁴:¹ᵃτῇ δὲ μιᾷ	¹Τῇ δὲ μιᾷ τῶν

GP 12:50–14:60	Matt 28	Mark 16	Luke 24	John 20
τῆς κυριακῆς	σαββάτων, τῇ ἐπιφωσκούσῃ εἰς μίαν σαββάτων...	πρωῒ τῇ μιᾷ τῶν σαββάτων... ἀνατείλαντος τοῦ ἡλίου.	τῶν σαββάτων ὄρθρου βαθέως...	σαββάτων... πρωῒ σκοτίας ἔτι οὔσης
Μαριὰμ ἡ Μαγδαληνὴ μαθήτρια τοῦ κυρίου φοβουμένη διὰ τοὺς Ἰουδαίους, ἐπειδὴ ἐφλέγοντο ὑπὸ τῆς ὀργῆς, οὐκ ἐποίησεν ἐπὶ τῷ μνήματι τοῦ κυρίου ἃ εἰώθεσαν ποιεῖν αἱ γυναῖκες ἐπὶ τοῖς ἀποθνήσκουσι καὶ τοῖς ἀγαπωμένοις αὐταῖς	²⁶:¹²βαλοῦσα γὰρ αὕτη τὸ μύρον τοῦτο ἐπὶ τοῦ σώματός μου πρὸς τὸ ἐνταφιάσαι με ἐποίησεν.	¹⁴:⁸ὃ ἔσχεν ἐποίησεν· προέλαβεν μυρίσαι τὸ σῶμά μου εἰς τὸν ἐνταφιασμόν.	¹ᶜφέρουσαι ἃ ἡτοίμασαν ἀρώματα.	¹⁹:⁴⁰ἔλαβον οὖν τὸ σῶμα τοῦ Ἰησοῦ καὶ ἔδησαν αὐτὸ ὀθονίοις μετὰ τῶν ἀρωμάτων, καθὼς ἔθος ἐστὶν τοῖς Ἰουδαίοις ἐνταφιάζειν.
⁵¹λαβοῦσα μεθ᾽ ἑαυτῆς τὰς φίλας ἦλθε ἐπὶ τὸ μνημεῖον ὅπου ἦν τεθείς. ⁵²καὶ ἐφοβοῦντο μὴ ἴδωσιν αὐτὰς οἱ Ἰουδαῖοι καὶ ἔλεγον· εἰ καὶ μὴ ἐν ἐκείνῃ τῇ ἡμέρᾳ ᾗ ἐσταυρώθη ἐδυνήθημεν κλαῦσαι καὶ κόψασθαι, καὶ νῦν ἐπὶ τοῦ μνήματος	²⁸:¹ᵇἦλθεν Μαριὰμ ἡ Μαγδαληνὴ καὶ ἡ ἄλλη Μαρία θεωρῆσαι τὸν τάφον.	¹⁶:²...ἔρχονται ἐπὶ τὸ μνημεῖον...	¹ᵇ...ἐπὶ τὸ μνῆμα ἦλθον...	²⁰:¹...Μαρία ἡ Μαγδαληνὴ ἔρχεται...εἰς τὸ μνημεῖον,

GP 12:50–14:60	Matt 28	Mark 16	Luke 24	John 20
αὐτοῦ ποιήσωμεν ταῦτα. ⁵³τίς δὲ ἀποκυλίσει ἡμῖν καὶ τὸν λίθον τὸν τεθέντα ἐπὶ τῆς θύρας τοῦ μνημείου, ἵνα εἰσελθοῦσαι παρακαθεσθῶμεν αὐτῷ καὶ ποιήσωμεν τὰ ὀφειλόμενα;		³καὶ ἔλεγον πρὸς ἑαυτάς, Τίς ἀποκυλίσει ἡμῖν τὸν λίθον ἐκ τῆς θύρας τοῦ μνημείου;		
⁵⁴μέγας γὰρ ἦν ὁ λίθος. καὶ φοβούμεθα μή τις ἡμᾶς ἴδη καὶ εἰ μὴ δυνάμεθα, κἂν ἐπὶ τῆς θύρας βάλωμεν ἃ φέρομεν εἰς μνημοσύνην αὐτοῦ, κλαύσομεν καὶ κοψόμεθα ἕως ἔλθωμεν εἰς τὸν οἶκον ἡμῶν.		⁴καὶ ἀναβλέψασαι θεωροῦσιν ὅτι ἀποκεκύλισται ὁ λίθος, ἦν γὰρ μέγας σφόδρα.		
¹³·⁵⁵καὶ ἀπελθοῦσαι εὗρον τὸν τάφον ἠνεωγμένον			²εὗρον δὲ τὸν λίθον ἀποκεκυλισμένον ἀπὸ τοῦ μνημείου,	²⁰·¹Μαρία ἡ Μαγδαληνή... βλέπει τὸν λίθον ἠρμένον ἐκ τοῦ μνημείου.
				¹¹Μαρία δὲ εἱστήκει πρὸς τῷ μνημείῳ ἔξω κλαίουσα.
καὶ προσελθοῦσαι παρέκυψαν		⁵καὶ εἰσελθοῦσαι εἰς τὸ	³εἰσελθοῦσαι δὲ οὐχ εὗρον τὸ σῶμα τοῦ	ὡς οὖν ἔκλαιεν παρέκυψεν εἰς

GP 12:50–14:60	Matt 28	Mark 16	Luke 24	John 20
ἐκεῖ καὶ ὁρῶσιν ἐκεῖ τινα νεανίσκον καθεζόμενον μέσῳ τοῦ τάφου ὡραῖον καὶ περιβεβλημέ-νον στολὴν λαμπροτάτην,		μνημεῖον εἶδον νεανίσκον καθήμενον ἐν τοῖς δεξιοῖς περιβεβλημέ-νον στολὴν λευκήν,	κυρίου Ἰησοῦ. ⁴καὶ ἐγένετο ἐν τῷ ἀπορεῖσθαι αὐτὰς περὶ τούτου καὶ ἰδοὺ ἄνδρες δύο ἐπέστησαν αὐταῖς ἐν ἐσθῆτι ἀστραπτούσῃ.	τὸ μνημεῖον, ¹²καὶ θεωρεῖ δύο ἀγγέλους ἐν λευκοῖς καθεζομένους, ἕνα πρὸς τῇ κεφαλῇ καὶ ἕνα πρὸς τοῖς ποσίν, ὅπου ἔκειτο τὸ σῶμα τοῦ Ἰησοῦ.
		καὶ ἐξεθαμβήθη-σαν.	⁵ἐμφόβων δὲ γενομένων αὐτῶν καὶ κλινουσῶν τὰ πρόσωπα εἰς τὴν γῆν εἶπαν πρὸς αὐτάς, Τί ζητεῖτε τὸν ζῶντα μετὰ τῶν νεκρῶν;	
ὅστις ἔφη αὐταῖς· ⁵⁶τί ἤλθατε; τίνα ζητεῖτε; μὴ τὸν σταυρωθέντα ἐκεῖνον;	⁵ἀποκριθεὶς δὲ ὁ ἄγγελος εἶπεν ταῖς γυναιξίν, Μὴ φοβεῖσθε ὑμεῖς, οἶδα γὰρ ὅτι Ἰησοῦν τὸν ἐσταυρωμένον ζητεῖτε·	⁶ὁ δὲ λέγει αὐταῖς, Μὴ ἐκθαμβεῖσθε· Ἰησοῦν ζητεῖτε τὸν Ναζαρηνὸν τὸν ἐσταυρωμέ-νον·		¹³ᵃκαὶ λέγουσιν αὐτῇ ἐκεῖνοι, Γύναι, τί κλαίεις;
⟨ἀνέστη⟩ καὶ ἀπῆλθεν. εἰ δὲ μὴ πιστεύετε, παρακύψατε καὶ ἴδετε τὸν τόπον ἔνθα ἔκειτο ὅτι οὐκ ἔστιν. ἀνέστη γὰρ καὶ ἀπῆλθεν ἐκεῖ ὅθεν ἀπεστάλη.	⁶οὐκ ἔστιν ὧδε, ⟨ἠγέρθη⟩ γὰρ ⟨καθὼς⟩ εἶπεν· δεῦτε ἴδετε τὸν τόπον ὅπου ἔκειτο.	⟨ἠγέρθη⟩, οὐκ ἔστιν ὧδε· ἴδε ὁ τόπος ὅπου ἔθηκαν αὐτόν.	⁶ᵃοὐκ ἔστιν ὧδε, ἀλλὰ ⟨ἠγέρθη.⟩	²τρέχει οὖν καὶ ἔρχεται πρὸς Σίμωνα Πέτρον καὶ πρὸς τὸν ἄλλον μαθητὴν ὃν ἐφίλει ὁ Ἰησοῦς, καὶ λέγει αὐτοῖς, ηραν τὸν κύριον ἐκ τοῦ μνημείου, καὶ οὐκ οἴδαμεν ποῦ ἔθηκαν αὐτόν.
	⁷καὶ ταχὺ πορευθεῖσαι εἴπατε τοῖς μαθηταῖς αὐτοῦ ὅτι Ἠγέρθη ἀπὸ τῶν νεκρῶν,	⁷ἀλλὰ ὑπάγετε εἴπατε τοῖς μαθηταῖς αὐτοῦ καὶ τῷ Πέτρῳ ὅτι Προάγει ὑμᾶς εἰς τὴν		

GP 12:50–14:60	Matt 28	Mark 16	Luke 24	John 20
	καὶ ἰδοὺ προάγει ὑμᾶς εἰς τὴν Γαλιλαίαν, ἐκεῖ αὐτὸν ὄψεσθε· ἰδοὺ εἶπον ὑμῖν.	Γαλιλαίαν· ἐκεῖ αὐτὸν ὄψεσθε, καθὼς εἶπεν ὑμῖν.		
⁵⁷τότε αἱ γυναῖκες φοβηθεῖσαι ἔφυγον.	⁸καὶ ἀπελθοῦσαι ταχὺ ἀπὸ τοῦ μνημείου μετὰ φόβου καὶ χαρᾶς μεγάλης ἔδραμον ἀπαγγεῖλαι τοῖς μαθηταῖς αὐτοῦ.	⁸καὶ ἐξελθοῦσαι ἔφυγον ἀπὸ τοῦ μνημείου, εἶχεν γὰρ αὐτὰς τρόμος καὶ ἔκστασις· καὶ οὐδενὶ οὐδὲν εἶπαν, ἐφοβοῦντο γάρ.	⁸καὶ ἐμνήσθησαν τῶν ῥημάτων αὐτοῦ, ⁹καὶ ὑποστρέψασαι ἀπὸ τοῦ μνημείου ἀπήγγειλαν ταῦτα πάντα τοῖς ἕνδεκα καὶ πᾶσιν τοῖς λοιποῖς. ¹⁰ἦσαν δὲ ἡ Μαγδαληνὴ Μαρία καὶ Ἰωάννα καὶ Μαρία ἡ Ἰακώβου· καὶ αἱ λοιπαὶ σὺν αὐταῖς ἔλεγον πρὸς τοὺς ἀποστόλους ταῦτα. ¹¹καὶ ἐφάνησαν ἐνώπιον αὐτῶν ὡσεὶ λῆρος τὰ ῥήματα ταῦτα, καὶ ἠπίστουν αὐταῖς.	
¹⁴:⁵⁸ἦν δὲ τελευταία ἡμέρα τῶν ἀζύμων καὶ πολλοί τινες ἐξήρχοντο ὑποστρέφοντες εἰς τοὺς οἴκους αὐτῶν τῆς ἑορτῆς	¹⁶Οἱ δὲ ἕνδεκα μαθηταὶ ἐπορεύθησαν εἰς τὴν Γαλιλαίαν εἰς τὸ ὄρος οὗ ἐτάξατο αὐτοῖς ὁ Ἰησοῦς	¹⁰ἐκείνη πορευθεῖσα ἀπήγγειλεν τοῖς μετ' αὐτοῦ γενομένοις πενθοῦσι καὶ κλαίουσιν (Mark 16:9-20 is a later	

GP 12:50–14:60	Matt 28	Mark 16	Luke 24	John 20
παυσαμένης. [59]ἡμεῖς δὲ οἱ δώδεκα μαθηταὶ τοῦ κυρίου ἐκλαίομεν καὶ ἐλυπούμεθα καὶ ἕκαστος λυπούμενος διὰ τὸ συμβὰν ἀπηλλάγη εἰς τὸν οἶκον αὐτοῦ.		addition)		[19]Οὔσης οὖν ὀψίας τῇ ἡμέρᾳ ἐκείνῃ τῇ μιᾷ σαββάτων, καὶ τῶν θυρῶν κεκλεισμένων ὅπου ἦσαν οἱ μαθηταὶ διὰ τὸν φόβον τῶν Ἰουδαίων, ἦλθεν ὁ Ἰησοῦς καὶ ἔστη εἰς τὸ μέσον καὶ λέγει αὐτοῖς, Εἰρήνη ὑμῖν. [21:1]Μετὰ ταῦτα ἐφανέρωσεν ἑαυτὸν πάλιν ὁ Ἰησοῦς τοῖς μαθηταῖς ἐπὶ τῆς θαλάσσης τῆς Τιβεριάδος· ἐφανέρωσεν δὲ οὕτως.
[60]ἐγὼ δὲ Σίμων Πέτρος καὶ Ἀνδρέας ὁ ἀδελφός μου λαβόντες ἡμῶν τὰ λίνα ἀπήλθαμεν εἰς τὴν θάλλασσαν. καὶ ἦν σὺν ἡμῖν Λευεὶς ὁ τοῦ Ἀλφαίου ὃν κύριος				[2]ἦσαν ὁμοῦ Σίμων Πέτρος καὶ Θωμᾶς ὁ λεγόμενος Δίδυμος καὶ Ναθαναὴλ ὁ ἀπὸ Κανὰ τῆς Γαλιλαίας καὶ οἱ τοῦ Ζεβεδαίου καὶ ἄλλοι ἐκ τῶν μαθητῶν αὐτοῦ δύο. [3]λέγει αὐτοῖς Σίμων Πέτρος, Ὑπάγω ἁλιεύειν. λέγουσιν αὐτῷ,

GP 12:50–14:60	Matt 28	Mark 16	Luke 24	John 20
				Ἐρχόμεθα καὶ ἡμεῖς σὺν σοί. ἐξῆλθον καὶ ἐνέβησαν εἰς τὸ πλοῖον, καὶ ἐν ἐκείνῃ τῇ νυκτὶ ἐπίασαν οὐδέν. (John 21 is a later addition)

More than any previous section of GP, the empty tomb visit has similarities to Mark. On this point, there is a consensus among commentators.[1] Yet when it comes to determining the specific nature of the relationship between GP and Mark, there is a peculiar case of scholarly role reversal. Brown, who typically finds GP to be dependent on the canonical gospels when there are similarities, concludes that "the tomb-story similarities leave too slim a basis for positing *GPet* dependence on Mark."[2] Crossan, on the other hand, includes the visit to the tomb in the redactional stratum of GP, meaning that it was not original but was added later to bring it into alignment with the canonical stories.[3] For him, GP is dependent on Mark here. Similarly, Koester concludes that "there is nothing in this account that could not have been derived from Mark or from the source that Mark used."[4] It is almost as if each side in this issue has crossed over here, only to realize that the other has done likewise. What is it about the story that has caused this? The following analysis will serve to explicate the matter.

Because everyone who had been guarding the tomb has left the place in order to bring news of the resurrection to Pilate, there is apparently no one present when the women arrive, except for the man who descended from heaven and entered the grave earlier (GP 11:44). The women come to the tomb "at dawn of the Lord's day" (ὄρθου δὲ τῆς κυριακῆς) (GP 12:50). This is the first clear chronological marker since "in the night in which the Lord's day dawned" at GP 9:35. All the NT gospels use a form of μία

---

[1] For example, Vaganay, *Évangile de Pierre*, 315; Crossan, *Cross That Spoke*, 281–90; Koester, *Ancient Christian Gospels*, 238–39; Brown, *Death of the Messiah*, 2:1327–28.

[2] Brown, *Death of the Messiah*, 2:1328.

[3] Crossan, *Cross That Spoke*, 284.

[4] Koester, *Ancient Christian Gospels*, 239.

σαββάτων, not κυριακή, to indicate the day of the visit (Matt 28:1; Mark 16:2; Luke 24:1; John 20:1).[5]

Those who come to the tomb are identified as Mary Magdalene and "her friends" (GP 12:50). Perhaps this a natural way to harmonize the various women named in the earlier accounts.[6] GP is unique in referring to Mary Magdalene as a μαθήτρια τοῦ κυρίου, and it alone adds the comment about fear of the Jews.[7] The women have come to do "what women are accustomed to do for their dead loved ones" (GP 12:50). This probably represents the same reason that the women come to the tomb in Mark 16:1 and Luke 23:56–24:1. Matthew says nothing of anointing by the women, while John implies that it was done by Joseph and Nicodemus at Friday's burial (John 19:40).[8]

The women's statement about fearing the Jews and lamenting the death of Jesus (GP 12:52) is without parallel in the NT accounts. Once at the tomb the women ask, "But who will roll away for us the stone that was laid at the door of the sepulcher, so that we may go in and sit beside him and do the things that are due?" (GP 12:53). Mark is the only NT gospel to include a question from the women, and it is very similar to the first half of the Petrine one: "Who will roll away the stone for us from the entrance to the tomb?" (Mark 16:3). Likewise, statements about the immensity of the stone follow immediately in the two accounts (GP 12:54; Mark 16:4), while no other NT writer mentions this.

After the women express fear of the Jews and mourn, they discover that the tomb is open (GP 12:54–13:55). Three NT evangelists include a similar comment, though each of their particular descriptions is different from the others (Mark 16:4; Luke 24:2; John 20:1). In order to enter the sepulcher, the women must stoop down (παρακύπτω) (GP 13:55). The angelic figure will also use this term when bringing the resurrection news to them (GP 13:56). Both Luke and John use παρακύπτω to describe the movement of

---

[5] As I stated in Chapter Five, this is possibly an indication that GP is to be dated later than the NT parallels. Luke 24:1 also includes the adjective ὄρθος when describing the time, as in GP.

[6] Crossan, *Cross That Spoke*, 285–86.

[7] μαθήτρια appears in the NT only once, in Acts 9:36. Other statements about the fear and piety of the women appear in GP 12:52, 54.

[8] Earlier allusions to anointing for burial come in Matt 26:12; Mark 14:8. On this practice in early Roman Palestine, see McCane, *Roll Back the Stone*, 31–32. Those anointing the body would wash it, sometimes with ointments or perfumes, before wrapping and binding it. McCane refers to the description of Lazarus in John 11:44 as an example of the manner in which bodies were wrapped.

those at the tomb (Luke 24:12; John 20:5, 11), perhaps indicating that GP has been influenced by one or both of the NT accounts.[9]

Once inside the sepulcher, the women see "a young man sitting in the middle of the tomb, beautiful and clothed with a brightly shining robe" (GP 13:55). Again, this most closely resembles Mark, who identifies this figure as "a young man, dressed in a white robe, sitting on the right side" (Mark 16:5). In Luke, two men are in the tomb, and in the Fourth Gospel two angels are sitting where Jesus' body had been lying (Luke 24:4; John 20:12). Matthew is ambiguous as to whether anyone (i.e., the women or angel) ever enters the tomb (Matt 28:2–6).

The man in the tomb asks the women three questions: "Why have you come? Who[m] do you seek? Not that one who was crucified?" (GP 13:56). These are paralleled by Mark, though he gives them as statements rather than questions. The women in Mark have come because they are "looking for Jesus of Nazareth, who was crucified" (Mark 16:6). This tells why they have come (to look for Jesus), whom they seek (Jesus), and, yes, he is the one who was crucified. The angelic statement in Matt 28:5 closely resembles the Petrine and Markan ones.

After the three questions, the figure at the grave continues, "He is risen and gone hence. But if you do not believe, stoop down and see the place where he lay: He is not (there)" (GP 13:56). Again, Mark is similar: "He has been raised; he is not here. Look, there is the place they laid him" (Mark 16:6). Matthew also follows Mark closely: "He is not here; for he has been raised, as he said. Come, see the place where he lay" (Matt 28:6). After the statement from the man in the tomb, GP includes the comment that "the women feared and fled," which is closest to the summary of Mark 16:8.

In light of these substantial agreements between GP and Mark, Koester's judgment appears to be on target: GP 12:50–13:57 is derived from either Mark or a pre-Markan source.[10] What does Koester offer in support of a pre-Markan source here? He claims that there are three Markan redactional elements that are absent from GP: 1) the commanding of the women to tell the disciples to go to Galilee (Mark 16:7); 2) "the exaggerated emphasis upon fear and astonishment (Mark 16:5, 8)"; and 3)

---

[9] So Crossan, *Cross That Spoke,* 289–90. He also suggests that Jesus going to "the place from which he was sent" echoes Johannine thought.

[10] Koester, *Ancient Christian Gospels,* 238–39. Frans Neirynck ("The Apocryphal Gospels and the Gospel of Mark," in *The New Testament in Early Christianity* [ed. Jean-Marie Sevrin; BETL 86; Leuven: Leuven University Press, 1989], 123–75) is perhaps closest to my own position. He claims that GP is a reflection upon and retelling of the Markan episode. The opening verse of the GP account answers questions such as "Who is Mary Magdalene, why does she go to the tomb, and why now, and not on the day of Jesus' death?" (ibid., 146).

"perhaps also the reference to the purchase of spices (Mark 16:1)."[11] The first of these I addressed in Chapter Five. There is a consistent trend in GP to lessen the role of women as witnesses to the resurrection. Crossan reaches a conclusion similar to my own, though he assigns this not to the original author of GP (his Cross Gospel) but to a later editor: "The redactor did not deem it appropriate to send messages to them [i.e., the disciples] through the women but preferred to have Jesus encounter them directly."[12]

Koester's second item – an exaggerated emphasis on fear and amazement – is not actually missing from GP, as he claims. He cites Mark 16:5, 8 as instances where GP is lacking this element of fear. With regard to the first instance, he is correct; the women are not afraid of the man in the tomb, which is the reason for the fear in Mark 16:5 (cf. GP 13:55). However, the parallel to Mark 16:8 does include a reference to fear (GP 13:57), though it is not emphasized to the same level as in Mark. More important, though, is Koester's silence regarding *three other places* in the Petrine account where the women are fearful (GP 12:50, 52, 54).[13] Certainly, then, I cannot agree with Koester when he says that GP is lacking the Markan emphasis on fear or astonishment.[14]

The third instance of alleged missing Markan redaction – the purchase of spices – is offered tentatively by Koester. But as is true of the element of fear, GP is not necessarily lacking this one. Granted, the women are not said explicitly to buy spices. However, it is possible that this act is inferred as part of their preparations to do "what women are accustomed to do for their dead loved ones" (GP 12:50). Moreover, Matthew omits completely the purchase of spices, yet it is obvious that he is otherwise dependent on Mark for his empty tomb story. The same can be said of GP.

Koester's proposals for dependence on a pre-Markan source are not compelling. Therefore, it appears best to conclude that the Petrine evangelist does know the Markan empty tomb account. In addition, he gives indications that he may also be familiar with elements of Luke and John at this point as well.

After the flight of the women from the tomb, GP includes what looks to be the opening of an epiphany story, though the text breaks off before Jesus actually appears to his disciples (GP 14:58–60). In these three verses there are elements in common with Matthew, Mark, and John. In a fashion typical of the Petrine evangelist, another chronological indicator marks a

---

[11] Koester, *Ancient Christian Gospels*, 239.

[12] Crossan, *Cross That Spoke*, 290.

[13] On this point, see Crossan, *Cross That Spoke*, 286–88; Neirynck, "Apocryphal Gospels," 146–47.

[14] I will say more about this below. John 19:38 and 20:19 refer to fear of the Jews. These verses may be the source of the theme throughout GP 12:50–13:57.

shift of scene: "But it was the last day of the unleavened bread" (GP 14:58). None of the NT gospels has such a reference. Because the feast has ended, many have departed Jerusalem and returned home (GP 14:58). The disciples have done this while mourning the death of Jesus (GP 14:59). Presumably, this means that they have gone back to Galilee. In Matthew and the Johannine epilogue the disciples certainly do return to Galilee after the crucifixion (Matt 28:16; John 21:1).[15]

Simon Peter, his brother Andrew, and Levi, son of Alphaeus, take their nets to the sea, and it is at this point that the extant portion of GP ends (GP 14:60). The verse is written in the first person, Simon Peter being the narrator.[16] Aside from this narrative perspective, the story is not unlike John 21:1–14, where Jesus appears to seven disciples by the Sea of Tiberias.[17] In John, these disciples are identified as "Simon Peter, Thomas called the Twin, Nathanael of Cana in Galilee, the sons of Zebedee, and two others of his disciples" (John 21:2). Because the text of GP ends, we do not know how many or which disciples accompanied Simon Peter, Andrew, and Levi.[18] In comparing GP to John, Koester claims that "the discrepancies in the list of names argues against any dependence."[19] This is odd in that Koester judges GP's story of the visit to the tomb to be dependent on Mark, despite the fact that, besides Mary Magdalene, "not one of the other names [from Mark] ... appears" in GP.[20] Aside from the difference in the list of names, Koester offers no further reason for rejecting GP's dependence on John here. It is therefore not clear why the issue

---

[15] Mark apparently knows of appearance stories that are set in Galilee (see Mark 14:28; 16:7). Luke keeps the disciples in the area around Jerusalem. Robert H. Lightfoot (*Locality and Doctrine in the Gospels* [London: Hodder & Stoughton, 1938]) was among the first to suggest that Mark 14:28 and 16:7 refer not to post-resurrection appearances but to the parousia. Against this proposal, see Robert H. Stein, "A Short Note on Mark xiv.28 and xvi.7," *NTS* 20 (1974): 445–52; Ernest Best, *Mark: The Gospel as Story* (Edinburgh: T&T Clark, 1983), 76–78; Andrew T. Lincoln, "The Promise and the Failure: Mark 16:7, 8," *JBL* 108 (1989): 283–300.

[16] This will be a topic of further discussion below. The narrator also employs first-person language in GP 7:26–27. No NT gospel includes a first-person narrator.

[17] Many have suggested a relationship between GP 14:58–60 and John 21:1–14. See, for example, Swete, *Akhmîm Fragment*, 24; Vaganay, *Évangile de Pierre*, 338–39; Mara, *Évangile de Pierre*, 210–12; Crossan, *Cross That Spoke*, 291–93.

[18] Crossan conjectures 1) that the author "intended to name twelve disciples since he had mentioned twelve in the preceding verse," and 2) that he may have replaced Judas Iscariot with Levi (*Cross That Spoke*, 293).

[19] Koester, *Ancient Christian Gospels*, 240.

[20] Ibid., 239. Crossan (*Cross That Spoke*, 292) shares my sentiments here when he remarks that "there were also major differences even in the first verse of the last intracanonical excerpt in 12:50–13:57."

should be an obstacle in the present instance when it did not count against judging in favor of dependence in the case of the women at the tomb.

It is interesting that the name "Levi, the son of Alphaeus" (Λευεὶς ὁ τοῦ Ἀλφαίου) occurs in earlier gospels only at Mark 2:14. This indicates a further possible parallel between the uses of this name in GP and Mark. In GP, it is "Levi, the son of Alphaeus, whom the Lord..." (Λευεὶς ὁ τοῦ Ἀλφαίου ὃν κύριος) who is mentioned just as the text breaks off (GP 14:60). In Mark 2:14 an individual with the same name is sitting at his tax booth when Jesus calls him to follow and he does so. Does the missing portion of GP's text continue with something like "whom the Lord *called*"? Whether GP gets this name from the Markan story is impossible to determine, but the suggestion is certainly plausible. We know nothing more of what follows in the original text of GP.

This synoptic analysis has shown that the story of the women's visit to the tomb in GP is based primarily on Mark's version for its structure. As I mentioned briefly and hope to elaborate upon in my subsequent discussion, the theme of the women's fear of the Jews may have been picked up from John. Because of the fragmentary nature of the closing verses of GP, I have tentatively suggested that it is a retelling of an appearance story like that found in John 21:1–14. Therefore, our final section of GP has the most in common with Mark and John.

6.2 GP 12:50–14:60: Fearing the Jews and Providing Apostolic Testimony

Because this final extant section of GP is best divided into two units – the tomb visit and the beginning of an appearance story – I will address one feature from each that exemplifies the ways in which the Petrine author has reworked the NT material. In the account of the women at the tomb, I will examine the theme of the fear of the Jews. Following this, I will discuss the role of apostolic witness in the closing epiphany story. In the course of reviewing this material I will be suggesting that both features are integral to the motives behind the rewriting of earlier texts and traditions.

6.2.1 Fearing the Jews

In the synoptic analysis, I contended that GP 12:50–13:57 is by far the most "Markan" section of the gospel. So, if we grant this knowledge of Mark, how has our author retold the story of the women at the tomb? Both Crossan and Neirynck are among the many who have concluded, despite Koester's claims to the contrary, that fear is a guiding motif in GP's version.[21] I will be echoing many of their conclusions throughout this section. Neirynck identifies the women's fear of being seen by the Jews as the "dominant theme" of the Petrine tomb story.[22] Crossan judges that both this fear and the mourning for Jesus are the most noteworthy themes.[23] Before looking further at GP, I will collect and assess Mark's references to fear.

Mark employs multiple words and expressions to convey fearfulness in his gospel. The most common Greek verb indicating fear is φοβέω, and Mark uses it in the tomb story, in the final phrase of his gospel: "And they said nothing to anyone, *for they were afraid* (ἐφοβοῦντο γάρ)" (Mark 16:8). But there is another Markan term that also warrants discussion. The verb ἐκθαμβέω appears only four times in the entire NT, and all of these are in Mark (Mark 9:15; 14:33; 16:5, 6).[24] Two of these four uses appear at the tomb: 1) the women are "alarmed" when they see the young man in the tomb (Mark 16:5); and 2) the young man reassures them by telling them not to be "alarmed" (Mark 16:6). In BDAG this term is defined as "to be moved to a relatively intense emotional state because of someth. causing great surprise or perplexity, be very excited."[25] Surprise or shock is the idea conveyed in Mark 16:5–6. This can also be deduced from looking at the other two instances where ἐκθαμβέω is used (Mark 9:15; 14:33). Therefore, in Mark the women are not afraid of the young man in particular; rather, the focus is on their fear and amazement at all they have witnessed at the tomb.

In addition to the references discussed thus far, there is one further occasion in Mark 16 where the women are fearful, and this comes near the very end of the story: "So they went out and fled from the tomb, for terror and amazement (τρόμος καὶ ἔκστασις) had seized them" (Mark 16:8a). The NRSV is not literal in its translation here. It would be better to describe what seizes them as "trembling and amazement." So what is causing their fear?

Taylor claims that the message from the figure at the tomb leads to the women's trembling and astonishment in the first half of v. 8, but then he finds a different explanation for the concluding ἐφοβοῦντο γάρ statement.[26] He alleges that what would naturally follow ἐφοβοῦντο γάρ would be a μή clause, which in itself is entirely possible.[27] But he goes

---

[21] Crossan, *Cross That Spoke,* 281–90; Neirynck, "Apocryphal Gospels," 146–47.

[22] Neirynck, "Apocryphal Gospels," 146.

[23] Crossan, *Cross That Spoke,* 285.

[24] The same is true of the related verb θαμβέω, which appears in the NT only in Mark 1:27; 10:24, 32.

[25] BDAG, s.v. "ἐκθαμβέω," 303.

[26] Taylor, *Gospel according to St. Mark,* 609–10.

[27] Taylor's position is that the original ending of Mark has been lost.

further in surmising that the subsequent μή clause would refer to "the Jews or to the charge of madness."[28] This stretches the evidence beyond what it is capable of providing. There is no reference to fear of the Jews anywhere in Mark, nor is there anything in the context of Mark 16:1–8 to indicate that Jews are in mind.[29] Thus, the closing Markan statement, "for they were afraid," does not refer to Jews; it is most likely a summary of the emotions that have resulted from their experience at the tomb. Crossan refers to this as "numinous awe," and I think that this is the idea in Mark.[30] Mark exhibits a flair for the dramatic. It is therefore only fitting that he ends on such a note.

Likewise, in Matthew the cause of the women's fear is left unstated. The angel at the tomb tells the women not to be afraid (μὴ φοβεῖσθε) (Matt 28:5). Here, Matthew is following Mark but has changed the verb from Mark's ἐκθαμβέω to φοβέω (cf. Mark 16:6). When the women depart from the tomb, Matthew again stays close to his Markan source in his description of them going away "with fear" (μετὰ φόβου) (Matt 28:8; cf. Mark 16:8). Then, as the women leave the tomb they encounter Jesus, who instructs them, "Do not be afraid" (μὴ φοβεῖσθε) (Matt 28:10). In none of these three instances is there an explanation regarding the cause of the fear. Matthew appears to be dependent upon Mark for this idea, though, like his source, he does not expound on the reason for it.

Luke also includes the apprehension of the women in his account. When they see two men in the tomb, they are "terrified" (ἔμφοβος) (Luke 24:5). This appears to indicate that the women are fearful of the figures at the tomb. Crossan's notion of "numinous awe" is the best explanation for their emotional state in each of these accounts. In contrast, something quite different affects Mary and her friends in GP.

There is a very specific type of fear that pervades the visit to the tomb in GP: fear of the Jews. To be sure, the closing statement of GP's story ("Then the women feared and fled" in 13:57) has retained the expression of fear from its parallel to Mark 16:8, and it leaves unstated the specific cause. However, this has been preceded by three occasions on which the Petrine evangelist indicates that the women are afraid of the Jews (GP 12:50, 52, 54). In addition, GP lacks the expressions of awe at the sight of the young man in the tomb (GP 13:55; cf. Mark 16:5). But this merely highlights what is significant about the women's apprehension. They are not afraid of the angel or in awe over what they are experiencing; rather, their fear is due solely to the threat posed by the Jews.

---

[28] Taylor, *Gospel according to St. Mark,* 610.

[29] As noted in Neirynck, "Apocryphal Gospels," 146–47.

[30] Crossan, *Cross That Spoke*, 290.

The synoptic chart at the beginning of this chapter reveals three points at which the author of GP has inserted additional dialogue or commentary that is not found in Mark or the other NT gospels. The first instance comes in GP 12:50, where the "fear of the Jews who were burning with rage" is what has prevented Mary Magdalene from doing "what women are accustomed to do for their dead loved ones." She and her friends have not been able to come to the tomb because of the rage-filled Jews who, presumably, are out to harm followers of Jesus. Neirynck suggests that GP is answering the question as to why the women did not carry out this act on the day of Jesus' death.[31] They were too afraid of the Jews. This is questionable, though, since the women still appear to be fearful two days later.

The second comment about fearing the Jews comes a short time later: "And they feared that the Jews should see them" (GP 12:52). Clearly, again, the inference is that harm will befall the women if the Jews should happen upon them. The synoptic table earlier in this chapter shows how GP 12:52 fits between the parallel material in Mark 16:2 and 16:3. The author of GP has inserted this to reiterate his claim about the nature and cause of the women's fear.

The third insertion comes after the description of the size of the stone: "And we fear that anyone should see us" (GP 12:54). This appears to be a simple restatement of the previous two comments about fear. While Jews are not mentioned specifically here, the fact that both of the preceding references speak explicitly of "the Jews" suggests that they are also the referent here. It is not a matter of just anyone seeing Mary and her companions. Instead, the concern is that the Jews will find them.

From where has this motif come? Crossan and Neirynck suggest that GP has picked it up from John, where Joseph of Arimathea is said to be a secret disciple of Jesus because of his "fear of the Jews" (φόβος τῶν Ἰουδαίων), and the disciples are hiding in a locked house on the day of the resurrection because of their "fear of the Jews" (φόβος τῶν

---

[31] Neirynck, "Apocryphal Gospels," 146. McCane (*Roll Back the Stone*, 31) notes that "Jewish funerals in this region and period, whether in Judea or the Galilee, generally took place as soon as possible after death, most often before sunset on the same day." It is not entirely clear what is meant in GP by the women doing "what women are accustomed to do for their dead loved ones" (GP 12:50), but most likely this refers to the practice of anointing and wrapping the body for burial. McCane (ibid., 32) notes the interesting detail that "some rabbinic texts argue that the task of 'wrapping and binding' must be gender specific: men, the rabbis suggest, may wrap and bind the corpse of a man, but not that of a woman. Women, by contrast, may wrap and bind either a male or a female corpse." It is rare to find gender roles within ancient Jewish societies that allowed greater freedom for a woman than a man. This would seem to imply that women were more often involved with burial preparations.

Ἰουδαίων) (John 19:38; 20:19).[32] If we consider that GP's author has exhibited familiarity with John at other points, it is indeed likely that he has borrowed this idea as well.[33] This is all the more likely when we remember that earlier in our gospel there is an episode very similar to John 20:19. In GP 7:26–27 Peter and the disciples are hiding after the crucifixion because they are being sought by the Jews as ones who want to burn down the temple. This additional scene well exemplifies the same fear of the Jews that arises from the women at the sepulcher. In light of this, I concur with Crossan's conclusion about the women's visit to the tomb in GP: the structure and sequence of Mark's account has been supplemented with John's theme of fearing the Jews.[34] The story has been retold by combining elements of two earlier gospels to form an entirely new account, one that continues to cast aspersions on the Jewish people much as it did in its revision of the crucifixion scene.

6.2.2 Apostolic Testimony

While this study has reviewed many similarities between GP and antecedent texts, our gospel is unique in its narrative perspective. The NT gospels are the only texts that antedate GP and include appearance stories. Mark includes no such account, though he seems to know of them (Mark 14:28; 16:7). Matthew and Luke recount epiphanies, yet both work strictly within a third-person narrative framework.[35] These two authors do not claim to

---

[32] Crossan, *Cross That Spoke*, 285; Neirynck, "Apocryphal Gospels," 146–47. Crossan (*Cross That Spoke*, 285) on two occasions cites John 20:9 as the source of the motif of fearing the Jews, but this should be John 20:19. Earlier in the Fourth Gospel, no one will speak openly about Jesus because of their "fear of the Jews" (φόβος τῶν Ἰουδαίων) (John 7:13). Vaganay (*Évangile de Pierre*, 320) offers two alternatives for explaining the fear of the Jews in GP: 1) borrowing from John; and 2) an interpretation of Mark 16:8. I have already offered some reasons for doubting the second proposal.

On the nature and background of the anti-Jewish tendency in John, see D. Moody Smith, "Judaism and the Gospel of John," in *Jews and Christians: Exploring the Past, Present, and Future* (ed. James H. Charlesworth; New York: Crossroad, 1990), 76–96; Robert Kysar, "Anti-Semitism and the Gospel of John," in Evans and Hagner, *Anti-Semitism and Early Christianity*, 113–27; J. Louis Martyn, *History and Theology in the Fourth Gospel* (3d ed.; Louisville: Westminster John Knox, 2003).

[33] For example, GP shows an awareness of the Johannine leg-breaking scene. Regarding GP 12:50–13:57 alone, Neirynck ("Apocryphal Gospels," 147 n. 126) lists no fewer than ten possible points of contact with John 19–20, although some are less compelling than others.

[34] Crossan, *Cross That Spoke*, 285.

[35] Luke's second volume includes first-person narratives (Acts 16:10–17; 20:5–21:17; 27:1–28:31). These, however, are not related to any accounts in his or any of the other NT gospels. The "we" passages in Acts have of course been the object of intense scholar-

have witnessed any of the events they describe. John, the likeliest source, if any, for GP's appearance story, is unique among the NT gospels in the perspective of its narrator.[36] My focus will be on John 19:35, though I will not try to sort through the entire maze of proposals regarding this issue, especially as it relates to John 21:24: "This is the disciple who is testifying to these things and has written them, and we know that his testimony is true." Who is the disciple? To what do "these things" refer? In what sense is it being claimed that the disciple wrote the gospel? Who are the "we" that are mentioned? Addressing all of these questions in detail would lead us too far afield.

We first note that John claims to have an eyewitness as one of his sources, and perhaps the author himself is claiming to be such a witness (John 19:35).[37] This source should in all probability be identified with "the disciple whom Jesus loved" (John 13:23; 19:26; 20:2; 21:7, 20).[38] The exact identity of this disciple is not important for our purposes, nor is the disciple's historicity.[39] It is only relevant to note that the Fourth Gospel claims to have a disciple of Jesus as an eyewitness to some of the events in John 19–21. Bauckham has argued, persuasively in my opinion, that "the portrayal of the Beloved Disciple qualif[ies] him to be the ideal witness to Jesus, his story, and its meaning."[40] The disciple's putative status as a witness grants him the authority to interpret the significance of the events

---

ly scrutiny at least since the groundbreaking work in Martin Dibelius, *Studies in the Acts of the Apostles* (London: SCM, 1956).

[36] This matter is complicated further by the fact that John 21, where this story occurs, is a later addendum whose authorship may differ from that of John 1–20. See the comments on this in Barrett, *Gospel according to St. John*, 479–80; Raymond E. Brown, *The Gospel according to John XIII–XXI: A New Translation with Introduction and Commentary* (AB 29A; New York: Doubleday, 1970), 1077–82. I follow the judgment of Brown (*Gospel according to John XIII–XXI*, 1080), that ch. 21 was composed by a later redactor, not by the original author. Brown later changed much of his reconstruction of the development of John's gospel in subsequent publications. See, for example, idem, *The Community of the Beloved Disciple* (New York: Paulist, 1979).

[37] Bauckham (*Jesus and the Eyewitnesses*, 358–437) argues at length that the Fourth Gospel was written by someone who claimed to be an eyewitness of many of the events he describes and that this individual was not a member of Jesus' inner circle of twelve disciples.

[38] Brown, *Gospel according to John XIII–XXI*, 936–37.

[39] Brown (ibid., xcii–xcviii) summarizes various proposals regarding the identity of the beloved disciple and the question of whether the term is intended to refer to a real person or is merely symbolic.

[40] Bauckham, *Jesus and the Eyewitnesses*, 399. We need not concur with Bauckham's judgment about the veracity of the Fourth Evangelist's claim to be an eyewitness in order to appreciate his point about the way in which the *portrayal* of the beloved disciple functions at the narrative level.

he narrates. Most importantly, the scene of John 21:1–14 – the potential source of GP 14:58–60 – is one at which the beloved disciple is present.

In summary, there are two items to be noted about John. First, it claims to be based on the testimony of someone who was present at some of the events it describes, yet the Fourth Evangelist still writes from a third-person perspective. Second, the source of this gospel is anonymous. The beloved disciple is never named.

GP differs from John in these two regards. The narrator speaks in the first person and his identity is made explicit. In GP 14:59 we read, "But we, the twelve disciples of the Lord, wept and were grieved." This indicates that the author is one of the "twelve disciples." The exact individual is noted in the next verse: "But I, Simon Peter, and my brother Andrew..." (GP 14:60). The story is told from a first-person perspective by Peter, one of the twelve disciples. There is also an instance of first-person narration earlier in GP:

> But I mourned with my companions, and having been wounded in heart we concealed ourselves. For we were being sought after by them as malefactors, and as persons who wanted to set fire to the temple. Because of all these things we fasted and sat mourning and weeping night and day until the Sabbath. (GP 7:26–27)

On those occasions where Peter is presumed to have been present, the account is given from his vantage point.

GP, then, is unlike any of its known potential sources in two respects. First, it includes first-person narrative. While John claims to be based on the witness of the beloved disciple, this is at least one step further removed from the perspective of GP. Second, the implied source of GP is not anonymous, as in John, but is explicitly named as a prominent apostle in the early Christian movement.

6.3 Early Christian Parallels

Expressions of fearing the Jews and works written in the name of a well-known Christian leader are common in early texts. I will review these separately because they are not directly related to one another in GP. This survey will lay the groundwork for the next section, in which I will make some proposals regarding the religio-social background that gave rise to the presence of these features.

6.3.1 Fearing the Jews

Because there are few accounts of the discovery of the empty tomb outside of GP and the NT gospels, we will need to look more broadly at the early

Christian literature in order to situate this motif of fearing the Jews. As I stated above, GP is most similar to John in locating Christian fear of the Jews in the aftermath of Jesus' death (John 19:38; 20:19). More often, though, Christian authors refer to a general fear of the Jews, particularly as it relates to the social contexts in which they were writing. This review will focus on those texts that refer to fear of the Jews or to circumstances in which Jews are said to threaten or harm Christians.

Paul claims to have been a persecutor of Christians prior to his conversion to the movement, though he never expounds on the precise nature of his opposition (1 Cor 15:9; Gal 1:13, 22–23; Phil 3:6).[41] Eventually Paul goes from persecutor to one of the persecuted. The clearest expression of his own experience comes in 2 Corinthians:

Five times I have received from the Jews the forty lashes minus one. Three times I was beaten with rods. Once I received a stoning. Three times I was shipwrecked; for a night and a day I was adrift at sea; on frequent journeys, in danger from rivers, danger from bandits, danger from my own people, danger from Gentiles, danger in the city, danger in the wilderness, danger at sea, danger from false brothers and sisters. (2 Cor 11:24–26)[42]

Reference is made to Jewish persecution of Christians in 1 Thess 2:13–16:

And we also thank God constantly for this, that when you received the word of God which you heard from us, you accepted it not as the word of men but as what it really is, the word of God, which is at work in you believers. For you, brethren, became imitators of the churches of God in Christ Jesus which are in Judea; for you suffered the same things from your own countrymen as they did from the Jews, who killed both the Lord Jesus and the prophets, and drove us out, and displease God and oppose all men by hindering us from speaking to the Gentiles that they may be saved – so as always to fill up the measure of their sins. But God's wrath has come upon them at last! (1 Thess 2:13–16)[43]

Paul's testimony that he once persecuted Christians indicates that threats or real acts of violence were carried out by Jews against Christians during

---

[41] On the nature of Paul's opposition to the sect of Christians, see Arland J. Hultgren, "Paul's Pre-Christian Persecutions of the Church: Their Purpose, Locale, and Nature," *JBL* 95 (1976): 97–111. Substantial treatments of Paul's life and travels, including his pre-Christian activities, are given in Martin Hengel, *The Pre-Christian Paul* (trans. John Bowden; Philadelphia: Trinity Press International, 1991); Martin Hengel and Anna M. Schwemer, *Paul between Damascus and Antioch: The Unknown Years* (trans. John Bowden; Louisville: Westminster John Knox, 1997); Udo Schnelle, *Apostle Paul: His Life and Theology* (trans. M. Eugene Boring; Grand Rapids: Baker, 2005); James D. G. Dunn, *Beginning from Jerusalem: Christianity in the Making*, vol. 2 (Grand Rapids: Eerdmans, 2009), esp. 322–77, 497–954.

[42] Paul may also allude to persecution in Rom 15:30–31; Gal 5:11; 6:12.

[43] See also my discussion of these verses in Chapter Two above. As I stated there, even if this is an interpolation, it is a very early one and is relevant to the question of Jewish-Christian relations during the first two centuries.

the first few years of the movement.[44] His later experience as a missionary provides a firsthand account of one who came to be on the receiving end of persecution from certain Jews.

Luke's second volume gives the same general presentation as Paul does on this topic.[45] The pre-Christian Paul opposed the followers of Jesus (Acts 7:58–9:2), and Paul himself is eventually opposed violently by some Jews after his own conversion (e.g., Acts 9:23–25; 14:2–5, 19; 17:5–9; 18:12–17; 20:3, 19; 21:27–32; 23:12–27). In addition, other Christians besides Paul faced persecution at the hands of certain Jews (Acts 4:1–22; 5:17–42; 8:1–3; 12:1–3).

Reading the NT gospels with an eye toward their original audience reveals several points at which hostility from Jews is indicated. Jesus tells his followers that the Jews will persecute them violently (Matt 10:17–18; 23:34; Mark 13:9; Luke 12:11; 21:12; John 15:18–25).[46] In some of these accounts, most notably John, the fear of the Jews is tied to the expulsion of Christians from the synagogues (John 9:22; 12:42–43; 16:2–3).[47] The Fourth Evangelist alleges that some will even push this opposition to the point of trying to kill the followers of Jesus (John 16:2–3).

As we move into the second century, further examples appear. In the *Martyrdom of Polycarp,* Jews in Smyrna are among those who assist in executing the bishop (*Mart. Pol.* 12.2; 13.1).[48] An interesting example is found in the second-century *Epistle to Diognetus*, where Christians are made enemies (πολεμόω) by Jews (*Diogn.* 5.17).[49] Without a doubt, though, Justin Martyr provides the greatest number of references to opposition from and persecution by Jews.

---

[44] It is not possible to date Paul's conversion with precision, but most have concluded that it occurred within two to six years after the death of Jesus. A summary of the data appears in Hengel and Schwemer, *Paul between Damascus and Antioch*, 24–35. Echoing a near-consensus among modern scholars, they date the conversion to approximately three years after the crucifixion, in which case Paul's opposition to the Christian sect would necessarily have come very early in its development.

[45] Setzer (*Jewish Responses*, 44–82) groups the reactions of Jews to Christians in Acts into four categories: 1) neutral curiosity; 2) general tolerance; 3) plots and spontaneous violence; and 4) the use of official channels to punish Christians.

[46] On this subject in Matthew and, to a lesser extent, the other NT gospels, see Douglas R. A. Hare, *The Theme of Jewish Persecution of Christians in the Gospel according to St. Matthew* (SNTSMS 6; Cambridge: Cambridge University Press, 1967).

[47] On the issue of synagogue expulsion in John, see Martyn, "A Gentile Mission That Replaced an Earlier Jewish Mission?" in *Exploring the Gospel of John: In Honor of D. Moody Smith* (ed. R. Alan Culpepper and C. Clifton Black; Louisville: Westminster John Knox, 1996), 124–44; idem, *History and Theology*, 56–65.

[48] ET and Greek text in Holmes, *Apostolic Fathers*, 318–21.

[49] ET and Greek text in ibid., 702–3.

Space will not allow discussion of all of Justin's accusations in this area. Setzer has placed Justin's comments about Jewish actions into the following categories: 1) verbal attacks against Christians; 2) hatred of Christians; 3) actual or desired harm of Christians.[50] I will survey examples from each of these groups. According to Justin, the verbal attacks include slander (*1 Apol.* 49) and cursing of Christians (*Dial.* 16; 93; 95; 96; 108; 123; 133). The two most illustrative quotations are included here:

Now you spurn those who hope in Him, and in Him who sent Him, namely, Almighty God, the Creator of all things; to the utmost of your power you dishonor (ἀτιμάζω) and curse (καταράομαι) in your synagogues all those who believe in Christ. (*Dial.* 16; Falls 172)[51]

For, in your synagogues you curse (καταράομαι) all those who through Him have become Christians, and the Gentiles put into effect your curse by killing all those who merely admit that they are Christians. (*Dial.* 96; Falls 299)[52]

At several points Justin refers to Jewish hatred of Christians (*1 Apol.* 36; *Dial.* 35; 39; 133; 136). Examples of this type are reflected in these statements:

The Jews, who possess the writings of the Prophets, did not understand this; not only did they not recognize Christ when He came, but they even hate (μισέω) us who declare that He has come. (*1 Apol.* 36; Falls 73)[53]

For this reason, too, we pray for you and for everyone else who hates (ἐχθραίνω) us. (*Dial.* 35; Falls 201)[54]

Slander and hatred, verbal abuses as it were, are not the only accusation Justin lodges against the Jews of his day.

Many times, especially in his *Dialogue with Trypho*, Justin claims that Jews pursue violence toward Christians, even to the point of seeking their death (*1 Apol.* 31; *Dial.* 16; 35; 95; 96; 110; 122; 133; 136). He does, however, indicate that Jews are relatively powerless to carry out their wishes, though he has no doubt that they would kill Christians if given the opportunity. I include here a few representative quotations:

But these Jews, though they read the books, fail to grasp their meaning, and they consider us as their enemies and adversaries, killing and punishing us, just as you do, whenever they are able to do so, as you can readily imagine. In the recent Jewish war, Bar Koche-

---

[50] Setzer, *Jewish Responses*, 131–32. She has other categories as well, but these are the most relevant to my discussion. Similar descriptions are provided in Stanton, "Aspects," 377–92.

[51] Greek text in Edgar J. Goodspeed, ed., *Die ältesten Apologeten: Texte mit kurzen Einleitungen* (Göttingen: Vandenhoeck & Ruprecht, 1914), 109.

[52] Greek text in ibid., 210.

[53] Greek text in ibid., 51.

[54] Greek text in ibid., 131.

ba, the leader of the Jewish uprising, ordered that only the Christians should be subjected to dreadful torments, unless they renounced and blasphemed Jesus Christ. (*1 Apol.* 31; Falls 67)

But if you curse Him and those who believe in Him, and, whenever it is in your power, put them to death, how will you prevent retribution from being demanded of you for having laid hands on Him, as of unjust and sinful men who are completely devoid of feeling and wisdom? (*Dial.* 95; Falls 299)

Whenever you and all other men have the power, you cast out every Christian not only from his own property but even from the whole world, for you allow no Christian to live. (*Dial.* 110; Falls 318)

But the proselytes not only do not believe, they blaspheme His name twice as much as you do and they, too, strive to torture and kill us who believe in Him, for they endeavor to follow your example in everything. (*Dial.* 122; Falls 336–37)

Indeed, your hand is still lifted to do evil, because, although you have slain Christ, you do not repent; on the contrary, you hate and (whenever you have the power) kill us who through Him believe in God, the Father of All, and you cease not to curse Him and those who belong to Him. (*Dial.* 133; Falls 354–55)

Later writers, including Origen and Tertullian, also make passing reference to Jewish persecution, as does Eusebius, who quotes some earlier writers in this regard.[55]

The fear of the women in GP is not unlike the sentiments expressed in other Christian texts of the first two centuries. How much was this grounded in the actual experience of early Christians, and how often was it merely a literary fiction used to disparage those outside the movement? This remains to be seen, but I will attempt a brief answer later in this chapter.

6.3.2 Apostolic Testimony

Appeals to apostolic authority even predate the NT texts. Twice in 1 Corinthians Paul criticizes his audience for their factionalism, their move to align with particular Christian apostles or missionaries:

For it has been reported to me by Chloe's people that there are quarrels among you, my brothers and sisters. What I mean is that each of you says, "I belong to Paul," or "I belong to Apollos," or "I belong to Cephas," or "I belong to Christ." (1 Cor 1:11–12)

For when one says, "I belong to Paul," and another, "I belong to Apollos," are you not merely human? What then is Apollos? What is Paul? Servants through whom you came to believe, as the Lord assigned to each. I planted, Apollos watered, but God gave the growth. (1 Cor 3:4–6)

Paul's defense of his status as an apostle also reveals its importance at a very early point in the emerging Christian movement (1 Cor 9:1–27; 2 Cor 11:1–15; Gal 1:11–24). We find that most early Christian texts carry the

---

[55] Examples in Setzer, *Jewish Responses,* 151–57.

name of an early Christian leader, are told from one's perspective, or have some close connection to one. This is true both of texts that came to be included in the NT canon and of those that did not.

Within the NT canon, the four gospels bear the name of an apostle or one affiliated with an apostle.[56] The author of Acts implies that he was occasionally in the company of Paul, at least judging by his use of "we" at times in the narrative. Thirteen letters purport to have been written by the apostle Paul. Two epistles are attributed to Peter, foremost among the twelve apostles. Of the remaining seven NT books, six (James, the Johannine epistles, Jude, and Revelation) bear an apostolic name or the name of one of Jesus' alleged siblings.[57] Some scholars have also proposed "schools" that were associated with various apostles during the first few centuries and in which Christians claimed to carry on the legacy of apostolic figures.[58]

Among texts that did not find their way into the NT canon, the majority of them are named after one of the first followers of Jesus or are purportedly based on their testimony. This extends to the four main literary genres: gospels, acts, epistles, and apocalypses. Early Christian gospels exemplifying this include the *Gospel of Thomas, Gospel of Philip, Gospel of Mary, Gospel of Nicodemus, Infancy Gospel of Thomas,* and the *Protoevangelium of James.* The various acts that circulated in the first few centuries include the *Acts of Peter, Acts of John, Acts of Paul, Acts of Andrew, Acts of Philip, Acts of Andrew and Matthias,* and the *Acts of Thaddaeus.* Apostolic epistles are represented by *Third Corinthians,* the *Epistle to the Laodiceans,* the *Epistles of Paul and Seneca,* the *Epistle of Titus,* and the *Epistle to the Alexandrians.* Lastly, apocalypses that carry the name of an apostle include the *Apocalypse of Peter, First Apocalypse of James, Se-*

---

[56] There is disagreement about whether the titles of the gospels are original or were added later (i.e., in the second century). Hengel ("Titles of the Gospels," 64–84) advocates the former position, while Koester ("From the Kerygma-Gospel to Written Gospels," *NTS* 35 [1989]: 361–81) represents the latter. In any case, by the mid- to late second century all four gospels were associated with an apostle or a figure connected to one.

[57] Of course, in the case of the Johannine epistles and Revelation it is uncertain whether the authors were claiming to have been the apostle John. A helpful summary of pseudepigraphal issues related to NT epistles in particular is found in Bauckham, "Pseudo-Apostolic Letter," *JBL* 107 (1988): 469–94.

[58] Examples of these "school" theories appear in Krister Stendahl, *The School of St. Matthew* (2d ed.; Philadelphia: Fortress, 1968); Oscar Cullman, *The Johannine Circle* (trans. John Bowden; Philadelphia: Westminster, 1976); James H. Charlesworth, *The Beloved Disciple: Whose Witness Validates the Gospel of John?* (Valley Forge, Pa.: Trinity Press International, 1995); Gregory J. Riley, *Resurrection Reconsidered: Thomas and John in Controversy* (Minneapolis: Fortress, 1995).

cond Apocalypse of James, Apocalypse of Paul, and the *Apocryphon of John.*

It is not surprising that Peter, who was perhaps the most well-known apostle of the early Christian era, is associated with numerous texts: 1 Peter, 2 Peter, GP, the *Apocalypse of Peter,* the *Acts of Peter,* the *Kerygma Petri,* the *Acts of Peter and the Twelve Apostles,* and the *Kerygmata Petrou* (pseudo-Clementine source). In the final section of this chapter I will discuss apostolic authority in early Christian texts, especially GP.

6.4 Apologetics and Polemics in GP 12:50–14:60

I will now offer explanations for the two features that we have surveyed in this chapter. Why is there an emphasis on the fear of the Jews? Why is the gospel written from the perspective of Peter? In my estimation, anti-Jewish polemic lies behind the answer to the first question, and intra-Christian apologetics are the motivating factor behind the second.

6.4.1 Fearing the Jews

As I mentioned in my treatment of Jewish responsibility for the death of Jesus in Chapter Two, any discussion of anti-Jewish polemic in the first centuries C.E. must strive to recognize that the subsequent two millennia of history had not yet unfolded. At the time GP was composed, Jews were a much larger social group than Christians, were much more widely recognized by outsiders, and generally had a higher social standing.[59] What little political power Jews had in communities, Christians possessed even less.

John's gospel, which refers to fear of the Jews, has generally been judged to have arisen during the aftermath of the exclusion of Christians from Jewish synagogues. The portrait in John, therefore, is of "a defensive and threatened Christian community, attempting to reshape its identity isolated from the synagogue and its Jewish roots."[60] The *Sitz im Leben* of this gospel can be detected in verses such as John 9:22; 12:42; and 16:2. Martyn has gone so far as to argue that John 16:2 indicates that some of those from the Johannine community who had been expelled from the

---

[59] On the relative social status of the two groups, see Grant, *Jews in the Roman World,* 97–169; Jack T. Sanders, *Schismatics, Sectarians, Dissidents, Deviants: The First One Hundred Years of Jewish-Christian Relations* (Valley Forge, Pa.: Trinity Press International, 1993); Wilson, *Related Strangers;* Lieu, *Image and Reality;* Smallwood, *Jews under Roman Rule.*

[60] Kysar, "Anti-Semitism and the Gospel of John," 120. Martyn (*History and Theology*) is perhaps foremost among those who have suggested that the setting of John lies in the aftermath of the Jewish expulsion of Christians from the synagogue.

synagogue were put to death by Jews for their religious devotion to Jesus.[61] Kysar contends that Martyn has overstated matters, although he acknowledges that there may have been some level of violence between Jews and Christians affiliated with the Johannine community.[62] What is really at issue in John is the question of religious identity: what defines a particular religious group? What distinguishes "us" from "them"? Allegiance to Jesus appears to be at the core of this question. Martyn suggests that if the Jewish authorities had been asked why they act violently against expelled Christian synagogue members, they would have responded in theological terms: "We persecute Jewish Christians because they worship Jesus as a second god."[63]

It is this same formation of a group's religious identity that is important for understanding the fear of the Jews in GP. The author of this text has self-identified in a way that draws a clear distinction between Christians and "Jews." Christians appear further removed from their Jewish roots than they do in John. Setzer remarks that in GP, "Christians hardly appear as any kind of insiders to the Jewish community."[64] There is nothing in GP that could be construed as "in-house" Jewish polemic, such as what is commonly found in the Synoptic Gospels. It is completely an "us vs. them" mentality that is resonating throughout our text. Jews oppose Jesus and anyone aligned with him.

Some have suggested that the reason Christians are afraid of Jews in GP is that the polemic between the two groups in the region where the gospel was written had risen to the point of violence.[65] This is possible, but I think it is more likely that the picture of Jews is being painted in the worst possible light simply to disparage them. Perhaps, as may be the case with Justin, the Petrine evangelist has merely heard of Jewish hostilities towards Christians in his day, though it is possible that some in his community have experienced this firsthand. Jews were one of the religious groups competing with Christians for adherents. The author of GP sees Jews as a socially stronger group, which leads him to present them as the aggressor in the competition with Christians. He uses Jews as the persecutors of Christians to reflect this idea, though he has inherited this motif from John in order to color his story of the women's visit to the tomb.

Theories from the social sciences prove illuminating on this matter. John G. Gager was one of the first to employ conflict theory to explain the

---

[61] Martyn, *History and Theology*, esp. 69–83.

[62] Kysar, "Anti-Semitism and the Gospel of John," 120–21.

[63] Martyn, *History and Theology*, 75.

[64] Setzer, *Jewish Responses*, 125.

[65] Ibid., 124.

growth and development of the early Christian movement.[66] Conflict, both internal and external, played a formative role in this process. Internal conflict manifests itself in areas such as questions of orthodoxy and orthopraxy within a religious sect. The group develops its identity by defining itself around such issues. More importantly for our present subject, though, is the issue of a religious group's external conflicts. Gager summarizes matters this way:

> The search for identity is often reached through a process of rebellion against one's immediate parentage. Inevitably, this task of self-definition involves conflict in one form or another. Externally, this conflict took the form of dialogues with and diatribes against the Jewish and pagan background of nascent Christianity. The polemical tone of these interchanges reflects the urgency that often accompanies the efforts of young, minority communities to establish their own identity in the context of a larger world.[67]

The emphasis in GP on fearing the Jews reflects the efforts of those who wish to portray themselves as the minority community (Christians) to establish its identity in relation to its stronger parent group from which it has separated (Jews).

Another aspect of conflict theory states that the closer the relationship between two competing groups, the more intense the conflict.[68] The portrait of Jews in GP might indicate that this text was composed by a Gentile who had contact with (non-Christian) Jewish groups or individuals. By depicting Jews as people to be feared by Christians, this gospel bears some resemblance to Justin's *Dialogue with Trypho*. Perhaps the Petrine evangelist was a Gentile Christian who viewed Jews in much the same way that Justin did.

6.4.2 Apostolic Testimony

In the emerging Christian movement the appeal to apostolic witness as support for one's position extended to written texts, a trend indicated by the proliferation of works composed in the name or from the perspective of one or more of the earliest Christian leaders. I cataloged this proliferation earlier with my list of works bearing the names of, or purporting to have

---

[66] Gager, *Kingdom and Community: The Social World of Early Christianity* (Englewood Cliffs, N.J.: Prentice-Hall, 1975). Gager is consciously dependent on the work of Lewis Coser (*The Functions of Social Conflict: An Examination of the Concept of Social Conflict and Its Use in Empirical Sociological Research* [New York: Free, 1956]). Coser's theory, in turn, is an exposition of the earlier efforts of Georg Simmel. More recently, Sanders (*Schismatics, Sectarians, Dissidents, Deviants*, 125–29) has advocated conflict theory as one of the most helpful lenses through which to view the relationship between emerging Christianity, Judaism, and the larger Greco-Roman world.

[67] Gager, *Kingdom and Community*, 80.

[68] Ibid., 83–85.

been written by, well-known figures. In early Christian communities, texts judged to have been written by apostles stood a better chance of being considered authoritative.[69]

The appeal to apostolic authority was widespread in early Christianity. In his review of this trend, Everett Ferguson contends that the impetus behind these appeals was the belief that the apostles provided the standard for the church's beliefs and praxis.[70] Christians of all persuasions looked to the age of the apostles as their foundation. This holds true regardless of whether the individuals would come to be identified as orthodox or heterodox in their theological claims. The church originated from the apostles, who formed its foundation, and this was apparently the view of most early Christians.[71] Writers such as Ignatius, Justin, Irenaeus, Tertullian, and Origen appealed to apostolic authority. Those who were eventually deemed heterodox did likewise. Basilides claimed to have received his teachings from Glaucias, an associate of Peter.[72] The Valentinians alleged that their founder was taught by Theudas, a student of Paul.[73]

Speaking specifically of written texts, Irenaeus argues that the four gospels which came to be included in the NT were the gospels "of the apostles" that "have been handed down to us from the apostles" (*Haer.* 3.11.9). For Tertullian, only writings that come from apostolic men are authoritative (*Marc.* 4.2). Christian doctrine, according to Clement, derives from the apostles and their associates, and is preserved in writings (*Strom.* 1.1). This practice of appealing to apostolic authority gives us some background to our discussion of GP.

---

[69] It is anachronistic to refer to the "NT canon" in the mid-second century. Thus, I use the term authoritative to indicate the status granted to texts for use in Christian worship and praxis. On the criterion of apostolicity for determining the authoritative status of texts and its role in the development of the NT canon, see Robert W. Funk, *Parables and Presence: Forms of the New Testament Tradition* (Philadelphia: Fortress, 1982), 182–86; Bruce M. Metzger, *The Canon of the New Testament: Its Origin, Development, and Significance* (Oxford: Clarendon, 1987), 253; Lee M. McDonald, "Identifying Scripture and Canon in the Early Church: The Criteria Question," in idem and Sanders, *Canon Debate*, 416–39, esp. 424–27.

[70] Ferguson, "The Appeal to Apostolic Authority in the Early Centuries," *ResQ* 50 (2008): 49–62. Ferguson and I are not making judgments as to the validity of any particular appeal to apostolic authority. That lies outside the purview of this project. The point is that these appeals were commonplace. See also the contributions in Anthony Hilhorst, ed., *The Apostolic Age in Patristic Thought* (VCSup 70; Leiden: Brill, 2004). The essays in this volume concern the various ways in which Christians of the second through fourth centuries viewed the age of the apostles and attempted to trace many of their claims back to them.

[71] Irenaeus, *Haer.* 3.12.7; 4.21.3; Origen, *Cels.* 3.28.

[72] Clement, *Strom.* 7.17.

[73] Ibid.

The comments of Serapion about the alleged authorship of this gospel are instructive, and we are fortunate that Eusebius has preserved the bishop's words:

> For our part, brethren, we receive both Peter and the other apostles as Christ, *but the writings which falsely bear their names* (τὰ δὲ ὀνόματι αὐτῶν ψευδεπίγραφα) we reject, as men of experience, knowing that such were not handed down to us. For I myself, when I came among you, imagined that all of you clung to the true faith; and, without going through the Gospel put forward by them in the name of Peter, I said: If this is the only thing that seemingly causes captious feelings among you, let it be read. (*Hist. eccl.* 6.12.3–4; Lake and Oulton, 2:40–41)

The gospel bears the name of Peter, but this attribution is false, according to Serapion. Hengel notes that this is the first time the rare word ψευδεπίγραφα appears in Christian literature.[74] The implication of these comments is that writings were put forward falsely in the name of early Christian leaders in an attempt to lend them a degree of credence or authority. In the estimation of the second-century bishop, GP was written in Peter's name and from his perspective in order to ascribe it an authoritative status. In a world of competing gospels, a stamp of approval by an apostle or other early Christian leader was almost essential. There are good reasons for understanding why Peter was chosen in this case.

Vaganay, Koester and others have noted that several pieces of evidence indicate that the authority of Peter was prominent in the area around Antioch and Western Syria during the first two centuries.[75] Peter's importance in this region can be traced back at least to the 40s C.E., as can be inferred from Paul's statements in Galatians 2. Peter is the leading apostle in Matthew's gospel, which most often is assigned a provenance in or around Syrian Antioch.[76] Theophilus of Antioch, still in the second century, alludes to the *Apocalypse of Peter* (*Autol.* 1.14; 2.19). In light of this, it should not be surprising that in Serapion's day GP was being read (and had been composed?) in the region. Swete claims that, when it comes to GP's provenance, "all the evidence points to Western Syria as the place of origin."[77]

---

[74] Hengel, *Four Gospels*, 218 n. 49.

[75] Vaganay, *Évangile de Pierre*, 94; Helmut Koester, "GNOMAI DIAPHOROI: The Origin and Nature of Diversification in the History of Early Christianity," in *Trajectories through Early Christianity* (ed. James M. Robinson and idem; Philadelphia: Fortress, 1971), 119–26; Terence V. Smith, *Petrine Controversies in Early Christianity* (WUNT 2.15; Tübingen: Mohr [Siebeck], 1985), 41–42. David H. Schmidt ("The Peter Writings: Their Redactors and Their Relationships" [Ph.D. diss., Northwestern University, 1972]) has examined the widespread appeal to Peter in early Christian texts that was done in order to garner acceptance for the claims in such works.

[76] Koester, "GNOMAI DIAPHOROI," 123; Hagner, *Matthew 1–13*, lxxv.

[77] Swete, *Akhmîm Fragment*, xliv.

While simply attributing a text to a particular apostle might help gain it a readership, it is even more compelling in granting authority if the text is written by one who participated in the events it describes. The *Gospel of Thomas* might be the earliest gospel to claim direct apostolic authority in this regard, as its opening line reads, "These are the secret words which the living Jesus spoke, and which Didymus Judas Thomas wrote down" (*Gos. Thom.* 1).[78] GP, like the *Gospel of Thomas*, places its apostolic author within its stories. There is no secondhand reporting; rather, one of the alleged eyewitnesses is recounting his own experiences. In this sense, then, writing a gospel in the name and from the perspective of a leading apostle is a form of intra-Christian apologetics. It is an effort to lend it apostolic authority, a key supporting foundation for theological claims.

6.5 Conclusions

The synoptic analysis of GP 12:50–14:60 revealed that the story of the women's visit to the tomb is likely based on Mark 16:1–8 and that the account of the disciples at the Sea of Tiberias may be related to John 21:1–14. In the second section of this chapter I argued that, while GP's empty tomb account is based on Mark, it has inherited the theme of fearing the Jews from John. What Mark leaves unstated – the cause of the fear – GP makes explicit. I then briefly summarized the role of the apostle Peter as the narrator and primary figure of this gospel and noted that this differs from all of the NT gospels. The shift to Peter as narrator resembles the practices of certain Second Temple rewritten Bible texts. For example, the author of the Qumran *Temple Scroll* has omitted the name of Moses when quoting the Pentateuch in order to make it appear as though God was giving the law directly to the *Temple Scroll* writer. This narrative maneuver attempts to lend greater authority to the text.

In reviewing early Christian parallels, I noted several texts, most notably Justin's, that refer to violence directed by Jews against Christians. Examples of works bearing the name of an early Christian leader were also provided in order to reflect the frequency of the practice. Finally, I suggested that, as we discovered in GP's crucifixion story, anti-Jewish polemics underlie the women's fear of the Jews. Christians considered themselves the socially weaker of the two groups, which led them to portray Jews as the aggressor in the competition between the sects. Finally, I showed that the proliferation of texts in the early Christian movement

---

[78] I have noted already that John is indirect in its claim to the authority behind it. The beloved disciple is anonymous and in this sense John differs from both the *Gospel of Thomas* and GP.

frequently led writers to associate their work with a well-known leader and that GP is one example of this. By appealing to the testimony of the most respected apostle – especially within some circles near Antioch during the first two centuries – the author of GP attempted to lend greater authority to his gospel.

Conclusion

Sometime in the middle part of the second century, a Christian author composed a new story of the life, death, and resurrection of Jesus. He did this by using as his primary sources the NT Gospels and other pieces of tradition with which he was acquainted. In this rewritten gospel there are many details that differ from the antecedent works, changes that were made in order to make the story more fitting for the new setting in which this author wrote. By all appearances, he was familiar with some of the criticisms that had been directed against Christian claims in general – and the NT Gospels in particular – by some of those outside the Christian movement. Many of the changes he makes to his sources seem to have been done in response to such objections. His anti-Jewish sentiments are obvious, which is perhaps an indication of real or perceived conflict that existed between his Christian community and a local Jewish group.

In Chapter One I first reviewed the early history of GP and noted that it was well known among Christian writers of the earliest centuries. I offered some reasons for judging that the text in the Akhmîm manuscript is indeed to be identified as a portion of the work known in antiquity as the "Gospel according to Peter." Next, I surveyed the history of scholarship on this text, summarizing the ways in which previous studies had viewed the relationship between GP and the canonical gospels and the proposals that had been made as to the context in which GP was written. I then outlined my twofold thesis: that GP is best understood as a "rewritten gospel," and that criticism from and competition with those outside the Christian movement played a formative role in the reworking of earlier gospel accounts.

Chapter Two examined the Passion Narrative and, in particular, the way in which the author of GP alters the identity of those responsible for crucifying Jesus. While the Romans are depicted as the executioners in the NT gospels, Herod and the Jews have this role in GP. Many of the abuses of Jesus that occur in the NT gospels are also in GP, yet all of them are carried out by Jews rather than Romans. Our author has done this in order to cast all of the blame for this event on to the Jews. He highlights the Jews' refusal to wash their hands, the primacy of Herod over Pilate in the proceedings, and the heightened malevolency of the Jews in their treatment of

Jesus. He also uses the Scriptures of Israel in a way that casts the Jews in a negative light. At the same time that the Jews are made guilty of killing Jesus, Pilate and the Romans are exonerated. The Petrine evangelist was not unlike Paul, Luke (the author of Acts), Justin, and Melito in sometimes referring solely to Jews as the ones responsible for Jesus' death, while neglecting to mention Roman involvement in the event. The religious and social competition with Jews that the author of GP likely experienced was a factor in his negative portrayal of them. He also was apologetically motivated to avoid having an enemy in the person of a Roman governor, which leads him to portray this political official as innocent of any wrongdoing.

In Chapter Three I contended that the author employs four specific signs as warnings to the Jews for their involvement in Jesus' death: darkness at the crucifixion, the torn temple veil, an earthquake, and the destruction of Jerusalem. He has drawn these four signs from the NT gospels, but their meaning has been dramatically altered in the rewritten gospel. While in the NT accounts these symbols serve primarily to indicate the identity of Jesus, they are portents of judgment in GP. Similar interpretations of these signs are found in Melito, Justin, the *Gospel of Bartholomew*, the Pseudo-Clementine *Recognitions*, the *Testament of Levi*, Tertullian, and Origen's report about Celsus. The author of GP uses these signs in an effort to show that God was on the side of Christians and not that of Jews. From his perspective, it showed the superiority of Christianity over Judaism.

Chapter Four reviewed the account of the guard in GP. The writer has retold the Matthean story and has altered it in seven ways in an effort to assure readers that the tomb of Jesus was secure. These changes involve the chronology of the guard's deployment, the timing of the placement of the stone, the identity of those who move the stone, the sealing of the tomb, an alibi for the disciples, the diligence of those guarding the tomb, and the visit of a crowd from Jerusalem. Cumulatively, these redactional choices reveal the apologetic motives of our author and his attempt to demonstrate that the disciples could not have stolen Jesus' body from its burial place. In early Christian literature the guards at the tomb are inextricably linked to the claim that the disciples had stolen Jesus' body, as evidenced in the *Gospel of Nicodemus*, the *Gospel of the Hebrews*, the Pseudo-Clementine *Recognitions*, the *Martyrdom and Ascension of Isaiah*, Tertullian, and Origen. The Petrine evangelist has changed the Matthean account because he is attempting to alleviate some of the difficulties in the earlier version that would allow for the possibility that the disciples could have stolen the body.

I examined the resurrection account of GP in Chapter Five. While none of the NT gospels describes the resurrection – the actual emergence of Jesus from the tomb – the noncanonical author adds this scene in an attempt to provide a better case for the reality of the event. He is meticulous in his description of witnesses to this event. Those present at the tomb see everything that transpires. By repeatedly mentioning that the guards and Jewish leaders saw the occasion, the author assures that there were witnesses. Furthermore, his first witnesses have distinctly different characteristics than the NT counterparts. The NT stories have friends (i.e., disciples) in this role; GP has enemies. The NT has women discover the empty tomb; in GP men have this role. Those who first see evidence of the resurrection in the NT initially doubt; the witnesses in GP are certain of what they are witnessing. Evidence from Codex Bobbiensis and the *Martyrdom and Ascension of Isaiah* indicates that the author may have borrowed his resurrection account from an earlier story, one not preserved in the NT gospels. The *Epistula Apostolorum* provides an example of how apologetic motivations sometimes influenced resurrection stories in early Christianity, interests that were shared by the author of GP. He rewrites the story in response to certain objections that were common among critics of the early Christian movement. Celsus is an example of a skeptic who ridicules the fact that Jesus never appeared to his enemies, and who scoffs at the idea that the resurrection claim rested its foundations on the testimony of a "hysterical woman." The Petrine evangelist was acquainted with sentiments like these and took them into consideration when writing his own account.

In Chapter Six I reviewed the final two pericopes of GP: the discovery of the empty tomb and what seems to be the beginning of a post-resurrection appearance story. The account of the women's visit to the tomb in GP is based largely on the Markan parallel. The primary change made to the Markan story is to offer an explanation for the women's fear: they are afraid of the Jews. He has imported this theme from John's gospel, and the motif aligns with his anti-Jewish sentiments elsewhere. The appearance story that comes at the end of the GP fragment resembles the scene of John 21:1–14. A key difference, though, is that our evangelist has placed Peter in the role of first-person narrator. Evidence of real or perceived aggression from Jews towards Christians can be found in many early writers and texts, including Paul, Luke, John, the *Martyrdom of Polycarp*, the *Epistle to Diognetus*, Justin, Tertullian, and Origen. It is likely that the author of GP was familiar with instances of conflict between Jews and Christians, and that his portrayal of them as aggressors may be rooted in the fact that Jews were a larger and more socially powerful group at the time. As for the apostolic testimony implied by depicting Peter as the narrator of GP, appeals to apostolic authority were commonplace during the first few centuries of the Common Era. This reflects an attempt to lend greater authority to his text and its claims.

Various theories have been made concerning the relationship of GP and the canonical gospels, and the social context in which GP was written. I have proposed a fresh analogy for understanding and appreciating the manner in which the author of GP viewed and handled the canonical gospels, having identified this noncanonical text as "rewritten gospel." Furthermore, I have identified apologetics as the primary motive behind the reworking of the NT accounts. Koester has claimed that those who view GP as being in some way dependent on the canonical works have failed to offer an adequate explanation for its structure and the setting in which it originated:

The judgment about the passion narrative of the *Gospel of Peter* and its relationship to the canonical gospels depends upon one's general view of the development of the passion narrative. If one assumes that there was once an older historical report which was later supplemented with materials drawn from scriptural prophecy, the *Gospel of Peter* with its rich references and allusions to such scriptural passages will appear as secondary and derivative. There are, however, serious objections to this hypothesis. Form, structure, and life situation of such a historical passion report and its transmission have never been clarified.[1]

I offer this study as a reply to Koester and an effort to account for the form, structure, and the social setting of this gospel.

It is my hope that this examination of GP has shone a new light on old questions. The category "rewritten gospel" that I have proposed may have other members in addition to GP. The *Epistula Apostolorum* and the *Gospel of the Ebionites* are two of the leading candidates for nomination, although further study is necessary on this front. By understanding the way that authoritative religious texts were rewritten by Jews in antiquity, we might better appreciate this practice by Christians of the same era. More importantly, this study has sought to focus on one particular motive that influenced our author – apologetics. In a world of competing religious claims and ideas, the contentions of outsiders and opponents are always present. Sometimes they are dismissed, other times they are heard and a response is offered. In the case of GP, the response has come in the form of a new story about the death, burial, and resurrection of Jesus.

Postscript

As a citizen of a post-Holocaust world, it has not always been easy to write on this subject matter. Throughout this study I have written as a historian and exegete, someone attempting to understand a text from antiquity. But a few comments about its relevance today are in order.

---

[1] Koester, "Apocryphal and Canonical Gospels," 127.

While I have noted at several points that the author of GP likely lived in an area in which there was some type of conflict or tension between Christians and Jews, this is part of the requisite conjecture that is needed when attempting to reconstruct history. We can never be certain of precisely what the author's Jewish "opponents" (as he viewed them) were doing or saying. This gospel is an important source of information about the so-called "parting of the ways" that took place between Judaism and Christianity during the course of the first few centuries. It is clear that the Petrine evangelist considered Christians and Jews to be two distinct and separate groups. From his vantage point, the ways had clearly parted.

It is ironic that at a time when today's Christians and Jews have made great strides toward a cooperative spirit, tolerance, and mutual appreciation of one another, it might appear as though some of the conclusions that I have reached about GP result in taking two (or three or four) steps back. However, this need not be the case. To remember the past is not necessarily a call to endorse it. In fact, I hope that in instances such as the present one, our memory of the past can serve as a reminder of the implications that our theology has on the world around us. Continued improvement in Jewish-Christian relations today will not come about simply by ignoring difficult texts such as GP. In this sense, then, my work on this gospel has most certainly not been prescriptive. But it is still able to serve as a lesson from history to a world that has always needed reminding.

Bibliography

1. Reference Works

Bauer, Walter, Frederick W. Danker, William F. Arndt, and Wilbur Gingrich. *A Greek-English Lexicon of the New Testament and Other Early Christian Literature*. 3d ed. Revised and edited by Frederick W. Danker. Chicago: University of Chicago Press, 2000.

Brown, Francis, Samuel R. Driver, and Charles A. Briggs, eds. *A Hebrew and English Lexicon of the Old Testament*. Rev. ed. Oxford: Clarendon, 1952.

Fuchs, Albert, ed. *Das Petrusevangelium*. Studien zum Neuen Testament und seiner Umwelt B2. Linz: A. Fuchs, 1978.

Hatch, Edwin, and Henry A. Redpath. *Concordance to the Septuagint and the Other Greek Versions of the Old Testament, Including the Apocryphal Books*. 2 vols. Oxford: Clarendon, 1897. Repr., 2 vols. in 1, Grand Rapids: Baker, 1998.

Kittel, G., and G. Friedrich, eds. *Theological Dictionary of the New Testament*. Translated by G. W. Bromiley. 10 vols. Grand Rapids: Eerdmans, 1964–1976.

Lampe, G. W. H., ed. *Patristic Greek Lexicon*. Oxford: Clarendon, 1961.

Liddell, Henry G., Robert Scott, and Henry S. Jones. *A Greek-English Lexicon*. 9th ed. with revised supplement. Oxford: Clarendon, 1996.

Louw, Johannes P., and Eugene A. Nida, eds. *Greek-English Lexicon of the New Testament: Based on Semantic Domains*. 2d ed. New York: United Bible Societies, 1989.

Resch, Alfred. *Aussercanonische Paralleltexte zu den Evangelien*, Vol. 2. Texte und Untersuchungen zur Geschichte der Altchristlichen Literatur 10.2. Leipzig: Hinrichs, 1894.

Smyth, Herbert W. *Greek Grammar*. Rev. ed. Cambridge, Mass.: Harvard University Press, 1956.

2. Primary Sources

Aland, Barbara, Kurt Aland, Johannes Karavidopoulos, Carlo M. Martini, and Bruce M. Metzger, eds. *The Greek New Testament*. 4th ed. Stuttgart: Deutsche Bibelgesellschaft, 1993.

Aland, Kurt, ed. *Synopsis of the Four Gospels: Greek-English Edition of the Synopsis Quattuor Evangeliorum*. 10th ed. Stuttgart: German Bible Society, 1993.

–. *Synopsis Quattuor Evangeliorum*. 15th ed. Stuttgart: Deutsche Bibelgesellschaft, 1997.

The Ante-Nicene Fathers. Edited by Alexander Roberts and James Donaldson. 1885–1887. 10 vols. Repr. Peabody, Mass.: Hendrickson, 1994.

Attridge, Harold W., ed. *The HarperCollins Study Bible with Apocrypha: New Revised Standard Version*. Rev. ed. New York: HarperOne, 2006.

Bernhard, Andrew E. *Other Early Christian Gospels: A Critical Edition of the Surviving Greek Manuscripts*. London: T&T Clark, 2006.

Bouriant, Urbain. "Fragments du texte grec du livre d'Énoch et de quelques écrits attribués à saint Pierre." Pages 91–147 in *Mémoires publiés par les membres de la mission archéologique française au Caire* 9.1. Paris: Libraire de la Société asiatique, 1892.

Cameron, Ron, ed. *The Other Gospels: Non-Canonical Gospel Texts*. Philadelphia: Westminster, 1982.

Chadwick, Henry. *Origen: Contra Celsum*. Cambridge: Cambridge University Press, 1953.

Charles, R. H. *The Apocrypha and Pseudepigrapha of the Old Testament Books in English: With Introduction and Critical and Explanatory Notes to the Several Books*. 2 vols. Oxford: Clarendon, 1913.

Falls, Thomas B. *Saint Justin Martyr*. Fathers of the Church 6. Washington, D.C.: The Catholic University of America Press, 1948.

Goodspeed, Edgar J., ed. *Die ältesten Apologeten: Texte mit kurzen Einleitungen*. Göttingen: Vandenhoeck & Ruprecht, 1914.

Hall, Stuart G. *Melito of Sardis: On Pascha and Fragments*. Oxford Early Christian Texts. Oxford: Clarendon, 1979.

Harris, J. Rendel, ed. *The Apology of Aristides on Behalf of the Christians*. Cambridge: Cambridge University Press, 1893.

Holmes, Michael W., ed. and trans. *The Apostolic Fathers: Greek Texts and English Translations*. 3d ed. Grand Rapids: Baker, 2007.

Kraus, Thomas J., and Tobias Nicklas. *Das Petrusevangelium und die Petrusapokalypse: Die griechischen Fragment mit deutscher und englischer Übersetzung*. Die griechische christliche Schriftsteller der ersten Jahrhunderte. Second Series 11. Berlin: de Gruyter, 2004.

Lake, Kirsopp, and J. E. L. Oulton, trans. *The Ecclesiastical History*. 2 vols. Loeb Classical Library. Cambridge, Mass.: Harvard University Press, 1926–1932.

Lods, Adolphe. "L'Évangile et l'Apocalypse de Pierre avec le texte grec du livre d'Hénoch. Text publié en facsimile, par l'héliogravure d'après les photographies du manuscrit de Gizéh." Pages 217–31, 322–35 in *Mémoires publiés par les membres de la mission archéologique française au Caire* 9.3. Paris: Libraire de la Société asiatique, 1893.

Lührmann, Dieter, and Egbert Schlarb. *Fragmente apokryph gewordener Evangelien in griechischer und lateinischer Sprache*. Marburger theologische Studien 59. Marburg: Elwert, 2000.

Moore, Clifford H., and John Jackson, trans. [Tacitus]. *The Histories*. 4 vols. Loeb Classical Library. Cambridge, Mass.: Harvard University Press, 1937.

Nestle, Eberhard, Erwin Nestle, Barbara Aland, Kurt Aland, Johannes Karavidopoulos, Carlo M. Martini, and Bruce M. Metzger, eds. *Novum Testamentum Graece*. 27th ed. Stuttgart: Deutsche Bibelgesellschaft, 1993.

The Nicene and Post-Nicene Fathers. Series 2. Edited by Philip Schaff. 1886–1889. 14 vols. Repr. Peabody, Mass.: Hendrickson, 1994.

Rahlfs, Alfred, ed. *Septuaginta id est Vetus Testamentum graece iuxta LXX interpretes*. Stuttgart: Deutsche Bibelgesellschaft, 1979.

Schneemelcher, Wilhelm, and R. McL. Wilson, eds. *New Testament Apocrypha*. 2 vols. Rev. ed. Louisville: Westminster John Knox, 1991.

Schubert, Hans von. *The Gospel of Peter: Synoptic Tables, with Translations and Critical Apparatus*. Translated by John MacPherson. Edinburgh: T&T Clark, 1893.

Tischendorf, Constantin von. *Evangelia Apocrypha*. 2d ed. Leipzig: Mendelssohn, 1876. Repr., Hildesheim: Georg Olms, 1966.

Wise, Michael, Martin Abegg, Jr., and Edward Cook. *The Dead Sea Scrolls: A New Translation*. New York: HarperCollins, 1996.

3. Secondary Sources

Aland, Kurt, and Barbara Aland. *The Text of the New Testament: An Introduction to the Critical Editions and to the Theory and Practice of Modern Textual Criticusm*. Translated by Erroll F. Rhodes. 2d ed. Grand Rapids: Eerdmans, 1989.

Albl, Martin C. *"And Scripture Cannot Be Broken": The Form and Function of the Early Christian Testimonia Collections*. Supplements to Novum Testamentum 96. Leiden: Brill, 1999.

–. *Pseudo-Gregory of Nyssa: Testimonies against the Jews*. Society of Biblical Literature Writings from the Greco-Roman World 8. Atlanta: Society of Biblical Literature, 2004.

Alexander, Philip S. "Retelling the Old Testament." Pages 99–121 in *It Is Written: Scripture Citing Scripture, Essays in Honour of Barnabas Lindars, SSF*. Edited by D. A. Carson and H. G. M. Williamson. Cambridge: Cambridge University Press, 1988.

Alsup, John E. *The Post-Resurrection Appearance Stories of the Gospel Tradition: A History-of-Tradition Analysis, with Text-Synopsis*. Calwer theologische Monographien A5. Stuttgart: Calwer, 1975.

Andresen, Carl. *Logos und Nomos: Die Polemik des Kelsos wider das Christentum*. Arbeiten zur Kirchengeschichte 30. Berlin: de Gruyter, 1955.

Attridge, Harold W. "Liberating Death's Captives: Reconsideration of an Early Christian Myth." Pages 103–15 in *Gnosticism and the Early Christian World: In Honor of James M. Robinson*. Edited by James E. Goehring, Charles W. Hedrick, Jack T. Sanders, and Hans D. Betz. Forum Fascicles 2. Sonoma, Calif.: Polebridge, 1990.

Bammel, Ernst. "Der Jude des Celsus." Pages 265–83 in vol. 1 of *Judaica*. Edited by Ernst Bammel. 2 vols.

Barnard, Leslie W. *Justin Martyr: His Life and Thought*. London: Cambridge University Press, 1967.

Barrett, C. K. *The Gospel according to St. John: An Introduction with Commentary and Notes on the Greek Text*. London: SPCK, 1955.

Bauckham, Richard J. "The Lord's Day." Pages 197–220 in *From Sabbath to Lord's Day: A Biblical, Historical, and Theological Investigation*. Edited by D. A. Carson. Grand Rapids: Zondervan, 1982.

–. "Pseudo-Apostolic Letter." *Journal of Biblical Literature* 107 (1988): 469–94.

–. "The *Acts of Paul* as a Sequel to Acts." Pages 105–52 in *The Book of Acts in Its Ancient Literary Setting*. Edited by Bruce W. Winter and Andrew D. Clarke. Vol. 1 of *The Book of Acts in Its First Century Setting*. Edited by Bruce W. Winter. Grand Rapids: Eerdmans, 1993.

–. "The Ascension of Isaiah: Genre, Unity, and Date." Pages 363–90 in *The Fate of the Dead: Studies on the Jewish and Christian Apocalypses*. Edited by Richard J. Bauckham. Supplements to Novum Testamentum 93. Leiden: Brill, 1998.

–. *Gospel Women: Studies of the Named Women in the Gospels*. Grand Rapids: Eerdmans, 2002.

–. *Jesus and the Eyewitnesses: The Gospels as Eyewitness Testimony.* Grand Rapids: Eerdmans, 2006.

Bauer, Walter. *Das Leben Jesu: Im Zeitalter der Neutestamentlichen Apokryphen.* Tübingen: Mohr, 1909. Repr., Darmstadt: Wissenschaftliche Buchgesellschaft, 1967.

Bellinzoni, Arthur J. *The Sayings of Jesus in the Writings of Justin Martyr.* Supplements to Novum Testamentum 17. Leiden: Brill, 1967.

Benko, Stephen. "Pagan Criticism of Christianity during the First Two Centuries A.D." *ANRW* 23.2:1055–1118. Part 2, *Principat*, 23.2. Edited by H. Temporini and W. Haase. New York: de Gruyter, 1980.

Berchman, Robert M. *Porphyry against the Christians.* Studies in Platonism, Neoplatonism, and the Platonic Tradition 1. Leiden: Brill, 2005.

Best, Ernest. *Mark: The Gospel as Story.* Edinburgh: T&T Clark, 1983.

Bond, Helen K. *Pontius Pilate in History and Interpretation.* Society for New Testament Studies Monograph Series 100. Cambridge: Cambridge University Press, 1998.

Bonner, Campbell. *The Homily on the Passion by Melito Bishop of Sardis and Some Fragments of the Apocryphal Ezekiel.* Studies and Documents 12. Philadelphia: University of Pennsylvania Press, 1940.

Bousset, Wilhelm. *Kyrios Christos: Geschichte des Christglaubens von den Anfangen des Christentums bis Irenaeus.* Göttingen: Vandenhoeck & Ruprecht, 1913.

Bovon, François. *The Last Days of Jesus.* Translated by Kristin Hennessy. 2d ed. Louisville: Westminster John Knox, 2006.

Brock, Ann Graham. "Peter, Paul, and Mary: Canonical vs. Non-Canonical Portrayals of Apostolic Witnesses." Pages 173–202 in *SBL Seminar Papers, 1999.* Society of Biblical Literature Seminar Papers 38. Atlanta: Society of Biblical Literature, 1999.

Brodie, Thomas L. *The Quest for the Origin of John's Gospel: A Source-Oriented Approach.* New York: Oxford University Press, 1993.

Brown, Raymond E. *The Gospel according to John XIII–XXI: A New Translation with Introduction and Commentary.* Anchor Bible 29A. New York: Doubleday, 1970.

–. *The Community of the Beloved Disciple.* New York: Paulist, 1979.

–. "The *Gospel of Peter* and Canonical Gospel Priority." *New Testament Studies* 33 (1987): 321–43.

–. *The Death of the Messiah: From Gethsemane to the Grave, A Commentary on the Passion Narratives in the Four Gospels.* 2 vols. Anchor Bible Reference Library. New York: Doubleday, 1994.

Bruce, F. F. *1 & 2 Thessalonians.* Word Biblical Commentary 45. Waco: Word, 1982.

Bultmann, Rudolf. "New Testament and Mythology." Pages 1–44 in *Kerygma and Myth: A Theological Debate.* Edited by Hans Werner Bartsch. Translated by Reginald H. Fuller. New York: Harper & Row, 1961.

–. *History of the Synoptic Tradition.* Translated by J. Marsh. Rev. ed. Peabody, Mass.: Hendrickson, 1963.

Cassels, Walter. *The Gospel according to Peter: A Study by the Author of "Supernatural Religion."* London: Longmans, Green, 1894.

Charlesworth, James H. "Christian and Jewish Self-Definition in Light of the Christian Additions to the Apocryphal Writings." Pages 27–55 in *Aspects of Judaism in the Graeco-Roman Period.* Edited by E. P. Sanders, A. I. Baumgarten, and A. Mendelson. Philadelphia: Fortress, 1981.

–. *The Beloved Disciple: Whose Witness Validates the Gospel of John?* Valley Forge, Pa.: Trinity Press International, 1995.

Conzelmann, Hans. *1 Corinthians: A Commentary on the First Epistle to the Corinthians.* Translated by James W. Leitch. Hermeneia. Philadelphia: Fortress, 1975.

Cook, John Granger. *The Interpretation of the New Testament in Greco-Roman Paganism.* Studien und Texte zu Antike und Christentum 3. Tübingen: Mohr Siebeck, 2000. Repr., Peabody, Mass.: Hendrickson, 2002.

Corley, Kathleen E., and Robert L. Webb, eds. *Jesus and Mel Gibson's Passion of the Christ: The Film, The Gospels and the Claims of History.* New York: Continuum, 2004.

Coser, Lewis. *The Functions of Social Conflict: An Examination of the Concept of Social Conflict and Its Use in Empirical Sociological Research.* New York: Free, 1956.

Cosgrove, Charles H. "Justin Martyr and the Emerging New Testament Canon: Observations on the Purpose and Destination of the *Dialogue with Trypho.*" *Vigiliae Christianae* 53 (1982): 209–32.

Craig, William L. "The Guard at the Tomb." *New Testament Studies* 30 (1984): 273–81.

Crawford, Sidnie White. *Rewriting Scripture in Second Temple Times.* Grand Rapids: Eerdmans, 2008.

Crossan, John Dominic. *Four Other Gospels: Shadows on the Contours of Canon.* Minneapolis: Seabury, 1985.

–. *The Cross That Spoke: The Origins of the Passion Narrative.* San Francisco: Harper & Row, 1988.

–. "Thoughts on Two Extracanonical Gospels." *Semeia* 49 (1990): 155–68.

–. *Who Killed Jesus?: Exposing the Roots of Anti-Semitism in the Gospel Story of the Death of Jesus.* New York: HarperCollins, 1995.

–. *The Birth of Christianity: Discovering What Happened in the Years Immediately after the Execution of Jesus.* San Francisco: HarperCollins, 1998.

–. "The Gospel of Peter and the Canonical Gospels: Independence, Dependence, or Both?" *Forum* n.s. 1 (1998): 7–51.

–. "The *Gospel of Peter* and the Canonical Gospels." Pages 117–34 in Kraus and Nicklas, *Evangelium nach Petrus.*

Cullman, Oscar. *The Johannine Circle.* Translated by John Bowden. Philadelphia: Westminster, 1976.

Cumont, Franz. "Un rescrit impérial sur la violation de sepulture." *Revue Historique* 163 (1930): 241–66.

Dalton, William J. *Christ's Proclamation to the Spirits: A Study of 1 Peter 3:18–4:6.* Analecta biblica 23. Rome: Pontifical Biblical Institute, 1965.

Danove, Paul L. *The End of Mark's Story: A Methodological Study.* Biblical Interpretation 3. Leiden: Brill, 1993.

Davies, William D., and Dale C. Allison, Jr. *A Critical and Exegetical Commentary on the Gospel according to Saint Matthew.* 2 vols. International Critical Commentary. Edinburgh: T&T Clark, 1988–1991.

Davis, Stephen T. *Risen Indeed: Making Sense of the Resurrection.* Grand Rapids: Eerdmans, 1993.

Denker, Jürgen. *Die theologiegeschichtliche Stellung des Petrusevangeliums: Ein Beitrag zur Frühgeschichte des Doketismus.* Europäische Hochschulschriften. Twenty-third Series 36. Frankfurt: Lang, 1975.

Dewey, Arthur J. "'Time to Murder and Create': Visions and Revisions in the *Gospel of Peter.*" *Semeia* 49 (1990): 101–27.

Dibelius, Martin. "Die alttestamentliche Motive in der Leidensgeschichte des Petrus- und Johannes-Evangeliums." Beihefte zur Zeitschrift für die neutestamentliche Wissenschaft 33 (1918): 125–50.

–. *Studies in the Acts of the Apostles.* London: SCM, 1956.

Dodd, C. H. *According to the Scriptures: The Sub-structure of New Testament Theology*. London: Nisbet, 1952.

Draguet, René. Review of Léon Vaganay, *L'Évangile de Pierre*. *Revue d'histoire ecclési-astique* 27 (1931): 854–56.

Dungan, David L. *Constantine's Bible: Politics and the Making of the New Testament*. Minneapolis: Fortress, 2007.

Dunn, James D. G. *The Partings of the Ways: Between Christianity and Judaism and their Significance for the Character of Christianity*. 2d ed. London: SCM Press, 2006.

–. *Beginning from Jerusalem: Christianity in the Making*, vol. 2. Grand Rapids: Eerdmans, 2009.

Elgvin, Torleif. "Jewish Christian Editing of the Old Testament Pseudepigrapha." Pages 278–324 in Skarsaune and Hvalvik, *Jewish Believers in Jesus*.

Elliott, John H. *1 Peter*. Anchor Bible 37B. New York: Doubleday, 2000.

Evans, Craig A. "The Jewish Christian Gospel Tradition." Pages 241–77 in Skarsaune and Hvalvik, *Jewish Believers in Jesus*.

Evans, Craig A., and Donald A. Hagner, eds. *Anti-Semitism and Early Christianity: Issues of Polemic and Faith*. Minneapolis: Fortress, 1993.

Ferguson, Everett. "The Appeal to Apostolic Authority in the Early Centuries." *Restoration Quarterly* 50 (2008): 49–62.

Foster, Paul. "Are There Any Early Fragments of the So-Called *Gospel of Peter*?" *New Testament Studies* 52 (2006): 1–28.

–. "The Discovery and Initial Reaction to the So-Called Gospel of Peter." Pages 9–30 in Kraus and Nicklas, *Evangelium nach Petrus*.

–. "The Gospel of Peter." *Expository Times* 118 (2007): 318–25.

–. "The Writings of Justin Martyr and the So-Called *Gospel of Peter*." Pages 104–12 in Parvis and Foster, *Justin Martyr and His Worlds*.

–. *The Gospel of Peter: Introduction, Critical Edition and Commentary*. Texts and Editions for New Testament Study 4. Leiden, Brill, 2010.

Fuller, Reginald H. *The Formation of the Resurrection Narratives*. 2d ed. Philadelphia: Fortress, 1980.

Funk, Robert W. *Parables and Presence: Forms of the New Testament Tradition*. Philadelphia: Fortress, 1982.

Gager, John G. *Kingdom and Community: The Social World of Early Christianity*. Englewood Cliffs, N.J.: Prentice-Hall, 1975.

Gamble, Harry Y. *Books and Readers in the Early Church: A History of Early Christian Texts*. New Haven: Yale University Press, 1995.

Gardner-Smith, Percival. "The Gospel of Peter." *Journal of Theological Studies* 27 (1926): 255–71.

–. "The Date of the Gospel of Peter." *Journal of Theological Studies* 27 (1926): 401–7.

–. *Saint John and the Synoptic Gospels*. Cambridge: Cambridge University Press, 1938.

Gebhardt, Oscar von. *Das Evangelium und die Apokalypse des Petrus: Die neuentdeckten Bruchstücke nach einer Photographie der Handschrift zu Gizeh in Lichtdruck herausgegeben*. Leipzig: Hinrichs, 1893.

Goulder, Michael. "The Baseless Fabric of a Vision." Pages 48–61 in *Resurrection Reconsidered*. Edited by Gavin D'Costa. Rockport, Mass.: Oneworld, 1996.

Gounelle, Rémi. *La descente du Christ aux enfers: Institutionnalisation d'une croyance*. Série Antiquité 162 of Collection des études augustiniennes. Paris: Institut d'Études Augustiniennes, 2000.

Grant, Michael. *The Jews in the Roman World*. New York: Scribner, 1973.

Grant, Robert M. *Augustus to Constantine: The Thrust of the Christian Movement into the Roman World*. New York: Harper & Row, 1970.

–. *Early Christianity and Society: Seven Studies*. San Francisco: Harper & Row, 1977.

Green, Joel B. "The Gospel of Peter: Source for a Pre-Canonical Passion Narrative?" *Zeitschrift für die neutestamentliche Wissenschaft und die Kunde der älteren Kirche* 78 (1987): 293–301.

Greschat, Katharina. "Justins 'Denkwürdigkeiten der Apostel' und das Petrusevangelium." Pages 197–214 in Kraus and Nicklas, *Evangelium nach Petrus*.

Gundry, Robert H. *Matthew: A Commentary on His Handbook for a Mixed Church under Persecution*. 2d ed. Grand Rapids: Eerdmans, 1994.

Gurtner, Daniel M. *The Torn Veil: Matthew's Exposition of the Death of Jesus*. Society for New Testament Studies Monograph Series 139. Cambridge: Cambridge University Press, 2007.

Hagner, Donald A. *Matthew 14–28*. Word Biblical Commentary 33B. Nashville: Thomas Nelson, 1995.

Hall, Stuart G. "Melito in the Light of the Passover Haggadah." *Journal of Theological Studies* n.s. 22 (1971): 29–46.

Hanfmann, George M. A. *Sardis from Prehistoric to Roman Times: Results of the Archaeological Exploration of Sardis, 1958–1975*. Cambridge: Mass.: Harvard University Press, 1983.

Hannah, Darrell D. "The Four-Gospel Canon in the Epistula Apostolorum." *Journal of Theological Studies* n.s. 59 (2008): 598–633.

Hare, Douglas R. A. *The Theme of Jewish Persecution of Christians in the Gospel according to St. Matthew*. Society for New Testament Studies Monograph Series 6. Cambridge: Cambridge University Press, 1967.

Harnack, Adolf von. "Bruchstücke des Evangeliums und der Apokalypse des Petrus." *Sitzungsberichte der königlichen Preussischen Akademie der Wissenschaften zu Berlin* 44 (1892): 895–903.

–. "Bruchstücke des Evangeliums und der Apokalypse des Petrus." *Sitzungsberichte der königlichen Preussischen Akademie der Wissenschaften zu Berlin* 45 (1892): 949–65.

–. *Bruchstücke des Evangeliums und der Apokalypse des Petrus*. 2d ed. Texte und Untersuchungen zur Geschichte der altchristlichen Literatur 9.2. Leipzig: Hinrichs, 1893.

Harrington, Daniel J. "Palestinian Adaptations of Biblical Narratives and Prophecies: I. The Bible Rewritten." Pages 239–47 in *Early Judaism and Its Modern Interpreters*. Edited by Robert A. Kraft and George W. E. Nickelsburg. The Bible and Its Modern Interpreters 2. Atlanta: Scholars Press, 1986.

Harris, J. Rendel. *A Popular Account of the Newly-Recovered Gospel of Peter*. London: Hodder & Stoughton, 1893.

–. *Testimonies*. 2 vols. Cambridge: Cambridge University Press, 1916–1920.

Hays, Richard B. *Echoes of Scripture in the Letters of Paul*. New Haven: Yale University Press, 1989.

Head, Peter M. "On the Christology of the Gospel of Peter." *Vigiliae Christianae* 46 (1992): 209–24.

Hengel, Martin. "The Titles of the Gospels and the Gospel of Mark." Pages 64–84 in *Studies in the Gospel of Mark*. Edited by Martin Hengel. Translated by John Bowden. Philadelphia: Fortress, 1985.

–. *The Pre-Christian Paul*. Translated by John Bowden. Philadelphia: Trinity Press International, 1991.

–. *The Four Gospels and the One Gospel of Jesus Christ: An Investigation of the Collection and Origin of the Canonical Gospels.* Translated by John Bowden. Harrisburg, Pa.: Trinity Press International, 2000.

Hengel, Martin, and Anna M. Schwemer. *Paul between Damascus and Antioch: The Unknown Years.* Translated by John Bowden. Louisville: Westminster John Knox, 1997.

Hieke, Thomas. "Das Petrusevangelium vom Alten Testament her gelesen: Gewinnbringende Lektüre eines nicht-kanonischen Textes vom christlichen Kanon her." Pages 91–115 in Kraus and Nicklas, *Evangelium nach Petrus.*

Hilgenfeld, Adolf. "Das Petrus-Evangelium über Leiden und Auferstehung Jesu." *Zeitschrift für wissenschaftliche Theologie* 36/1 (1893): 439–54.

–. "Das Petrus-Evangelium." *Zeitschrift für wissenschaftliche Theologie* 36/2 (1893): 220–67.

Hilhorst, Anthony, ed. *The Apostolic Age in Patristic Thought.* Supplements to Vigiliae Christianae 70. Leiden: Brill, 2004.

Hill, Charles E. "Was John's Gospel among Justin's *Apostolic Memoirs*?" Pages 88–94 in Parvis and Foster, *Justin Martyr and His Worlds.*

Hills, Julian V. *Tradition and Composition in the Epistula Apostolorum.* Exp. ed. Harvard Theological Studies 57. Cambridge, Mass.: Harvard University Press, 2008.

Holmes, Michael W. "To Be Continued … The Many Endings of the Gospel of Mark." *Bible Review* 17, no. 4 (August 2001): 12–23, 48–50.

Hultgren, Arland J. "Paul's Pre-Christian Persecutions of the Church: Their Purpose, Locale, and Nature." *Journal of Biblical Literature* 95 (1976): 97–111.

Hurd, John C. "Paul Ahead of His Time: 1 Thess. 2:13–16." Pages 21–36 in Richardson and Granskou, *Anti-Judaism in Early Christianity*, vol. 1.

Hurtado, Larry W. *Lord Jesus Christ: Devotion to Jesus in Earliest Christianity.* Grand Rapids: Eerdmans, 2003.

James, Montague R. Review of Léon Vaganay, *L'Évangile de Pierre. Journal of Theological Studies* 32 (1931): 296–99.

Johnson, Benjamin A. "Empty Tomb Tradition in the Gospel of Peter." Th.D. diss., Harvard University Divinity School, 1965.

Jones, F. Stanley. "The Gospel of Peter in Pseudo-Clementine Recognitions 1,27–71." Pages 237–44 in Kraus and Nicklas, *Evangelium nach Petrus.*

Jonge, Marinus de. "Matthew 27:51 in Early Christian Exegesis." *Harvard Theological Review* 79 (1986): 67–79.

Kalin, Everett. "The New Testament Canon of Eusebius." Pages 386–404 in McDonald and Sanders, *Canon Debate.*

Karmann, Thomas R. "Melito von Sardes und das Petrusevangelium." Pages 215–35 in Kraus and Nicklas, *Evangelium nach Petrus.*

Kirk, Alan. "Examining Priorities: Another Look at the *Gospel of Peter*'s Relationship to the New Testament Gospels." *New Testament Studies* 40 (1994): 572–95.

–. "The Johannine Jesus in the Gospel of Peter: A Social Memory Approach." Pages 313–22 in *Jesus in Johannine Tradition.* Edited by Robert T. Fortna and Tom Thatcher. Louisville: Westminster John Knox, 2001.

–. "Tradition and Memory in the *Gospel of Peter*." Pages 135–58 in Kraus and Nicklas, *Evangelium nach Petrus.*

Kittel, G., and G. Friedrich, eds. *Theological Dictionary of the New Testament.* Translated by G. W. Bromiley. 10 vols. Grand Rapids: Eerdmans, 1964–1976.

Klijn, A. F. J. *Jewish-Christian Gospel Tradition.* Supplements to Vigiliae Christianae 17. Leiden: Brill, 1992.

Klijn, A. F. J., and G. J. Reinink. *Patristic Evidence for Jewish-Christian Sects.* Supplements to Novum Testamentum 36. Leiden: Brill, 1973.

Koester, Helmut. "GNOMAI DIAPHOROI: The Origin and Nature of Diversification in the History of Early Christianity." Pages 114–43 in *Trajectories through Early Christianity.* Edited by James M. Robinson and Helmut Koester. Philadelphia: Fortress, 1971.

–. "From the Kerygma-Gospel to Written Gospels." *New Testament Studies* 35 (1989): 361–81.

–. *Ancient Christian Gospels: Their History and Development.* Philadelphia: Trinity Press International, 1990.

–. "Apocryphal and Canonical Gospels." *Harvard Theological Review* 73 (1980): 105–30. Repr. pages 3–23 in *From Jesus to the Gospels: Interpreting the New Testament in Its Context.* Minneapolis: Fortress, 2007.

Koskenniemi, Erkki, and Pekka Linqvist. "Rewritten Bible, Rewritten Stories: Methodological Aspects." Pages 11–39 in *Rewritten Bible Reconsidered: Proceedings of the Conference in Karkku, Finland August 24–26 2006.* Edited by Antti Laato and Jacques van Ruiten. Studies in Rewritten Bible 1. Winona Lake, Ind.: Eisenbrauns, 2008.

Kraus, Thomas J., and Tobias Nicklas, eds. *Das Evangelium nach Petrus: Text, Kontexte, Intertexte.* Texte und Untersuchungen zur Geschichte der altchristlichen Literatur 158. Berlin: de Gruyter, 2007.

Kraus, Thomas J., Michael J. Kruger, and Tobias Nicklas, eds. *Gospel Fragments.* Oxford Early Christian Gospel Texts. New York: Oxford University Press, 2009.

Kysar, Robert. "Anti-Semitism and the Gospel of John." Pages 113–27 in Evans and Hagner, *Anti-Semitism and Early Christianity.*

Labriolle, Pierre de. *La réaction païenne: Étude sur la polémique antichrétienne du Ier zu VIe siècle.* 2d ed. Paris: Artisan du Livre, 1948.

Lampe, G. W. H. "A.D. 70 in Christian Reflection." Pages 153–71 in *Jesus and the Politics of His Day.* Edited by Ernst Bammel and C. F. D. Moule. Cambridge: Cambridge University Press, 1984.

Lessing, G. E. *Fragmente des Wolfenbüttelschen Ungennanten: Ein Anhang zu dem Fragment vom Zweck Jesu und seiner Jünger.* Berlin: Wever, 1784.

Lieu, Judith M. *Image and Reality: The Jews in the World of the Christians in the Second Century.* Edinburgh: T&T Clark, 1996.

Lightfoot, Robert H. *Locality and Doctrine in the Gospels.* London: Hodder & Stoughton, 1938.

Lincoln, Andrew T. "The Promise and the Failure: Mark 16:7,8." *Journal of Biblical Literature* 108 (1989): 283–300.

Lindars, Barnabas. *New Testament Apologetic: The Doctrinal Significance of the Old Testament Quotations.* Philadelphia: Westminster, 1961.

Lüdemann, Gerd. *What Really Happened to Jesus?: A Historical Approach to the Resurrection.* Louisville: Westminster John Knox, 1995.

Lührmann, Dieter. *Die apokryph gewordenen Evangelien: Studien zu neuen Texten und zu neuen Fragen.* Supplements to Novum Testamentum 112. Leiden: Brill, 2004.

MacDonald, Margaret Y. *Early Christian Women and Pagan Opinion: The Power of the Hysterical Woman.* Cambridge: Cambridge University Press, 1996.

MacMullen, Ramsay. *Christianizing the Roman Empire: A.D. 100–400.* New Haven: Yale University Press, 1984.

Mara, Maria G. *Évangile de Pierre: Introduction, Texte Critique, Traduction, Commentaire et Index.* Sources chrétiennes 201. Paris: Cerf, 1973.

Martyn, J. Louis. "A Gentile Mission That Replaced an Earlier Jewish Mission?" Pages 124–44 in *Exploring the Gospel of John: In Honor of D. Moody Smith*. Edited by R. Alan Culpepper and C. Clifton Black. Louisville: Westminster John Knox, 1996.

–. *History and Theology in the Fourth Gospel*. 3d ed. Louisville: Westminster John Knox, 2003.

McCane, Byron R. *Roll Back the Stone: Death and Burial in the World of Jesus*. Harrisburg, Pa.: Trinity Press International, 2003.

McCant, Jerry W. "The Gospel of Peter: The Docetic Question Re-Examined." Ph.D. diss., Emory University, 1978.

–. "The Gospel of Peter: Docetism Reconsidered." *New Testament Studies* 30 (1984): 258–73.

McConville, J. Gordon. *Deuteronomy*. Apollos Old Testament Commentary 5. Leicester: Apollos, 2002.

McDonald, Lee M. "Identifying Scripture and Canon in the Early Church: The Criteria Question." Pages 416–39 in McDonald and Sanders, *Canon Debate*.

McDonald, Lee M., and James A. Sanders, eds. *The Canon Debate*. Peabody, Mass.: Hendrickson, 2002.

Meiselman, Moshe. *Jewish Woman in Jewish Law*. New York: KTAV, 1978.

Metzger, Bruce M. "Names for the Nameless in the New Testament: A Study in the Growth of Christian Tradition." Pages 79–99 in volume 1 of *Kyriakon: Festschrift Johannes Quasten*. Edited by Patrick Granfield and Josef A. Jungmann. 2 vols. Münster: Aschendorff, 1970.

–. "The Nazareth Inscription Once Again." Pages 221–38 in *Jesus und Paulus: Festschrift für Werner Georg Kümmel zum 70. Geburtstag*. Edited by E. Earle Ellis and Erich Gräßer. Göttingen: Vandenhoeck & Ruprecht, 1975.

–. *The Early Versions of the New Testament: Their Origin, Transmission and Limitations*. Oxford: Clarendon, 1977.

–. *The Canon of the New Testament: Its Origin, Development, and Significance*. Oxford: Clarendon, 1987.

–. *A Textual Commentary on the Greek New Testament*. 2d ed. Stuttgart: Deutsche Bibelgesellschaft, 1994.

Metzger, Bruce M., and Bart D. Ehrman. *The Text of the New Testament: Its Transmission, Corruption, and Restoration*. 4th ed. New York: Oxford University Press, 2005.

Minnen, Peter van. "The Akhmîm *Gospel of Peter*." Pages 53–60 in Kraus and Nicklas, *Evangelium nach Petrus*.

Mohri, Erika. *Maria Magdalena: Frauenbilder in Evangelientexten des 1. bis 3. Jahrhunderts*. Marburger theologische Studien 63. Marburg: Elwert, 2000.

Morford, Mark. "Tacitus' Historical Methods in the Neronian Books of the 'Annals.'" *ANRW* 33.2:1582–627. Part 2, *Principat*, 33.2. Edited by H. Temporini and W. Haase. New York: de Gruyter, 1990.

Neirynck, Frans. "The Apocryphal Gospels and the Gospel of Mark." Pages 123–75 in *The New Testament in Early Christianity*. Edited by Jean-Marie Sevrin. Bibliotheca ephemeridum theologicarum lovaniensium 86. Leuven: Leuven University Press, 1989.

Nickelsburg, George W. E. *Resurrection, Immortality, and Eternal Life in Intertestamental Judaism and Early Christianity*. Exp. ed. Harvard Theological Studies 56. Cambridge, Mass.: Harvard University Press, 2006.

Nicklas, Tobias. "Die 'Juden' im Petrusevangelium (PCair 10759): Ein Testfall." *New Testament Studies* 46 (2000): 206–21.

Norelli, Enrico. "Situation des apocryphes pétriniens." *Apocrypha* 2 (1991): 31–83.

Omerzu, Heike. "Die Pilatusgestalt im Petrusevangelium: Eine erzählanalytische Annäherung." Pages 327–47 in Kraus and Nicklas, *Evangelium nach Petrus*.

Osborn, Eric F. *Justin Martyr*. Beiträge zur historischen Theologie 47. Tübingen: Mohr (Siebeck), 1973.

Osiek, Carolyn. "The Women at the Tomb: What Are They Doing There? *Ex Auditu* 9 (1993): 97–107.

Paley, William. *A View of the Evidences of Christianity*. London: Faulder, 1794.

Parvis, Sara, and Paul Foster, eds. *Justin Martyr and His Worlds*. Minneapolis: Fortress, 2007.

Patterson, Stephen J. "Why Did Christians Say: 'God Raised Jesus from the Dead'?" *Forum* 10 (1994): 135–60.

Pearson, Birger A. "1 Thessalonians 2:13–16: A Deutero-Pauline Interpolation." *Harvard Theological Review* 64 (1971): 79–94.

Perkins, Pheme. *Resurrection: New Testament Witness and Contemporary Reflection*. Garden City, N.Y.: Doubleday, 1984.

Pilhofer, Peter. "Justin und das Petrusevangelium." *Zeitschrift für die neutestamentliche Wissenschaft und die Kunde der älteren Kirche* 81 (1990): 60–78.

Piovanelli, Pierluigi. "Pre- and Post-Canonical Passion Stories: Insights into the Development of Christian Discourse on the Death of Jesus." *Apocrypha* 14 (2003): 99–128.

Porter, Stanley, E. "The Greek of the Gospel of Peter." Pages 77–90 in Kraus and Nicklas, *Evangelium nach Petrus*.

Reinhartz, Adele. "'Rewritten Gospel': The Case of Caiaphas the High Priest." *New Testament Studies* 55 (2009): 160–78.

Remus, Harold. "Justin Martyr's Argument with Judaism." Pages 59–80 in Wilson, *Anti-Judaism in Early Christianity*, vol. 2.

Richardson, Peter, and David Granskou, eds. *Anti-Judaism in Early Christianity*, vol. 1: *Paul and the Gospels*. Studies in Christianity and Judaism 2. Waterloo: Wilfrid Laurier University Press, 1986.

Riley, Gregory J. *Resurrection Reconsidered: Thomas and John in Controversy*. Minneapolis: Fortress, 1995.

Robinson, J. Armitage, and Montague R. James. *The Gospel according to Peter, and the Revelation of Peter: Two Lectures on the Newly Discovered Fragments together with the Greek Texts*. London: Clay, 1892.

Sanders, Jack T. *Schismatics, Sectarians, Dissidents, Deviants: The First One Hundred Years of Jewish-Christian Relations*. Valley Forge, Pa.: Trinity Press International, 1993.

Satran, David. "Anti-Jewish Polemic in the Peri Pascha of Melito of Sardis: The Problem of Social Context." Pages 49–58 in *Contra Iudaeos: Ancient and Medieval Polemics between Christians and Jews*. Edited by Ora Limor and Guy G. Stroumsa. Tübingen: Mohr (Siebeck), 1996.

Schaeffer, Susan E. "The Guard at the Tomb (Gos. Pet. 8:28–11:49 and Matt 27:62–66; 28:2–4, 11–16): A Case of Intertextuality?" Pages 499–507 in *SBL Seminar Papers, 1991*. Edited by E. H. Lovering. Society of Biblical Literature Seminar Papers 30. Atlanta: Scholars Press, 1991.

–. "The *Gospel of Peter*, the Canonical Gospels, and Oral Tradition." Ph.D. diss., Union Theological Seminary, 1997.

Schmidt, David H. "The Peter Writings: Their Redactors and Their Relationships." Ph.D. diss., Northwestern University, 1972.

Schnelle, Udo. *Apostle Paul: His Life and Theology*. Translated by M. Eugene Boring. Grand Rapids: Baker, 2005.

Setzer, Claudia J. *Jewish Responses to Early Christians: History and Polemics, 30–150 C.E.* Minneapolis: Fortress, 1994.

–. "Excellent Women: Female Witnesses to the Resurrection." *Journal of Biblical Literature* 116 (1997): 259–72.

–. *Resurrection of the Body in Early Judaism and Early Christianity: Doctrine, Community, and Self-Definition.* Boston: Brill, 2004.

Skarsaune, Oskar. *The Proof from Prophecy: A Study in Justin Martyr's Proof-Text Tradition: Text-type, Provenance, Theological Profile.* Supplements to Novum Testamentum 56. Leiden: Brill, 1987.

Skarsaune, Oskar, and Reidar Hvalvik, eds. *Jewish Believers in Jesus: The Early Centuries.* Peabody, Mass.: Hendrickson, 2007.

Smallwood, E. Mary. *The Jews under Roman Rule: From Pompey to Diocletian, A Study in Political Relations.* 2d ed. Boston: Brill, 2001.

Smith, D. Moody. "Judaism and the Gospel of John." Pages 76–96 in *Jews and Christians: Exploring the Past, Present, and Future.* Edited by James H. Charlesworth. New York: Crossroad, 1990.

Smith, Terence V. *Petrine Controversies in Early Christianity.* Wissenschaftliche Untersuchungen zum Neuen Testament 2.15. Tübingen: Mohr (Siebeck), 1985.

Smyth, Kevin. "The Guard at the Tomb." *Heythrop Journal* 2 (1961): 157–59.

Soden, Hans von. "Das Petrus Evangelium und die kanonischen Evangelien." *Zeitschrift für Theologie und Kirche* 3 (1893): 52–92.

Stanton, Graham N. "Aspects of Early Christian-Jewish Polemic and Apologetic." *New Testament Studies* 31 (1985): 377–92.

–. *Jesus and Gospel.* Cambridge: Cambridge University Press, 2004.

–. "Jewish Christian Elements in the Pseudo-Clementine Writings." Pages 305–24 in Skarsaune and Hvalvik, *Jewish Believers in Jesus.*

Stein, Robert H. "A Short Note on Mark xiv.28 and xvi.7." *New Testament Studies* 20 (1974): 445–52.

Stendahl, Krister. *The School of St. Matthew.* 2d ed. Philadelphia: Fortress, 1968.

Stewart, Robert B., ed. *The Resurrection of Jesus: John Dominic Crossan and N. T. Wright in Dialogue.* Minneapolis: Fortress, 2006.

Stewart-Sykes, Alistair. "Melito's Anti-Judaism." *Journal of Early Christian Studies* 5 (1997): 271–83.

Stillman, Martha K. "The Gospel of Peter: A Case for Oral-Only Dependency?" *Ephemerides theologicae lovanienses* 73 (1997): 114–20.

Strecker, Georg. *Das Judenchristentum in den Pseudoklementinen.* 2d ed. Texte und Untersuchungen 70. Berlin: Akademie, 1981.

Swete, Henry B. *The Akhmîm Fragment of the Apocryphal Gospel of St. Peter.* London: Macmillan, 1893.

Taylor, Vincent. *The Gospel according to St. Mark: The Greek Text with Introduction, Notes, and Indexes.* 2d ed. London: Macmillan, 1966.

Temporini, Hildegard, and Wolfgang Haase, eds. *Aufstieg un Niedergang der römischen Welt: Geschichte und Kultur Roms im Spiegel der neueren Forschung.* Part 2. *Principat,* 23.2. New York: de Gruyter, 1980.

–. *Aufstieg un Niedergang der römischen Welt: Geschichte und Kultur Roms im Spiegel der neueren Forschung.* Part 2. *Principat,* 33.2. New York: de Gruyter, 1990.

Thiselton, Anthony C. *The First Epistle to the Corinthians.* The New International Greek Testament Commentary. Grand Rapids: Eerdmans, 2000.

Tuckett, Christopher, ed. *The Gospel of Mary.* Oxford Early Christian Gospel Texts. New York: Oxford University Press, 2007.

Vaganay, Léon. *L'Évangile de Pierre.* 2d ed. Études bibliques. Paris: Gabalda, 1930.

VanderKam, James C. "Questions of Canon Viewed through the Dead Sea Scrolls." Pages 91–109 in McDonald and Sanders, *Canon Debate.*

Verheyden, Joseph. "Silent Witnesses: Mary Magdalene and the Women at the Tomb in the Gospel of Peter." Pages 457–82 in *Resurrection in the New Testament: Festschrift J. Lambrecht.* Edited by R. Bieringer, V. Koperski, and B. Lataire. Bibliotheca ephemeridum theologicarum lovaniensium 165. Leuven: Leuven University Press, 2002.

Vermes, Geza. *Scripture and Tradition in Judaism.* Studia post-biblica 4. Leiden: Brill, 1961.

Weatherly, Jon A. "The Authenticity of 1 Thessalonians 2.13–16: Additional Evidence." *Journal for the Study of the New Testament* 42 (1991): 79–98.

–. *Jewish Responsibility for the Death of Jesus in Luke-Acts.* Journal for the Study of the New Testament: Supplement Series 106. Sheffield: Sheffield Academic, 1994.

Wegner, Judith Romney. *Chattel or Person? The Status of Women in the Mishnah.* New York: Oxford University Press, 1988.

Weinfeld, Moshe. *Deuteronomy and the Deuteronomic School.* Oxford: Clarendon, 1972.

Wilckens, Ulrich. *Die Missionsreden der Apostelgeschichte.* 3d ed. Wissenschaftliche Monographien zum Alten und Neuen Testament 5. Neukirchen-Vluyn: Neukirchner, 1973.

Wilken, Robert L. *The Christians as the Romans Saw Them.* 2d ed. New Haven: Yale University Press, 2003.

Wilson, Stephen G. "The Jews and the Death of Jesus in Acts." Pages 155–64 in Richardson and Granskou, *Anti-Judaism in Early Christianity*, vol. 1.

–. "Melito and Israel." Pages 81–102 in Wilson, *Anti-Judaism in Early Christianity*, vol. 2.

–. *Related Strangers: Jews and Christians 70–170 C.E.* Minneapolis: Fortress, 1995.

–, ed. *Anti-Judaism in Early Christianity*, vol. 2: *Separation and Polemic.* Studies in Christianity and Judaism 3. Waterloo: Wilfrid Laurier University Press, 1986.

Winter, Paul. *On the Trial of Jesus.* Revised and edited by T. A. Burkill and Geza Vermes. 2d ed. Studia judaica 1. Berlin: de Gruyter, 1974.

Wright, David F. "Apologetic and Apocalyptic: The Miraculous in the *Gospel of Peter.*" Pages 401–18 in *Gospel Perspectives*, vol. 6: *The Miracles of Jesus.* Edited by David Wenham and Craig Blomberg. Sheffield: JSOT Press, 1986.

Wright, N. T. *Jesus and the Victory of God.* Minneapolis: Fortress, 1996.

–. *The Resurrection of the Son of God.* Minneapolis: Fortress, 2003.

Zahn, Theodor. *Das Evangelium des Petrus: Das kürzlich gefundene Fragment seines Textes.* Erlangen/Leipzig: Deichert, 1893.

Index of Ancient Sources

1. Hebrew Bible and Apocrypha

2. Pseudepigrapha, Dead Sea Scrolls, and Other Jewish Sources

3. New Testament

23:11	47, 54
23:12	53
23:16	54
23:22	54
23:24–25	44–45, 52
23:25	46, 53, 76
23:28–31	59
23:33	48, 54
23:34	48, 54
23:36	51, 53–54
23:38	48, 54
23:39–43	49, 54
23:44	50, 55, 73, 99, 103
23:45	98, 102
23:46	52
23:47	53, 110
23:48	22, 101, 105–107
23:50–51	52, 77, 99–100
23:50–52	45–46, 52, 103
23:50–53	77, 104
23:50–56	126
23:52	99
23:53	98, 100, 104, 134–135
23:55	171, 173
23:56	160, 171, 191
23:56–24:1	198
24	168
24:1	155, 160, 171, 191–192, 198
24:1–9	174
24:2	133–134, 161, 198
24:2–6	172, 193–194
24:3	165
24:4	155–156, 199
24:5	166, 204
24:8–9	173
24:8–11	195
24:10	171
24:11	175, 186
24:12	165, 168, 199
24:13–32	165
24:23	168
24:24	168
24:34	142, 164–166, 168
24:35	169
24:36–53	165
24:37	168
24:37–38	175
24:39	168
24:41	175

| 24:49 | 66 |

John
3:3	39
3:33	137
7:13	206
9:22	210, 214
11:44	198
12:38–41	74
12:42	214
12:42–43	210
13:23	207
15:18–25	210
16:2	214
16:2–3	210
18:8	106
19:1–5	63
19:1–7	53, 54
19:2	47, 53
19:2–3	54
19:3	47, 54, 59
19:5	53
19:13	47, 53, 63, 72
19:16	45–46, 52, 76
19:18	54
19:18–19	48
19:19	54
19:23	48–49
19:23–24	54
19:23–25	53
19:25	172
19:26	207
19:28–29	51
19:29–30	55
19:30	52
19:31	46, 53, 60, 62
19:31–33	49–50, 54
19:31–34	53
19:31–36	60
19:31–37	60
19:35	207
19:38	45, 52–53, 77, 98–99, 103–104, 106, 200, 206, 209
19:38–42	77, 99–100, 103–104, 126
19:40	104, 192, 198
19:41	104
19:41–42	134
19:42	171

4. Gospel of Peter

5. Early Christian Sources

6. Greco-Roman Sources

Index of Modern Authors

182
Celan

185 ~ fill in
gaps

200 appearance,
205

208   —146—   160 ✓
    few   Guards   167 ✓
             Jewish   199 ✓

          156 500
          brother &
            sisters

Doubt is
completely
175 eliminated   181 Text of
     in Peter   women
                            insignificant

        185 why
        not appear
        to Senate

Subject Index

Extended Information

NOTE:
NOTE:
NOTE:
COMMENT:
NOTIFY USER VIA: PHONE
PREVIOUS ID: 21544001500513
USE COUNT: 74
INACTIVE IDS: 21544001500513

Active checkouts
Total: 5
*BRANCHES OF THE GOSPEL OF JOHN

11/12/2013. 19:42

— John not Clare
   repeated
witnessin

burning with
       rage

1.70" stark"
       contrast

Wissenschaftliche Untersuchungen zum Neuen Testament

Alphabetical Index of the First and Second Series

Becker, Michael: Wunder und Wundertäter im frührabbinischen Judentum. 2002. *Vol. II/144.*

Becker, Michael and *Markus Öhler* (Ed.): Apokalyptik als Herausforderung neutestamentlicher Theologie. 2006. *Vol. II/214.*

Bell, Richard H.: Deliver Us from Evil. 2007. *Vol. 216.*

– The Irrevocable Call of God. 2005. *Vol. 184.*

– No One Seeks for God. 1998. *Vol. 106.*

– Provoked to Jealousy. 1994. *Vol. II/63.*

Bennema, Cornelis: The Power of Saving Wisdom. 2002. *Vol. II/148.*

Bergman, Jan: see *Kieffer, René*

Bergmeier, Roland: Das Gesetz im Römerbrief und andere Studien zum Neuen Testament. 2000. *Vol. 121.*

Bernett, Monika: Der Kaiserkult in Judäa unter den Herodiern und Römern. 2007. *Vol. 203.*

Betz, Otto: Jesus, der Messias Israels. 1987. *Vol. 42.*

– Jesus, der Herr der Kirche. 1990. *Vol. 52.*

Beyschlag, Karlmann: Simon Magus und die christliche Gnosis. 1974. *Vol. 16.*

Bieringer, Reimund: see *Koester, Craig.*

Bittner, Wolfgang J.: Jesu Zeichen im Johannesevangelium. 1987. *Vol. II/26.*

Bjerkelund, Carl J.: Tauta Egeneto. 1987. *Vol. 40.*

Blackburn, Barry Lee: Theios Aner and the Markan Miracle Traditions. 1991. *Vol. II/40.*

Blanton IV, Thomas R.: Constructing a New Covenant. 2007. *Vol. II/233.*

Bock, Darrell L.: Blasphemy and Exaltation in Judaism and the Final Examination of Jesus. 1998. *Vol. II/106.*

– and *Robert L. Webb* (Ed.): Key Events in the Life of the Historical Jesus. 2009. *Vol. 247.*

Bockmuehl, Markus: The Remembered Peter. 2010. *Vol. 262.*

– Revelation and Mystery in Ancient Judaism and Pauline Christianity. 1990. *Vol. II/36.*

Bøe, Sverre: Cross-Bearing in Luke. 2010. *Vol. II/278.*

– Gog and Magog. 2001. *Vol. II/135.*

Böhlig, Alexander: Gnosis und Synkretismus. Vol. 1 1989. *Vol. 47* – Vol. 2 1989. *Vol. 48.*

Böhm, Martina: Samarien und die Samaritai bei Lukas. 1999. *Vol. II/111.*

Börstinghaus, Jens: Sturmfahrt und Schiffbruch. 2010. *Vol. II/274.*

Böttrich, Christfried: Weltweisheit – Menschheitsethik – Urkult. 1992. *Vol. II/50.*

– and *Herzer, Jens* (Ed.): Josephus und das Neue Testament. 2007. *Vol. 209.*

Bolyki, János: Jesu Tischgemeinschaften. 1997. *Vol. II/96.*

Bosman, Philip: Conscience in Philo and Paul. 2003. *Vol. II/166.*

Bovon, François: New Testament and Christian Apocrypha. 2009. *Vol. 237.*

– Studies in Early Christianity. 2003. *Vol. 161.*

Brändl, Martin: Der Agon bei Paulus. 2006. *Vol. II/222.*

Braun, Heike: Geschichte des Gottesvolkes und christliche Identität. 2010. *Vol. II/279.*

Breytenbach, Cilliers: see *Frey, Jörg.*

Broadhead, Edwin K.: Jewish Ways of Following Jesus Redrawing the Religious Map of Antiquity. 2010. *Vol. 266.*

Brocke, Christoph vom: Thessaloniki – Stadt des Kassander und Gemeinde des Paulus. 2001. *Vol. II/125.*

Brunson, Andrew: Psalm 118 in the Gospel of John. 2003. *Vol. II/158.*

Büchli, Jörg: Der Poimandres – ein paganisiertes Evangelium. 1987. *Vol. II/27.*

Bühner, Jan A.: Der Gesandte und sein Weg im 4. Evangelium. 1977. *Vol. II/2.*

Burchard, Christoph: Untersuchungen zu Joseph und Asenath. 1965. *Vol. 8.*

– Studien zur Theologie, Sprache und Umwelt des Neuen Testaments. Ed. by D. Sänger. 1998. *Vol. 107.*

Burnett, Richard: Karl Barth's Theological Exegesis. 2001. *Vol. II/145.*

Byron, John: Slavery Metaphors in Early Judaism and Pauline Christianity. 2003. *Vol. II/162.*

Byrskog, Samuel: Story as History – History as Story. 2000. *Vol. 123.*

Cancik, Hubert (Ed.): Markus-Philologie. 1984. *Vol. 33.*

Capes, David B.: Old Testament Yaweh Texts in Paul's Christology. 1992. *Vol. II/47.*

Caragounis, Chrys C.: The Development of Greek and the New Testament. 2004. *Vol. 167.*

– The Son of Man. 1986. *Vol. 38.*

– see *Fridrichsen, Anton.*

Carleton Paget, James: The Epistle of Barnabas. 1994. *Vol. II/64.*

– Jews, Christians and Jewish Christians in Antiquity. 2010. *Vol. 251.*

Carson, D.A., O'Brien, Peter T. and *Mark Seifrid* (Ed.): Justification and Variegated Nomism.
Vol. 1: The Complexities of Second Temple Judaism. 2001. *Vol. II/140.*

Vol. 2: The Paradoxes of Paul. 2004.
Vol. II/181.

Chae, Young Sam: Jesus as the Eschatological Davidic Shepherd. 2006. *Vol. II/216.*

Chapman, David W.: Ancient Jewish and Christian Perceptions of Crucifixion. 2008. *Vol. II/244.*

Chester, Andrew: Messiah and Exaltation. 2007. *Vol. 207.*

Chibici-Revneanu, Nicole: Die Herrlichkeit des Verherrlichten. 2007. *Vol. II/231.*

Ciampa, Roy E.: The Presence and Function of Scripture in Galatians 1 and 2. 1998. *Vol. II/102.*

Classen, Carl Joachim: Rhetorical Criticsm of the New Testament. 2000. *Vol. 128.*

Colpe, Carsten: Griechen – Byzantiner – Semiten – Muslime. 2008. *Vol. 221.*

- Iranier – Aramäer – Hebräer – Hellenen. 2003. *Vol. 154.*

Cook, John G.: Roman Attitudes Towards the Christians. 2010. *Vol. 261.*

Coote, Robert B. (Ed.): see *Weissenrieder, Annette.*

Coppins, Wayne: The Interpretation of Freedom in the Letters of Paul. 2009. *Vol. II/261.*

Crump, David: Jesus the Intercessor. 1992. *Vol. II/49.*

Dahl, Nils Alstrup: Studies in Ephesians. 2000. *Vol. 131.*

Daise, Michael A.: Feasts in John. 2007. *Vol. II/229.*

Deines, Roland: Die Gerechtigkeit der Tora im Reich des Messias. 2004. *Vol. 177.*

- Jüdische Steingefäße und pharisäische Frömmigkeit. 1993. *Vol. II/52.*

- Die Pharisäer. 1997. *Vol. 101.*

Deines, Roland and *Karl-Wilhelm Niebuhr* (Ed.): Philo und das Neue Testament. 2004. *Vol. 172.*

Dennis, John A.: Jesus' Death and the Gathering of True Israel. 2006. *Vol. 217.*

Dettwiler, Andreas and *Jean Zumstein* (Ed.): Kreuzestheologie im Neuen Testament. 2002. *Vol. 151.*

Dickson, John P.: Mission-Commitment in Ancient Judaism and in the Pauline Communities. 2003. *Vol. II/159.*

Dietzfelbinger, Christian: Der Abschied des Kommenden. 1997. *Vol. 95.*

Dimitrov, Ivan Z., James D.G. Dunn, Ulrich Luz and *Karl-Wilhelm Niebuhr* (Ed.): Das Alte Testament als christliche Bibel in orthodoxer und westlicher Sicht. 2004. *Vol. 174.*

Dobbeler, Axel von: Glaube als Teilhabe. 1987. *Vol. II/22.*

Docherty, Susan E.: The Use of the Old Testament in Hebrews. 2009. *Vol. II/260.*

Dochhorn, Jan: Schriftgelehrte Prophetie. 2010. *Vol. 268.*

Downs, David J.: The Offering of the Gentiles. 2008. *Vol. II/248.*

Dryden, J. de Waal: Theology and Ethics in 1 Peter. 2006. *Vol. II/209.*

Dübbers, Michael: Christologie und Existenz im Kolosserbrief. 2005. *Vol. II/191.*

Dunn, James D.G.: The New Perspective on Paul. 2005. *Vol. 185.*

Dunn , James D.G. (Ed.): Jews and Christians. 1992. *Vol. 66.*

- Paul and the Mosaic Law. 1996. *Vol. 89.*

- see *Dimitrov, Ivan Z.*

-, *Hans Klein, Ulrich Luz,* and *Vasile Mihoc* (Ed.): Auslegung der Bibel in orthodoxer und westlicher Perspektive. 2000. *Vol. 130.*

Ebel, Eva: Die Attraktivität früher christlicher Gemeinden. 2004. *Vol. II/178.*

Ebertz, Michael N.: Das Charisma des Gekreuzigten. 1987. *Vol. 45.*

Eckstein, Hans-Joachim: Der Begriff Syneidesis bei Paulus. 1983. *Vol. II/10.*

- Verheißung und Gesetz. 1996. *Vol. 86.*

-, *Christoph Landmesser* and *Hermann Lichtenberger* (Ed.): Eschatologie – Eschatology. The Sixth Durham-Tübingen Research Symposium. 2011. *Vol. 272.*

Ego, Beate: Im Himmel wie auf Erden. 1989. *Vol. II/34.*

Ego, Beate, Armin Lange and *Peter Pilhofer* (Ed.): Gemeinde ohne Tempel – Community without Temple. 1999. *Vol. 118.*

- and *Helmut Merkel* (Ed.): Religiöses Lernen in der biblischen, frühjüdischen und frühchristlichen Überlieferung. 2005. *Vol. 180.*

Eisele, Wilfried: Welcher Thomas? 2010. *Vol. 259.*

Eisen, Ute E.: see *Paulsen, Henning.*

Elledge, C.D.: Life after Death in Early Judaism. 2006. *Vol. II/208.*

Ellis, E. Earle: Prophecy and Hermeneutic in Early Christianity. 1978. *Vol. 18.*

- The Old Testament in Early Christianity. 1991. *Vol. 54.*

Elmer, Ian J.: Paul, Jerusalem and the Judaisers. 2009. *Vol. II/258.*

Endo, Masanobu: Creation and Christology. 2002. *Vol. 149.*

Ennulat, Andreas: Die 'Minor Agreements'. 1994. *Vol. II/62.*

Ensor, Peter W.: Jesus and His 'Works'. 1996. *Vol. II/85.*

Eskola, Timo: Messiah and the Throne. 2001. *Vol. II/142.*

– Theodicy and Predestination in Pauline Soteriology. 1998. *Vol. II/100.*

Farelly, Nicolas: The Disciples in the Fourth Gospel. 2010. *Vol. II/290.*

Fatehi, Mehrdad: The Spirit's Relation to the Risen Lord in Paul. 2000. *Vol. II/128.*

Feldmeier, Reinhard: Die Krisis des Gottessohnes. 1987. *Vol. II/21.*

– Die Christen als Fremde. 1992. *Vol. 64.*

Feldmeier, Reinhard and *Ulrich Heckel* (Ed.): Die Heiden. 1994. *Vol. 70.*

Finnern, Sönke: Narratologie und biblische Exegese. 2010. *Vol. II/285.*

Fletcher-Louis, Crispin H.T.: Luke-Acts: Angels, Christology and Soteriology. 1997. *Vol. II/94.*

Förster, Niclas: Marcus Magus. 1999. *Vol. 114.*

Forbes, Christopher Brian: Prophecy and Inspired Speech in Early Christianity and its Hellenistic Environment. 1995. *Vol. II/75.*

Fornberg, Tord: see *Fridrichsen, Anton.*

Fossum, Jarl E.: The Name of God and the Angel of the Lord. 1985. *Vol. 36.*

Foster, Paul: Community, Law and Mission in Matthew's Gospel. *Vol. II/177.*

Fotopoulos, John: Food Offered to Idols in Roman Corinth. 2003. *Vol. II/151.*

Frank, Nicole: Der Kolosserbrief im Kontext des paulinischen Erbes. 2009. *Vol. II/271.*

Frenschkowski, Marco: Offenbarung und Epiphanie. Vol. 1 1995. *Vol. II/79 –* Vol. 2 1997. *Vol. II/80.*

Frey, Jörg: Eugen Drewermann und die biblische Exegese. 1995. *Vol. II/71.*

– Die johanneische Eschatologie. Vol. I. 1997. *Vol. 96. –* Vol. II. 1998. *Vol. 110. –* Vol. III. 2000. *Vol. 117.*

Frey, Jörg and *Cilliers Breytenbach* (Ed.): Aufgabe und Durchführung einer Theologie des Neuen Testaments. 2007. *Vol. 205.*

– *Jens Herzer, Martina Janßen* and *Clare K. Rothschild* (Ed.): Pseudepigraphie und Verfasserfiktion in frühchristlichen Briefen. 2009. *Vol. 246.*

– *Stefan Krauter* and *Hermann Lichtenberger* (Ed.): Heil und Geschichte. 2009. *Vol. 248.*

– and *Udo Schnelle (Ed.):* Kontexte des Johannesevangeliums. 2004. *Vol. 175.*

– and *Jens Schröter* (Ed.): Deutungen des Todes Jesu im Neuen Testament. 2005. *Vol. 181.*

– Jesus in apokryphen Evangelienüberlieferungen. 2010. *Vol. 254.*

–, *Jan G. van der Watt,* and *Ruben Zimmermann* (Ed.): Imagery in the Gospel of John. 2006. *Vol. 200.*

Freyne, Sean: Galilee and Gospel. 2000. *Vol. 125.*

Fridrichsen, Anton: Exegetical Writings. Edited by C.C. Caragounis and T. Fornberg. 1994. *Vol. 76.*

Gadenz, Pablo T.: Called from the Jews and from the Gentiles. 2009. *Vol. II/267.*

Gäbel, Georg: Die Kulttheologie des Hebräerbriefes. 2006. *Vol. II/212.*

Gäckle, Volker: Die Starken und die Schwachen in Korinth und in Rom. 2005. *Vol. 200.*

Garlington, Don B.: 'The Obedience of Faith'. 1991. *Vol. II/38.*

– Faith, Obedience, and Perseverance. 1994. *Vol. 79.*

Garnet, Paul: Salvation and Atonement in the Qumran Scrolls. 1977. *Vol. II/3.*

Gemünden, Petra von (Ed.): see *Weissenrieder, Annette.*

Gese, Michael: Das Vermächtnis des Apostels. 1997. *Vol. II/99.*

Gheorghita, Radu: The Role of the Septuagint in Hebrews. 2003. *Vol. II/160.*

Gordley, Matthew E.: The Colossian Hymn in Context. 2007. *Vol. II/228.*

– Teaching through Song in Antiquity. 2011. *Vol. II/302.*

Gräbe, Petrus J.: The Power of God in Paul's Letters. 2000, ²2008. *Vol. II/123.*

Gräßer, Erich: Der Alte Bund im Neuen. 1985. *Vol. 35.*

– Forschungen zur Apostelgeschichte. 2001. *Vol. 137.*

Grappe, Christian (Ed.): Le Repas de Dieu / Das Mahl Gottes. 2004. *Vol. 169.*

Gray, Timothy C.: The Temple in the Gospel of Mark. 2008. *Vol. II/242.*

Green, Joel B.: The Death of Jesus. 1988. *Vol. II/33.*

Gregg, Brian Han: The Historical Jesus and the Final Judgment Sayings in Q. 2005. *Vol. II/207.*

Gregory, Andrew: The Reception of Luke and Acts in the Period before Irenaeus. 2003. *Vol. II/169.*

Grindheim, Sigurd: The Crux of Election. 2005. *Vol. II/202.*

Gundry, Robert H.: The Old is Better. 2005. *Vol. 178.*

Gundry Volf, Judith M.: Paul and Perseverance. 1990. *Vol. II/37.*

Häußer, Detlef: Christusbekenntnis und Jesus-überlieferung bei Paulus. 2006. *Vol. 210.*

Hafemann, Scott J.: Suffering and the Spirit. 1986. *Vol. II/19.*

– Paul, Moses, and the History of Israel. 1995. *Vol. 81.*

Hahn, Ferdinand: Studien zum Neuen Testament.
Vol. I: Grundsatzfragen, Jesusforschung, Evangelien. 2006. *Vol. 191.*
Vol. II: Bekenntnisbildung und Theologie in urchristlicher Zeit. 2006. *Vol. 192.*

Hahn, Johannes (Ed.): Zerstörungen des Jerusalemer Tempels. 2002. *Vol. 147.*

Hamid-Khani, Saeed: Relevation and Concealment of Christ. 2000. *Vol. II/120.*

Hannah, Darrel D.: Michael and Christ. 1999. *Vol. II/109.*

Hardin, Justin K.: Galatians and the Imperial Cult? 2007. *Vol. II /237.*

Harrison; James R.: Paul's Language of Grace in Its Graeco-Roman Context. 2003. *Vol. II/172.*

Hartman, Lars: Text-Centered New Testament Studies. Ed. von D. Hellholm. 1997. *Vol. 102.*

Hartog, Paul: Polycarp and the New Testament. 2001. *Vol. II/134.*

Hasselbrook, David S.: Studies in New Testament Lexicography. 2011. *Vol. II/303.*

Hays, Christopher M.: Luke's Wealth Ethics. 2010. *Vol. 275.*

Heckel, Theo K.: Der Innere Mensch. 1993. *Vol. II/53.*

– Vom Evangelium des Markus zum vier-gestaltigen Evangelium. 1999. *Vol. 120.*

Heckel, Ulrich: Kraft in Schwachheit. 1993. *Vol. II/56.*

– Der Segen im Neuen Testament. 2002. *Vol. 150.*

– see *Feldmeier, Reinhard.*

– see *Hengel, Martin.*

Heemstra, Marius: The Fiscus Judaicus and the Parting of the Ways. 2010. *Vol. II/277.*

Heiligenthal, Roman: Werke als Zeichen. 1983. *Vol. II/9.*

Heininger, Bernhard: Die Inkulturation des Christentums. 2010. *Vol. 255.*

Heliso, Desta: Pistis and the Righteous One. 2007. *Vol. II/235.*

Hellholm, D.: see *Hartman, Lars.*

Hemer, Colin J.: The Book of Acts in the Setting of Hellenistic History. 1989. *Vol. 49.*

Henderson, Timothy P.: The Gospel of Peter and Early Christian Apologetics. 2011. *Vol. II/301.*

Hengel, Martin: Jesus und die Evangelien. Kleine Schriften V. 2007. *Vol. 211.*

– Die johanneische Frage. 1993. *Vol. 67.*

– Judaica et Hellenistica. Kleine Schriften I. 1996. *Vol. 90.*

– Judaica, Hellenistica et Christiana. Kleine Schriften II. 1999. *Vol. 109.*

– Judentum und Hellenismus. 1969, ³1988. *Vol. 10.*

– Paulus und Jakobus. Kleine Schriften III. 2002. *Vol. 141.*

– Studien zur Christologie. Kleine Schriften IV. 2006. *Vol. 201.*

– Studien zum Urchristentum. Kleine Schriften VI. 2008. *Vol. 234.*

– Theologische, historische und biographische Skizzen. Kleine Schriften VII. 2010. *Vol. 253.*

– and *Anna Maria Schwemer:* Paulus zwischen Damaskus und Antiochien. 1998. *Vol. 108.*

– Der messianische Anspruch Jesu und die Anfänge der Christologie. 2001. *Vol. 138.*

– Die vier Evangelien und das eine Evangelium von Jesus Christus. 2008. *Vol. 224.*

Hengel, Martin and *Ulrich Heckel* (Ed.): Paulus und das antike Judentum. 1991. *Vol. 58.*

– and *Hermut Löhr* (Ed.): Schriftauslegung im antiken Judentum und im Urchristentum. 1994. *Vol. 73.*

– and *Anna Maria Schwemer* (Ed.): Königsherrschaft Gottes und himmlischer Kult. 1991. *Vol. 55.*

– Die Septuaginta. 1994. *Vol. 72.*

–, *Siegfried Mittmann* and *Anna Maria Schwemer* (Ed.): La Cité de Dieu / Die Stadt Gottes. 2000. *Vol. 129.*

Hentschel, Anni: Diakonia im Neuen Testament. 2007. *Vol. 226.*

Hernández Jr., Juan: Scribal Habits and Theological Influence in the Apocalypse. 2006. *Vol. II/218.*

Herrenbrück, Fritz: Jesus und die Zöllner. 1990. *Vol. II/41.*

Herzer, Jens: Paulus oder Petrus? 1998. *Vol. 103.*

– see *Böttrich, Christfried.*

– see *Frey, Jörg.*

Hill, Charles E.: From the Lost Teaching of Polycarp. 2005. *Vol. 186.*

Hoegen-Rohls, Christina: Der nachösterliche Johannes. 1996. *Vol. II/84.*

Hoffmann, Matthias Reinhard: The Destroyer and the Lamb. 2005. *Vol. II/203.*

Hofius, Otfried: Katapausis. 1970. *Vol. 11.*
- Der Vorhang vor dem Thron Gottes. 1972. *Vol. 14.*
- Der Christushymnus Philipper 2,6–11. 1976, ²1991. *Vol. 17.*
- Paulusstudien. 1989, ²1994. *Vol. 51.*
- Neutestamentliche Studien. 2000. *Vol. 132.*
- Paulusstudien II. 2002. *Vol. 143.*
- Exegetische Studien. 2008. *Vol. 223.*
- and *Hans-Christian Kammler:* Johannes-studien. 1996. *Vol. 88.*

Holloway, Paul A.: Coping with Prejudice. 2009. *Vol. 244.*
- see *Ahearne-Kroll, Stephen P.*

Holmberg, Bengt (Ed.): Exploring Early Christian Identity. 2008. *Vol. 226.*
- and *Mikael Winninge* (Ed.): Identity Formation in the New Testament. 2008. *Vol. 227.*

Holtz, Traugott: Geschichte und Theologie des Urchristentums. 1991. *Vol. 57.*

Hommel, Hildebrecht: Sebasmata.
Vol. 1 1983. *Vol. 31.*
Vol. 2 1984. *Vol. 32.*

Horbury, William: Herodian Judaism and New Testament Study. 2006. *Vol. 193.*

Horn, Friedrich Wilhelm and *Ruben Zimmermann* (Ed.): Jenseits von Indikativ und Imperativ. Vol. 1. 2009. *Vol. 238.*

Horst, Pieter W. van der: Jews and Christians in Their Graeco-Roman Context. 2006. *Vol. 196.*

Hultgård, Anders and *Stig Norin* (Ed): Le Jour de Dieu / Der Tag Gottes. 2009. *Vol. 245.*

Hume, Douglas A.: The Early Christian Community. 2011. *Vol. II/298.*

Hvalvik, Reidar: The Struggle for Scripture and Covenant. 1996. *Vol. II/82.*

Jackson, Ryan: New Creation in Paul's Letters. 2010. *Vol. II/272.*

Janßen, Martina: see *Frey, Jörg.*

Jauhiainen, Marko: The Use of Zechariah in Revelation. 2005. *Vol. II/199.*

Jensen, Morten H.: Herod Antipas in Galilee. 2006; ²2010. *Vol. II/215.*

Johns, Loren L.: The Lamb Christology of the Apocalypse of John. 2003. *Vol. II/167.*

Jossa, Giorgio: Jews or Christians? 2006. *Vol. 202.*

Joubert, Stephan: Paul as Benefactor. 2000. *Vol. II/124.*

Judge, E. A.: The First Christians in the Roman World. 2008. *Vol. 229.*
- Jerusalem and Athens. 2010. *Vol. 265.*

Jungbauer, Harry: „Ehre Vater und Mutter". 2002. *Vol. II/146.*

Kähler, Christoph: Jesu Gleichnisse als Poesie und Therapie. 1995. *Vol. 78.*

Kamlah, Ehrhard: Die Form der katalogischen Paränese im Neuen Testament. 1964. *Vol. 7.*

Kammler, Hans-Christian: Christologie und Eschatologie. 2000. *Vol. 126.*
- Kreuz und Weisheit. 2003. *Vol. 159.*
- see *Hofius, Otfried.*

Karakolis, Christos: see *Alexeev, Anatoly A.*

Karrer, Martin und *Wolfgang Kraus* (Ed.): Die Septuaginta – Texte, Kontexte, Lebenswelten. 2008. *Vol. 219.*
- see *Kraus, Wolfgang.*

Kelhoffer, James A.: The Diet of John the Baptist. 2005. *Vol. 176.*
- Miracle and Mission. 1999. *Vol. II/112.*
- Persecution, Persuasion and Power. 2010. *Vol. 270.*
- see *Ahearne-Kroll, Stephen P.*

Kelley, Nicole: Knowledge and Religious Authority in the Pseudo-Clementines. 2006. *Vol. II/213.*

Kennedy, Joel: The Recapitulation of Israel. 2008. *Vol. II/257.*

Kensky, Meira Z.: Trying Man, Trying God. 2010. *Vol. II/289.*

Kieffer, René and *Jan Bergman* (Ed.): La Main de Dieu / Die Hand Gottes. 1997. *Vol. 94.*

Kierspel, Lars: The Jews and the World in the Fourth Gospel. 2006. *Vol. 220.*

Kim, Seyoon: The Origin of Paul's Gospel. 1981, ²1984. *Vol. II/4.*
- Paul and the New Perspective. 2002. *Vol. 140.*
- "The 'Son of Man'" as the Son of God. 1983. *Vol. 30.*

Klauck, Hans-Josef: Religion und Gesellschaft im frühen Christentum. 2003. *Vol. 152.*

Klein, Hans, Vasile Mihoc und *Karl-Wilhelm Niebuhr* (Ed.): Das Gebet im Neuen Testament. Vierte, europäische orthodox-westliche Exegetenkonferenz in Sambata de Sus, 4. – 8. August 2007. 2009. Vol. 249.
- see Dunn, James D.G.

Kleinknecht, Karl Th.: Der leidende Gerechtfertigte. 1984, ²1988. *Vol. II/13.*

Klinghardt, Matthias: Gesetz und Volk Gottes. 1988. *Vol. II/32.*

Kloppenborg, John S.: The Tenants in the Vineyard. 2006, student edition 2010. *Vol. 195.*

Koch, Michael: Drachenkampf und Sonnenfrau. 2004. *Vol. II/184.*

Koch, Stefan: Rechtliche Regelung von Konflikten im frühen Christentum. 2004.
Vol. II/174.

Köhler, Wolf-Dietrich: Rezeption des Matthäusevangeliums in der Zeit vor Irenäus. 1987.
Vol. II/24.

Köhn, Andreas: Der Neutestamentler Ernst Lohmeyer. 2004. *Vol. II/180.*

Koester, Craig and *Reimund Bieringer* (Ed.): The Resurrection of Jesus in the Gospel of John. 2008. *Vol. 222.*

Konradt, Matthias: Israel, Kirche und die Völker im Matthäusevangelium. 2007. *Vol. 215.*

Kooten, George H. van: Cosmic Christology in Paul and the Pauline School. 2003. *Vol. II/171.*

– Paul's Anthropology in Context. 2008. *Vol. 232.*

Korn, Manfred: Die Geschichte Jesu in veränderter Zeit. 1993. *Vol. II/51.*

Koskenniemi, Erkki: Apollonios von Tyana in der neutestamentlichen Exegese. 1994. *Vol. II/61.*

– The Old Testament Miracle-Workers in Early Judaism. 2005. *Vol. II/206.*

Kraus, Thomas J.: Sprache, Stil und historischer Ort des zweiten Petrusbriefes. 2001. *Vol. II/136.*

Kraus, Wolfgang: Das Volk Gottes. 1996. *Vol. 85.*

– see *Karrer, Martin.*

– see *Walter, Nikolaus.*

– and *Martin Karrer* (Hrsg.): Die Septuaginta – Texte, Theologien, Einflüsse. 2010. *Bd. 252.*

– and *Karl-Wilhelm Niebuhr* (Ed.): Frühjudentum und Neues Testament im Horizont Biblischer Theologie. 2003. *Vol. 162.*

Krauter, Stefan: Studien zu Röm 13,1-7. 2009. *Vol. 243.*

– see *Frey, Jörg.*

Kreplin, Matthias: Das Selbstverständnis Jesu. 2001. *Vol. II/141.*

Kuhn, Karl G.: Achtzehngebet und Vaterunser und der Reim. 1950. *Vol. 1.*

Kvalbein, Hans: see *Ådna, Jostein.*

Kwon, Yon-Gyong: Eschatology in Galatians. 2004. *Vol. II/183.*

Laansma, Jon: I Will Give You Rest. 1997. *Vol. II/98.*

Labahn, Michael: Offenbarung in Zeichen und Wort. 2000. *Vol. II/117.*

Lambers-Petry, Doris: see *Tomson, Peter J.*

Lampe, Peter: Die stadtrömischen Christen in den ersten beiden Jahrhunderten. 1987, ²1989. *Vol. II/18.*

Landmesser, Christof: Wahrheit als Grundbegriff neutestamentlicher Wissenschaft. 1999. *Vol. 113.*

– Jüngerberufung und Zuwendung zu Gott. 2000. *Vol. 133.*

– see *Eckstein, Hans-Joachim.*

Lange, Armin: see *Ego, Beate.*

Lau, Andrew: Manifest in Flesh. 1996. *Vol. II/86.*

Lawrence, Louise: An Ethnography of the Gospel of Matthew. 2003. *Vol. II/165.*

Lee, Aquila H.I.: From Messiah to Preexistent Son. 2005. *Vol. II/192.*

Lee, Pilchan: The New Jerusalem in the Book of Relevation. 2000. *Vol. II/129.*

Lee, Sang M.: The Cosmic Drama of Salvation. 2010. *Vol. II/276.*

Lee, Simon S.: Jesus' Transfiguration and the Believers' Transformation. 2009. *Vol. II/265.*

Lichtenberger, Hermann: Das Ich Adams und das Ich der Menschheit. 2004. *Vol. 164.*

– see *Avemarie, Friedrich.*

– see *Eckstein, Hans-Joachim.*

– see *Frey, Jörg.*

Lierman, John: The New Testament Moses. 2004. *Vol. II/173.*

– (Ed.): Challenging Perspectives on the Gospel of John. 2006. *Vol. II/219.*

Lieu, Samuel N.C.: Manichaeism in the Later Roman Empire and Medieval China. ²1992. *Vol. 63.*

Lindemann, Andreas: Die Evangelien und die Apostelgeschichte. 2009. *Vol. 241.*

Lincicum, David: Paul and the Early Jewish Encounter with Deuteronomy. 2010. *Vol. II/284.*

Lindgård, Fredrik: Paul's Line of Thought in 2 Corinthians 4:16–5:10. 2004. *Vol. II/189.*

Livesey, Nina E.: Circumcision as a Malleable Symbol. 2010. *Vol. II/295.*

Loader, William R.G.: Jesus' Attitude Towards the Law. 1997. *Vol. II/97.*

Löhr, Gebhard: Verherrlichung Gottes durch Philosophie. 1997. *Vol. 97.*

Löhr, Hermut: Studien zum frühchristlichen und frühjüdischen Gebet. 2003. *Vol. 160.*

– see *Hengel, Martin.*

Löhr, Winrich Alfried: Basilides und seine Schule. 1995. *Vol. 83.*

Lorenzen, Stefanie: Das paulinische Eikon-Konzept. 2008. *Vol. II/250.*

Luomanen, Petri: Entering the Kingdom of Heaven. 1998. *Vol. II/101.*

Luz, Ulrich: see *Alexeev, Anatoly A.*

– see *Dunn, James D.G.*

Mackay, Ian D.: John's Raltionship with Mark. 2004. *Vol. II/182.*

Mackie, Scott D.: Eschatology and Exhortation in the Epistle to the Hebrews. 2006. *Vol. II/223.*

Magda, Ksenija: Paul's Territoriality and Mission Strategy. 2009. *Vol. II/266.*

Maier, Gerhard: Mensch und freier Wille. 1971. *Vol. 12.*

– Die Johannesoffenbarung und die Kirche. 1981. *Vol. 25.*

Markschies, Christoph: Valentinus Gnosticus? 1992. *Vol. 65.*

Marshall, Jonathan: Jesus, Patrons, and Benefactors. 2009. *Vol. II/259.*

Marshall, Peter: Enmity in Corinth: Social Conventions in Paul's Relations with the Corinthians. 1987. *Vol. II/23.*

Martin, Dale B.: see *Zangenberg, Jürgen.*

Maston, Jason: Divine and Human Agency in Second Temple Judaism and Paul. 2010. *Vol. II/297.*

Mayer, Annemarie: Sprache der Einheit im Epheserbrief und in der Ökumene. 2002. *Vol. II/150.*

Mayordomo, Moisés: Argumentiert Paulus logisch? 2005. *Vol. 188.*

McDonough, Sean M.: YHWH at Patmos: Rev. 1:4 in its Hellenistic and Early Jewish Setting. 1999. *Vol. II/107.*

McDowell, Markus: Prayers of Jewish Women. 2006. *Vol. II/211.*

McGlynn, Moyna: Divine Judgement and Divine Benevolence in the Book of Wisdom. 2001. *Vol. II/139.*

Meade, David G.: Pseudonymity and Canon. 1986. *Vol. 39.*

Meadors, Edward P.: Jesus the Messianic Herald of Salvation. 1995. *Vol. II/72.*

Meißner, Stefan: Die Heimholung des Ketzers. 1996. *Vol. II/87.*

Mell, Ulrich: Die „anderen" Winzer. 1994. *Vol. 77.*

– see *Sänger, Dieter.*

Mengel, Berthold: Studien zum Philipperbrief. 1982. *Vol. II/8.*

Merkel, Helmut: Die Widersprüche zwischen den Evangelien. 1971. *Vol. 13.*

– see *Ego, Beate.*

Merklein, Helmut: Studien zu Jesus und Paulus. Vol. 1 1987. *Vol. 43.* – Vol. 2 1998. *Vol. 105.*

Merkt, Andreas: see *Nicklas, Tobias*

Metzdorf, Christina: Die Tempelaktion Jesu. 2003. *Vol. II/168.*

Metzler, Karin: Der griechische Begriff des Verzeihens. 1991. *Vol. II/44.*

Metzner, Rainer: Die Rezeption des Matthäusevangeliums im 1. Petrusbrief. 1995. *Vol. II/74.*

– Das Verständnis der Sünde im Johannesevangelium. 2000. *Vol. 122.*

Mihoc, Vasile: see *Dunn, James D.G.*

– see *Klein, Hans.*

Mineshige, Kiyoshi: Besitzverzicht und Almosen bei Lukas. 2003. *Vol. II/163.*

Mittmann, Siegfried: see *Hengel, Martin.*

Mittmann-Richert, Ulrike: Magnifikat und Benediktus. 1996. *Vol. II/90.*

– Der Sühnetod des Gottesknechts. 2008. *Vol. 220.*

Miura, Yuzuru: David in Luke-Acts. 2007. *Vol. II/232.*

Moll, Sebastian: The Arch-Heretic Marcion. 2010. *Vol. 250.*

Morales, Rodrigo J.: The Spirit and the Restorat. 2010. *Vol. 282.*

Mournet, Terence C.: Oral Tradition and Literary Dependency. 2005. *Vol. II/195.*

Mußner, Franz: Jesus von Nazareth im Umfeld Israels und der Urkirche. Ed. von M. Theobald. 1998. *Vol. 111.*

Mutschler, Bernhard: Das Corpus Johanneum bei Irenäus von Lyon. 2005. *Vol. 189.*

– Glaube in den Pastoralbriefen. 2010. *Vol. 256.*

Myers, Susan E.: Spirit Epicleses in the Acts of Thomas. 2010. *Vol. 281.*

Nguyen, V. Henry T.: Christian Identity in Corinth. 2008. *Vol. II/243.*

Nicklas, Tobias, Andreas Merkt und *Joseph Verheyden* (Ed.): Gelitten – Gestorben – Auferstanden. 2010. *Vol. II/273.*

– see *Verheyden, Joseph*

Niebuhr, Karl-Wilhelm: Gesetz and Paränese. 1987. *Vol. II/28.*

– Heidenapostel aus Israel. 1992. *Vol. 62.*

– see *Deines, Roland.*

– see *Dimitrov, Ivan Z.*

– see *Klein, Hans.*

– see *Kraus, Wolfgang.*

Nielsen, Anders E.: "Until it is Fullfilled". 2000. *Vol. II/126.*

Nielsen, Jesper Tang: Die kognitive Dimension des Kreuzes. 2009. *Vol. II/263.*

Nissen, Andreas: Gott und der Nächste im antiken Judentum. 1974. *Vol. 15.*

Noack, Christian: Gottesbewußtsein. 2000. *Vol. II/116.*

Noormann, Rolf: Irenäus als Paulusinterpret. 1994. *Vol. II/66.*

Norin, Stig: see *Hultgård, Anders.*

Novakovic, Lidija: Messiah, the Healer of the Sick. 2003. *Vol. II/170.*

Obermann, Andreas: Die christologische Erfüllung der Schrift im Johannesevangelium. 1996. *Vol. II/83.*

Öhler, Markus: Barnabas. 2003. *Vol. 156.*
– see *Becker, Michael.*

Okure, Teresa: The Johannine Approach to Mission. 1988. *Vol. II/31.*

Onuki, Takashi: Heil und Erlösung. 2004. *Vol. 165.*

Oropeza, B. J.: Paul and Apostasy. 2000. *Vol. II/115.*

Ostmeyer, Karl-Heinrich: Kommunikation mit Gott und Christus. 2006. *Vol. 197.*
– Taufe und Typos. 2000. *Vol. II/118.*

Pao, David W.: Acts and the Isaianic New Exodus. 2000. *Vol. II/130.*

Park, Eung Chun: The Mission Discourse in Matthew's Interpretation. 1995. *Vol. II/81.*

Park, Joseph S.: Conceptions of Afterlife in Jewish Insriptions. 2000. *Vol. II/121.*

Parsenios, George L.: Rhetoric and Drama in the Johannine Lawsuit Motif. 2010. *Vol. 258.*

Pate, C. Marvin: The Reverse of the Curse. 2000. *Vol. II/114.*

Paulsen, Henning: Studien zur Literatur und Geschichte des frühen Christentums. Ed. von Ute E. Eisen. 1997. *Vol. 99.*

Pearce, Sarah J.K.: The Land of the Body. 2007. *Vol. 208.*

Peres, Imre: Griechische Grabinschriften und neutestamentliche Eschatologie. 2003. *Vol. 157.*

Perry, Peter S.: The Rhetoric of Digressions. 2009. *Vol. II/268.*

Philip, Finny: The Origins of Pauline Pneumatology. 2005. *Vol. II/194.*

Philonenko, Marc (Ed.): Le Trône de Dieu. 1993. *Vol. 69.*

Pilhofer, Peter: Presbyteron Kreitton. 1990. *Vol. II/39.*
– Philippi. Vol. 1 1995. *Vol. 87.* – Vol. 2 ²2009. *Vol. 119.*
– Die frühen Christen und ihre Welt. 2002. *Vol. 145.*
– see *Becker, Eve-Marie.*
– see *Ego, Beate.*

Pitre, Brant: Jesus, the Tribulation, and the End of the Exile. 2005. *Vol. II/204.*

Plümacher, Eckhard: Geschichte und Geschichten. 2004. *Vol. 170.*

Pöhlmann, Wolfgang: Der Verlorene Sohn und das Haus. 1993. *Vol. 68.*

Poirier, John C.: The Tongues of Angels. 2010. *Vol. II/287.*

Pokorný, Petr and *Josef B. Sou ek:* Bibelauslegung als Theologie. 1997. *Vol. 100.*
– and *Jan Roskovec* (Ed.): Philosophical Hermeneutics and Biblical Exegesis. 2002. *Vol. 153.*

Popkes, Enno Edzard: Das Menschenbild des Thomasevangeliums. 2007. *Vol. 206.*
– Die Theologie der Liebe Gottes in den johanneischen Schriften. 2005. *Vol. II/197.*

Porter, Stanley E.: The Paul of Acts. 1999. *Vol. 115.*

Prieur, Alexander: Die Verkündigung der Gottesherrschaft. 1996. *Vol. II/89.*

Probst, Hermann: Paulus und der Brief. 1991. *Vol. II/45.*

Puig i Tàrrech, Armand: Jesus: An Uncommon Journey. 2010. *Vol. II/288.*

Rabens, Volker: The Holy Spirit and Ethics in Paul. 2010. *Vol. II/283.*

Räisänen, Heikki: Paul and the Law. 1983, ²1987. *Vol. 29.*

Rehkopf, Friedrich: Die lukanische Sonderquelle. 1959. *Vol. 5.*

Rein, Matthias: Die Heilung des Blindgeborenen (Joh 9). 1995. *Vol. II/73.*

Reinmuth, Eckart: Pseudo-Philo und Lukas. 1994. *Vol. 74.*

Reiser, Marius: Bibelkritik und Auslegung der Heiligen Schrift. 2007. *Vol. 217.*
– Syntax und Stil des Markusevangeliums. 1984. *Vol. II/11.*

Reynolds, Benjamin E.: The Apocalyptic Son of Man in the Gospel of John. 2008. *Vol. II/249.*

Rhodes, James N.: The Epistle of Barnabas and the Deuteronomic Tradition. 2004. *Vol. II/188.*

Richards, E. Randolph: The Secretary in the Letters of Paul. 1991. *Vol. II/42.*

Riesner, Rainer: Jesus als Lehrer. 1981, ³1988. *Vol. II/7.*
– Die Frühzeit des Apostels Paulus. 1994. *Vol. 71.*

Rissi, Mathias: Die Theologie des Hebräerbriefs. 1987. *Vol. 41.*

Röcker, Fritz W.: Belial und Katechon. 2009. *Vol. II/262.*

Röhser, Günter: Metaphorik und Personifikation der Sünde. 1987. *Vol. II/25.*

Rose, Christian: Theologie als Erzählung im Markusevangelium. 2007. *Vol. II/236.*

– Die Wolke der Zeugen. 1994. *Vol. II/60.*

Roskovec, Jan: see *Pokorný, Petr.*

Rothschild, Clare K.: Baptist Traditions and Q. 2005. *Vol. 190.*

– Hebrews as Pseudepigraphon. 2009. *Vol. 235.*

– Luke Acts and the Rhetoric of History. 2004. *Vol. II/175.*

– see *Frey, Jörg.*

Rüegger, Hans-Ulrich: Verstehen, was Markus erzählt. 2002. *Vol. II/155.*

Rüger, Hans Peter: Die Weisheitsschrift aus der Kairoer Geniza. 1991. *Vol. 53.*

Ruf, Martin G.: Die heiligen Propheten, eure Apostel und ich. 2011. *Vol. II/300.*

Runesson, Anders: see *Becker, Eve-Marie.*

Sänger, Dieter: Antikes Judentum und die Mysterien. 1980. *Vol. II/5.*

– Die Verkündigung des Gekreuzigten und Israel. 1994. *Vol. 75.*

– see *Burchard, Christoph*

– and *Ulrich Mell* (Ed.): Paulus und Johannes. 2006. *Vol. 198.*

Salier, Willis Hedley: The Rhetorical Impact of the Semeia in the Gospel of John. 2004. *Vol. II/186.*

Salzmann, Jorg Christian: Lehren und Ermahnen. 1994. *Vol. II/59.*

Sandnes, Karl Olav: Paul – One of the Prophets? 1991. *Vol. II/43.*

Sato, Migaku: Q und Prophetie. 1988. *Vol. II/29.*

Schäfer, Ruth: Paulus bis zum Apostelkonzil. 2004. *Vol. II/179.*

Schaper, Joachim: Eschatology in the Greek Psalter. 1995. *Vol. II/76.*

Schimanowski, Gottfried: Die himmlische Liturgie in der Apokalypse des Johannes. 2002. *Vol. II/154.*

– Weisheit und Messias. 1985. *Vol. II/17.*

Schlichting, Günter: Ein jüdisches Leben Jesu. 1982. *Vol. 24.*

Schließer, Benjamin: Abraham's Faith in Romans 4. 2007. *Vol. II/224.*

Schnabel, Eckhard J.: Law and Wisdom from Ben Sira to Paul. 1985. *Vol. II/16.*

Schnelle, Udo: see *Frey, Jörg.*

Schröter, Jens: Von Jesus zum Neuen Testament. 2007. *Vol. 204.*

– see *Frey, Jörg.*

Schutter, William L.: Hermeneutic and Composition in I Peter. 1989. *Vol. II/30.*

Schwartz, Daniel R.: Studies in the Jewish Background of Christianity. 1992. *Vol. 60.*

Schwemer, Anna Maria: see *Hengel, Martin*

Scott, Ian W.: Implicit Epistemology in the Letters of Paul. 2005. *Vol. II/205.*

Scott, James M.: Adoption as Sons of God. 1992. *Vol. II/48.*

– Paul and the Nations. 1995. *Vol. 84.*

Shi, Wenhua: Paul's Message of the Cross as Body Language. 2008. *Vol. II/254.*

Shum, Shiu-Lun: Paul's Use of Isaiah in Romans. 2002. *Vol. II/156.*

Siegert, Folker: Drei hellenistisch-jüdische Predigten. Teil I 1980. *Vol. 20* – Teil II 1992. *Vol. 61.*

– Nag-Hammadi-Register. 1982. *Vol. 26.*

– Argumentation bei Paulus. 1985. *Vol. 34.*

– Philon von Alexandrien. 1988. *Vol. 46.*

Simon, Marcel: Le christianisme antique et son contexte religieux I/II. 1981. *Vol. 23.*

Smit, Peter-Ben: Fellowship and Food in the Kingdom. 2008. *Vol. II/234.*

Snodgrass, Klyne: The Parable of the Wicked Tenants. 1983. *Vol. 27.*

Söding, Thomas: Das Wort vom Kreuz. 1997. *Vol. 93.*

– see *Thüsing, Wilhelm.*

Sommer, Urs: Die Passionsgeschichte des Markusevangeliums. 1993. *Vol. II/58.*

Sorensen, Eric: Possession and Exorcism in the New Testament and Early Christianity. 2002. *Vol. II/157.*

Sou ek, Josef B.: see *Pokorný, Petr.*

Southall, David J.: Rediscovering Righteousness in Romans. 2008. *Vol. 240.*

Spangenberg, Volker: Herrlichkeit des Neuen Bundes. 1993. *Vol. II/55.*

Spanje, T.E. van: Inconsistency in Paul? 1999. *Vol. II/110.*

Speyer, Wolfgang: Frühes Christentum im antiken Strahlungsfeld. Vol. I: 1989. *Vol. 50.*

– Vol. II: 1999. *Vol. 116.*

– Vol. III: 2007. *Vol. 213.*

Spittler, Janet E.: Animals in the Apocryphal Acts of the Apostles. 2008. *Vol. II/247.*

Sprinkle, Preston: Law and Life. 2008. *Vol. II/241.*

Stadelmann, Helge: Ben Sira als Schriftgelehrter. 1980. *Vol. II/6.*

Stein, Hans Joachim: Frühchristliche Mahlfeiern. 2008. *Vol. II/255.*

Stenschke, Christoph W.: Luke's Portrait of Gentiles Prior to Their Coming to Faith. *Vol. II/108.*

Sterck-Degueldre, Jean-Pierre: Eine Frau namens Lydia. 2004. *Vol. II/176.*

Stettler, Christian: Der Kolosserhymnus. 2000. *Vol. II/131.*

– Das letzte Gericht. 2011. *Vol. II/299.*

Stettler, Hanna: Die Christologie der Pastoralbriefe. 1998. *Vol. II/105.*

Stökl Ben Ezra, Daniel: The Impact of Yom Kippur on Early Christianity. 2003. *Vol. 163.*

Strobel, August: Die Stunde der Wahrheit. 1980. *Vol. 21.*

Stroumsa, Guy G.: Barbarian Philosophy. 1999. *Vol. 112.*

Stuckenbruck, Loren T.: Angel Veneration and Christology. 1995. *Vol. II/70.*

–, *Stephen C. Barton* and *Benjamin G. Wold* (Ed.): Memory in the Bible and Antiquity. 2007. *Vol. 212.*

Stuhlmacher, Peter (Ed.): Das Evangelium und die Evangelien. 1983. *Vol. 28.*

– Biblische Theologie und Evangelium. 2002. *Vol. 146.*

Sung, Chong-Hyon: Vergebung der Sünden. 1993. *Vol. II/57.*

Svendsen, Stefan N.: Allegory Transformed. 2009. *Vol. II/269.*

Tajra, Harry W.: The Trial of St. Paul. 1989. *Vol. II/35.*

– The Martyrdom of St.Paul. 1994. *Vol. II/67.*

Tellbe, Mikael: Christ-Believers in Ephesus. 2009. *Vol. 242.*

Theißen, Gerd: Studien zur Soziologie des Urchristentums. 1979, ³1989. *Vol. 19.*

Theobald, Michael: Studien zum Corpus Iohanneum. 2010. *Vol. 267.*

– Studien zum Römerbrief. 2001. *Vol. 136.*

– see *Mußner, Franz.*

Thornton, Claus-Jürgen: Der Zeuge des Zeugen. 1991. *Vol. 56.*

Thüsing, Wilhelm: Studien zur neutestamentlichen Theologie. Ed. von Thomas Söding. 1995. *Vol. 82.*

Thurén, Lauri: Derhethorizing Paul. 2000. *Vol. 124.*

Thyen, Hartwig: Studien zum Corpus Iohanneum. 2007. *Vol. 214.*

Tibbs, Clint: Religious Experience of the Pneuma. 2007. *Vol. II/230.*

Toit, David S. du: Theios Anthropos. 1997. *Vol. II/91.*

Tolmie, D. Francois: Persuading the Galatians. 2005. *Vol. II/190.*

Tomson, Peter J. and *Doris Lambers-Petry* (Ed.): The Image of the Judaeo-Christians in Ancient Jewish and Christian Literature. 2003. *Vol. 158.*

Toney, Carl N.: Paul's Inclusive Ethic. 2008. *Vol. II/252.*

Trebilco, Paul: The Early Christians in Ephesus from Paul to Ignatius. 2004. *Vol. 166.*

Treloar, Geoffrey R.: Lightfoot the Historian. 1998. *Vol. II/103.*

Troftgruben, Troy M.: A Conclusion Unhindered. 2010. Vol. II/280.

Tso, Marcus K.M.: Ethics in the Qumran Community. 2010. *Vol. II/292.*

Tsuji, Manabu: Glaube zwischen Vollkommenheit und Verweltlichung. 1997. *Vol. II/93.*

Twelftree, Graham H.: Jesus the Exorcist. 1993. *Vol. II/54.*

Ulrichs, Karl Friedrich: Christusglaube. 2007. *Vol. II/227.*

Urban, Christina: Das Menschenbild nach dem Johannesevangelium. 2001. *Vol. II/137.*

Vahrenhorst, Martin: Kultische Sprache in den Paulusbriefen. 2008. *Vol. 230.*

Vegge, Ivar: 2 Corinthians – a Letter about Reconciliation. 2008. *Vol. II/239.*

Verheyden, Joseph, Korinna Zamfir and *Tobias Nicklas* (Ed.): Prophets and Prophecy in Jewish and Early Christian Literature. 2010. *Vol. II/286.*

– see *Nicklas, Tobias*

Visotzky, Burton L.: Fathers of the World. 1995. *Vol. 80.*

Vollenweider, Samuel: Horizonte neutestamentlicher Christologie. 2002. *Vol. 144.*

Vos, Johan S.: Die Kunst der Argumentation bei Paulus. 2002. *Vol. 149.*

Waaler, Erik: The *Shema* and The First Commandment in First Corinthians. 2008. *Vol. II/253.*

Wagener, Ulrike: Die Ordnung des „Hauses Gottes". 1994. *Vol. II/65.*

Wagner, J. Ross: see *Wilk, Florian.*

Wahlen, Clinton: Jesus and the Impurity of Spirits in the Synoptic Gospels. 2004. *Vol. II/185.*

Walker, Donald D.: Paul's Offer of Leniency (2 Cor 10:1). 2002. *Vol. II/152.*

Walter, Nikolaus: Praeparatio Evangelica. Ed. von Wolfgang Kraus und Florian Wilk. 1997. *Vol. 98.*

Wander, Bernd: Gottesfürchtige und Sympathisanten. 1998. *Vol. 104.*

Wardle, Timothy: The Jerusalem Temple and Early Christian Identity. 2010. *Vol. II/291.*

Wasserman, Emma: The Death of the Soul in Romans 7. 2008. *Vol. 256.*

Waters, Guy: The End of Deuteronomy in the Epistles of Paul. 2006. *Vol. 221.*

Watt, Jan G. van der: see *Frey, Jörg*
– see *Zimmermann, Ruben*

Watts, Rikki: Isaiah's New Exodus and Mark. 1997. *Vol. II/88.*

Webb, Robert L.: see *Bock, Darrell L.*

Wedderburn, Alexander J.M.: Baptism and Resurrection. 1987. *Vol. 44.*
– Jesus and the Historians. 2010. *Vol. 269.*

Wegner, Uwe: Der Hauptmann von Kafarnaum. 1985. *Vol. II/14.*

Weiß, Hans-Friedrich: Frühes Christentum und Gnosis. 2008. *Vol. 225.*

Weissenrieder, Annette: Images of Illness in the Gospel of Luke. 2003. Vol. II/164.
–, and *Robert B. Coote* (Ed.): The Interface of Orality and Writing. 2010. *Vol. 260.*
–, *Friederike Wendt* and *Petra von Gemünden* (Ed.): Picturing the New Testament. 2005. *Vol. II/193.*

Welck, Christian: Erzählte ‚Zeichen‘. 1994. *Vol. II/69.*

Wendt, Friederike (Ed.): see *Weissenrieder, Annette.*

Wiarda, Timothy: Peter in the Gospels. 2000. *Vol. II/127.*

Wifstrand, Albert: Epochs and Styles. 2005. *Vol. 179.*

Wilk, Florian and *J. Ross Wagner* (Ed.): Between Gospel and Election. 2010. *Vol. 257.*
– see *Walter, Nikolaus.*

Williams, Catrin H.: I am He. 2000. *Vol. II/113.*

Wilson, Todd A.: The Curse of the Law and the Crisis in Galatia. 2007. *Vol. II/225.*

Wilson, Walter T.: Love without Pretense. 1991. *Vol. II/46.*

Winn, Adam: The Purpose of Mark's Gospel. 2008. *Vol. II/245.*

Winninge, Mikael: see *Holmberg, Bengt.*

Wischmeyer, Oda: Von Ben Sira zu Paulus. 2004. *Vol. 173.*

Wisdom, Jeffrey: Blessing for the Nations and the Curse of the Law. 2001. *Vol. II/133.*

Witmer, Stephen E.: Divine Instruction in Early Christianity. 2008. *Vol. II/246.*

Wold, Benjamin G.: Women, Men, and Angels. 2005. *Vol. II/2001.*

Wolter, Michael: Theologie und Ethos im frühen Christentum. 2009. *Vol. 236.*
– see *Stuckenbruck, Loren T.*

Wright, Archie T.: The Origin of Evil Spirits. 2005. *Vol. II/198.*

Wucherpfennig, Ansgar: Heracleon Philologus. 2002. *Vol. 142.*

Yates, John W.: The Spirit and Creation in Paul. 2008. *Vol. II/251.*

Yeung, Maureen: Faith in Jesus and Paul. 2002. *Vol. II/147.*

Zamfir, Corinna: see *Verheyden, Joseph*

Zangenberg, Jürgen, Harold W. Attridge and *Dale B. Martin* (Ed.): Religion, Ethnicity and Identity in Ancient Galilee. 2007. *Vol. 210.*

Zimmermann, Alfred E.: Die urchristlichen Lehrer. 1984, ²1988. *Vol. II/12.*

Zimmermann, Johannes: Messianische Texte aus Qumran. 1998. *Vol. II/104.*

Zimmermann, Ruben: Christologie der Bilder im Johannesevangelium. 2004. *Vol. 171.*
– Geschlechtermetaphorik und Gottesverhältnis. 2001. *Vol. II/122.*
– (Ed.): Hermeneutik der Gleichnisse Jesu. 2008. *Vol. 231.*
– and *Jan G. van der Watt* (Ed.): Moral Language in the New Testament. Vol. II. 2010. *Vol. II/296.*
– see *Frey, Jörg.*
– see *Horn, Friedrich Wilhelm.*

Zugmann, Michael: „Hellenisten“ in der Apostelgeschichte. 2009. *Vol. II/264.*

Zumstein, Jean: see *Dettwiler, Andreas*

Zwiep, Arie W.: Christ, the Spirit and the Community of God. 2010. *Vol. II/293.*
– Judas and the Choice of Matthias. 2004. *Vol. II/187.*

For a complete catalogue please write to the publisher
Mohr Siebeck • P.O. Box 2030 • D–72010 Tübingen/Germany
Up-to-date information on the internet at www.mohr.de